MW01676369

Last of the Barefoot Tycoons

THE STORY OF FRASER ISLAND'S SID MELKSHAM AND THE $1,000,000 DEBACLE

Angela Burger

Thanks for everything
Sid

To Ann
with much love
Angela Burger

First published 2008
M&B Publishing,
P.O.Box 10809,
Southport B.C.
Queensland 4125
Australia.
Tel: 61 7 5591 6499
Email: sidangela@hotmail.com

Copyright © Angela Burger 2008

All rights reserved. No part of this publication may be reproduced, stored in or introduced into a retrieval system or transmitted in any form or by any means (electronic, mechanical, photocopying, recording or otherwise) without the prior written permission of the copyright owner.

Printed and bound in Australia by Print Finishing, 16, Northview St., Mermaid Beach, Q 4218.

National Library of Australia
Cataloguing–in-publication data:

Author: Angela Burger
Title: Last of the Barefoot tycoons – The story of Fraser Island's Sid Melksham and the $1,000,000 debacle.
ISBN 978-0-646-49673-3 (pbk)

Subjects: Melksham Sid.
Businessmen-Queensland-Fraser Island – Biography.
Tourism-Queensland-Fraser Island.
Fraser Island (Qld)

Dewey Number 338.04092

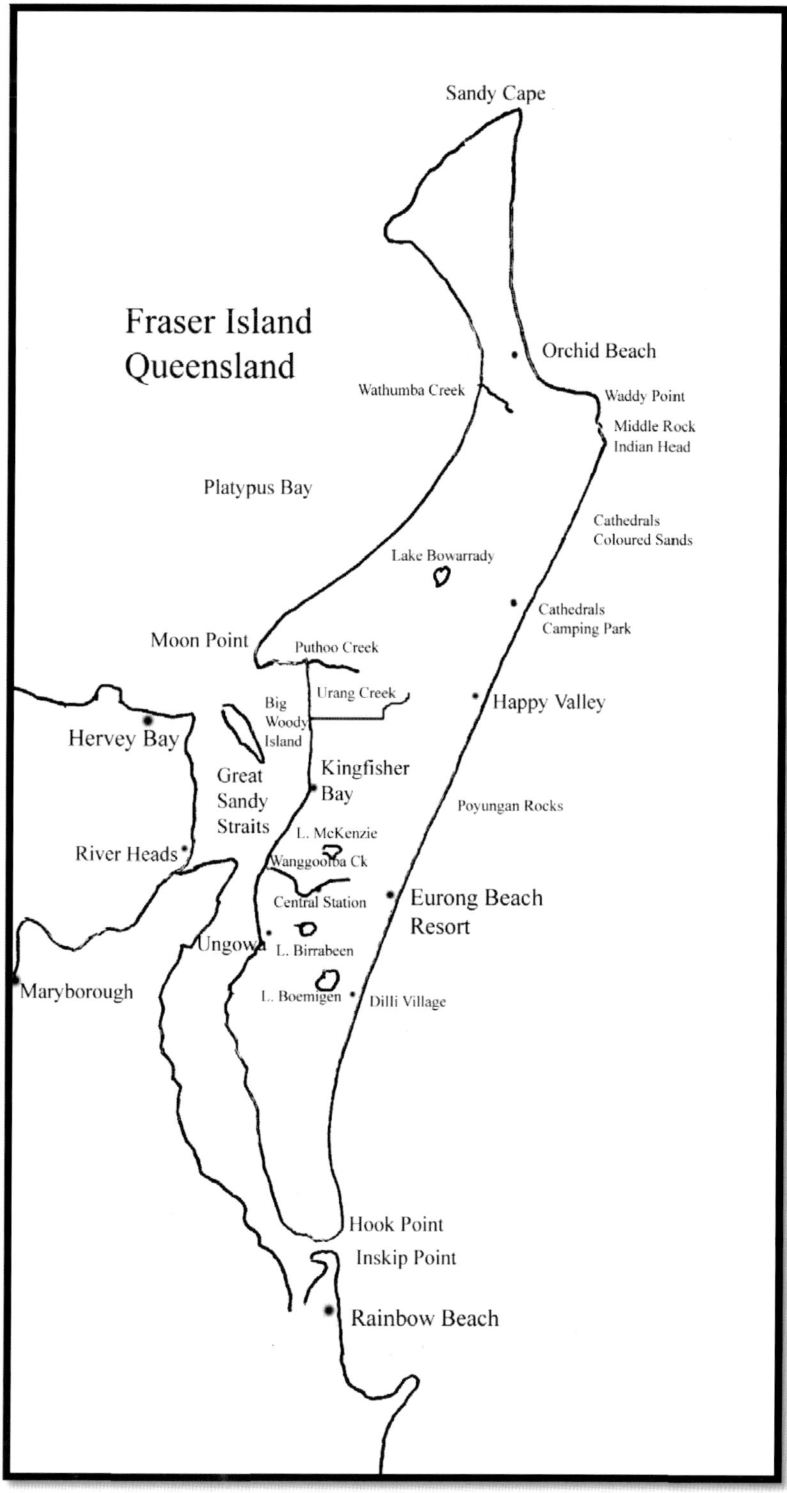

Fraser Island
Queensland
Sandy Cape
Orchid Beach
Wathumba Creek
Waddy Point
Middle Rock
Indian Head
Platypus Bay
Cathedrals
Coloured Sands
Lake Bowarrady
Cathedrals
Camping Park
Moon Point
Puthoo Creek
Urang Creek
Happy Valley
Big
Woody
Island
Hervey Bay
Great
Sandy
Straits
Kingfisher
Bay
Poyungan Rocks
L. McKenzie
River Heads
Wanggoolba Ck
Central Station
Eurong Beach
Resort
Ungowa
L. Birrabeen
Maryborough
L. Boemigen
Dilli Village
Hook Point
Inskip Point
Rainbow Beach

Chapter 1

Cyclone Dora blew in to Fraser Island off the south east Queensland coast on February 17 1971 with little warning.

At Eurong on the surf beachfront, a burly chap called Sid Melksham had just tacked new corrugated roofing iron on to a building he was putting up. As the winds gathered strength, he feared the iron would be blown off and twisted beyond use, and he couldn't afford to buy more.

He had himself strapped spread eagled on the roof and there he stayed through howling winds and pouring rain for 15 hours holding his roofing iron down until the cyclone passed.

The incident illustrated Sid's utter determination in pioneering a tourism industry on the world's largest sand island. It was just one of many astonishing feats in a lifetime of working against the odds in near isolation that made Sid a legend, and changed the face of Fraser Island and the entire region.

* * * *

The first time Sid saw Fraser Island was when he went there on honeymoon on 6 July 1959. The only people living on the island then were people employed in the timber industry, cutters and forestry workers, about 40 people all told.

They had to be a very self reliant breed for life on Fraser was primitive in the extreme. There were no services. If they needed power they bought and installed a generator; if they needed water they put a spear down into the island water table and they dug their own septic trenches for toilets.

Roads across the island were sand tracks forged through dense forest and over high sand dunes that turned into dry bogs in the winter and wet bogs in heavy summer rains.

The 120 km long surf beach was the main north south "road" with outcrops of hard coffee rock, fast running creeks and treacherous hidden soft patches to negotiate and always the fear of breakdown that could lead to a vehicle getting swamped by the incoming tide.

The island was hard to reach. There were no ferry or boat services to take people across the Great Sandy Straits from the collection of little townships that bordered the mainland shores of Hervey Bay. The few who wanted to visit, mainly to go fishing, had to get over on one of two small boats owned by people who had fishing shacks on the island.

The only reason Sid and his new wife, Beryl, both Maryborough people, went to the island was because it was all they could afford. Sid's cousin, Joe Cunningham was a timber cutter there, and he arranged for the newlyweds to travel over to the island on the launch that brought the Forestry Department workers from the mainland.

Joe also organised for them to borrow a tent, and assigned one of his employees, Jimmy Campbell to meet them off the Forestry Department's launch and take them the hour and a half hour drive across the island through the rainforest to the surf beach to Eurong.

Originally a winter gathering place for tribal Aborigines on Fraser, the name Eurong means "place of many camps".

That first drive across Fraser Island through dense rainforest punctuated by some of the biggest trees in Australia was an eye opener for Sid. "I was 22 years old and had seen nothing like them."

When they reached the surf beach Sid was even more amazed. "I had never seen surf before and here were great waves thundering onto a broad white sandy beach that stretched as far as I could see in both directions."

Sid and Beryl spent ten days in splendid isolation in the tent under a pandanus palm at on the beach at Eurong, about 40 km from the southern tip of Fraser. They didn't see another soul the whole time. They ran out of food. They caught no fish. And it poured rain for the second half of their stay.

When Jimmy turned up to take them back to the launch as arranged, it was on foot. He'd got his car bogged in a big rain washout on the track. So the luckless pair had to carry their gear half way back across the island to the car and help Jimmy push it out of the bog. They arrived back at the launch landing hungry, exhausted, dirty and wet through.

The timber cutters thought Sid would never want to set foot on Fraser Island again. They were wrong.

That week was to change Sid's life - and Fraser Island.

For in spite of the rain and the hunger pangs - and this a chap so keen on his tucker that when he was doing National Service in the army a few years before, he had joined the boxing squad to qualify for bigger rations - he recognized that Fraser Island was a extraordinary place, and thought if he found it magnificent, so would other people - if they could only get to see it.

"The island was so close to Maryborough and so different and no-one was doing anything about it," Sid says.

He had the glimmerings of an idea for a business, doing trips to Fraser from Hervey Bay, nine kilometres across the Great Sandy Straits.

For him the surf beach was the big attraction, and he was sure it would attract many more people if they could get to Fraser Island.

"I had never seen surf before and not many people in Maryborough would have seen it either, for Hervey Bay, where most Maryborough folk went for their holidays, is sheltered by Fraser Island and has calm water.

"Rainbow Beach and the Sunshine Coast to the south with surf beaches weren't developed then, so the only place to see surf was on the Gold Coast - and not many folk I knew could afford to go there for holidays. It was a grueling drive of at least two days from Maryborough in rattle trap cars on a very rough road."

But here on Fraser Island was surf and huge trees in luxuriant forest, creeks of clear water, and lovely blue lakes rimmed with white sand beaches all on the doorstep as it were, but a place that was inaccessible to folk if they didn't own a boat.

The only vessels which crossed the Great Sandy Straits to Fraser Island regularly were involved in the timber business, barges that picked up logs from where they had been dumped in creek mouths on the island's western shore to take to the big sawmills, Hynes and Wilson Harts in Maryborough, four hours steaming up the Mary River. Their access to the island was at high tide only.

There was nowhere for a vessel to land except a little Forestry jetty at Ungowa for the once weekly Forestry launch to tie up.

When Sid contemplated taking people across the island to the surf beach which had so captivated him, he knew it would be in virtual isolation. Unless by chance there was one of the timber cutters around, there would be no-one to give him a hand if he had any problems.

He would be thrown entirely on his own skill and ingenuity.

The conditions of the island roads alone would have daunted a less determined man. Made by loggers to give access to commercial timber stands or by Forestry Department workers as firebreaks they were just rough tracks blazed through the forest and only one vehicle wide.

In dry seasons the sand was loose and powdery and in wet weather washouts presented another challenge. The tracks were criss crossed by exposed tree roots and not infrequently after high wind, by whole trees blown down.

Sid was very aware that any tourist venture to Fraser Island meant starting from scratch. This prospect didn't worry him in the least. "Had it been easy someone else probably would have had the idea before I did," he says.

Two other factors had to be considered. He had no financial resources and no knowledge of boats. But he regarded neither as a deterrent. He had great confidence in his ability to cope, and work hard, for he had been working hard since childhood.

* * * *

Sid was born in August 1936 and, during the early years of World War II, he lived with his mother, grandmother and First World War veteran Uncle Willy in Maryborough.

His mother did laundry for airmen stationed at the Maryborough airport during World War II across the road from the family home.

Sid with his mother at the 1938 Maryborough Show.

Sid on his third birthday.

In May 1943 Sid was six years old when his mother married Ernie Baumgart, a dairy and cane farmer from Prawle, 16 km out of town. Sid stayed with his grandmother and Uncle Willy in Maryborough so he could go to school.

His longest trips away from home were when he was sent off to spend occasional holidays with an aunt and a brood of cousins at Bauple, a little village about 30 km south of Maryborough.

When he was just 11, his mother took Sid to live on the farm, and he was immediately pressed into working alongside his stepfather.

Feeding a calf at Grandma's

He had to change from the city school he had been attending to the little one teacher country school of St. Helens between Prawle and Maryborough.

"On school days I was wakened at 4 am to go on the milk run, delivering milk in Maryborough with Ernie. He'd drop me at school when the milk run was finished. At the end of the school day I'd ride 10 km home on my push bike, then wash the milk cans, and on weekends, I'd go and chip cane alongside him and mum. In the cane season I'd be cutting cane by hand and walking with a bundle of it over my shoulder up a ramp to throw into the truck," he remembers. "Most of the time at school I was too tired to take in the lessons.

"At weekends and school holidays it was even harder. I'd have to get up at 2 am to milk the cows as well as everything else, and milk them in the afternoon as well. They were 16 hour days, seven days a week, then I'd go to bed with a kerosene lantern.

"I learned to drive when I was 12, so I could drive the milk cart from Prawle to Maryborough in the early hours while Ernie had a sleep. I had to leave school at Grade 5 to work full time on the farm. Mum got correspondence lessons for me, but after a full day's work on the farm I was too tired to do them at night."

"Ernie worked me as hard as any adult. When I was 14, I could carry more cane up the ramp to load the trucks than he could.

There was no electricity on the farm. Milking the cows had to be done by kerosene lamps and torchlight. This meant there were always a lot of flat torch batteries lying around. Inventive and practical, Sid rigged up a lighting system in a disused pig shed, warming the batteries in the oven to give them an extra spark of life and connecting a wire from them to an on-off switch. Here in the shed he says "I was always pulling first my pushbike, then farm machinery and trucks to pieces and fixing them."

The only relaxation the family had was every Saturday night, when Ernie's parents had seats permanently booked at the Embassy picture theatre in Maryborough.

"We went to town in the three ton 1938 Bedford truck they had for carting the cane, the only vehicle they had. The parents sat in the front, while Ernie, Mum and I sat on a tarpaulin in the open back. They always parked in the same car park and always sat in the same picture theatre seats."

Sid's life on the farm was not unusual for his generation when youngsters were expected to work alongside their parents, but he hated the farm life.

"It wasn't for me. Apart from the unending grind, I wanted the big smoke. I wanted to be a mechanic, but when I was old enough I went for all sorts of jobs I was so desperate to get away. The only good thing about those years on the farm was that I developed into a bigger, stronger person.

"My poor education went against me when I applied for a job as a storeman in the local hardware store, Horsburgh's, and I didn't get it."

Many years later, when he was a multi millionaire resort, ferry and tour owner, Sid was asked what the future could have held if he had had a better education. He replied "I could have been unemployed by now. If I'd got the job at Horsburgh's, I could have stayed there and I'd have been put off when the firm was closed down. That's what happened to the chap who did get the job."

Then an apprenticeship as a panel beater was offered and Sid took it because at least it meant working on cars and trucks. While he was doing his apprenticeship, Sid went back to live with his grandmother and his much loved Uncle Willy in Maryborough.

Sid, front right, on a course at Brisbane Technical College during his apprenticeship as a panel beater.

He saved up to buy a motorbike and became one of a small gang of tearaways. The story was told for many years of how Sid and his mates chained Maryborough's solitary police vehicle, a 1947 Ford utility, to the police station fence then roared by on their motorbikes. The police raced out of the station and leapt into the vehicle to chase them, taking the fence with them.

"The police were always after us for making a noise," Sid recalls. "They always used to carry a steel rod. When they stopped us for making a racket on our motorbikes, they would push this rod up the tailpipes to see if they were fitted with baffles to reduce the noise. Of course none of them were, but we all went to endless trouble fitting fake baffles, metal discs which we welded inside the tail pipes.

"They didn't reduce the noise at all, but they'd block the policeman's rod going far up the tailpipe so we would be given the benefit of the doubt."

He was stopped for speeding one day on the motorbike. The policeman asked to see his licence and Sid replied "I don't have one." The policeman told him to go and get one. So Sid put up his age by a year or so and went and applied for a licence. "I was so big that no-one doubted I was 17," he says.

Some months later someone did a check. There was a knock on the door and it was a policeman to get the licence back until he was old enough to have it.

The panel beating apprenticeship was for five years and Sid used it to become a first class tradesman and learn everything he could about vehicles. His first boss, Ron Vickers, sacked him when he and three mates were convicted as juveniles of stealing petrol out of a car in a sales yard to put in their motorbikes, and each ordered to pay a small fine.

Sid's reputation for good work and aptitude was such that another panel beater, Ken Yates put him straight on to finish his time.

* * * *

His interest in vehicles led over the years to him buying and restoring some powerful motorcycles and such cars as an XK120 Jaguar, a Mark 7 Jaguar, an E Type Jaguar and a 1927 six seat Lancia that today's collectors would give their eye teeth to own, as indeed would Sid.

He still remembers how his love affair with Jaguar cars came about. "I had a Ford Customline I'd done up," says Sid "and one day I passed an XK120 towing a caravan. I pulled up alongside and put my foot down. So did the Jaguar driver and he pulled away from me, caravan and all. I thought I'd better get one of them."

"I always wanted something better for my own satisfaction," Sid acknowledges. "I know when I got the XK120 I couldn't afford to put petrol in it except once a week on pay day, but I had a Jaguar."

When Sid's apprenticeship was completed, Ken Yates could not afford to keep him on, so still in his late teens, Sid started his own panel beating business.

He and Uncle Willy went out into the bush and cut posts and battens to build a shed behind the family home for Sid's workshop with a sign out the front *"Maryborough Panel Service"*. Sid sacrificed his beloved XK 120 Jaguar car for the business, selling it for the money to buy the tools he needed. "The man who bought it still has it in his shed and I go and look at it now and again," he says.

No sooner had he started his own business than he had to stop for three months while he was called to do National Service in the army at Wacol, near Brisbane.

"We were asked what experience we had and I said was a panel beater and had been driving a tow truck. The chap next to me said he had been driving a furniture pantechnicon, so both of us were sent to the transport section for an interview," Sid remembers. "We were both rejected and sent back to Able Company, the infantry. I think the Army wanted to teach its drivers its way. But for the first two weeks I peeled spuds in the kitchen," he recalls. "They didn't have a uniform to fit me across the shoulders so I was given overalls and kept out of sight."

Once a uniform was made and he allowed out of the kitchen, he took up boxing. "The boxers often got steak," he explains his sporting involvement. He rapidly became battalion heavyweight boxing champion.

Once his basic training was finished, Sid immediately resumed his panel beating business. He still had to serve an obligatory two years part time in the Maryborough Citizens Military Force, and was rapidly promoted to transport sergeant.

His panel beating skills came in very useful when a group of senior personnel rolled a utility over at a CMF camp. They asked Sid and a fellow panel beater, Col Wolstencroft if they would repair it. It took Sid and Col two days, and no-one ever knew it had been in an accident.

By time he was 21 Sid had several employees – but once his army service was over he was always looking for something better.

After visiting Fraser Island on his honeymoon, the prospect of an island lifestyle as he imagined it, doing something different every day and meeting the challenges of isolation, was much more exciting.

Chapter 2

If Sid were to make a business of taking people to show them the splendour of Fraser Island, the first thing he needed was a boat.

His boating experience was limited to a childhood exercise when he "built" a boat to sail on the farm dam. He took an old sheet of galvanized iron and bent it. To seal the ends and holes in the iron, he rode his bike to the nearest bitumen road on a hot day and picked melted tar from the surface.

In any case he had no money to buy a boat. Every penny he made went into setting up a home with Beryl.

As well as panel beating in his workshop in the backyard, Sid took another job, cleaning offices at night, at the Maryborough Adult Education Centre and the *Maryborough Chronicle* newspaper, where Beryl was office manager, to save for his island dream.

When Sid's grandmother died she left the family home, an old weatherboard house on high stumps, to Uncle Willy for his lifetime and then to Sid. When Sid and Beryl married, Uncle Willy moved out and gave the house to them.

Sid had big plans to modernize it, and got a carpenter to come and give him ideas. This chap told him some of the internal walls would have to come out, and the front verandah knocked down so they could be replaced with new materials.

To save money and have a good time as well, Sid got some of his mates round and they had a wrecking party, punching out walls, chopping down the front verandah and such.

Unfortunately the party was a tad premature for then Sid heard of an opportunity to start his new island business career that was just too good to ignore – and improving the house came to a standstill.

The couple lived in the dilapidated house for the first year of their marriage before they could afford to start rebuilding bit by bit.

The business opportunity which had diverted Sid's attention and funds was a home built nine metre wooden boat owned by a Maryborough schoolteacher, Aub Werder.

It was sitting four metres underwater on the bottom of a muddy creek running into Hervey Bay. Werder did not consider it worth the effort of raising.

When Sid appeared on Aub's doorstep with an offer to buy the boat "as is where is", Aub said it would cost £60. Sid paid him with three cheques, two of them post dated because he could not afford the full sum all at once.

This was the start of a tourism empire that, 43 years of persistent hard work later, comprised a holiday resort with accommodation for 600 people, restaurants, bars, shops, five vehicle and passenger ferries, two large commercial catamarans and the largest 4WD coach fleet in Australia.

It saw Fraser Island turn into a major international tourist destination and Hervey Bay become one of the fastest growing cities in Queensland as a gateway to the island.

* * * *

For several weekends after Sid bought that first boat, which he named *Rio Marie,* he and Uncle Willy would go down to the creek and raise it bit by bit.

They got empty 44 gallon fuel drums, tied ropes around them, floated them out over the boat at low tide, then Sid would dive down and tie the ropes on the boat, and when the tide came in the drums would lift the boat off the bottom. The two men would stand on the bank and haul the drums, with boat attached dangling below, inshore as far as they could before the boat hit bottom again.

Then they'd have to go home to Maryborough and return the following weekend to repeat the laborious process at the next high tide, shortening the ropes from which the boat was suspended, until they got enough of it out of the water to investigate why it had sunk in the first place - a leak where the propeller shaft entered the boat.

They repaired the old Dodge car engine and gear box in the boat, installed a battery, and motored quietly along the shores of Hervey Bay and 35 km up the Mary River to Maryborough to run it aground on the river bank.

Sid continued to work on his treasure at weekends for the next four months. He rebuilt and fibreglassed over the deck; installed a reconditioned Perkins diesel engine, and gearbox and bought fire extinguishers and lifebelts. Finally the boat was thoroughly cleaned and given a new paint job.

The Rio Marie is ready to go to work.

The harbour-master gave the *Rio Marie* a thorough inspection, declared it seaworthy, and certified it as capable of carrying eight passengers.

A Forestry Department launch skipper and builder, Jack Pashley, who had watched Sid working on the *Rio Marie,* offered to teach him boat handling and navigation.

"Sid had no difficulty getting his launch master's ticket," Jack recalls.

"There wasn't much to it really," Sid says now. "It only took us one trip before I got the hang of everything."

With the *Rio Marie* Sid could now get passengers to the Forestry jetty at Ungowa on Fraser Island's calm water western shore opposite Hervey Bay.

To get them across the island to the surf beach, the big attraction, he bought a 1928 A Model Ford utility, one of a few of these reliable old vehicles still chugging around Maryborough.

To fit it for the island's sand tracks he stripped it down, and put big balloon tyres on its back wheels, having already learned from his honeymoon trip across that you could get bogged in the sand with ordinary tyres. He installed a second hand gear box in reverse to give it lower gearing and more pulling power, and gathered driftwood to make bench seats across the back.

He talked the skipper of the *Sarawak,* a coastal boat, into taking the A Model to the island, and it was hoisted aboard at Maryborough and off loaded at Ungowa jetty.

Such was his satisfaction at taking his first trip after so long in preparation that he still remembers the names of every one of his eight passengers.

It was a rough and ready day trip that Sid was offering, to say the least, but it was the only way to go, and it was a very cheap day out, at about £1 per adult.

Passengers watch while Sid fixes a tyre on the A Model Ford utility.

He began to do regular day trips to the island on Sundays and holiday times, still working at his panel beating business and office cleaning during the week.

During the first Christmas holiday, when Maryborough people would traditionally flock to one of the five little suburbs that lined the shore of Hervey Bay, Point Vernon, Pialba, Scarness, Torquay and Urangan, Sid moored the *Rio Marie* just off the beach at Torquay, the most popular holiday spot.

He bought a caravan to act as a holiday home and booking office and parked it on the foreshore with a hand written sign advertising Fraser Island trips. He couldn't afford to do anything more in the way of promotion, but in an era when men were almost all clean shaven, he grew a big bushy beard to draw attention. If any out-of-towners missed his sign, but enquired of a local how they could get to Fraser Island, which loomed interestingly on the horizon, the local would tell them "Just go down the beach and look for the fellow with the beard. He'll take you."

The *Rio Marie* and the old Ford could only carry eight passengers, so it was not hard to get a full complement of trippers most days. Neither was it very profitable, due to its small scale. But Sid persevered. He adopted as his business philosophy the tale of the little elf who made one pair of shoes and when he had sold that he could afford to buy the leather to make two pairs.

It took up to four hours to cross the straits from Torquay, skirting Woody Island then following the mangrove ridden west coast of Fraser for many kilometres until he came to Ungowa, where Sid would offload his people on the Forestry jetty.

It took another three hours to drive across the island on a timber truck route and back, if the A Model didn't break down or get one of its tyres speared by a tree root, and four hours chugging back to Torquay.

"I realized very quickly that with this long boat trip, it wasn't workable," says Sid. "So I looked for a shorter sea crossing and saw the ideal would be from River Heads, the northern bank of the Mary River mouth across to the Forestry jetty at Ungowa only about an hour's sea crossing.

"River Heads was about 11 km south of Hervey Bay. There was a rough road through farmland ending in a little track through the scrub to the rocky shore.

The road to River Heads in 1960.

"I widened the track to take a vehicle and I made a concrete footpath over the rocks so my passengers could walk out to get aboard *Rio Marie.*

"I had to make a mooring there for the boat, so one weekend I borrowed a little Fordson truck from a mate, Bev Whitaker who had a truck business in Maryborough and took chains and weights to River Heads.

"On my way home I ran into a bull wandering on the road and damaged the radiator, the grill and one of the mudguards. The bull fell over so I stopped and went back to look at it. Next thing it got up and charged me. I ran for the truck, jumped up on the wooden tray at the back and the bull, with its head down, hit the truck hard, and dropped dead on the road.

"I plugged the radiator to get the truck going, then went to the wreckers in Maryborough and found an identical truck, in the same standard colours and all. I bought the parts off it and over the weekend bolted them all on and took the truck back to Bev so he never knew it had been in an accident."

To get his customers to River Heads from Hervey Bay, Sid bought a former PMG dual cab truck into which eight people could fit and drove them there and back ***(below).***

There were no facilities on the island for the tourists. Going to the toilet was a matter of men to the bushes on the right; ladies on the left, until Sid paid for the Forestry Department to build a very basic corrugated iron dunny in the heart of the rainforest at Central Station.

This was his first stop to let his passengers walk down a bank to look at the crystal clear Wanggoolba Creek which ran through a palm studded valley there.

The early trips just had time to cross the island to the surf beach, where the passengers ate their picnic lunches, and return, but once Sid moved his operation to River Heads, he could take his passengers to Lake Birrabeen as well.

One of Fraser's lovely and unique perched lakes, it is a broad expanse of blue water rimmed by a pure white sand beach. Sid was first shown the lake by one of the timber cutters, Roy Fish, who had built a shack on its beach for himself and his wife.

Sid immediately realized the lake would be another attraction to show to his passengers, and after the rough trip on the island tracks, most people were glad to plunge into its usually warm waters.

Sid, in the rear, takes his passengers in a dinghy out to the Rio Marie at River Heads. Before he got an outboard motor, he rowed them out.

* * * *

In 1963 Sid's fortunes took a forward leap. A big American company, Petty Geophysical Engineering of San Antonio, Texas, came to Fraser to prospect for oil. Pettys used seismic exploration, drilling holes in the sand, putting a canister of explosives down, then setting off an explosion while geophones would send shock wave readings back to specialised recording equipment.

This enabled them to "read" the formation of the terrain, and ascertain whether there were any underground hollows that might contain oil.

Sid won the contract to take whatever they needed from their stockpile of equipment on a farm outside Maryborough to wherever they were working on Fraser Island. He urgently needed more vehicles for the job.

For the mainland side of the operation, he bought an old VW kombi van and transported quantities of explosives, bran to hold the sides of the drill holes from collapsing, packages of drillers' mud, and groceries to River Heads then on his boat across to Fraser.

In a stroke of good timing the Forestry Department offered a 1942 ex-army Chevrolet Blitz truck that its staff had used on the island for sale for £70. Sid snapped it up, as ideal to carry the materials to the sometimes remote Petty campsites ***(below).***

He had to stop doing his day trips for the time being. "I couldn't be everywhere and I earned good wages from Petty's," he says. "For bringing the gear from Maryborough and the hire of the boat they paid £50 a week, plus paying for all my fuel, and they used to feed me when I got to their camp."

As Pettys moved north up the island, Sid had to find new landing spots to be able to take the gear ashore in a dinghy, manhandling it many times to get it ashore.

It was a good steady income for him, but not all plain sailing. On one of his trips in the VW Kombi from Maryborough to River Heads, probably overloaded, the motor caught fire and the Kombi burned.

Sid didn't want to have to buy another vehicle, but arranged instead to intercept the *Sarawak*, the coastal steamer which brought Petty's supplies from Brisbane to Maryborough, at River Heads, and have the supplies passed over to him in the *Rio Marie* at sea. But that didn't work well with the boats banging into each other, so Sid had to buy another vehicle and run from Maryborough again.

Sid's strength both mental and physical became legendary. He had to be strong to do the heavy tasks he set himself, lifting a succession of 44 gallon drums of petrol on to his truck for delivery to the Petty crew.

He would grasp a drum, bounce it lengthwise on one knee and heave it on to the back of the truck, to be followed by another and another until he had a full load.

But the work took its toll. When Pettys wanted to move their drilling gear north they asked Andy Postan, an island timber cutter who had a small bulldozer, if he would cut a track through an outcrop of hard indurated rocks on the surf beach for them to drive through.

Andy asked Sid, known for his resourcefulness, if he would come with him to help. The two of them set off well before day break, for Pettys wanted the job done quickly, and when they came to the rocks, Sid had to show the way with a spot light.

He jumped up on the side of the dozer shining the light ahead, but unknowingly was standing on a part of the frame that the dozer blade came up hard against when Andy raised it. Sid was barefoot, as always, and his big toe was totally crushed.

It ballooned straight away and the pain was excruciating. But Sid, knowing the job had to be done that day, kept on working. With the track cut through the rocks and camp set up for Pettys by evening, Sid then had to drive across the island, motor across the straits in the *Rio Marie* and drive to Maryborough to get to hospital, arriving some 18 hours after the accident.

The doctor looked at the ghastly crushed toe and said "If you'd got here earlier I might have been able to do something with it. But it's too late now." He bandaged it up and Sid went straight back to work.

Some short time later when Sid took the *Rio Marie* with a load way up to the north western shore of Fraser Island, to land in the huge estuary at Wathumba Creek, night fell as he finished unloading and the Petty workers invited him to bunk down with them for the night and go back at daylight next day.

At that time there was no broadcasting of weather forecasts, so they did not know a northerly front was coming through. The *Rio Marie* riding unmanned at anchor just offshore was exposed to the strong wind.

During the night with the pulling and jerking of the high waves, the anchor rope wore through as it crossed the bulwark and the *Rio Marie* was washed ashore and badly damaged.

Sid left it there. It was proving too small to carry everything needed as the oil exploration job gained momentum, and later he sold it, still beached at Wathumba Creek, for salvage to a fisherman.

With his Petty's job at stake, Sid went looking for another bigger boat straight away. The boat he found was a 15 metre launch. It was laying on the bank of the Burnett River in Bundaberg, at high tide the river running through broken hull timbers. He still couldn't afford a boat that was actually floating.

Undeterred Sid and Uncle Willy worked fast and got the bottom repaired well enough so the boat would stay afloat long enough to get it to Maryborough. Sid bought a second hand 40hp Southern Cross motor and drove with it to Bundaberg with a young deckhand to give him a hand to install it and help him bring the boat south.

They did very basic work to get the boat able to cruise. They just connected the motor to the shaft but had no controls like a throttle or battery to start the motor.

Sid's second vessel was this old launch lying on the banks of the Burnett River in Bundaberg. He repaired it and named it the Lady Fraser.

It was a long haul down the coast and it was well dark before they arrived at their overnight destination, a small concrete jetty at Urangan, the most southerly of the Hervey Bay suburbs.

Not only was it dark, a storm blew up. It was not a happy homecoming. The boat had no lights, but Sid with great forethought had equipped himself with a torch to shine ahead to see the jetty so they didn't run into it.

Sid instructed his deckhand to climb down the hatch into the bottom of the boat, where the engine was, and when Sid flashed the torch down the hatch, he was to stop the motor so they would just drift into the jetty, and then the deckhand had to clamber hurriedly up onto the deck to help Sid tie up.

They chugged on closer, then lightning flashed. The deckhand, down below, thinking this was Sid's signal with the torch to cut the motor, did so. Without batteries and unable to restart the engine from the wheelhouse, Sid had to abandon the wheel and race down into the hold to start the motor up again by hand cranking it. They set off again. The lightning flashed; the deckhand cut the motor…

Next day they continued on to Maryborough, where Sid and his uncle spent two weeks getting the launch, which he named the *Lady Fraser,* in good order, with new hull timbers and decking, a repaired wheelhouse, gearbox, batteries and all.

To save himself the back breaking work of lifting all his cargo on and off the *Lady Fraser* by hand, Sid built himself a basic cargo hoist on the front deck out of second hand scrap and parts. He commandeered a long pipe, abandoned by Petty Geophysical when they moved sites, to make a boom and mast. He bought a second hand winch, which he powered with a second hand Ford Prefect engine from the local wreckers, and he had his hoist ***(left).***

From then on he could sling the drums of fuel, bundles of timber, pipes and whatever else was waiting for him, from the Maryborough wharf on to the *Lady Fraser's* deck. It made life a lot easier for him. He was back working for Pettys within a few weeks, and was able to carry much bigger and heavier loads without having to manhandle everything.

Soon he was earning enough to be able to give up panel beating, which he didn't mind at all. "I'd much rather have been doing island things than being stuck in a hot shed beating metal all day," he says. In a symbolic gesture that there was no going back, he threw his panel beating tools in the ocean.

It was to take almost seven years before his and Beryl's house was completely finished to their satisfaction. Sid remembers the last job on it was a new roof, and the roofer was paid in the new decimal currency.

Chapter 3

When Petty's oil survey was completed, Sid was ready to start his day trips again, bigger and better than before with the *Lady Fraser* and the Blitz.

He lengthened the chassis of the old truck, put a tray back on and made up a bank of seats to bolt across it, built a canopy over the open back, and panel beat and painted it to look really smart. He even painted the wheel nuts bright red! He had it taken back to Fraser Island on a timber barge.

Sid, second from left, watches anxiously as his newly converted Chevy Blitz bus is hoisted aboard the timber barge, Kgari, in Maryborough to take to Fraser Island.

In those early years visitors must have been a tolerant lot because anything could happen and often did. On one trip, when a Forestry boat was tied up at the jetty at Ungowa, Sid had to put his passengers ashore on a nearby beach. They had to step off the *Lady Fraser* into a small dinghy for Sid to row them to land.

One rather large lady point blank refused. So Sid had her sit in the cargo sling, and hoisted her up and over into the dinghy.

The Lady Fraser is transformed into a passenger as well as cargo boat. There was no anchor winch at first so Sid and his deckhand had to pull the anchor in by hand.

Passengers had to be rowed ashore from the Lady Fraser by Sid, pictured pushing the dinghy from the rear, while brother, Dennis, guides from the side.

Sid was so shy with his customers that they got little in the way of commentary – but he was great at getting them over and back on the island, no matter what happened.

Usually he could fix breakdowns or flat tyres on the spot, although on a couple of occasions he remembers, a lot of running to get help was required.

On one occasion the Blitz stripped a camshaft gear at Lake Birrabeen. Sid left his load of day trippers swimming happily, while he raced on foot through the scrub taking the shortest way to the Forestry camp at Central Station.

He had seen four timber cutters there earlier in the day, each with his own vehicle, none bought for more than £10, an old Landrover, an A Model Ford, a two wheel drive Mystery Overland and a Chevrolet sedan, and trusted to luck they were still there. They were, and encouraged by the offer of two cartons of beer on Sid's next trip, they willingly helped transport the tourists back to the *Lady Fraser* in odd procession.

Another time someone stole petrol from Sid's bus left from one weekend to the next parked at Ungowa, and it sputtered to a stop midway between Ungowa and Central Station.

Again Sid had to run several kilometres to borrow enough petrol to get his bus going again.

A scenic stop for day trip passengers among the satinay trees in the island rainforest.

Now and again his frustration at a breakdown would lead to amazing scenes. On one occasion he was transporting a group and they had endured a long run of problems with an engine overheating.

The trip was punctuated by ever shorter runs and ever longer stops while the engine cooled, and Sid could start it again with a crank handle. After the nth time, Sid got so exasperated he took the crank handle and rained blows on the bus bonnet.

"It didn't go any better or worse after that," he says wryly and remembers how one of his passengers came to him at the end of the day and said "I wouldn't want you working on my car."

But with the *Lady Fraser* capable of carrying 58 people, he needed more vehicles and he had earned enough money with Petty's to buy them. The only big four wheel drive vehicles in Australia then were trucks left behind by the American Army after World War II.

Cousin Joe had three of these, 20 year old six wheel drive GMC timber trucks which he was ready to replace, so Sid bought them. He converted two of them into open buses by building new, longer bodies with bench seats on the chassis and added canopies to protect drivers and passengers from rain, sun and sand.

He cut off the cab tops and removed the windscreens, not only to give his passengers a better view through the front, but because he had learned from the Blitz that the cab created a vacuum, sucking sand behind and liberally spraying it over passengers. Removing the cab eliminated the vacuum and kept passengers cleaner and happier.

With six wheels, the GMC's gave much smoother rides than the Blitz. The Fraser Island tourism industry really got a shot in the arm with the introduction of the GMC's.

As his tour business grew Sid began to employ drivers, always choosing men with enough mechanical knowledge to get themselves out of trouble. One such was Jimmy Schmidt, who worked for Sid for many years.

One day Jimmy was driving a day tour when his bus had, as he describes it, "a heart attack" at Central Station. While the passengers explored the beautiful Wanggoolba Creek flowing through a little valley there, Jimmy investigated and diagnosed a problem with the fuel pump.

When his passengers returned, Jimmy noticed one woman was carrying a leather hand bag. He asked if he might borrow it. Curiously she handed it over – and Jimmy cut a gasket out of the side of it.

* * * *

As the *Lady Fraser* was the only commercial launch operating to Fraser, Sid was called on to do all sorts of jobs with it during the week.

One of his most memorable trips was to tow an old punt loaded with cattle from the island to the mainland. A River Heads farming family, the Bengstons had run cattle around Moon Point for years. These cattle had been running wild on the island until the Bengston boys, Selwyn and Garnet, decided they were ready for market. Sid took the Bengstons over to the island, towing their old punt behind the *Lady Fraser*.

They rounded up the 20 steers they could find, and herded them on to the punt. The cattle were trouble from the start, and it took time to load them aboard, then the tow back across the straits began.

Half way across the restless cattle began milling about. They stamped their way right through the bottom of the punt, and it sank quickly. The cattle found themselves swimming in deep water and panicked.

For the next five hours Sid had to manoeuvre the *Lady Fraser* up to each panic stricken beast, then lasso it, haul it in tight to the sides of the *Lady Fraser* and tie its head up out of the water to the hand rails. When he had rounded up the 19 he could find, he had them tied all the way around the vessel. They were far from happy and as he set off to Hervey Bay, the cattle started pulling against the ropes nearly wrenching the rails off the vessel.

Sid realized he was going to have great difficulty landing this cargo. Once they felt ground beneath their feet they were likely to stampede. To save the *Lady Fraser* there was nothing for it but to unhitch them within swimming distance of the Hervey Bay beachfront. His last sight of them was as they charged along the beach, scattering fishermen in every direction, the Bengstons racing after them.

Occasionally local folk would ask Sid to take them and their vehicles across to the island so they could go fishing.

To make it possible to get their vehicles ashore on Fraser, Sid and his timber cutter mate, Roy Fish, built a rough log ramp on a coffee rock outcrop at Ungowa next to the Forestry wharf. The timbers ended at about the height of the *Lady Fraser* deck above the water at low tide.

Sid and timber cutter Roy Fish build a ramp at Ungowa for passengers and vehicles to disembark.

Once the ramp was finished Sid started the first commercial car carrying business to Fraser. Small vehicles could be hoisted on the front deck from the Maryborough fishermen's wharf, but owners of larger ones would have to wait until the tide brought the rear deck level with the wharf, then drive gingerly over a couple of planks placed across to the back deck.

Three vehicles at a time could be fitted on the *Lady Fraser*, two large ones on the back deck behind the wheelhouse, one small one on the front deck.

It was a long four hour haul up and down the Mary River and Sid always used the tide to speed the trip. This meant that quite often when the *Lady Fraser* arrived at Ungowa, the boat deck was far higher than the ramp, and the planks for the vehicles to drive off were at a steep downward angle.

Many a vehicle owner baulked at having to drive off under these conditions, but Sid forcefully persuaded them, suggesting that if they didn't drive off right there and then, he would have to push their vehicle into the drink, as he had to get going to catch the tide on his return trip.

There was little wonder than once a vehicle was on Fraser Island it very rarely came off. Repairs and maintenance were done bush fashion until the vehicle was past repair. Then it was just abandoned.

At one time to make some extra money, Sid and a couple of mates went around the island salvaging engine blocks from all the dumped vehicles and sold them to the iron foundry in Maryborough.

At different times a couple of small aircraft crashed on the island and Sid brought them back.

Among the more unusual loads on the Lady Fraser to be taken to Maryborough were aircraft which had crashed on the island.

The owner of one of the planes, Don Adams had developed a private airport in Scarness, Hervey Bay and ran an air charter business, *Island Air.* Always looking for more opportunities for his business, he cleared Fraser's first airstrip in 1960.

This was on a large area of flat land near Wanggoolba Creek on the west coast of the island and Don began doing regular supply trips for the Forestry and timber workers on the island.

"Wanggoolba was a wet swampy area and one of my pilots, bringing a timber cutter and his family from the island, bogged on the strip and turned a brand new plane over," Don remembers.

Sid says "One of Don's engineers came with me, and at high tide I took the *Lady Fraser* into Wanggoolba Creek mouth, the closest point to the airstrip.

"We stood the plane upright, then he removed the wings and we carried them back to the boat. We hiked back to the plane and wheeled the fuselage back along a track made for timber trucks, and hoisted it aboard."

The second aircraft was a Fox Moth which had nosedived while landing on the surf beach near Happy Valley. Its pilot had been showing off to friends, came in too low over the surf and hit the top of a wave. A timber cutter trucked the plane across to Urang Creek, where it was loaded on to the *Lady Fraser.*

Another unusual job was taking local surveyor, Don Mathiesen, out into the Sandy Straits, where there was a deep water channel between Big Woody Island and Fraser, to mark a measured mile for the big Maryborough engineering firm of Walkers Ltd., so they could test the speed of the large ships they built. Sid set up shipping leads on Big Woody, cruised for the mile as directed by Don, then went ashore and put two more leads in position.

* * * *

The mainstay of Sid's cargo carrying business from 1962 on was delivering 44 gallon drums of fuel to the Forestry Department workers and four of the island timber cutters, his cousin, Joe Cunningham, Andy Postan, Taffy Lewis and Warwick Cornwall. They were all working in the forests about 60 km from the southern tip of the 160 km long island.

Sid's delivery contracts involved him picking up 63 drums of fuel on the Maryborough wharf and delivering them right to the timber cutters' camps on one of the GMC trucks, decanting the fuel into their tanks and taking the empty drums back again to Maryborough to be refilled.

To land the drums on the island, he and Joe built a little wooden jetty into deep water at high tide in Urang Creek on Fraser's west coast.

Sid and cousin Joe Cunningham, standing at the rear, build a jetty at Urang Creek for Sid's fuel deliveries.

Once Sid arrived with a full load of fuel in drums on the deck and in the hold of the *Lady Fraser*, he would have to wait for high tide to get the vessel into the shallow creek mouth and tie up alongside the jetty.

He would back the truck he kept at Urang down the ramp and would sling 21 drums, two at a time on to its tray back, where he would stand them up straight and wrestle them into position. Then he would set off on the trips to the timber cutters' camps.

Doing regular fuel runs for the timber cutters meant Sid got to know them and their families and workers well, and a real bond of mutual respect developed between these hard working, self reliant men.

Sid's running the *Lady Fraser* to the island made a big difference to the cutters. They were no longer reliant only on timber barges, or the Forestry launch, which came on Mondays and went back to the mainland on Thursdays, to get to and from the island.

In spite of his busy work schedule, Sid went out of his way for them.

"I ran my day trips on Saturdays and Sundays and then on Sunday night I would take the *Lady Fraser* all the way up the Mary River to load up with fuel drums for the Forestry delivery at Ungowa on a Monday," he says.

"One Sunday night I'd just got into the wharf in Maryborough around 11 pm, when my wife, Beryl came to tell me Roy Fish had phoned her to ask if I would back to the island for his brother, John, who'd had an accident.

"I had to go all the way back down the river and across to the island again, pick up John and bring him back to Maryborough. It took about nine hours to get him to hospital.

"Another time I got a call to go over and pick up another timber cutter, who'd had a chainsaw accident. The chainsaw had bounced off a hard bit of timber and cut him right across the face through his nose. When I got to the island he was sitting on the jetty holding a rag to his face. Again it took hours to get him to Maryborough, but that's how life was on the island then. There was no other way to get to medical help.

"We all got on together, helping each other out when we could," says Sid. "Roy Fish was a particular friend. I saw him and his wife, June, regularly because my day trips went to Lake Birrabeen, where they had a bush humpy.

Timber cutter Roy Fish

"Eventually Roy bought a caravan to improve his lifestyle, and had me bring it over on the back deck of the *Lady Fraser*, then he towed it to wherever he was cutting timber.

"He told me one day he'd found a beaut spot with views of the ocean on both sides of the island. I went to see and found the camp surrounded by bush. I asked Roy where the sea view was and he said in all seriousness 'You just have to climb up that tree.'

"Roy was always ready to give me a hand. One time it was coming up to the Christmas holidays, so I decided to smarten up the *Lady Fraser*. I got a couple of gallons of white paint and Roy and I painted her up in a little creek in Hervey Bay. Then we went for a couple of beers.

"We both had our cars so I set off home to Maryborough and Roy followed. I saw a police car pass in the opposite direction but thought nothing of it.

"Next morning Roy turned up exhausted at my place. He said he'd swerved or something when he saw the police car, so it had turned and followed him. Roy pulled in to the side of the road, jumped out of his car and ran into the bush, then climbed up a tree. The police ran after him, but didn't see him up the tree and one of them got out his pistol and started firing into the air. Roy had bullets whistling past him, but never gave himself away.

"They didn't catch him, so when they'd gone, he walked miles into Maryborough and came for me to take him back to pick up his car."

* * * *

On another occasion Sid was taking an early scientific study group around the island, but they couldn't keep to the busy schedule they had set themselves.

Late one afternoon Sid ended up driving them along the surf beach at high tide back to their campsite on the dunes above Poyungan Rocks, an outcrop of indurated coffee rock.

Big tides had washed a lot of sand from around the rocks and left deep water filled holes at the front of them. Rather than try to drive his bus over the rocks, Sid drove around the front, and one of his front wheels fell into a hole, and the engine stalled.

The battery terminal came off, and before Sid could put it back on, a big wave came and swamped the bus. He had to leave it until the tide fell, running back the eight km to Eurong in the meantime to enlist Roy Fish's help.

Working all night, the two men towed the bus out of the hole, drained the oil out of the sump, gear box and differential, replaced it with sump oil they had brought, removed the starter motor, cleaned sand out of it, and put it back in, then got the bus started and running again.

Next morning at 8 am there was Sid waiting to pick up the scientists, who were happily unaware of anything amiss – and that with a less conscientious or capable guide they could well have been stranded.

* * * *

Sid and Roy's greatest escapade was when Sid was approached by Maryborough iron foundry owners, Cockburn and Watson, to ask if he could recover some of the cast iron from the wreck of the *Maheno* on Fraser's surf beach to sell to them.

A one time luxury liner, the *Maheno* was rusting away on the beach about 40 km north of Eurong. It had been blown ashore in a cyclone in 1935 while being towed to Japan for breaking up. During the Second World War the wreck was used for all sorts of target practice. Pilots from an aviation school in Bundaberg flew over and aimed bombs down on her. She was also shelled from the sea and her masts and funnels blown up for demolition practice by Commandoes training on Fraser Island.

The wreck of the Maheno on Fraser's surf beach.

When Sid and Roy had no work for a week, they decided to take up the foundry request, and earn some money. They knew they would have to blow up sections of the *Maheno* to get manageable pieces of iron, but they knew nothing about explosives. However a friend of Roy's did and gave him instruction on mixing fertilizer and diesel in a container, then setting it off with a detonator and a small piece of explosive.

"It didn't sound as if it would be much good, so for our first charge we made up the mix in a 5lb milk tin and put it down a hollow bollard on the deck," says Roy. "Then we raced back to our camp in the dunes and crouched behind an old kerosene fridge I'd brought with the food and drinks for the week.

"Well there was an enormous explosion. The bollard flew to pieces and flying metal dinted all the *Maheno* deck and the front of the fridge.

"We knew then to make up much smaller charges and used stubby beer bottles. There were plenty of those lying around the beach, left by fishermen.

"There were only one or two vehicles on the island in those days, but we had to look out for them when we were setting off our charges. I had a lad working for me, and we got him to stand up the beach and stop any vehicles that came along. I remember one chap refused to stop, just gave the lad the finger and drove on. Of course he was just passing the *Maheno* when the explosive went off. He didn't get hurt, but he got the fright of his life.

"We got tons of iron off the wreck, and trucked it to the wharf at Ungowa then slung it aboard the *Lady Fraser* and took it to Maryborough. Cockburn and Watson were mostly making manhole covers, so somewhere in Australia are a lot of manhole covers made from the *Maheno*."

* * * *

Sometimes it seemed as if nothing went smoothly for Sid. Battling with old equipment in the hard and isolated island environment as he did, he often gave vent to an explosive temper when things went wrong, and earned himself the nickname "Savage Sid." But an angry outburst never lasted long and within minutes it was as if it had never happened. Often it was pent up frustration that gave him the strength to do what few others could.

"Soon after I bought the GMC's, the head bloke in the Forestry said if one had a tipper body, he'd give me some work carting sand to make a causeway to a landing being built for timber barges at Puthoo Creek, on the island's west coast," Sid says.

"I bought a second hand tip body from a wrecking yard and put it on one of the GMCs. I was all ready to head off to Puthoo to start the next day.

"Then the Forestry blokes asked if I'd put their Drott tracked digger on the back of the truck and take it up for them, as they didn't have a truck big enough. I had no idea how to carry the Drott, but got it on board, drove it right to the front of the tip body and tied it down, instead of leaving it over the rear wheels that could take the weight.

"The track to Puthoo Creek through the middle of the island was a shocker. The heavy Drott bounced around and bent the truck chassis. I was lucky that I was near my cousin Joe's house, a short distance from Puthoo. He was away on the mainland, but his workshop was open. I drove the Drott off the truck, then got the tip body off with Joe's hoist and with Joe's hydraulic ram, managed to straighten the chassis.

"I welded some plates on, dropped the tip body back on the chassis, drove the Drott on and got to Puthoo just in time for work. I was by myself and no-one knew what I'd had to go through to get there, all in one day and night. I can't imagine anyone else doing that."

It was the GMC, still with the tip body and now with bus seats bolted on to it, that was used to bring a group from the Maryborough Trampoline Club across the island for a weekend camp. Sid was driving the club members through the forest, when a chap sitting up front next to him accidentally kicked the tip lever. The first Sid knew of it was when he heard a loud shout and looked around to see his passengers rising in the air, hanging on to their seats with white knuckles.

He quickly knocked the tip lever back into place to lower them, and not knowing what else to do, put his head down and kept on driving as if nothing had happened.

Another drama happened with one of his first drivers, Johnny Lenthall, when he was bringing a football club to the beach. The lads played up in the back of the truck and their coach swung himself out to sit on the front mudguard to face backwards and keep them in order. He fell off the mudguard and the rear wheels of the truck went over him.

Fortunately the accident happened in soft sand and the coach stood up, shook the sand off himself and continued with his weekend.

When he got back to Maryborough he took a couple of hours off work to get himself checked out, but was found fit and well except for bruised ribs.

* * * *

To make the *Lady Fraser* pay, Sid would occasionally do a charter trip out to Lady Elliott or Lady Musgrave Islands, which mark the southern extremity of the Great Barrier Reef.

The attraction there was the excellent fishing. To reach these coral atolls involved a 14 hour journey for the *Lady Fraser* at her steady speed of eight knots.

Sid's wife, Beryl with some of the fish caught on the first trip to Lady Musgrave.

On one return journey from Lady Elliott, the party was caught in cyclonic conditions. Sid managed to get the *Lady Fraser* into the lee of Fraser Island before the full force of the wind hit. Even so the launch could only make one or two knots against waves which washed right over the front deck and wheelhouse. From the northern end of Fraser to harbour took eight hours and the launch lost its dinghy and handrails.

One Lady Musgrave trip with a group of divers ended in tragedy. One of their number was a young medical student whose name had been put forward for a medal for bravery for his part in the rescue of crewmen from a dredge, the *Captain Nielsen* when it sank in Moreton Bay.

The student was a keen diver, and no sooner had Sid reached the reef than he and two others hopped in the dinghy they'd had towed behind the *Lady Fraser* and went off. Sid had to continue around the reef to anchor at the entrance to the island's lagoon. When the three divers did not rejoin the *Lady Fraser* as planned, Sid motored back around the reef looking for them.

He found the young student had gone too deep and drowned. The stricken group managed to recover his body, and then set off straight back to Hervey Bay. The young man's medal was given posthumously to his parents.

* * * * *

Sid often had the help of a great mate, Johnny Stevenson, a linotype operator at the *Maryborough Chronicle.* The two of them met when Sid was cleaning the Chronicle offices and immediately hit it off, with their shared enthusiasm for motorcycles and Jaguar cars.

Stevo *(right)* matched Sid in size, height and girth, and when John grew a beard people often believed them to be brothers.

John used to work nights and would show up at the Maryborough wharf to help Sid load during the day. On days off he would go along on the *Lady Fraser* trips. "He'd help me whenever he could," says Sid, "and was always keen to go to Fraser Island, especially after he met the daughter of a Forestry worker, Denise Fletcher, whom he later married."

Sid also acquired an employee from his cousin, Joe Cunningham. Sid was to take building materials, including a plate glass door, to the island for Joe to build an extension to his house at Bogimbah.

Joe informed him that the builder, Kelly Page, would be making the trip with him.

Sid had the *Lady Fraser* loaded and ready to cast off at Maryborough, but Kelly did not show up. Sid fretted about time and tides, but eventually spotted a rather portly, bespectacled figure ambling slowly, and not at all surely, down to the wharf. When he identified himself as Kelly, Sid shouted at him to get a move on.

Kelly clambered onboard, missed his footing, fell and smashed through the plate glass door.

Three weeks later Sid was handling another shipment for Joe, and was again waiting for Kelly. Kelly arrived late and under the influence again, was shouted at, scrambled aboard and crashed into Joe's replacement glass door.

Joe did not particularly want Kelly back after the second incident, and there was certainly no reason why Kelly would have impressed Sid enough to be offered a job. But somehow Sid ended up with Kelly.

He seemed to sense when Sid was loading in Maryborough for a trip to the island and would turn up at the wharf. Sid told him repeatedly to go and look for another job, and Kelly would amble away, but would always come back.

Sid tried to line up other jobs for him, but Kelly never lasted long in any of them. Sid found out why when he was taken severely to task by a Forestry officer. "You know that Kelly Page you sent to us for a job," said the officer. "We sent him out to plant trees and do you know what he did?" Sid could not imagine. "He planted them upside down."

Sid finally succumbed to Kelly's Irish blarney and gave him a job and, when he got land at Eurong, a home for more than 20years.

Sid also employed relatives from time to time, and on different occasions invited one of his half brothers and a brother-in - law to go into partnership with him. They didn't have to buy in to the business, just help with the work. Both declined. They said they could see no future in Fraser Island.

Chapter 4

Sid was often asked to take groups over to camp on the island. He would have liked to buy some land at Eurong to make a camping ground, but there was no private land available there. It was all State Forest.

In the 1930's a few timber cabins had been built for visitors at Happy Valley, 25 km notrth of Eurong, but Happy Valley Resort, as it was grandly named, didn't survive the Depression. At Eurong there was nothing but beach and bush.

Nonetheless Sid applied to the local Burrum Shire Council for land at Eurong on April 12 1962. His application was passed to the Lands Department, but he heard nothing more.

Coincidentally in the same year two businessmen applied to the Lands Department for four acre land leases at Eurong. One was Don Adams, who had formed the airstrip near Wanggoolba Creek mouth, and the other a Maryborough businessman, Keith Williams, whose family ran the coastal steamer, *Sarawak* between Brisbane and Maryborough, among many other businesses.

Don says "I thought we might look at supplementing the flights we did for the Forestry staff by flying tourists to the airstrip and then driving them across the island to the beach. In 1962 I applied for a special lease on four acres of land at Eurong as a day trip destination."

Keith Williams applied for a similar size lease to build a holiday house for himself.

The four acre leases were granted to these influential businessmen. Their interest in island land spurred the Queensland Lands Department into creating small townships at Eurong and Happy Valley and surveying subdivisions of about 20 small house blocks at each place in an effort to regulate demand.

In 1963, the survey complete, the Department held an auction offering the blocks for lease for about £9 a year rent. Sid bid successfully for three blocks at Eurong, and a few others were taken up, but by no means all, for with the difficulties involved in getting there, interest in Fraser Island was minimal.

Sid was asked by the handful of new landholders to bring materials to the island for them to build holiday houses, and this kept him busy, but the work was hard and more than once Sid nearly lost a truck when he had a breakdown on the surf beach on an incoming tide on his way to Happy Valley.

From the early to mid 1960's all building materials for Fraser Island had to be transported on the Lady Fraser. Sid is pictured guiding a load of bricks on to the front deck.

Soon after Don Adams obtained his four acre lease at Eurong, another chap entered the Fraser Island scene. This was Sir Reginald Barnewall, a third generation Australian from a long line of Irish baronets. He had been the chief pilot and founder of Polynesian Airlines in Samoa, and came to Fraser in 1964 with the idea of building a Samoan style holiday resort. He applied for land on high sand cliffs overlooking the surf beach and a rocky headland called Waddy Point, some 100 km north of Eurong.

With flying interests in common, Don Adams went into partnership with Sir Reg and the pair of them set about making their idea of an exclusive resort, which they called Orchid Beach, a reality.

Don had done nothing on the Eurong land and was no longer interested in it. When Sid asked if he could buy it from him, Don agreed to sell for £600. But the sale stalled when the Lands Department would not transfer the lease to Sid, until Don fulfilled one of the lease conditions and put at least £2000 worth of improvements on the land.

Don didn't want to do that. He had enough on his plate. So it was agreed on a handshake that Sid would put on the improvements, and then the sale could go through.

Nowadays everyone thinks the land was the real estate bargain of the century. Then everyone in Maryborough and Hervey Bay thought Sid was crazy paying so much for a block of land on Fraser Island. It was so isolated they did not imagine there would be anything Sid could do with it to make it worth £600.

They did not count on the amazing persistence, willingness to work hard and dedication to a dream that Sid was to show.

The land was covered in thick lantana, which had to be cleared, leaving only bigger trees, clumps of gnarled coastal banksias, casuarinas and the occasional pandanus.

In between running his trips and doing whatever work came up for his trucks and boat, Sid set about clearing it.

"I bought a little Fordson tractor with a bucket on the front and had it brought over to the island on a timber barge," Sid recounts. "I'd charge into a mass of lantana and it would get heaped up in the front of the tractor and it would stall. The tractor needed petrol to get it started then ran on kerosene, which was cheaper. So when it stalled, I had to cut my way with a brush hook through the heap of prickly lantana to the front of the tractor, drain the kerosene out of the carburetor, turn it on to petrol, wait for it to cool, and crank it with a handle to get it started again. I did my level best not to stall the tractor too often."

As he cleared one patch of land at a time, he would hand plant grass turfs on it, to hold the sand from blowing away.

There were no services at all on the island then, no electricity, water supply, or sewerage. Sid had to provide them all for himself. "It was a beautiful place and I wasn't at all frightened of the challenge," he says.

Eurong township was split in two by a large sand blow, a bare dune blown up from the beach, steadily moving inland, covering the trees in its path, for more than a kilometre. Half the houses and Sid's land was on the northern side of it; the other houses on the southern side. The track from the western side of the island, through Central Station to the beach, ran south of the blow. It was so steep that in the often long spells of dry winter weather, it was hard to drive up or down in the soft sand.

Sid and his fellow Eurong landowners heard of a disused timber wharf that was being pulled down on the island, and said they would remove the timber if they could have it.

In a series of working bees they got the timber, trucked it across the island, and laid it on the soft track. But they only had enough to lay it lengthwise and it didn't take long before it kicked up and was more trouble than it was worth.

"The only option was to find a better route with less gradient and the only one was north of the blow," Sid recalls. "With the tractor, I cleared two kilometres of new road to the beach, following natural gradients to the northern section of the township. I followed the survey pegs between my lease and those of half a dozen house blocks, and that became the main road to Eurong."

In so doing, Sid cleverly positioned his land on what was to become the crossroads of Fraser Island, with the main east west road along one side of his lease and the surf beach, the main north south thoroughfare, along its frontage.

* * * *

Jack Pashley, the man who had taught Sid boat handling on the *Rio Marie* some years before, was first and foremost a builder and Sid asked him to build a little shed, four metres by four metres, at Eurong for him.

Jack says they bartered "I knew Sid was a first class panel beater, and it so happened I had a Land Rover, which had a rusted out chassis through being in the salt on Fraser Island, and I asked Sid if he could get it going again. He suggested I buy another second hand chassis, for him to mount the body on, which I did. It took him some weeks to get the Land Rover back in good order and by then I was ready to build his shed in return."

Once complete, Sid bought eight ex-army wire beds and chained them to the walls for himself and his employees, Kelly Page and Johnny Lenthall, to sleep in and for friends and relatives staying over - and to stay over usually meant friends were put to work anyway.

The men acquired a bush shower and had to cart buckets of water from lagoons in front of the land to fill it. No more than half a gallon of water per shower was the rule.

The next little building was a shed to house a 5 kva generator driven by a 10 h.p motor to produce 240 volt power, so Sid would have lights to work at night.

A Forestry worker, Bob Oldfield, who built the first little house of bush timber at Eurong, scoffed when it was being installed. "Why are you putting in such a big power system? You'll never need 240 volt power over here," he told Sid.

Neighbours across the road from Sid's land were delighted when he got his generator. One of them, Cedric Keller, craftily dug a channel across the road, ran a power lead across it and plugged into Sid's electricity.

"Well it was only fair," says Cedric. "I got Sid to take a new cement mixer to the island for me, and when I went over to use it, Sid had hired it out to a chap in Happy Valley."

Sid was quite well aware of the power sharing. "A lot of the neighbours tapped in to my power at Cedric's place. They thought I didn't know, but I used to turn the power out late at night to save fuel, and I would see all their lights go off at the same time."

Pinching Sid's power continued for many years, and one cheeky chap used it to run a freezer to make blocks of ice to sell in opposition to Sid's ice sales. His power lead got chopped into a dozen pieces when Sid found out.

* * * *

Work at Eurong ground to a halt for lack of funds, until one of the transport jobs Sid did was to cart blocks for a holiday house in Happy Valley for a chap who owned a country sawmill and brickworks. In return the man gave him the timber for two A Frame cottages that Sid wanted to build to let to visitors.

Again Sid asked Jack Pashley to do the building for him.

"I cut out the timber on the wharf in Maryborough. When Sid saw the timber he wasn't happy, because it wasn't straight, and I had to calm him down telling him to wait until I'd cut it out and he'd see it was all right," Jack recounts.

"I remember one time I was working on the timber there, Sid turned up at the wharf in a former Brisbane City Council bus he'd bought second hand, and it seemed down at the springs.

"I looked inside and saw bags of cement laid out everywhere on the floor. He'd brought about four tons with him because it was a lot cheaper to buy in Brisbane.

"I asked 'How did you go at the weighbridges?'

"He said 'All right, because I found an 'out of service' sign and put it in the front of the bus and the inspectors could see there were no passengers in it, so waved me on by."

The bus was intended to attract more custom to the day trips. When he had time Sid put it in good working order, and painted it red with white sign writing advertising the island trips, and a logo of a top hatted little character sitting on the tip of Fraser Island.

To attract more custom to his tours, Sid bought this Brisbane City Council bus to carry his passengers from Maryborough, restored it and painted it red, even down to the wheel nuts.

An employee, Max Williams drove the bus bringing people from Maryborough to Hervey Bay, then out to River Heads to board the *Lady Fraser*, while his wife, Pam ran a tour booking office in Maryborough with Fraser Island its only destination.

Max was working for a Brisbane bus company when he first met Sid. He brought a group of people on one of Sid's day tours. At the end of the day he took the group back to Brisbane, gave his notice and returned with Pam and two young daughters, Ricki and Robyn, to live in Maryborough and work as a driver for Sid. He was to stay with him for more than 30 years.

Jack Pashley will never forget another day when Sid had to do a run to the island with supplies.

"He came down to the *Lady Fraser,* which was tied up at the wharf, and asked me if his deckhand had come down to take empty 44 gallon fuel drums out of the hold, "Jack recounts.

"I told him no-one had been and in sheer frustration he went down the hold, and next thing I saw these 44 gallon drums come flying up on to the wharf. I had to look out so they didn't roll on me.

"How he managed to handle these drums and throw them up on to the wharf from down the hold amazes me to this day. I survived the onslaught of the drums, and soon the frames of the A Frame cottages were completed and ready for shipment to the island, once the foundations were finished."

Sid by now was juggling so many projects, building at Eurong, transporting building materials for other folk by boat and truck, doing regular runs to keep the timber cutters supplied with fuel, and running his day trips that it was amazing he had the mental as well as physical capacity to keep them all going.

Progress on the building at Eurong was slow, because Sid was always hindered by lack of money, but it never stopped. As he could afford to buy it, he would have gravel for foundations along with timber or roofing iron left for him on the wharf in Maryborough.

Jack Pashley describes how the gravel was brought to Eurong: "Sid would line up open 44 gallon drums on the Maryborough wharf. Then Byrne Brothers would bring four yards of gravel in a tip truck and dump it in the drums.

"When Sid arrived, he had to shovel up what missed the drums, and then hoist them all on to the *Lady Fraser's* deck and pile other materials on top.

"He'd motor all the way down the Mary River on the outgoing tide and across the straits to the Forestry jetty at Ungowa, and tie up. The hoist on the *Lady Fraser* only had enough reach to sling the drums on to the jetty, so Sid would have to tip the gravel out into a heap, and shovel it by hand up into the back of one of his trucks.

"Then he would drive across the island and start shoveling the gravel off the truck again. It used to take him a day and part of the night to get just four yards of gravel to Eurong. " says Jack.

"Even the sand had to be brought the same way, for island sand is too fine and too round to use for building.

"It was exhausting and backbreaking work. I don't know of anyone else who would have persisted with it day after day.

"Water for the concrete mixing was bucketed from a beach front lagoon into drums on the back of an old utility and transported to the building site.

"There was as much pushing as driving involved because, weighed down with drums of water, the poor old two wheel drive ute bogged down in the sand every few yards."

When Sid and his workers sat back, often well after dusk, having poured and screeded a slab of concrete, they would have to stay alert to stop dingoes and brumbies from running over it until it set.

The island brumbies were a major problem. Each herd had its own territory and once Sid started making a lawn, a stallion and eight mares made his land theirs. They would pull out the new turf and churn it up with their hooves. Sid would run about shouting and waving his arms and throwing sticks at them and the horses would drift away, but not for long.

When they threatened his new concrete floors or pathways, it was the last straw. One night Sid crept up on the brumbies and with a bloodcurdling yell and a bound, he leapt upon the back of one. The brumby took off full pelt down the beach in the darkness with Sid hanging on for dear life. No-one knew when they would see Sid again, but he soon turned up more angry than hurt. The brumby had thrown him off and he had lost his watch.

"Sid picked out the site for the A Frames cottages, towards the back of his lease, and I started to assemble the A Frames in position," says Jack Pashley, "I had the first strut braced and the others locked in when Sid looked at them and said what a bendy lot of frames they were.

"I calmed him down by telling him to wait until I had stood them all up. No more was said and when everything was up, they were plumb and straight. And there they stand to this day.

"I remember while I was working on the first cottage a chap named Fred Jarvis, who lived at Eurong, came over for a chat.

"Sid was not far away and as we watched, he picked up a full 44 gallon fuel drum, rolled it on to his knee, then heaved it on to his trailer and stood it upright.

I said to Fred "That drum is full of petrol you know," and Fred said "No way. It's got to be empty."

No more was said and a bit later when Sid had gone, I saw Fred wander over to the trailer, grab the top of the drum and give it a pull. The drum didn't move. Fred came back and said "You're right. The darned thing is full."

* * * *

If life was primitive for Sid and his workers at Eurong, it was not a great deal better for the first guests.

Jack had almost completed building the first A Frame when a group of fishermen approached Sid and asked if they could book it for a week.

Sid explained "It's not quite finished, but you can stay if you don't mind making your own beds." Expecting sheets, the fishermen said "Not at all." Sid gave them planks of wood, hammer and nails.

No-one complained. If they did they faced Sid's temper. He had so much work to get through every day, that he had no time for niceties or holidaymaker demands.

One guest asked Sid if he could expect to have a quiet and peaceful weekend at Eurong. Sid replied "Well I've been here for years and I haven't had one yet."

Another man, later an airline executive, recalls a staying at Eurong in 1968 with a couple of fishing mates.

"We stayed in an A Frame cottage which had a kero fridge. Sid lent us an old vehicle to get around the island. One day the vehicle ran out of petrol and the fridge ran out of kero, so we had to ask Sid for both things as once.

"The reception we got was such that when it happened a second time, we did without the vehicle for a couple of days so we could space out our requests.

"When we got the vehicle fuelled again and set off up the beach, it broke down. The three of us worked like beavers to get it going again – we just weren't game to go back to Eurong without it. For all that I became a regular at Sid's place."

Sid was hopeless at public relations. He saw his island enterprise as a series of practical building and vehicle challenges to be overcome, and not in terms of people.

His success at meeting the challenges was remarkable – but guests always had to take him as they found him.

He felt his guests and passengers should recognise how hard won everything was and not take anything for granted, even inadvertently, by driving over the lawn or leaving a tap turned on.

He became a very well known and controversial character because he had a strong personality and an uncertain temper.

But he was greatly admired by those who got to know him, even slightly, for the nonstop hard work he put in to establish and develop his business from scratch in very difficult conditions.

Sid always lived under pressure, both self imposed by his ambition and imposed upon him by the isolation. It would have beaten most men, but his tremendous will power and his dream of a resort drove him on relentlessly.

"There have been many times that I have asked myself if it is all worth it," he said at the time. "I thought of walking away from the whole thing but I know I couldn't do that. It's too much part of my life."

Sadly he felt his poor education and limited experience outside the island meant he had little to offer in the way of sociability. He had a terrible memory for names. Hence he was a very shy man and communicated little until familiarity made him more sure of himself.

Then he revealed great depth of character, compassion, understanding of people and a dry wit of such quality that his remarks and responses were repeated endlessly by others.

* * * *

The A Frame cottages.

Sid showed great foresight in planning his resort. Many years later he was asked if, when he started, he envisaged how big it would grow. Sid pointed to his two A Frame cottages and replied "If I had thought they were the best buildings I was ever going to be able to build, I would have put them right at the front of the resort, instead of towards the back. I knew better buildings would come and saved the frontage for them."

Similarly he can point to concrete paths he laid in the early days. Without exception the ends were left rough so connecting paths to later buildings could readily be joined on to them.

Sid couldn't put his plans for Eurong on paper, but he had them clearly in mind, and his vision for a resort, and confidence in his ability to develop it, were such that he early realized the front four acres would not be enough.

The Forestry Department granted him an occupation permit, the least secure of land tenures at the time, on another four acres of land behind his lease. He planned to use it initially as a camping ground, and later for more resort buildings.

This land too was infested with dense lantana and again Sid had to clear it before he could do anything more. It was all punishing work, and Sid started to become a legend among the small island community for never giving up, no matter what the odds.

* * * *

Before the second A Frame was completed, building priorities had to change. A camping group of 80 people booked to come to Eurong for a long weekend. Left and right hand bushes for toilets and a shower, laboriously filled with one bucket at a time, would not suffice.

Sid, Kelly Page and Johnny Lenthall set about building a concrete block amenities building with showers, toilets and laundry tubs. Kelly was a plasterer by trade, which, in Sid's view, qualified him as a bricklayer and plumber too.

Kelly was willing but felt he needed a beer at more frequent intervals than Sid would allow while he was working. Sid thought he had won the battle of the booze until, as land clearing progressed at Eurong, caches of beer bottles were uncovered everywhere.

Not surprisingly the amenities block walls Kelly built ended up not being quite straight, but he had done his best.

Jack Pashley came to put the timber roof beams and the roofing iron on, and says "When I got to the end of the building I found the back of it was a foot longer than the front. I managed to dummy things up so it looked O.K., and only Sid and I knew."

There was no time to re-build better, for the 80 campers were due. The night before their arrival the amenities block was completed, but the water supply had not been connected.

At midnight Sid, Kelly and Johnny finished erecting a tall wooden tank stand on a nearby hill, hoisted a 2000 litre corrugated iron water tank on it, and connected water pipes from this tank to the amenities block. All that remained was to fill the overhead tank, so water would run from it under pressure to the toilets and showers.

Down to the lagoon they bumped in the old ute with a smaller 1000 litre water tank on its back from which they could fill the pressure tank. Sid by this time had been prevailed upon to buy a little petrol pump, so at least they did not have to bucket the tank full.

They set off back up the hill. As usual Sid and Johnny had to push the ute as Kelly drove it, but as it lurched up the hill, the full tank of water started to slide backwards.

"Hold it on Johnny. Just put your shoulder to it," Sid shouted, his shoulder already bearing the load. So there were the two of them in the middle of the night, in the middle of the bush, pushing an old ute up a steep hill and stopping a 1000 litre tank full of water slipping off the back at the same time.

It was 3.30 am when they finally pumped the water into the overhead pressure tank on the stand. There was no time to check that the water actually ran down to the new amenities block. Sid and Johnny had to dash off to the *Lady Fraser* on the other side of the island, and then motor over to the mainland to pick up the campers.

When Sid and Johnny drove in to Eurong that afternoon, and pulled up, all 80 jumped off the open buses and raced to the toilets. The two men just sat looking at each other, keeping their fingers crossed the water had run through.

Then was heard the welcome sound of the first toilet flushing.

* * * *

The next building project was a small workshop so buses and trucks could be repaired, out of the all pervading salt spray from the surf. When it was finished, it was judged there was indeed £2000 worth of improvements on the land, so Don Adams could sell the lease to Sid. Don was as good as his word and the sale went through for £600.

Many years later when Sid had made a viable resort at Eurong and Orchid Beach, which Don had chosen to become involved with, was struggling with access and erosion problems, Don was to say to Sid "I made the wrong decision." Being one of nature's gentlemen, it was said entirely without rancour or envy.

Chapter 5

While Sid was slowly starting to clear the land and erect very small buildings at Eurong, work on the far more up market Orchid Beach resort had begun in 1965, on land selected in Marloo Bay by the flamboyant Sir Reginald Barnewall for its beauty of outlook. Sir Reg and Don Adams, both pilots, planned to fly their guests in so did not see it being hard to access was a handicap – except when it came to building.

Jack Pashley became construction manager for the Orchid Beach project. The first thing he did was employ Sid's cousin, Joe Cunningham and his dozer driver, Jimmy Campbell to clear the site; and Sid with two of his GMC trucks to cart sand to level the land for an airstrip and building sites.

Getting the trucks, even empty, to Orchid Beach was extremely difficult. Sid and his brother-in-law, Gary Milera, had to drive some 90 km along the surf beach and the beach was fraught with dangers.

If a truck bogged in a soft patch of sand, or while being driven through one of the many large freshwater creeks that flow across the beach, or round the front of one of the many coffee rock outcrops, it could have been swamped by incoming tide and lost. Those beach hazards still exist, but nowadays so many people drive the surf beach that help is always at hand. Then there was no-one at all.

The major barriers to travelling up the surf beach are two huge rock headlands, Indian Head and Middle Rock, which jut well out to sea just a few miles south of Orchid Beach.

Indian Head stands alone in a landscape of bare sand dunes, and to pass behind it was a matter of ploughing through deep, powdery sand. Middle Rock was worse, being the southern edge of a rock plateau. Its steep scree covered rock face had to be climbed.

Jimmy Campbell bulldozed a road through the scrub from Orchid Beach to the top of Middle Rock and a track of sorts up the side of Middle Rock.

He did his best to avoid the steepest sections, but this meant putting a dog leg half way up.

Indian Head with a soft sand track behind it.

Sid was well aware of the difficulties that faced them in getting trucks to Orchid Beach, but there was three weeks' work in leveling the airstrip and it was too big an opportunity to ignore, so he went.

Sir Reginald asked Sid one day what he thought of the Orchid Beach site, expecting admiration for the tremendous view over the great sweep of Marloo Bay, terminating at the most northerly of Fraser Island's rock headlands, Waddy Point in one direction, and a surf beach as far as the eye could see in the other.

Ever practical, Sid replied he thought the site was a poor choice. He foretold it would be prone to erosion, and pointed out that a ship, the *Marloo*, had run aground in 1912 in the bay.

"You can still see the remains of the *Marloo* more than half a mile out to sea," Sid told Sir Reg. "The wreck hasn't shifted – the land has been lost to erosion."

Sir Reg would not be dissuaded. It had been a long and difficult process for him to get a lease on the land from the Queensland Government to want to start the whole procedure again in another location.

Jack Pashley recounts "My next job was to find a reliable way to get all the building materials to the site.

" It wasn't possible to bring goods up the surf beach because, with the cyclones we'd been having, a lot of sand had been washed off the beach leaving big outcrops of coffee rock exposed, and laden trucks couldn't get up the steep rock face at Middle Rock.

"The only alternative was by sea to Wathumba Creek, a big estuary on the north west coast of Fraser Island, then about 13 km across the island by truck to the resort site on the eastern shore. There was a narrow fisherman's track across the island and Joe Cunningham and Jimmy Campbell made it wider, clearing a lot of trees with Joe's bulldozer, so we could get our truck across.

"I had to find someone to transport the materials by boat to Wathumba, a hard job as the northern beach is so unpredictable with big soft patches. There were no barges going to the island then, but I had seen what Sid could do in his little boat and told Sir Reg that Sid was the only bloke I knew that could do the work."

Sid, keen for employment of any kind, agreed to bring materials into Wathumba Creek. He found he was working for people who had absolutely no concept of what was involved for him. When he pulled in to the Maryborough wharf for his first load for Orchid Beach, he found much of it was a huge quantity of timber, all strapped up into half ton bundles, far too big and heavy to lift aboard the *Lady Fraser.*

Sid got on the phone to Sir Reginald in Hervey Bay and complained long and loud, but when nothing happened and it was obvious he and his deckhand, Chummy Nielsen's lad, were going to have to break up the bundles and load the timber without any help, he had to delay his first trip to Wathumba Creek by two days until they could get it all aboard.

There were no wharves or ramps to off load at Wathumba, and the *Lady Fraser* couldn't get right into the beach.

Jack Pashley, a co-worker, Don Tyndall and one of Don Adam's pilots, Darcy Walters had driven over in a small truck to collect the materials. They, with Sid and his deckhand, young Nielsen, had to form a human chain to get the materials off the boat through the sea to the shore.

"Sid had to come in at high tide so there was enough water to get his boat as close in to the beach as possible, and we had to get unloaded before the tide dropped," Jack Pashley recalls.

"If we didn't do that and Sid's boat sat on the bottom with the heavy load, it could have split her timbers. Unloading was always a race against time and tide.

"We had a small Blitz truck, and Sid suggested we use the hardwood planks he'd brought, to make a ramp across the soft sand and patches of mud, so we could back the truck closer to the boat. We had to lay four lengths of the timber side by side for each wheel track for about 100 metres between the boat and the firmer beach. Sid passed each length of timber down from the boat, and there were three of us to carry it and lay it in place, one piece at a time.

"It was so soft closer to the boat that the planks just sank under the weight of the Blitz so we still had to carry everything 20 metres between boat and truck in the squelchy sand. Sid said the rest of the timber would have to be unloaded first and he and his deckie passed it down to us and we staggered to the truck and loaded it on.

"Next came big sheets of corrugated fibro-cement roofing. It was tremendously heavy, and it took two of us to carry each one. We had just got that unloaded when we had to stop as the tide was coming in over the plank tracks. Sid said we'd have to wait until the tide started to drop again in the afternoon to offload the rest of the cargo."

It was 3 pm before they could get started again and there was no chance of them finishing the unloading before dark. Jack and his two co-workers were not relishing sleeping on the beach, but Sid took them on board the *Lady Fraser*, fed them and gave them a place to sleep in the wheelhouse under a tarp.

He got them up again before first light, made breakfast of instant coffee and Vegemite on bread and the unloading continued.

"Sid was on the deck passing everything to us in the chain at great speed," says Jack. "You got a case of louvres or nails or a sheet of fibro or roofing iron on your shoulder, and you sank into the sand a foot or more, and staggered ashore, put it down above the tide and went back for another load. The only light we had was one off the boat.

"We had material spread all along the beach, and then we had to load it on to the truck, and do the long slow trip across the island to Orchid Beach to offload."

Once all the materials that needed to be kept dry were taken off the *Lady Fraser*, Sid, anxious to get going, threw the rest of the hardwood timber off the deck into the ocean for the Orchid Beach fellows to pick up when the tide fell.

But Sid didn't get away as fast as he hoped, and it was fortunate for the Orchid Beach fellows that he didn't. A mooring rope tied to a large mangrove tree fouled the propeller.

Sid had to dive at least a dozen times to get the tangle of ropes free and was all ready to start up again, when he saw Darcy Walters waving his arms and shouting they were in trouble.

"Don Tyndall was driving our truck fully laden up the beach and it got two flat tyres on the back," says Jack. "We were below high tide mark and the tide was coming in fast. We only had one spare wheel and managed to change one wheel, then tried to drive the tuck above high tide mark with just one flat. Don stuffed things in the gear box and, trying to rev up to get out of a soft sand bog, he made a big hole in the beach.

"We were completely stuck. None of us had any mechanical knowledge to sort things out.

"Then I saw Sid coming along the beach. I told him about the gear box and the flat tyres. I soon realized how lucky we were that Sid was there. He got his toolbox from the boat and set to work.

"Don had tangled the gears but Sid delved in and fixed them. We tried again to get the truck out of the bog but ended up screwing the flat tyre to pieces. We managed to get the truck above the high tide mark but couldn't drive it any further.

"In the meantime Sir Reg flew over from Orchid Beach in his little Cessna plane to see what had happened to us, and when he saw us still struggling away on the western beach, he landed to find out what was going on.

"I explained everything to him and he said he knew where he could get another wheel in a hurry, from a fire truck at the little airport in Hervey Bay. Sid knew of this truck, and told Reg the wheel on it wouldn't fit our truck as ours was an 8 stud wheel and the fire truck was a 10 stud. This didn't register with Reg, so he took off and brought back the wheel, and on landing, one back wheel of his plane went smack into the hole in the beach and damaged the undercarriage.

"We took the fire truck wheel off the plane to put it on our truck, and of course it didn't fit. Sid watched with interest, and then came up with a temporary solution that we take the tube out of the fire truck wheel and put it in our wheel.

"Fortunately we had a foot pump to inflate it. So we were mobile, but now had the problem of the damaged plane.

"Reg decided he'd better take the plane above the high tide mark, so he hopped in to taxi it up the beach while we pushed it. As soon as the nose wheel hit the soft sand, down it dropped. The propeller hit the ground and bent one of the blades. Reg decided he would try to take off on the narrow strip of hard beach that was left and fly to Scarness airport to get repairs done.

"We said he was crazy, but he said worse things than this had happened in war time. With the condition the prop was in, Reg said he had to take the weight off the front of the plane, so the nose wheel was kept off the beach. He told Darcy and I to sit on the tail, one either side of the rudder, while he taxied up the beach to take off.

"Darcy told me that he'd nod his head when we had to jump off. Reg taxied slowly up the beach and that was all right. Then he turned into the wind and put the power on. We were blasted with sand.

"We were doing at least 60 km p h when I saw Darcy nod, and we dropped off the plane, careered along the beach and got all the skin scraped off our arms and legs by the sand. I reckon we were lucky just to get that."

* * * *

Sid's cargo trips to Wathumba Creek on the *Lady Fraser* varied between monthly and fortnightly as materials were needed.

Sir Reg went with the truck on the second trip to collect the building materials, and recollects "The *Lady Fraser* was more than ten metres out from the high water mark when Sid threw ropes ashore for Jack to tie to trees.

"We were all dressed ready to wade in the water and had old shoes on our feet to protect us from mangrove spikes. The tallest of us, who happened to be me, had to stand next to the boat to take the materials as Sid passed them off the boat.

"I was up to my armpits in water and, when I stepped back into a hole by mistake, the water came over my head.

"Once the human chain was in place, Sid began unloading. A barrage of 44 gallon drums of petrol came over the side in such rapid succession, that I found it hard to pull one clear of the drop zone before the next one came down.

"The carpenter, Alan Caplick managed to push the drums to Jack and another worker, Normie Palmer, who took an end each and pulled them to dry land."

When Sir Reg suggested a different order to the unloading, he learned very quickly a Melksham characteristic, that Sid had his methods and, having worked out how he thought things should be done, would brook no opposition or diversion. If anyone demurred, as Sir Reg did, then Sid would put on a show of temper to get his way.

"I certainly cannot recall being on the receiving end of a lustier, more colourful blast of invective than I copped that morning," Sid Reginald recalls. "I thought if that's the tone of things so early on in the unloading, what's it going to be like when the pressure is really on."

But Sid had got his way. No-one gainsaid him again and as Sir Reg records "The expected repetition didn't come. Sid had let off steam and that was all that was required." Says Sid, who also remembers the incident well, "Of course I knew how the boat should be unloaded. I had loaded it."

Sir Reg continues "A dozen or so 100 pound gas cylinders came next. To my utter amazement I watched this great bear of a man above me, clad only in shorts, and with a cigarette dangling from somewhere in the middle of his beard, lay two gas cylinders on the deck simultaneously then, one in each hand – grasped by the handles on the top of each – effortlessly lift them both clear of the rail and hand them down to where he expected me to take them. I could barely manage one at a time.

"Six or so cases of nails, each weighing some 50 kilos followed. They had to be taken on my shoulders and, with Alan's assistance, passed to Jack and Normie. I asked Sid for a break but he said another 15 minutes would get the dry cargo ashore, then he would toss the hardwood off, and get going as the tide was falling rapidly.

"After Sid and his deckhand threw the timber off in almost frenzied haste, he checked the *Lady Fraser* was clear of all the timber he'd tossed overboard, started the motor and, without a word, had the boat edging out of the gutter into which he had brought her for unloading," says Sir Reginald. "He headed gingerly into the main channel and brought her about into the fast ebbing tide.

"He gave a blast on his horn, a wave and then disappeared into the wheelhouse to head to Maryborough."

* * * *

One can imagine how Sid regarded the apparent lack of organization that accompanied the first few deliveries of the Orchid Beach materials. "These blokes didn't really know what they were doing," he says, and more charitably, "It wasn't what they were used to. You can't be good at everything.

"Their truck was a stupid little thing, with a tray back not much bigger than a utility, far too small to carry the long lengths of timber. I couldn't put up with all the time wasting and mucking about."

He found a better landing spot in a small creek. Jack Pashley recalls "Sid said with all the gear he was going to have to bring over, a ramp would need to be built to get the truck closer. Well we tried, but Reg had different ideas from me, and the ramp turned into a total failure.

"I recall Sid getting up us for not doing a proper job by using army surplus steel matting or some such. We all had to keep offloading by hand."

After only a few trips, Sid suggested he deliver the loads right to Orchid Beach using two of his much bigger trucks.

From then on Sid, his deckhand and one of his drivers, Max Williams or Gary Milera or sometimes his mate Johnny Stevenson, would offload the *Lady Fraser.*

Young Nielsen, the deckhand, for some reason known only to himself, refused to take off his ex army greatcoat and when it came to summer, he got terribly hot. Sid found him dropping a few things over the side of the boat, so he could jump in after them, greatcoat and all, to cool off. Had Sid been able to get a replacement, he most likely would have sacked the lad, when he caught him deliberately dropping a bag of cement overboard.

Sid would moor the boat well out in deep water. Then he and his men would unload the vessel, and load the trucks by hand and drive them slowly and carefully over the dreaded soft sands of the Wathumba Creek estuary, and across the island to Orchid Beach on the rough track, offload, and drive back.

With the huge boomerang shaped bond wood covered beams for the roof and walls of the main restaurant building, a Samoan style *fale fono* as Sir Reg called it, this was an enormous struggle, every bit of strength needed to wrestle them off the boat and on to the trucks.

"There were eight or ten of these beams and we had to put them half on either side of the wheelhouse. They had to be kept dry and when it came to unloading, we had a terrible time wrestling them off the front deck." Sid says.

Time and again Sid needed all his strength and practical bent to keep deliveries to Orchid Beach going.

"One time Johnny Stevenson and I were on the *Lady Fraser* going through a gutter off Moon Point with a load of fibro sheeting on the deck," Sid remembers. "I misjudged the depth of water, the boat touched bottom and we got stuck on a falling tide. If the tide went right out, the boat would have keeled over and all the sheeting would have slid off. I had to take urgent action.

"I dropped the anchor, then jumped overboard, hauled the anchor into deep water and dug it into the sand with my feet.

"I climbed back on board, started up the motor and used the anchor winch to pull the boat forwards over the hump so it was floating again."

It was hardly surprising with all the heavy work that Sid got a severe hernia and had to be operated on. Jack Pashley took over skippering the *Lady Fraser* for one delivery while he was in hospital.

"All told it would take three days to take a load to Orchid Beach from Maryborough and get back to Maryborough," says Sid, "if things went well."

But many times as Sid was heading to Wathumba, strong northerly winds would blow, lashing the sea into big waves. Sid would have to go about and run for shelter behind Moon Point well to the south. Sometimes he would have to shelter in the lee of the big promontory for three or four days until the winds dropped.

While most of the building materials came on the *Lady Fraser*, Sid bought a second vessel from Maryborough sawmillers, Wilson Harts, a small tug called *Tradewinds* to carry the huge quantity of concrete blocks needed for guest rooms to Wathumba Creek.

Tradewinds, which had once pushed dumb barges, laden with timber from Fraser Island to Maryborough, had a deep hull with square windows at the back into it. The blocks would be stacked in the hold and, on arrival at Wathumba, would be passed through the windows to waiting hands outside.

So many of them were passed through over the following months, the windowsills were completely worn away.

Tradewinds when Sid bought it.

To get the really heavy equipment to Orchid Beach, Sir Reg relied on Sid again, but there was no possibility of landing it at Wathumba Creek and manhandling it ashore. The only way was to transport it up the surf beach on a truck.

Sid had taken empty trucks up the beach before but was now going to have to try with a heavy load. The first load to go this way was a big four and a half tonne electricity generator for the Orchid Beach power supply.

Sid organized for the big generator to be brought to a landing on Fraser on a timber barge, then trucked it across the island and prepared to drive it up the surf beach.

He set off with Max Williams and Johnny Lenthall. They took with them a few lengths of steel Marsden matting that had been used to make wartime airstrips on soft surfaces. With Sid at the wheel, the truck made it up the surf beach without incident, and then came to the loose sand behind Indian Head.

While Sid drove slowly, Max and Johnny lay lengths of the matting ahead of the truck. As it crawled along from one length to the next, they would run behind, pick up each piece of matting and run round to put it under the front wheels.

They had a brief respite when they reached firm sand in the cove between Indian Head and Middle Rock.

The three great rock headlands, Indian Head, Middle Rock and Waddy Point in the foreground.

They had to use the matting again to get through yet another long stretch of soft sand to the base of Middle Rock.

Sid gritted his teeth and began to ease the truck up the rock face. It was so steep that, with the weight of the generator on the back of the truck, the front wheels lifted off the ground.

Sid had Max and Johnny throw loose rocks under the back wheels to help skew the truck around the tight corner. More than once the truck seemed in danger of tipping over.

Hearts in mouths they finally made it to the top and from there it was comparatively straightforward driving on the bush track Jimmy Campbell had bulldozed to the Orchid Beach site.

In all five heavy loads had to go up the beach, and the headlands.

The most care had to be taken with a load of ten big satinay logs that Sir Reg wanted as features to hold the ceiling inside his *fale fono.* He specified that the bark had to be left on the logs and they be delivered undamaged.

Sir Reg got special approval from the Forestry Department to buy the logs, and had Joe Cunningham cut a satinay tree for him from Yidney Scrub behind Happy Valley.

Joe had a small crane and was to meet Sid to lift the logs on to his truck for the drive up the beach.

Timing, as always with beach driving was crucial, so the big loads could be taken up on an outgoing tide. But Joe was late, and when he finally arrived, he and Sid, both big men with big voices, had the biggest argument ever between them.

Each log had to be wrapped in tarpaulin or old bags, whatever they had, where chains were put around for the lift with the crane, so the bark would not be bruised.

By time Sid's truck was loaded the tide was already coming in. It was again a nerve wracking drive, but Sid made it safely to Orchid Beach – and there was Sir Reg waiting to inspect the precious logs. The bark on one of the logs was scarred.

Sir Reg exploded and blamed Sid. Sid exploded and blamed Joe. To this day neither Sid nor Sir Reg has forgotten the incident. "It wasn't that much of a scar," says Sid.

* * * *

Fishermen and experienced island drivers began to use the steep track up the side of Middle Rock in their small 4WD's, but only about one in twenty succeeded, and it became a good day's entertainment to sit perched on the side of the goat track, as it became known, watching the attempts to drive up it with lots of laughing at the failures and loud cheers if anyone made it.

It was so difficult and dangerous that other drivers formed a sand track behind Middle Rock, but this was so long, so powdery and soft that there was no improvement in the success rate unless tyres were let down to bulgy.

It became known as beep beep hill because the most frequently heard sound was the beep beeps that modern 4WD's make when they are reversing.

Then in 1992, when the National Parks Service took over the management of Fraser Island, and needed access to Orchid Beach for its huge rubbish compactor trucks, it had the sand track boarded all the way up with big timber planks. Now everyone can drive up Middle Rock, and the dangerous track up its face is visible today only as a gully filled with planted casuarinas trees.

* * * *

With only a few trips left to go for Sir Reg Barnewall, the death knell to Sid's cargo trips, not only to Orchid Beach but also the weekly fuel trips to the timber cutters, was sounded when a small steel barge, the *Way-Lillie,* was introduced to the Sandy Straits by a former Fisheries patrol officer, Kev Donnelly.

As Sir Reg well recalls "Donnelly was the protégé of the local harbourmaster, Captain Whiteman, who decreed that wooden ships could not carry fuel at all and any sort of cargo north of Moon Point. The object was obviously to send Sid broke, so Donnelly could take all his business – but those who tried to do that over the years found they had a bigger fight on their hands than ever they expected.

"I think a lot of people looked at this character struggling against the odds with this little boat and totally underestimated the incredibly strong sense of purpose he had."

Sid remembers it too "Within a week of Donnelly starting, the harbourmaster wrote to say it was illegal for me to carry fuel in drums on a wooden boat, although I had been carrying drums of fuel for the Forestry for years, and fuel was being brought up from Brisbane in a wooden boat, the *Sarawak.* It was pretty obvious that I was being put out of business so Donnelly could take it over.

"It may have been a good thing, because then I went off in a different direction."

By then Sid had done more than 450 return cargo trips up and down the Mary River in the *Lady Fraser* and the *Tradewinds* for Sir Reg; for himself to start building at Eurong; for the folk who wanted to take vehicles to the island and to build holiday houses, and for the Forestry Department and the timber cutters.

Sid had to sell *Tradewinds* to pay what was owed his crew in wages. Many years later he was surprised to see it working as a trawler out of Southport on the Gold Coast. "I could tell it was her because the windowsills hadn't been replaced."

The loss of most of his cargo carrying business on the *Lady Fraser* meant that Sid had lost the mainstay and biggest income earner of his infant enterprise. But he never for one moment considered abandoning it.

He put his considerable energy instead on bringing tourists to the island and building at Eurong, as well as trucking materials around the island for anyone and everyone, although Donnelly in an attempt to get rid of the competition Sid presented, persuaded a local pineapple farmer, Les Greensill to bring 4WD trucks to the island for cartage to Orchid Beach.

Sid says "I was happy to use Donnelly's barge myself because I thought it would make it easier for me to get my building materials to the island.

"But he was the wrong bloke for that kind of life. He had been a desk man in a collar and tie. If he should be setting off at 4 am to catch the tide, he'd probably still be in bed, and he'd turn up two hours late. Things were always going wrong.

"The first time he took me over was with a truckload of sand and gravel for building at Eurong. He was to take me into the old log dump in the mouth of Wanggoolba Creek at high tide, which was the only time a vessel could get in there.

"But he was running late as usual and when we got to Wanggoolba, the tide was running out fast and Donnelly couldn't get right up to land. He said he wouldn't take the truck back to the mainland and I'd got to get it off.

"There was a big stretch of mud between the barge door and the land, but he gave me no option so I drove off his barge and of course got bogged axle deep. Donnelly just sailed away and left me. I had to shovel all the gravel off the back of the truck on to the mud to lighten it enough to drive it out.

"It was still stuck fast. So then I had to walk miles to the Forestry camp at Ungowa to ask for help. One of the blokes got a tractor and came and pulled the truck out for me.

"I didn't want to lose the gravel, so then I put boards down and backed the truck on them down over the mud again to the gravel heap, and shoveled as much as I could collect out of the mud on to the truck again, then drove to Eurong. That was a long day's work.

"Donnelly never made a success of his barge business. I'd taken nearly all the building materials to Orchid Beach before he came on the scene, and there wasn't a great deal of other work. Before long he sold the barge away from the area, so I was back to carrying cargo as well as the day trips."

With all the work he was doing on the island, Sid was hardly ever home and Beryl had a full time job at the *Maryborough Chronicle,* so she could hardly ever go to Fraser. Their marriage ended in divorce in early 1969.

* * * *

Another unusual enterprise for Sid and the *Lady Fraser* was the start of an artificial reef in Hervey Bay. Abundant fish in the Great Sandy Straits was one of Hervey Bay's claims to fame, but after a few poor seasons it was stated the bay was "fished out".

Ill feeling flared between professional and amateur fishermen.

In early 1969 Maryborough engineer and professional diver, Roy Rufus conceived the idea of an artificial reef to improve fish breeding and make a good dive site.

He thought a good start would be the hulk of a 39 metre steel dumb barge that had been abandoned on the bank of Deep Creek, south of Ungowa.

Called *The Otter*, the vessel had outlived its usefulness firstly as a coastal lighter, and secondly as a timber barge.

When Roy put his plan of towing it to the proposed site of the reef, in a channel between Fraser and Big Woody Islands, authorities said he couldn't take it because it was too rusty and had been condemned.

Not one to give up, Roy approached Sid and the pair of them had a good look over the vessel, tapping the hull with hammers to see if it was sound.

"We felt it was in better condition than thought, and if it was empty there would be no risk of it sinking while it was being towed to the reef site," Sid explains. "It was, after all, only a short time after it had been carrying full loads of heavy logs. Then the sawmill company owners had cut holes in the bottom to scuttle it.

"Roy welded patches over the holes, then we let it float for a few tides and kept an eye on it. We believed we would have no problems at all, so one night at the end of July we towed it out with the *Lady Fraser* and sank it again on the reef site.

"Soon afterwards Roy dived on it with an underwater oxy acetylene set and cut off the wheelhouse to a safe navigation level for vessels to pass over it.

"Once the start on the reef had been made, enthusiasm mounted, and timber barges took old car bodies, concrete bombies and tyres to dump overboard in an arc around the old vessel. When two more old timber barges, the *Pelican* and the *Lass O'Gowrie,* had outlived their use by dates, they too were towed and sunk on the site in 1971 and 1975 respectively."

The artificial reef became the largest in the southern hemisphere. Within a short time myriads of fish had made it their home. The reef was named after Roy Rufus: a memorial to him for he died in 1983 while diving on it to do a fish count.

Chapter 6

In the mid 1960's there were big developments at Cooloola on the mainland immediately south of Fraser Island. Sand mining was planned for the mineral rich beaches by Queensland Titanium Mines Pty Ltd, a subsidiary of the American company, National Lead. In preparation a new township, Rainbow Beach was begun to service the industry, with a bitumen access road to join the Gympie-Tin Can Bay road.

Gordon Elmer, a bean farmer from Amamoor, near Gympie, realizing the road meant people could now access Fraser Island from the south, saw a business opportunity for himself. In 1967 he built a small ferro cement barge called *Fraser Dawn,* which he started to operate from the beach at Inskip Point about 11km from Rainbow Beach to Hook Point beach at the southern tip of Fraser.

His barge could only carry a couple of small vehicles at a time, but made it easier for anyone wanting to take a vehicle to the island. Few did in the beginning and Gordon ran his barge only at low tide and then not every day. As he said, on a busy long weekend he would carry only 22 vehicles.

Sid welcomed the new barge service, because it meant he could get a small load of stores or building materials on a 4WD International van from Maryborough to Eurong, without having to manhandle everything on and off the *Lady Fraser*. But before long, from Sid's viewpoint, things didn't go well.

He explains "Elmer used to work at low tide, never to a regular schedule. I'd go over on his barge in the morning to Maryborough, and come back all the way with a load of supplies, frozen goods and perishables, a round trip of 320 km, to find he'd knocked off early. He'd have only planned to work maybe a couple of hours at dead low tide, but hadn't told me when I was on the way over. If he wouldn't come to take me over I'd have to drive all the way back to Maryborough, 160 km each way on rough roads, to take all the frozen stuff back to the suppliers to put back in their freezers. Next morning I'd have to go and collect it and set off again.

"I never knew what hours Elmer was working, and he'd have knocked off regularly when I wanted to get back to island. Many times he'd still have his barge on the beach, but would say he'd finished for the day and it would be an extra $30 to take me over."

Sid with his International 4WD stores panel van at Gordon Elmer's first ferro cement barge at Inskip Point.

The southern beach from Hook Point was much narrower than at Eurong, and could change with every tide. One day it could be firm and the next have gutters running into it with "melon" holes, large patches of soupy sand. There were four big creeks between Eurong and Hook Point and, where they ran across the beach, they could change from wide and shallow one day to narrowly imprisoned torrents between steep banks the next.

This stretch of beach nearly caused Sid to lose two of his trucks.

"Max Williams and I were taking a load of timber up the beach from the barge in the International van," Sid says. "It bogged, and trying to drive it out of the soft sand, it broke its front wheel drive. We had no hope then of getting it out of the bog. We ran to Eurong and got another truck, the last remaining one of the GMC's, to tow it out.

"We took some of the timber planks off the load on the Inter to put under the wheels of the GMC across the soft sand to the Inter make the tow easier. We had just pulled the Inter out of the bog when something in the transfer case of the GMC broke so it had no drive at all. It was a desperate situation. I thought we lose both of the trucks as the tide was surging in fast right up to the top of the beach. But we managed to use the Inter, by now with only two wheel drive, to tow the GMC back to Eurong, before the tide swamped us."

"It was the closest shave I ever had with any of my trucks," Sid recalls. "It was lucky we had lengths of timber on the load. Those two vehicles were my entire fleet of freight vehicles at that time. Had we lost them it could have been the end of my trucking business."

If the beach could get two experienced island drivers like Sid and Max into so much trouble, novices, many in conventional cars, who could now come to the island on Elmer's barge often found themselves in dire straits.

With Eurong the most visible settlement on the beach front, Sid now found him called upon for help by people deceived by the island's beauty into ignoring or not realizing how treacherous it could be.

"One day a chap came running up to tell us he'd bogged his Holden ute while driving it across one of the four big creeks between us and Hook Point, and ask if we could tow it out for him.

"We raced down in a truck but couldn't find it. We thought someone else must have come along and towed it out for him, and were about to go home when I saw about 60cm of radio aerial sticking out of the sand. The fast flowing creek had washed the sand from under the ute's wheels and it had sunk right into the creek bed. We had no hope of recovering it and it is there still."

All another fellow thought to save from his vehicle, as it sank in a creek bed, was a snake he had caught and put in a cardboard box.

"Then there were the three fellows who came to ask for help in towing their vehicle out of the surf. It was well out and facing into the breakers," Sid remembers. "They sheepishly admitted to having a few beers as they were driving up the beach in the dark. They had mistaken the lights of prawn trawlers at sea for the resort lights. So they had turned and headed straight for them.

"There was the group of scientists renting one of the A Frame cottages, who had us out day after day rescuing them and their vehicle from creeks and sand bogs," Sid well remembers. "By way of thanks they left the fridge full of dead snakes, bush rats and other small animals they had caught and killed."

* * * *

One of the people to come on the first group tour on Elmer's barge to Eurong was Brisbane businessman, Phil Delaney. He recalls "I first met Sid through Max and Pam Williams. They had been working for Sid, and were trying to get a camping tour together from Brisbane to take to his place on Fraser Island."

Phil made up a pamphlet advertising the trip for them and spent hours printing copies out on a Roneo machine.

As a thank you Sid asked if Phil *(right)* would like to come to the island with the group.

"There were 14 of us and we traveled by bus to the Sunshine Coast then someone else took us to the barge over to Fraser. It started to pour rain as we got there," says Phil.

"We all had to stand on the open deck on Elmer's little concrete barge, which had no cover, and there was Sid in an open truck waiting for us on the other side.

"Sid had brought a plastic sheet for us all to hold over ourselves to keep this torrential rain off us and our luggage. Of course that blew away before we'd gone very far.

"By time we arrived at Eurong and lifted our sodden suitcases out of the truck they all fell apart. All we were left holding were the handles while the cases themselves fell open at our feet. It was a disastrous start, but by the next day the weather had cleared and we were having a ball. Everyone said it was the best weekend they had ever had.

"The following weekend another group was coming, and Sid asked if I'd like to stay over for a holiday and go back with them. At least this time it was fine and sunny, but not without incident.

"On the first night some soldiers from the army training camp at Tin Can Bay flew over in a helicopter and seeing our tents, landed for a better look. They ended up partying with us and staying all night. Early next morning another helicopter came looking for the first one because it hadn't returned. It too landed – and when the two helicopters took off they blew all our tents down and our stuff all over the place."

Phil ended up cooking for the groups and the resort staff and at the end of the week Sid obviously felt pangs of guilt about Phil working so hard on his holiday. So he offered him another week's holiday. "I cooked all the next week too," Phil recalls. "Sid and I became great mates, a friendship which has lasted to this day."

Phil became a regular visitor to Eurong and was invariably roped in to help, often driving the day trips.

"One time Sid and I were driving the day trip back to the *Lady Fraser* in the open buses and mine broke down, so I put it to the people that they all get on to the one bus, or they could stay and miss the boat.

"Sid just sat there saying nothing. The passengers grumbled a bit but by time they'd all squashed on, they started to see the funny side of things. I sat on the front mudguard facing backwards and told them stories about the island and then I heard Sid say 'Look at that.'

"I turned round and saw the biggest red bellied black snake I had ever seen in my life. It was gliding across the road and its head went in the bush but its tail was still coming.

"I looked in awe and forgot the passengers could see this snake as well. By time I turned back around the bus was empty. They'd all jumped off and ran down the road they way we'd come, thinking, I suppose, that the snake would come up the wheels into the bus."

Phil well remembers too the time he went to Brisbane with Sid to buy a Toyota.

"It was about two years old, and was the newest vehicle he'd ever bought. He and I got a lift to Brisbane to pick it up and bring it back to the island. By time we got to Elmer's barge at Inskip Point it was high tide.

"Elmer dropped us at Hook Point and the vehicle went straight down into soft sand and bogged.

"It took us until after dark to get it out and I have never known so many mosquitoes. They swarmed on us. We wiped them off and our arms were covered in blood and they came back for more.

"Sid said we'd drive fast to Ted Schiefelbein's house to get away from them. He was a fellow who ran cattle at the southern end of the island. The mosquitoes followed us into the Toyota. We raced to Ted's house and hammered on the door. He had an inside door and an outside door, both with screens, and we knew why.

"He peered out at us, black with mosquitoes, and asked the daftest question of all time: 'Do you want to come in?' "And I tell you those mosquitoes were so thick that they made the fly screen bulge with the sheer weight of them trying to get in after us."

* * * *

In March 1970 Sid married for the second time. A Brisbane teacher of the blind, Marietta Bono met Sid when she came to the island on a camping trip. They were to have two children, Monica born in November 1970 and Bill, born in January 1974.

Sid and Marietta took up residence on the top floor of the first A Frame, and at lunchtimes sold soft drinks and ice creams to the day trip visitors from a counter on the ground floor.

When he had spare time but no money for building materials, Sid would work away on the land, hand planting lawn to create an oasis in the wilderness, as well as make a fire break for there were frequent bushfires on Fraser, and make visible any snakes coming out of the surrounding forest.

Sid and Marietta set up shop in the ground floor of one of the A Frames.

Sid mowed the lawn himself with a motor mower, marching up and down for two days to cut the whole area. A ride-on mower would have made the job easier and faster, but Sid feared his weight on a ride-on would cause the mower wheels to dig grooves in the sand based lawn, break up the roots and the lawn would die.

At Eurong on low beachfront dunes, the island water table is close to the surface and by sinking a spear into it with an electric pump attached, Sid was able to tap into a bountiful supply.

Not one to waste time, while he planned how he was going to achieve his next project, he would now stand after work and water the precious lawn to get it established.

He spent so much time thinking and watering his lawn that one time a guest who had been watching him, and not knowing he owned the place, remarked to him "I don't know what your boss pays you mate but whatever it is you're not worth it." Sid was dumbfounded – and just as well.

This high water table did however create a major problem when Sid acquired a hand operated petrol bowser and decided to move into petrol retailing. He had to install underground fuel tanks, and thought it would be a simple matter of digging a large hole in the sand by the side of the road, rolling the tanks in and burying them.

He should have known by now nothing on Fraser Island was that simple. He began to dig. Only a metre or so below ground level, he struck water. He continued digging faster but the water slurried almost as much sand into the hole as Sid could dig out. Finally deciding the hole was big enough, he rolled the tanks in the hole, but they floated. Sid poured in all the drums of petrol he had trucked to Eurong, and at last they sank enough for him to mix batches of concrete to pour over them and bed them in.

* * * *

One of the biggest problems facing Sid at Eurong, in the early years, was the lack of communication with the mainland. If he needed to call for help for an emergency or arrange for a load of materials or supplies for his infant resort, he could do nothing unless he drove 9 km to use the Forestry phone at Central Station. The only telephone line to Fraser Island, installed seven years earlier, was to the Forestry Department headquarters at Ungowa, with branch lines to the Department's secondary camps.

An appeal to the Post Master General's Department, the forerunner of Telecom and Telstra, to run a party line across the island to Eurong brought refusal. It was too expensive a job for the benefit of a single subscriber.

After persisting for months with his requests for a phone and being refused, Sid finally got permission to tap on to the Forestry line at Central Station. But he would have to string his own line 9 km through the scrub to get there.

In early 1970 he did just that. He bought big rolls of fencing wire for the line. He took insulators from disused forestry lines that had been left in trees.

The Forestry Department said he would have to buy the trees he wanted to mount the insulators in for his line, and Sid agreed, but slyly pointed out that the timber would be worth a lot of money in time to come. The Forestry agreed then to hold him to a bond of $50 to remove the insulators, if and when the line became obsolete.

Over the next two months, whenever they had time between other jobs, Sid and one of his employees, Johnny Lenthall set off with an extension ladder, to install the insulators into the trees.

It was hard work, chopping off branches, then stretching up as high as their arms could reach to drill small holes in the chosen trees with an augur and bit to screw the insulators in, the same way all the Forestry lines were strung. Then they ran the fencing wire from insulator to insulator for the 9 km to Central Station.

The last insulator is put in the trees for the phone line.

"We had to make the line as high as possible where it crossed the road for timber trucks, often with big logs piled three high, were using the road, and we didn't want them to keep snagging the line and pulling it down as they passed," Sid says.

He bought a second hand phone of around 1926 design with a wind up handle, mounted it on the wall in the A Frame cottage where he lived, and joined it to his line.

He wound the handle and a voice answered. It was a telephone operator in Maryborough. Sid said he would like to speak to the Maryborough milk factory, so he could put in an order to have milk ready for collection. The operator connected him without demur.

Now people could contact Sid directly and he started to get bookings for his tours, A Frame cottage and camping ground – bookings which were written on the back of a cornflakes packet tacked to the wall next to the phone. It gave a big boost to his business.

The phone system worked well for its time and place, but the PMG was slow to accept Sid's highly unorthodox entry into its system, until everything changed on July 22 1970 when his telephone was needed more urgently than ever before or since.

* * * *

A year or so earlier a Urangan man, Jack Reville, had started running day trips from Hervey Bay with his boat, the *Island Queen,* and two Blitz trucks he'd mounted seats and metal roof canopies on, copying Sid's trucks.

Reville would land his people on McKenzies beach near a timber cutter's derelict jetty, 25 km north of Ungowa, and drive them to one of Fraser's lovely lakes, Lake McKenzie then to Central Station and return.

From time to time, Reville would call on Sid for help and on this particular July day he phoned asking Sid to meet him with one of his vehicles, as he had more people than would fit on to his truck. Sid agreed and, with ten passengers aboard one of his small vehicles, followed Jack's truck with some 40 people.

They were on their way back from Lake McKenzie to the *Island Queen,* and Sid was some way behind Reville. He breasted a steep hill and came upon a shocking scene. Reville's truck had careered out of control down a steep hill, smashed into a big tree stump at the bottom and turned over.

The metal truck canopy had detached and sliced into many of the passengers, who were lying everywhere, some dead, some with severed limbs and all screaming and crying out in pain.

Sid immediately asked his passengers to go and assist the injured as best they could, while he drove fast back to the Forestry HQ at Central Station to call for help. The Forestry response was to ground all its vehicles and men. Sid was left to handle the situation by himself.

Sid rang the police in Hervey Bay. "The police wouldn't believe me," Sid reports. "They could not seem to understand the enormity of the accident."

Frantic by now as time was passing and he was getting nowhere, Sid bypassed the authorities and rang Don Adams of *Island Air* at the Scarness airport, told him the situation and asked him to evacuate the injured by air. He said he would be waiting at the airstrip near Wanggoolba Creek mouth.

"Don knew me, and knew I was fair dinkum," he says.

Sid then rang two of his staff, Johnny Lenthall and Gary Milera, at Eurong and told them to bring blankets and torches and each drive a vehicle to the accident site.

The accident had happened about 2.30 pm but Sid knew it would be well dark before the rescue effort could be got under way with the time it took driving back and forth over the rough tracks.

The first sign of help was a single small plane with one of Don's pilots, Darcy Walters, who had brought lamps to light the airstrip ready for the evacuation planes. He and Sid hastily placed the lights around the strip.

Don had first had to get approval from the Civil Aviation Authority to fly into Wanggoolba at night, and then he had called a local G.P., Andy Mayne and the Hervey Bay hospital, which sent its matron to help. Don himself flew them over in a medium size Britten Norman Islander. Another of his pilots flew a six seater Cherokee.

"It was a high risk operation, piloting planes in the night on to the rough boggy sand strip and I thought I'd better go myself," says Don now.

Sid was waiting for him to land, to drive Dr. Mayne and the matron to the accident.

They immediately started to check the injured and prioritized them for Sid and his two men in their vehicles, to take back to the airstrip to be airlifted to the mainland, where ambulances were waiting.

It was a testing and traumatic time for the worst injured had to be transported so slowly. Don and his pilots continued well into the night, shuttling the victims to the mainland, as Sid and his men delivered them to the planes.

More than 30 were badly injured, too many for the little Hervey Bay hospital to cope with, so the majority was flown directly to Maryborough.Sid and the team worked through the night, until all the injured were evacuated.

Then Sid went back and collected the seven bodies, including Jack Reville's, put them in his vehicle and took them to a disused timber cutter's hut, a short distance from Lake McKenzie. He laid them inside, closed the door to keep the dingoes away and went home for a short rest.

Next morning he returned to the hut and took the bodies back to McKenzie's beach, carried them on board Reville's boat, the *Island Queen* and skippered the boat across the Sandy Straits to Urangan Boat Harbour, where the police and ambulances were waiting.

Thirty years later the survivors of the accident had a reunion on Fraser Island, and learned for the first time who the man was who had helped them, and who had undoubtedly saved some of their lives. Many wrote letters of personal thanks to Sid.

He simply says "If I hadn't been following Jack's bus, the injured would most likely have stayed there all night. The road was not used by the Forestry very much and in those days some of the tours were not very reliable, with people getting home at midnight or later, so no alarm would have been raised, nor a search begun until next morning."

This terrible accident highlighted the need for better communication on the island and the value of Sid's telephone was recognized.

At an inquest into the accident, it was found that Jack Reville had died of a heart attack at the wheel of his bus and it had careered out of control. It was also found he had no registration or insurance on his bus and the Queensland Government had to pay massive compensation to the victims.

In the aftermath of the accident, Fraser Island's infant tourist industry came to a halt. Sid had started to transport many school groups on camping tours around the island. Cancellations poured in and Sid had to spend weeks personally visiting all the schools, and showing that he had all the right documentation for his buses. But it was two years before his tour business recovered.

Reville's widow held an auction of the *Island Queen* some months after the accident, and put their house up for sale.

A chap who ran cattle on Facing Island, out from Gladstone, called Wally Toy bought it and the *Island Queen* to run it as a family venture for himself, his wife, Cec and his two sons, Laurie and Dennis.

Wally soon made contact with Sid and between them they agreed they would jointly run the day trips to Fraser, with the Toys looking after the marine side and bookings, and Sid driving the people across the island. At first they ran only one or two trips a week, but as the business grew more days were added.

"The *Lady Fraser* was pretty old now and I wanted to concentrate on developing Eurong, so it suited me," says Sid.

He sold the vessel to two brothers in Brisbane and was heartened many years later to find her in a yard being rebuilt with great care.

With the Toys organizing the mainland side of the day trips, and his daughters' schooling finished, Max Williams and his family moved to Eurong.

Sid's informal partnership with the Toys lasted for more than a decade, and as the day trips became more frequent and numbers built up, the Toy's needed a larger vessel, and bought a launch called the *Philanderer*.

Sid kept going to army auctions and buying more ex American Army, mainly Studebaker, trucks for conversion. Sid repainted the dark green Studebakers bright orange, so they would be very visible as they were driven through the rainforest.

"There wasn't a lot of traffic, but the timber trucks used to come hurtling along the road," he explains.

Most of Sid's 1970's tour fleet was converted from WW11 Studebakers.

Before one auction Sid was taken around the trucks for sale by an army chap who was a regular visitor to Eurong. He recounts how Sid noticed once truck had "Engine U.S." chalked on the bonnet. He lifted the bonnet, peered inside the engine, poked around and put the bonnet back down.

At the auction Sid was the only bidder and got the truck for a song. After the event the auctioneer asked Sid if he needed a tow truck to take the truck away.

Sid declined the offer, lifted the bonnet again, worked on the engine briefly, then drove the truck away.

Forestry worker Sandy Luck, Sid and his cousin, timber cutter Joe Cunningham at a Forestry Department meeting at Central Station

Chapter 7

By 1971 Sid was finding it almost impossible to run his growing business without access to the mainland other than by driving the 320 km round trip to Maryborough via Rainbow Beach, or going to Hervey Bay as a passenger on the *Philanderer,* which ran three times a week.

At Orchid Beach he had watched Sir Reginald Barnewall and Don Adams flying back and forth.

"It took them only 15 minutes to get to the mainland while it took me all day," he says. "I thought I'd got to get into this flying."

Undeterred by being taken on an acrobatic flight over Eurong by a mate of Darcy Walters, Sid bought a four seat Cessna 182 aircraft from his friend, Bev Whitaker, who had gone into charter flying in Maryborough, and was to found the regional airline, Sunstate Airlines.

Sid began flying lessons at the Aero Club in Maryborough, in the meantime employing a series of pilots to fly guests and small loads of urgently needed stores to Eurong. He soon mastered the practical aspects of flying, and understood how aircraft worked. But when it came to the written work and theory he was greatly disadvantaged by his lack of education. He could barely read or write.

His determination and persistence meant he did not give up. He had had four little brick accommodation units built at Eurong by this time, and for six months he shut himself away in one of these after his day's work, teaching himself how to read and write well enough to understand what he needed to know.

Gordon King, a tour operator at the time, recalls "I brought people regularly to Eurong from Brisbane, but I hardly ever saw Sid. He was always in his room studying. You have to hand it to him for his dedication."

When Sid felt he had absorbed all he could, he went periodically over the next two months to Archerfield airport in Brisbane, to top off his lessons by practical experience, flying into a large airport and making cross country flights.

When it came to the exams, he had no problem passing the practical flying, though he never forgot one examiner who accompanied him and criticized him for not changing from one fuel tank to another to keep the plane balanced part way through the flight.

"It wasn't necessary," Sid maintains. "The plane was balanced and I think his criticism was just to find something to say. I don't like criticism if it serves no purpose."

The first written exam was on aircraft engines and systems. Sid sat it with 12 others. When they finished they had to stand up, hand in their papers and leave the room. Sid was the first to leave and he got 92 per cent.

He did less well with navigation. "Calculations and mathematics beat me," he acknowledges. But at the end of it all, in early 1974, he got his private pilot's licence.

Flying became a great joy and over succeeding years, he owned and flew many different aircraft. He was a meticulous pilot. No matter how busy his schedule, he would not be hurried through the aircraft checks he did before every flight. Throughout his whole 30 year flying career he never had a single incident.

His first planes were kept on a flat grassed area just above the surf beach at Eurong, and landings and take-offs were on a hard stretch of sand, just south of the resort, kept damp by water seepage.

"It was most important to be able to read the beach before landing," he said, "learning to recognize a patch of soft sand into which a light plane's nose wheel could plough and break, by its colour.

"Another hazard was the dozens of freshwater outlets from tiny seepages to deep creeks which run from the island dunes across the beach to the sea.

"After heavy rain what could have been a trickle one day can be much faster flowing the next and have carved a channel into the beach – again a danger to nose wheels."

Many a time Sid came in to land to find a group of holidaymakers in occupation with a game of cricket in progress, and he would fly over low and waggle the plane wings as a signal for them to disperse. Often they thought it was an aerial greeting, and simply waved cheerily back.

At other times brumbies, the island's wild horses, would be ambling along on the strip, but they were easier to get moving as the plane zoomed in just over their heads.

Sid was not the only pilot to land and take off on the surf beach, but he always did so successfully, unlike one particular charter pilot. Sid could hardly believe his eyes when he drove his day trip into Eurong one lunchtime, and saw a plane bobbing about in the surf. The pilot had landed on a soft patch of sand, and his plane had slewed into the sea.

Under Sid's direction, 40 day trippers immediately took off their shoes, rolled up their trousers and waded out to the plane to push it and its terrified occupants back to safety.

Sid's new mobility meant that he could get to Maryborough in 12 minutes to do essential business. Many times he would take a member of staff with him on days off. Not all were happy at the prospect. Driver Jimmy Schmidt particularly hated flying. Sid had flown Jimmy over and back many times, and was surprised, as they were leaving Maryborough one day, to hear Jimmy remark in wonder "Just look at all those cane fields." He had never seen them on previous flights because he had always had his eyes shut.

* * * *

Sid and his family and workers usually had their meals cooked in an ex army mobile camp kitchen that he had bought from an army disposal store. It had a big Wiley's cast iron oven and steamer and a steamer wand for heating liquids. It was wood fired and it was part of the cook's job to chop the wood.

One time the resort was between cooks and the fellows were taking two day turns at the stove. When it came to Sid's turn, he boiled some eggs for breakfast. At lunchtime he boiled more eggs and at dinner, yet more boiled eggs appeared. The next day there were boiled eggs for breakfast and lunch. When they were again presented at dinner time, there was mutiny.

Sid marched out on his ungrateful staff, climbed in his plane and flew away, with all the workers very worried about the consequences of their revolt upon his return. Before anyone else could be persuaded to cook a meal, Sid was back – with a big parcel of fish and chips from the best fish shop in Maryborough.

* * * *

The early day trippers used to bring their own picnic lunches. A dining room was next on Sid's list of desired buildings so he could offer lunches to them. He heard of a former American Air Force hut that had been converted to a barn at Dundowran, just north of Hervey Bay, and was now for sale. Sid bought it for $20, dismantled it, brought it across to Eurong, and began rebuilding it to make a dining room.

It was almost finished with new roofing iron lightly tacked on it when on February 17 1971 Cyclone Dora blew in on the island with little warning.

Sid's first concern was his Cessna plane, parked on a small grassy rise above the surf beach. The sky became heavily overcast in the forefront of the cyclone before Sid had time to fly it to safety on the mainland.

The wind quickly picked up to gale force, and the chances of the plane's survival on the beachfront were minimal. Sid and Max Williams drove all the trucks around the plane and tied it to them with wire hawsers. Waves pushed by high winds came up to the rise and washed right up to the plane's undercarriage, but they didn't shift it.

Next Max ran to get a roll of wire to tie down the roof of the campers' amenities block. He was racing down a small slope, when the wind picked him up and carried him some distance. When Sid ran to pick him up and found he was all right, he commented wryly "It's lucky you were weighted down with that heavy wire, or goodness knows where the wind would have taken you."

All else secured as best they could, Sid climbed on the roof of the dining room to be, and had Max tie him spread eagled across the roof, to save his precious roofing iron from being blown off and buckled. He stayed there, all night through howling wind and pouring rain, until the cyclone moved on 15 hours later.

The dining room, called appropriately the Island Inn, was built on a slope at the back of the land with small wooden stumps at the back and longer ones at the front. Sid extended it at one end and added a kitchen at the other, and a large verandah all along the front. By time it was finished it could seat all the people on the day trip except on the busiest days, when the scenic stops on the tour would be juggled around so there could be two sittings for lunch.

Max Williams' daughters, Robyn and Rikki prepared the salads on the daily buffet for the day trip.

A small kitchen was built at the back of the new dining room, and the big cast iron stove from the mobile kitchen fitted into it. One young cook, when he was leaving, was asked if he wanted a reference. He had never experienced anything like the big wood stove, but coped well on it. He said if he could have the name plate off the stove to show future employers what he had been cooking on, it would stand him in better stead than the best reference.

Among other shortcomings the new kitchen had a gap in the wall. One cook resigned on the spot when he turned from the stove to be confronted by a large goanna standing on its hind legs and stealing a steak from the kitchen table.

* * * *

In the evenings the Island Inn became the social centre for the little community. Fishermen, holidaymakers, campers, holiday home owners, forestry workers and timber cutters would gather and the Saturday night parties became the biggest social event on the island with dancing to a record player.

A pool table was duly purchased for after dinner games, and covered with a lid and a tablecloth for the day trippers' buffet to be set out at lunchtimes.

Pool or cards, for lack of any other entertainment were very popular, but Sid was a terrible loser. One evening he was introduced to Pontoon and given a very rudimentary rule to play by: "You win if you get 21."

He lost consistently but finally got 21, only to be told another player had a better 21. Never having been told there were different levels, Sid was very upset. He marched out of the dining room, scattering chairs and tables in his wake, headed straight up to the generator shed, turned the power off and went to bed.

His luckless opponents were left to scramble over felled chairs in the dark to go home.

Mostly the gatherings were all male, and everyone would bring along their own bottles of beer. It was in such short supply, having had to be brought from the mainland, that many a time an argument would break out as to who had drunk all their beer and who had some left in the one and only fridge.

A scheme was devised whereby everyone marked their bottles, usually with X's in marker pen. Crafty Kelly Page's mark was four X's, so if he saw a stubby or two in the fridge with one, two or three Xs on, it was a simple matter for him to add more and claim the beer was his.

Sid, who drank very little, had a way of settling the men down if the arguments over the beer seemed to be getting out of hand. He would lead everyone outside to the workshop, where he had an old blacksmith's anvil, a heavy piece of cast iron, and declare if anyone could pick it up, lift it to chest height, walk a figure 8 with it and put it, not drop it, down again, he could make all the trouble he wanted.

Sid would then demonstrate. As no-one else could so much as pick it up, it was an effective end to most contention. Anvil lifting became an event in itself, and only one man besides Sid, his mate Phil Delaney, could walk the 8.

Often on Saturday nights Sid and his staff would gather for a barbecue in the camp ground surrounded by dense dark bush, from which dozens of red eyes shone out. There were dingoes galore but in those early days they were timid and kept their distance, even when the aroma of cooking steak must have sorely tempted them to break cover.

* * * *

Because of the isolation in which they lived and worked the Eurong staff had to be close knit and remain unworried by each other's foibles.

Sometimes newcomers found it hard to know what was going on, but Sid always had a great understanding of his workers.

Regularly throughout the year Kelly would announce it was his birthday so everyone would shout him a beer. When Sid found out, he changed the whole birthday tradition. From then on whoever celebrated a birthday at Eurong did so by shouting for the others.

Guests had no immunity from Kelly's tales. As the resort grew, he would accrue reflected glory, and hopefully a beer, by telling them he was Sid's father.

He did this once to impress a lady guest, and it worked. Kelly had two whole days of her undivided attention – until Sid's widowed mother arrived unannounced for a short holiday.

Over lunch Mum was introduced to the lady guest who, in some dismay, said "Oh I met your husband yesterday."

Kelly did not put in another appearance until guest and mother had safely departed the island.

Inadvertently Kelly and Sid were directly responsible for the departure of one Eurong cook, only two days after the fellow had arrived. With all the work to be done at Eurong, Kelly knew he wouldn't be given a day off by the simple process of asking. He took to announcing he was sick and, when that failed to achieve the desired result, he would elaborate on the theme.

New staff were obvious targets. One day, lazing in bed, Kelly called the new cook and took him into his confidence.

"When I was in town last week I went to the doctor and he told me I had only a short time to live," Kelly reported.

The new cook hastened to Sid to lodge an appeal on Kelly's behalf for the day off.

Sid was not as sympathetic as the cook expected. "Go and tell him to get out of bed and get to work. Say that if it kills him, we'll just have to put his body in the fridge until I'm ready to go to town for stores."

Sid was well used to Kelly's tales. What he had not anticipated was the new cook's reaction. A look of horror crossed the man's face. "I'm, not having any bodies in my fridge," he declared. "I resign."

* * * *

One of Sid's drivers was a cadaverous Finn called Victor. His surname was unpronounceable so everyone called him Victor Pyjamas. He worked for Sid for a while, then left on some pretext, but returned when he needed a job again and Sid re-employed him.

Soon after his return he came in one evening to announce he was leaving early next day. Sid was surprised but paid him up.

Next morning Sid discovered the reason for Victor's sudden departure. He had been filling a hole in the road near Lake Birrabeen and had run Sid's front end loader into a tree.

Sid grumbled but he realized it must have been an unavoidable accident and that Victor must have been too scared to own up. He knew Victor really needed a job, but had no way of getting in touch with him.

A short time later a form came from the Commonwealth Employment Service seeking information on Victor's work record because he had applied for unemployment benefit.

Sid phoned the CES but was told Victor's address could not be divulged.

He had a solution – to use the CES as intermediary. He wrote on the back of the form "Tell Victor all is forgiven." Three days later Victor was back at Eurong with a big grin.

Chapter 8

Regular cyclones were a fact of life on Fraser throughout the 1950's, 1960's and 1970's. Sometimes there were two a year; in 1976 two within two days.

In February 1971 Cyclone Dora crossed the coast between Fraser and Brisbane. Cyclone Daisy in February 1972 made a direct hit on the island and destroyed 200 homes in Hervey Bay. It was followed by Wanda in January 1974 which passed over the coast near Fraser then caused massive flooding in Brisbane.

Cyclone Pam in February 1974 passed well to the east of the island but sent a huge tidal surge lashing the island's surf beach. Beth in February 1976 brought waves with 10 metre high peaks crashing on to the surf beach.

Colin on March 4 1976 also generated huge waves after moving south of Fraser to southern NSW and just two days later, Dawn, on March 6, crossed the coast at Fraser causing damage and flooding.

Eurong on the surf beach front was totally exposed, but suffered no damage. Early experience of the violence of Fraser's weather taught Sid valuable lessons in building.

"I was always aware of cyclones and always used cyclone bolts in every building, even though there were no building standards in the early days," he says and adds proudly "We never lost a single building at Eurong facing the brunt of the cyclones, though hundreds of buildings were damaged in Hervey Bay and Maryborough."

His land at Eurong suffered no erosion, being on a straight stretch of beach and having a chain of freshwater lagoons in front, which broke the force of the waves. In clearing the land, Sid had wisely left lantana all along the small dunes fronting it, and their root systems held the sand together.

Elsewhere on the island the huge cyclonic waves would erode vast quantities of sand off the surf beach, exposing an under layer of indurated coffee rock, making it impassable north of Eurong for months on end.

"We could always get from Eurong to the southern end of the island, because there were no coffee rock outcrops there," Sid explains. "The first rock outcrop was One Tree Rocks about three kilometers north of Eurong. Normally you don't know these rocks even exist as they are completely covered by sand. But once the sand is washed away they form an impassable barrier.

"It would be months before anyone could travel the beach. When the sand started to build up around the rocks again, and we were close to getting through them, all the island people would get together and have working bees chopping the tops off the rocks with picks, axes, and mattocks to try and level them out and make tracks to drive through.

"One of the worst places was Yidney Rocks, just south of Happy Valley which was two or three metres sheer into deep water at low tide. It was such a barrier that the Forestry workers made an inland bypass around the rocks."

At the southern end of the island there was tremendous erosion of thousands of tonnes of sand from the fore dunes, leaving sand cliffs up to 10m high rising sheer off the beach, with fallen trees tangled at the base of them.

Orchid Beach suffered very badly in one cyclone soon after Sir Reginald Barnewall had sold his resort to a Brisbane consortium. Big seas undermined the high dunes upon which the resort was built, and 50 metres of land, where just four years before Sid had parked three of his trucks side by side between the swimming pool and the edge of the dunes, fell down overnight and the swimming pool was left hanging over the edge.

In the island's interior, high winds wreaked havoc in the forest. The tracks would be completely blocked by fallen timber.

"Immediately after a cyclone had passed the Forestry men would start clearing the road across the island from Ungowa and we would work our way from the other side," says Sid. "When we met, the road was clear. We all had chainsaws and cut up the branches. It would take us at least three days to get the road open.

"Cyclone Wanda dropped 1050mm of rain in two days on Fraser and that blocked any movement inland for a further three or four days. Even though the island is sand and normal rain is soaked up quickly, this downpour saturated the sand and made big ponds in the track all the way across."

When the surf beach was eroded after Cyclone Dora in 1971, a visitor saw what he thought was an unexploded bomb on the beach near the *Maheno* shipwreck. Knowing the ship had been used for war time target practice, the authorities were duly concerned and in September sent a team of Navy skin-divers to Fraser to investigate.

They stayed at Eurong resort and each morning set off to the *Maheno* where they tested the surrounding beach with metal detectors. Whenever they got a positive reading, often from deep in the sand, they would erect a timber tripod over the site, and hoist a large concrete pipe over it. Then by water jetting out the sand they would sink the pipe and when they reached the metal, one of the divers would be lowered down inside the pipe to see if it was a bomb.

They found lots of food cans, bits of the hawsers which had held the ship when it first stranded and lots of small, inexplicably shattered, pieces of the hull, but no bombs.

Navy divers search for unexploded bombs around the Maheno in 1972

The navy divers didn't bother to recover the concrete pipes they had sunk in the beach, so Sid asked if he could have them, and, when they agreed, sought a letter saying they were his. He just had to recover them from the beach, set them in the ground at Eurong, connect pipes, fit lids and presto, he would have a whole series of septic tanks.

Sid had bought a small, rusty but serviceable crane to speed building at Eurong, so off he went up the beach, with Kelly and the cook of the month, with the crane and a truck to collect the pipes. He came home in a bad mood.

One pipe was missing. He knew because had had counted them carefully when the divers had first brought them to the island. Someone had beaten him to it, and, by following the only other set of vehicle tracks to and from the *Maheno,* Sid discovered the someone was neighbour, Les Roper.

Sid went straight to Les's house and in spite of the pipe already being installed for exactly the same purpose Sid had planned, showed his letter of ownership and insisted Les dig it up and hand it over.

The prize, a left over concrete pipe finds a home. Sid and Paddy Doran roll it into place.

It was while he was collecting the pipes from around the *Maheno*, that Sid took a fancy to its anchor. It would go well as an attraction at his Eurong Beach resort. He intended to do something about it, and quickly, before he was beaten to it too.

Soon after the concrete pipes had been safely gathered Sid and his brother in law, Gary Milera set off to try and recover the anchor, taking with them packed lunches.

It mattered not that this anchor was very rusty, that it was inside the hull below decks, that it weighed five tons and that the crane was capable of lifting only two, Sid was determined to have it.

The pair had brought with them a couple of hacksaws with which to cut through the big four inch diameter pin holding the anchor stem to the fluke, so they could lift it out in two sections.

They discovered the anchor pin was so clogged with rust they could not use the hacksaws to cut it through.

Only the blades and not the frame would fit into the working space, so they took it in turns to sit hunched over the anchor sawing away with the little blades held between their fingers. Sid became so frustrated he threw the first thing to hand at the ship's hull a little way out to sea. It was the bag of packed lunches.

After three days they managed to cut through the pin, lift out the anchor and take it to Eurong, where it lay on the front lawn, still in two pieces for many years. Its recovery had strained the back of the old crane and there was nothing else to lift it into position for mounting.

Brisbane model, Merryl Geddes, on Fraser Island for a photo shoot, poses by the big anchor at Eurong, its stem still suspended from the crane.

Displaying the anchor properly became one of the "gonna" jobs around the resort, about which Sid spoke from time to time as in "I'm gonna mount the anchor", but about which he actually did nothing because there were always more important jobs to do.

One priority was replacing the generator. Up to this time the resort power had been supplied by the first little 5 kva generator Sid had brought to the island. To save fuel Sid used to close it down at bedtime.

He rigged up a fishing line from his bedroom in the A Frame to it in the shed about 90m away, so he could pull on the string and stop the generator without having to go outside. Often if he let go the string too early, the generator would pick up speed and start running again, and all the dimming lights would come back to life, so he would have to get out of bed, pull and hold the string for longer to make sure the generator had completely stopped.

With nine cabins and another toilet and shower block added to the resort by early 1972, the generator became too small and the supply of power it put out, completely unreliable.

Sid saw an advertisement in a *Country Life* newspaper that Golden Fleece had two generators for sale from a petrol station that was closing down at Moonie, more than 400 kilometres south west of Fraser Island. He and Kelly set out for Moonie in one of the trucks. If the generators were sound and could be purchased at Sid's price, they planned to bring them back.

"Kelly had worked out there at one time so he came with me as navigator," Sid tells the story.

"But our progress to Moonie was extremely slow because his navigation took us on a long drive from pub to pub. "He would say 'turn here' and 'go through there' and we'd find ourselves in a pub yard. He knew the back door to every pub on the way. After a bit of an argument that we weren't on a pub crawl, he finally got us there."

Sid bought both generators, a 30 kva and a 35 kva, loaded them on the truck and ignoring Kelly's protestations made a bee-line for home.

They arrived back on the island about an hour after sunset. As they drove up the beach Sid peered ahead for the lights of the resort. There were none. The old generator had expired just two hours earlier.

After days of driving, the last thing Sid wanted was more work that night. But he had no choice. The fridges had to be kept going or the food would spoil.

He didn't have time to lift the generators off the truck. By torchlight he oiled and greased the larger Moonie generator and made a few minor adjustments. It sprang into life still on the back of the truck.

He tells "I simply backed the truck alongside the generator shed, connected the resort wiring to the generators, started it up and ran it where it was on the back of the truck. It ran like that for three weeks until we extended the generator shed and got the two generators unloaded and installed properly."

Chapter 9

The 1970's was a decade of great significance in the history of Fraser Island. Afterwards it was never to be the same.

Fraser Island sands are rich in much sought after minerals, in particular rutile from which titanium is produced, as well as ilmenite, zircon, monazite and silica. Sand mining exploration leases were granted over much of the island as early as 1949, but it wasn't until the 1960's, when the growing international demand for these minerals made it worthwhile for sand mining companies to take a closer look at Fraser.

The mining companies with island leases were Murphyores Incorporated Pty. Ltd; Queensland Titanium Mines Pty Ltd and Offshore Minerals Pty Ltd.

Murphyores Incorporated Pty. Ltd. and Q.T.M. held leases along Fraser's surf beach and up to four kilometres inland.

In the days of the Petty Geophysical Engineering oil search in the early 1960's, a team of Murphyores representatives followed along and, as Petty's men drilled into the sand throughout the island, to insert explosives for seismic readings, Murphyores took their core samples to ascertain the mineral content of the sands.

Sums were done on the costs of establishment and operation on the island – the need for trafficable, hard surface access roads, barge ramps, an airstrip, and workers' accommodation to be built on Fraser, and processing plants on the adjacent mainland. Then there would be the high, on going costs of dredging, trucking in heavy machinery, fuel and supplies and taking out the sand. The sums came out in favour of mining.

Murphyores decided to go ahead and attracted the American industrial giant, Dillinghams as a major shareholder and partner.

Q.T.M. held 1160 acres in 10 dredging leases and a sand mining lease extending to Fraser Island from the mainland to the south.

In January 1971 Dillingham-Murphyores applied to the Maryborough Mining Warden's Court for mining leases over 6317 acres in the south east of the island and 1696 acres in the north east.

This was to signal the start of a conservation battle to stop sand mining on Fraser, which brought the relatively unknown island into national and international prominence.

The conservation movement in the area was small and newly formed but attention grabbing. Its members were forewarned that sand mining on Fraser Island was in prospect, for Q.T.M. had moved to start sand mining at Cooloola, on the mainland south of Fraser Island, and in 1970 had been blocked by the Queensland joint government parties in defiance of the Queensland Cabinet. With its base already established at Rainbow Beach it was logical it would move on to the island.

As soon as the Dillingham-Murphyores applications for island mining leases on Fraser Island were advertised, the conservation leaders, a Hervey Bay couple Dr. Andy Mayne and his wife, Frances set about rallying support, including those fresh from their Cooloola victory, who had tactical advice to give.

Within two weeks they called a meeting for anyone with an interest in Fraser Island, tourist and timber operators, local council members and business people from Maryborough and Hervey Bay. Although given the cold shoulder by local government and business people, who saw enormous economic benefit for their areas, the meeting led to the formation of the Fraser Island Defenders Organisation, F.I.D.O.

A Maryborough Adult Education officer, John Sinclair was elected president. Vocal and well aware of the value of media attention, he was to win a devoted following, and make a name for himself throughout Australia with the fight over Fraser Island.

The sand mining leases were granted by the Maryborough Mining Warden to Dillingham-Murphyores in June 1971. Sinclair and his supporters did not give up.

Neither were they assuaged when the Queensland Government created a new national park on Fraser Island, from Indian Head to the northern tip, Sandy Cape, a huge expanse with neither mineral sands nor commercial timber.

Rather they pressed on more determinedly than ever. When in 1972 the Gough Whitlam led Labor Party won the Federal election, F.I.D.O. was in at the start, lobbying for it to stop the export of minerals from Fraser Island.

The Federal Government could not stop mining. That was a State Government prerogative. But it did have control over what was exported from Australia. There was no call for mineral sand in Australia so, if the sand mining companies were stopped from selling it overseas, there would be no point mining on Fraser Island.

Q.T.M. did not waste any time. With its equipment and infrastructure well in place after the Cooloola effort, the company began dredging the surf beach at the southern end of Fraser in November 1971.

The company hired a barge, the *Tom Welsby,* to work from Hook Point to Inskip Point on the mainland, taking their mineral sands to the new sand mining township of Rainbow Beach, where the first stage of processing was done. The sand was then transported in big trucks to Gympie for further processing and onward shipment, eventually overseas.

Q.T.M. had earlier built a bitumen road connecting Rainbow Beach to the Gympie-Tin Can Bay road. Now the company built a road from Rainbow Beach to Inskip Point, and the first bitumen road on Fraser Island, from Hook Point to the northern limit of their mining lease at Fourth Creek, 16 km south of Eurong.

Dillingham-Murphyores was slower to get started because it had to begin its operation from scratch. Its mining was to be north of Q.T.M.'s leases, and its base was to be Maryborough.

Preparatory work involved setting up workers' accommodation in demountable buildings at Dilli Village, about six kilometres south of Eurong; a barge ramp being cut through a high bank at Buff Creek south of Ungowa on the west coast of Fraser; a gravel road between the two; a gravel airstrip inland from Dilli Village, and on the mainland, a concrete barge ramp at River Heads.

Two large barges were hired to bring supplies and vehicles from River Heads to Buff Creek and push dumb barges laden with the mineral sands up the Mary River to Maryborough for refining.

John Sinclair and FIDO turned their opposition into the first big conservation battle in Australia.

It received a vast amount of media attention, nationally and internationally. The conservationist case was built, in large part, on the island's unique scenic attractions and more and more folk wanted to see Fraser Island for themselves.

At the outset Sid did not involve himself in the controversy over sand mining. He was kept fully occupied trying to make a living with his day tours and at Eurong.

* * * *

Life at the resort became more hectic when an Australian film company came to Fraser in 1974 to make a film about a dramatic episode in the island's early history, the story of Eliza Fraser. The film crew booked out the accommodation at Eurong, and made it their base.

Eliza had been the wife of a Scottish sea captain, James Fraser and together with him and some of their crew had been stranded among the Aborigines on Fraser Island when their ship, the *Stirling Castle* was wrecked in 1836.

James and other crew members were killed, but Eliza continued to live with the Aborigines for some months until she was rescued by a convict and taken back to the penal colony of Moreton Bay, now Brisbane.

A stellar cast was gathered for the film headed by the British actors Susannah York as Eliza, and Trevor Howard as the commandant of Moreton Bay, and Australian actors Noel Ferrier as Captain Fraser, John Waters as the convict who rescues Eliza from the Aborigines and Gus Mercurio as a soldier. Tim Burstall was the director.

A Tasmanian brewery was one of the film sponsors, and the first thing to arrive, to Kelly Page's utter delight, was a plane filled with cartons of beer.

There were a couple of logistical problems with filming. There were no Aborigines living on Fraser by this time, so Aborigines from Mornington Island in the Gulf of Carpentaria were employed and flown in with all their authentic weaponry.

Neither were there kangaroos on the island and film director, Tim Burstall felt kangaroos important to give the Australian flavour to the international production.

He had kangaroos from a Brisbane wildlife sanctuary flown in too, and it was quite a spectacle as the plane landed on the beach with kangaroos in sugar bags strapped into the seats, peering anxiously out of the windows.

The kangaroos were not a great success. They were kept in a compound, but being from a sanctuary and used to being hand fed, as soon as the cameraman entered the compound to film them supposedly bounding through the bush, they raced towards him looking for a handout. All told the kangaroo hire was hardly worth the expense. They were so uncooperative that the only kangaroo footage able to be used was a one second shot of a solitary animal.

Also very expensive was the acquisition of a long boat. Burstall found one in a naval museum in Melbourne and had it transported to the island. Timber cutter Andy Postan hauled it across to the surf beach on his timber jinker.

Its appearance in the film was brief. The day set aside for shooting scenes of the Fraser party being washed ashore was windy and the surf was heavy. Burstall felt this would add authenticity. The problem was getting the unwieldy long boat, with all the actors aboard, out through the surf, so it could be washed in again. By the time this was achieved everyone was exhausted, not least Sid and his staff who were helping, but waves washed the boat in at an angle wrong for the camera, so out they had to push it out again and again. Finally and desperately Burstall had the boat pushers stay out in the surf, and hold on to the back of the boat to guide it into the beach. The camera crew had to use every skill to get footage without showing the pushers' fingers over the sides of the boat.

The film brought a great boost to Sid's day trip numbers. "Everyone wanted to see the stars, especially Susannah York. She was an aloof, very private person but not so private as to refrain from sunbathing topless on the lawn outside her A Frame cottage, so she could get a good tan for her role," Sid recalls.

"Trevor Howard kept to himself too, and became known to us for his drinking substantial quantities of whisky before appearing on camera."

The large space under the Island Inn dining room had been closed in to use as a storeroom, and the filmmakers asked if they could set up bush gunyahs in it to do close up shots and record some of the talking roles.

But above, in the dining room, all the locals wanted to play pool. There were more of them than usual too as everyone wanted to see the film crew, especially Susannah.

Sid quickly formulated a plan to keep all his patrons happy. When the film makers wanted to film, they would thump on the ceiling with the end of a broom handle. Above everyone froze and remained silent and motionless, until another thump meant they could carry on as usual.

More gunyahs were built on the beach at Lake Boemigen, the largest of the island's unique lakes, south of Eurong, where scenes of Eliza Fraser's rescue from the Aborigines by a convict was to be shot. At the filmmakers' request for a watchman, Sid appointed Kelly Page as guardian of the gunyahs.

Kelly settled down at the lake for the night with a carton of beer and some food, while everyone else returned to Eurong. Next day the weather was wrong for filming Eliza's rescue, as was the day after. In all the flurry of changed plans poor Kelly was forgotten.

Four days later they suddenly remembered him and dashed back. There he was still looking after the gunyahs but bitterly complaining, not because he had run out of food, but because he had run out of beer.

Next time he was on watchman duty he took ample beer supplies with him, and so Sid would not find out, hid the cartons in a sand dune – and then could not find which dune he had hidden them in.

The Aborigines were well worthy of their hire. They played their roles to the hilt, much to Noel Ferrier's discomfort on one particular occasion. They were shooting a scene, in which Aborigines were trying to get Captain Fraser to work harder. It called for Ferrier to be hauling a log in the bush and for the head of the tribe to kick him up the rear end.

The scene wasn't going right and Ferrier was worn out hauling his log around. Lindsay, the Aborigine involved, got fed up too with all the takes.

Finally the scene began to take shape until Lindsay gave Ferrier such a kick that it set him on his face. The air resounded with unscripted expletives.

One night one of the Aboriginal women could not be found and a suspicious husband put on his war paint, took up his spear and boomerang, and went looking for her.

Poor Kelly was sitting quietly in his cottage enjoying some of the brewery's largesse, when suddenly his door crashed open and there stood the Aborigine. It was the first time Kelly had been known to choke on a beer.

All night the hunt for the missing wife continued with the resort staff and film crew terrified of attack. The only man to stay unworried was the cook, Bill Wilson. By next morning everyone else was reduced to a state of nerves and when the Aborigine, still armed and painted, arrived for breakfast there was a mass exodus from the Island Inn.

Bill wasn't going to have his food go cold. With an enormous roar he told the Aborigine to take his weapons outside or he wouldn't get served. Meekly the man did. Breakfast continued, but the minute it was over the Aborigine was off on the war path again. Burstall organized a special flight to have him taken off the island that day, by popular request.

The Aborigines generally adapted well to Fraser, except one night when one of Sid's drivers, Jimmy Schmidt was bringing them back to Eurong from Boemigen in one of the open buses. The bus lights went out so Jimmy stopped to fix them. Immediately all the Aborigines jumped down from the bus and refused to board it again. They walked many kilometers back to Eurong.

When it came time for them to return to Mornington Island they really didn't want to go. They were getting good food and award wages and wanted this to last. They associated the good things more with Fraser Island than the film, and thought that as long as they stayed they would get fed and paid. When four planes came to fly them out, they went bush. It took three days before they trickled back into Eurong and could be sent on their way.

Actor Gus Mercurio, in Sid's opinion, was the outstanding character in the crew. "He was cheerful and always considerate. He liked a cold drink on a hot day and was always talking about walking up the beach to Happy Valley, some 25 km.

"There wasn't much there, a small shop and several houses, but it was somewhere else, so off he'd go.

"After a while I'd drive up the beach looking for him. He'd just be sitting on the sand and I'd bring him back. I don't think he ever got to Happy Valley."

Director, Tim Burstall gave the Eliza Fraser saga a light touch and it did not win much acclaim. In fact it made a loss and the production company went broke, or so Sid was informed when, after months of patient waiting, he tried to recover the $4000 worth of unpaid bills he was left holding.

His only profit was a fine collection of Aboriginal artifacts and a not-so-fine collection of grey army blankets that were left behind.

Chapter 10

From an estimated 5,000 people a year going to Fraser Island before the sand mining controversy, the number trebled within a year.

Gordon Elmer had a six vehicle steel barge built to cater for the demand and the *Tom Welsby*, the barge hired by Queensland Titanium Mines from the big Riverside barge company in Brisbane, carried private vehicles as well as mining trucks.

"When Riverside first put their barge in to operation for Q.T.M., I started to use it instead of Elmer's barge. It was much larger, and worked longer hours, 12 hours a day, to take the loads of sand back to Rainbow Beach," Sid explains.

"Elmer would never talk to me after I used the *Tom Welsby*. If he saw me, he'd turn his back and walk away."

When the Dillingham-Murphyores mining operation began in 1974 Sid got a job with one of his buses, picking up workers from the company airstrip as they were flown in by *Island Air* and driving them to Dilli Village at each shift change.

Fuel was brought to the Buff Creek ramp in the tank of one of the small barges, hired by D-M and pumped into a holding tank ashore. It would then be pumped out into a tank on the back of a truck when needed and taken to another holding tank at Dilli Village.

Sid had long been accustomed to taking whatever work he could find on the island for himself, his employees and his trucks.

Now he got the job, with one of his Studebaker trucks with a 2000 litre tank on the back, of delivering the fuel from Dilli Village to the different work sites every eight hours and filling the sand miners' machinery, dozers, graders, loaders and dredge.

Sid and his driver, Eric Everett worked 14 to 16 hours a day, seven days a week to maintain the supply.

When the contract for bringing the fuel from Buff Creek to Dilli Village also came up for tender in 1976, Sid remembered the enormous truck he had seen when he was doing flying training at Archerfield airport in Brisbane early in 1974. It was in a machinery sale yard near the airport.

It had gone underwater in the big Brisbane flood that January, and was cleaned up again when the flood subsided. Sid went to find out more about it, and learned it was a six wheel drive Peterbilt imported from America to West Australia to transport oil rigs round the desert. The work completed, it had ended up in Brisbane for sale. It was left hand drive, over width, weighed some 24 tons and could carry 50 tons.

On Fraser Island it really didn't matter that it was left hand drive and over width, and, when Sid won the contract to transport fuel from the barge landing at Buff Creek to Dilli Village. he bought the monster.

It was so big and wide that Sid had to get a special police permit to drive it from Brisbane. It came into its own on the island. Its carrying capacity and ability to traverse the island roads won Sid an excellent reputation for reliability.

The Peterbilt dwarfs its driver.

By working for D-M, Sid became a target for John Sinclair's hostility.

From initially regarding his fuel delivery contracts as a much needed source of income, the often virulent attacks on him led Sid to assess the sand mining situation for himself.

He did not arrive at his opinion lightly. Sid felt a great affinity to Fraser Island and he had great experience and practical knowledge of its conditions.

He observed the D-M mining operations at first hand in a hitherto inaccessible area of, to him, poor quality scrub with no outstanding features. He paid particular and intelligent attention to the rehabilitation work done in the wake of the dredging and mineral extraction process, and believed it would be successful. He had no reason to disbelieve the sand company representatives, when they stated publicly time and again that they would steer well clear of areas of significant natural beauty.

He says now "I did not think mining would be bad for Fraser Island. It wasn't going to happen near any of the beauty spots, the rainforest or lakes, because they were protected. Where it was going to take place was in a swampy area, that no-one thought much of at the southern end of the island.

"Fraser Island then was still isolated, with primitive little settlements and with at most 5,000 people a year coming to stay on the island, mainly to go fishing. Apart from the timber industry people, I don't think many folk at all appreciated Fraser Island.

"Less than a decade earlier the Federal Government had wanted to give it to the people from the South Pacific island of Nauru in return for their island being despoiled by guano mining. No-one objected to that. The Nauruans turned it down.

"I saw the economic benefits of sand mining as outweighing its effect on the part of the island where it was going to take place."

A Maryborough man through and through, Sid was very concerned about the future of the city.

"Maryborough was really suffering economically, with all its traditional industries winding down. Shipbuilding was at an end; the railway workshops were slowing. The big engineering firm of Walkers Ltd had closed one of its workshops. People were leaving their homes to look for work elsewhere. I believed sand mining would put Maryborough back on its feet," he says. "Of course I knew I would get work with the sand mining.

"I knew anyone who lived on the island, who was prepared to put in the effort, would get a job. And I was prepared to work day and night, when not many would. It was a big income earning opportunity for me, the biggest yet.

"If John Sinclair had owned land and planned a future at Eurong, I think he may have felt the same as I did," Sid said at the time. "But John was looking for a political career, either state or federally at the time, and he believed the conservation cause on Fraser Island could be the way to achieve it. In fact it didn't happen.

"He stood for election to the state seat of Maryborough as a Country Party, later National Party, candidate and got hardly any votes, because the people were so angry at his opposition to sand mining.

"I believe he still thought he had a political future federally because his mother, Beryl, who lived at Eurong at that time, told me 'John is going to be Prime Minister of Australia.'

"John, who earlier used to bring Adult Education groups to the island on my trips, from then on turned completely against me. I think as time went on he became increasingly bitter, when his planned political career went nowhere, and he saw me getting ahead."

Sid hardly ever expressed these opinions, never publicly, and no-one ever asked for them. He took no part in the decrying of John Sinclair that took place, particularly in Maryborough at the time. That wasn't Sid's style. He simply saw himself with a job to do, a job he was comfortable with and he did it to the best of his ability.

But he had the Peterbilt for less than a year, when on December 31 1976, he and it were out of work.

The conservationists won the most important battle against sand mining. Bowing to conservation and public pressure, the Whitlam Government held a major Environmental Inquiry into Fraser Island beginning in June 1975.

In October 1976, with Malcolm Fraser's Liberal Government now in office, the Inquiry handed down its recommendations – that export licences be refused for all mineral sands taken from above high water mark on the island. In November the Government adopted the recommendations.

Without being able to sell the minerals overseas there was no point in the mining operations continuing.

Q.T.M. and Dillinghams immediately began to wind down and stopped mining at the end of the year, removing all their equipment and, in Q.T.M.'s case, in such haste that they badly damaged the bitumen road they had made on the island.

D-M's left behind Dilli Village, the collection of demountable huts for their workers, and the barge ramps they had built at Buff Creek and River Heads.

Sid asked Dillingham's manager, Ron Cross if he could have the River Heads barge ramp, and Cross agreed. Years before Sid had loaded his day trip passengers at River Heads, and always aware that it provided the shortest crossing to Fraser Island, he had the idea it could be useful to him in the future.

Dilli Village was bought by the Queensland Government and made into a National Fitness camp.

Sid's accountant, Barry Keys applied for compensation, which the Federal Government promised for those disadvantaged by the cessation, and eventually Sid got $8,000 for the loss of his contracts, the purchase price of the Peterbilt.

Sid took the big fuel tank off the monster truck and used it himself to carry fuel in drums to Eurong, but it was such a heavy truck that on the mainland it couldn't carry much without being overweight for the roads – as well as being left hand drive.

Tourists pose by the Peterbilt with its load of fuel drums.

He did not consider selling it. He knew it would be irreplaceable and his conviction had never wavered that he would be building bigger and better at Eurong in the future and the Peterbilt would have a place in the scheme of things.

He simply took it to Maryborough, out of the island's salt laden atmosphere, and put it in mothballs.

* * * *

With all the attention, Fraser Island started to change from a place where people came just to go fishing to one where people started to enjoy its atmosphere and scenic beauty.

It was the beginning of an era too when city dwellers began to seek the "freedom" of the bush in their leisure time and to buy four wheel drive vehicles so they could "get away from it all". A 1976 Brisbane *Sunday Sun* newspaper article is headlined "Fraser Island – it's just like Queen Street now", and describes how the Christmas holidays saw the island teeming with people from all over Australia, "attracted by the furore over companies digging up Fraser's fabulous mineral wealth.".

Sid was in the box seat to meet the rapidly growing demand for accommodation, tours and supplies.

"The island was a different world with a different atmosphere and a different lifestyle," Sid describes. "I enjoyed the island and was happy to provide what people needed so they could enjoy it too. I gave them a safe place to stay, built amenities, helped them see and appreciate the beauty, and took care of many of them when they got into difficulty."

The same *Sunday Sun* article describes his five canopied buses as carrying an average of 160 people a day, and quotes Sid as saying "Not long ago we really had to scrape around to find passengers. Now we can barely cope."

He bought four little caravans to rent out, the most he could afford at the time, and had them brought over to the island by barge from Inskip Point. He well remembers that when he had bags of cement to make pads for their annexes on the truck coming to the island, it poured with rain.

As soon as he got the wet bags to Eurong late that evening, he set to work straight away making concrete before the wet cement set and was useless. "And the cement mixer motor kept stopping," he remembers. It took him all night.

There was an increasing demand for supplies. Sid had sold a few lines like ice creams and soft drinks for the day trippers, first from the A Frame he and his family lived in, then from the small hut originally built to house the first workers.

The need for a bigger shop became paramount. The only other shop on the whole island was at Happy Valley, 25 km north.

Sid asked Jack Pashley to help him level a site for the proposed shop. "I had my builder's level and Sid was leveling the land on his old Fordson tractor with the end loader," says Jack.

"I kept saying 'More off here, more off there Sid," and after a while he got off the tractor and told me what I could do with my level as it couldn't possibly be right. We had a heated argument and I ended up picking up my gear and leaving.

"We didn't see each other for a couple of months, but then I was going past Eurong one day on the way to my hut at Happy Valley and Sid was there. He called out to me and said 'That level you had was right, and I'm sorry I shouted at you.' That was Sid. He could tear strips off people and next day it was back to square one."

With his earnings from Dillinghams, in 1975 Sid had the foundations laid for a new shop, with a staff unit at one end. Bricklayer, Peter Young had built its concrete block walls, when Marietta decided she and the children would go and live on the mainland, so Monica could go to school. The new shop was put on hold, as Sid's priority became to buy a house for them in Maryborough.

When he received the $8000 government compensation for the loss of his sand mining contracts, Sid could go ahead with the shop. He employed Dennis Crooks, a builder from Maryborough to complete it, with two spacious two bedroom units on the second floor, grandly called the Penthouses, for the Christmas holiday of 1977.

The building was completed, plumbed, wired, painted and furnished in just 23 days.

Its painter, Gordon Pavey booked one of the Penthouses for his holiday. He finished painting on Christmas Eve, went home to collect his family and arrived back on Christmas Day as a guest.

Stocking the new shop was a bit of a problem. Goods were carried over from the shop in the old shed, but they were so few that there was more empty space on the shelves than items to sell. Sheets were hung over them to hide the emptiness.

The shop, ***(above)*** soon became a great success. Sid adopted the policy of keeping prices as low as possible so he would attract return trade and as a matter of personal philosophy.

"I knew what it was like to be poor, and didn't want high prices to prevent anyone visiting Fraser," he said.

Within two years the shop with its bare shelves had become far too small for all the goods crammed into it. A year later Sid successfully applied for a license to sell take away liquor from a small room next to it.

* * * *

Sid was also to find the growth in tourism was a situation that also demanded he shoulder even greater responsibilities.

Most visitors took advantage of the island's largely unregulated wilderness and chose to camp unhindered along its surf beach fore dunes. On an island with no mainland services the influx was to create problems and some claimed, do more environmental damage than sand mining would have done.

"There were no police stationed on the island and many took advantage of that to do whatever they wanted. The nearest police were at Tin Can Bay and they wouldn't come over unless it was something really serious," says Max Williams. "We'd always had some difficulties with drunken fishermen, then we got drunken hoons. It was mainly arguments and domestics."

At Eurong, Sid found himself and his staff, with locals' and regular holidaymakers' backup, having to be everything, rescuer, policeman and arbitrator.

"I remember one night there was a terrible hullabaloo in the camping ground and we found this chap beating his wife," Sid recalls. "He just wouldn't stop, so a couple of us grabbed him, put him in the back of a vehicle and drove a fair way up the beach. We did a couple of doughnuts so he wouldn't know which way was which, took him out and left him to sober up. Next morning when he walked back into Eurong, his wife was really happy to see him!"

Not all problem campers were as readily handled. Sid remembers "One tourist who came with a large group of campers, unknown to us and them, had to take medication regularly. We were to learn he had left it behind.

"Our first intimation of trouble was when he suddenly professed a hatred of all things German, raced off across the camping ground and began to kick a VW beach buggy belonging to other astonished campers.

"There was a nurse who had done some psychiatric training on staff as a temporary housemaid and she talked to him at length. She advised that without his medication he could become violent again very quickly and required expert help.

"I telephoned the Tin Can Bay police, explained the problem to them and asked if they would come and take him to hospital. They promised to come right away. It would take them at least two hours and meanwhile everyone was on tenterhooks. However the nurse managed to keep the man calm by promising to marry him.

"I began to worry that perhaps I had over reacted and would be in trouble for calling the police out on what looked like turning into a wild goose chase.

"But at the sight of the police uniforms the man went wild and had to be restrained before he could be bundled into the police van. We heard next day that on the barge to Inskip Point he had smashed a window in the van, escaped through it and had been about to jump overboard when the police managed to grab him."

* * * *

More seriously the island had no medical services to meet the accident rate which rose dramatically with the increased number of visitors.

The long surf beach was a temptation to drivers to speed, unaware of soft patches that could bring a vehicle to a dead halt and of the steep banks the freshwater creeks cut into the sand.

Passengers would often sit on vehicle bonnets or roof racks, the better to enjoy the sun and breeze. Many lost their hold and fell off.

"They would be safer doing that on the highway," said Sid. "At least there they are closer to medical help. But as soon as they get on the island too many put their vehicles into top gear and their brains in neutral."

With his plane in full view on the beachfront, and the speedy access it represented to the mainland and medical services, Sid found himself being asked to evacuate countless accident victims

On one occasion a lad on a motorbike rode it up a sand blow unaware of the sheer drop at the end of it. The fall broke his back. His companions came for help and said he would need to be carried out. Sid took a door off one of the units, and he and Max and some of the sand mining men, who'd been enjoying themselves playing pool in the Island Inn, walked with it up the blow for more than two kilometres.

The youth was placed gently on the door and carried out to the beach. By time they reached Eurong, it was dark. But with a vehicle driving in front of his plane to show him the way with its lights, and people with torches standing on either side of his beach landing strip, Sid was able to take off and get him to hospital.

On another occasion Sid was able to save the life of a man who dived into the surf to rescue a little girl in difficulties, then got into difficulties himself. By the time rescuers got him out of the water he was immobile and having difficulty breathing.

While others telephoned Maryborough to alert the ambulance and hospital, Sid had the man half way there in his plane. The ambulance was waiting for him at the airport and the man was given oxygen immediately. He made a full recovery.

Helping the sick and injured became a mounting burden, for Sid had no medical knowledge and neither did his regular staff. There was always a worry whether they were doing the right thing in moving people to get them into the plane.

Occasionally a doctor or nurse holidaying at Eurong would make the decision for Sid, but most times he had to make the decision himself. If time in getting someone to medical help appeared the most critical factor, he would take the responsibility and fly them to Maryborough.

"One of the worst accidents was when a group of deaf and dumb people came across from Inskip Point in two hired vehicles in the mid 1970's," Sid recalls.

"The first we knew was when I was woken at 11pm and told there was a bad accident at Poyungan Rocks, about 12 km north of Eurong. Max and I drove up in the dark and found they had driven one of their vehicles head on into a 3 m high wall of black coffee rock.

"It looked like five of them were badly injured. To our absolute amazement and dismay soon after we arrived, the leader of the party announced he and the others were going to continue on their way.

"They just drove off in the second vehicle, leaving us to cope, but it was hard for us because we could not communicate with them. We lay the injured down carefully in our vehicle and took them back to Eurong.

"We put them on mattresses on the floor of the A Frame so their bodies were supported. Once we got them settled I phoned for help. After a long wait, I was told I should wait for a doctor to fly in in the morning, and in the meantime we should do what we could to keep them warm and comfortable for the rest of the night.

"It was a terrible ordeal for the poor people not being able to tell us where they hurt or anything."

With some relief in the late 1970's, Sid learned a Maryborough doctor, Dennis Costigan, had a plane, and had offered to do a fortnightly surgery at Eurong and could be called upon in other emergencies.

The surgeries were short lived however and Dr. Costigan's real value for flying in to handle emergencies came to an end when, after 40 good beach landings, he ran over a creek bank on landing, breaking a nose wheel strut on his plane.

The nose dipped, the propeller twisted itself into the sand and the plane toppled over on to a wing. In two seconds some $20,000 of damage was caused.

His insurance company told the doctor beach landings from then on were out.

Not all calls for medical evacuation were as serious as they seemed to the victims.

"Two German couples came one day to ask me to fly one of the men to hospital because they had been camping up the beach and he had been bitten by a snake," Sid recounts. "I asked what sort of snake, but no-one had seen it. He had two distinct puncture marks on his leg and was in agony. I put him and his wife in the plane and took them to Maryborough where we had organized for an ambulance to be waiting."

"Next morning their friends came into the shop to ring the hospital. The man had been discharged and the friends had to drive all the way through Rainbow Beach to Maryborough to pick him and his wife up. They missed the last barge from Inskip Point to get back to the island so had to spend the night in a hotel.

"Two days later they were all back. The wife had been bitten by a snake, so we went through the same routine. She insisted on being flown to hospital. Next morning the hospital had discharged the woman and the friends had to go and pick her up. They said they were getting sick of all the driving.

"A couple of days later I went up to their beach camp to see how they doing – and found they had put their tent right on top of a big nest of bull ants."

Chapter 11

Sid was not the only person whose business got a boost from Fraser Island's developing tourism industry. Basking in their proximity to the island, Hervey Bay and Rainbow Beach grew steadily and people in both centres began to run trips to the island.

One of these was a real country character, Paddy Doran. He obviously thought if Sid could make a go of a tour and resort business on Fraser, then so could he. But Paddy lacked Sid's drive and single mindedness.

Like Sid he was heavily built, bearded and wore no shoes. After a tree limb nearly fell on his head, he invariably wore a construction worker's hard hat. Asked why, if falling trees were his problem, he wore the hat indoors, Paddy's guileless response was "In case the roof falls in."

He started to run trips from Rainbow Beach to Fraser in an old Blitz truck he had converted to an open air bus. Goodness knows what his day trippers thought when they saw the Blitz with wooden sides, wooden roof, even wooden doors and their guide wearing a hard hat. But the only way to go on a tour from Rainbow Beach in the mid 1970's was with Paddy.

He decided to expand into a resort. He didn't own any land on Fraser, but that was a minor impediment. He built a series of little wooden huts, mounted them on skids and towed them up the surf beach behind his truck. He parked them on a grassy spot in the frontal dunes just north of the *Maheno.*

In due course the Lands Department got to hear about Paddy's resort appearing from nowhere, and asked him to shift it. Paddy did – about 40 metres further along the dunes. Next he got a verbal instruction from a kindly Lands officer to shift it 80 kms, right off the island. It made no difference to Paddy. He just kept towing his mobile resort to a new location and by time the Lands officer had found it again, he would have had six month's occupancy.

It was a little confusing for his guests sometimes. They would go back after a fishing trip to find the resort had vanished.

Sid too fell foul of government. With more visitors coming to Fraser every year, regulation inevitably followed. The Transport Department sought to limit the number of people coming on tours, to the numbers each operator was carrying at the time.

Sid was confident that his business would keep growing, so to get as many passenger numbers as he possibly could, he had every one of his trucks counted as passenger carrying vehicles, even if they normally carried building materials or fuel.

The problem with most of Sid's trucks was that, being American, they were left hand drive and left hand drive vehicles were illegal in Queensland, so could not be counted. Transport inspectors made occasional forays to Fraser Island and threatened to ground Sid's fleet, and Paddy's open air bus

Between them they collected a handful of warning letters, and decided to go together to see the Minister for Transport in Brisbane and explain the conditions they were operating in on Fraser Island.

Alan Cullen, a former sand mining employee, who had begun tourist fishing trips went along for support. "He was the brains of the outfit," says Sid.

All were plain hard working bush fellows, none of them comfortable in shoes, which they didn't need in sand. Paddy had his hard hat. They put on their clean working clothes, for they didn't have suits, and went to Parliament House to see the Minister. On the way Sid went to Woolworth's and bought a little kiddy's lunch case to put the paperwork in, so they would look more official.

At Parliament House no-one quite knew what to do with them, for they had not thought to make an appointment, and they were eventually passed to the Minister's private secretary. Bemusedly this elegant gentleman looked the trio up and down, hard hat, kiddy's lunch case, work clothes, no shoes, and asked "Whom shall I say wishes to see the Minister?"

Sid replied "Melksham, Cullen and Doran."

"Ah," said the private secretary," solicitors I presume."

Probably out of curiosity the Minister agreed to see them, and they put their case. There and then Sid was given special permission to drive his left hand drive vehicles on Fraser Island.

By 1977 he had 17 trucks and buses.

Sid's bright orange Studebaker buses became a real island feature, each an individual with its own name, *Mystery, Jerky* and *Flappers.*

Sid remembers telephoning the motor vehicle inspector in Maryborough one time to ask for temporary cancellation of bus registration while one of the Studebakers underwent a major overhaul.

He asked which one, and Sid replied "*Mystery.*" The inspector replied, somewhat testily "I am not playing guessing games."

One of the old GMC's survived until the early 1980's. This was *Softly.* It worked hard and never missed a beat. It could stand idle for months but, encouraged by a well charged battery, would fire up straight away.

Driver Jimmy Schmidt tells of when he had to use *Softly* when it hadn't been used for some time. "The bus I was driving broke down right at Eurong, and I dashed to the workshop for *Softly.* Unusually I had trouble starting it. Eventually it coughed, backfired and spat out from the exhaust pipe a very startled bush rat which landed on the leg of a curious passenger who had followed me, and bit him."

* * * *

Sid's enterprise catered for every type of visitors, families, groups, and school children.

"Our camping ground and tours of the island soon became very popular with school groups, then teachers would tell each other about the island and soon they were coming from all over Queensland," says Sid.

Unforgettable was a group of 19 Aboriginal children who came to Eurong for a week from Normanton on the Gulf of Carpentaria.

Dingo scalps attracted a $10 bounty there and when the children saw the island dingoes, they thought they would be making a lot more pocket money than they had come with.

Next day Sid had to restrain the three cool characters in the group from leaping on to the backs of the brumbies for buck jumping practice for the Normanton rodeo.

When the youngsters practiced rap dancing in the bistro area, a woman visitor was most impressed by what she thought was a display of native dancing.

Many Maryborough and Hervey Bay people began to make Eurong their regular holiday spot. The Hervey Bay Little Theatre director, Lyn Dahl asked Sid if they could put on plays in the dining room during school holidays to help raise funds for the theatre.

Sid was only too pleased to have entertainment at Eurong, and the theatre group performances became a regular fixture on the Eurong social calendar. Its members came to look on Eurong as their holiday home and they even wrote a song about Sid and his day trips as the finale to their shows.

There were annual band concerts with Maryborough bands folk carrying over all their instruments for the weekend, ***(below).***

Another regular group was of motorcyclists organized by Maryborough motorbike shop owner Greg Ohls. They would come to Eurong year after year dressed in their best bibs and tucker, even elderly dinner suits purchased specially for their island sojourns from an op shop ***(below)***.

Then there were the "Ipswich boys", a group of characters who adopted Fraser Island and entertained themselves playing practical jokes on fellow holidaymakers.

"On one visit we brought a most realistic rubber shark fin mounted on a little raft, which we operated by remote control radio." Lance Robertson, one of the "boys", described.

"When Sid's day trippers were all swimming in Lake Birrabeen, we sat on the beach there and sent it across the lake. Everyone raced out of the water. Not one person stopped to think that you don't get sharks in freshwater lakes, especially ones perched up in the sand dunes with no access to the sea. "

The Ipswich boys earned everlasting fame when they arrived one Easter and unloaded 140 cartons of beer from their vehicles into the A Frames for the eight of them to consume over the four days.

They drank it all too. Fortunately they were a good natured group, even in their cups, but for what they saw of Fraser that long weekend they might as well have stayed home.

* * * *

Eurong became so busy that Sid's visits to his family became rushed as he raced to see them between calls on Maryborough businesses to organize supplies or work for the island.

His marriage to Marietta ended in 1978, and the couple was divorced two years later. Sid's love for his children, Monica and Bill, made the break harder to bear when Marietta moved back to her family home of Brisbane, taking them with her. He got access to them every second weekend in Brisbane and half of every school holiday on Fraser Island, but the latter were always the busiest times at the resort and it was hard to give them the time he wanted.

Bill remembers the freedom he experienced at Eurong and the mischief he and Ross Williams, Max's grandson, got up to. Ross was the same age as Bill.

As they grew older Sid tried to instill his work ethic in his children. Bill remembers "Dad told Ross and me to go and sweep up the workshop one day. We went off to play and Ross said we should smear ourselves with oil and dirt to make it look as if we had been working. Dad always had me picking up things, cigarette dumpers from the resort lawns, and sticks that might have speared bus tyres on the roads."

Daughter Monica was keen to do her share to help and one day when all the staff were busy, she persuaded off duty shop assistant Leslie Muller, to drive the resort rubbish truck, a Toyota tray back laden with wheelie bins to upend them in the dump. Backing it to the dump which was at that time a pit half full of burning rubbish, Leslie went too far, the side crumbled and the vehicle and bins fell in. She and Monica scrambled out, but by time they had run back to the resort for help, the vehicle and bins had burned.

Of course Sid had to be told. He was so relieved no harm had come to Monica and Leslie that if he was angry, he didn't show it. He simply gave the terse instruction to Leslie "Ring up and find out if those bins were insured."

Bill, Ross Williams and Monica camp out on the Eurong camping ground during the 1983 New Year holidays.

* * * *

In due course Sid sold his Cessna and bought a bigger aircraft, a six seat Cherokee. It wasn't new, but it was mechanically sound and when Sid and his friend, Phil Delaney spent a week sanding it down and painting it gleaming white with orange and green trim, it became his pride.

A pilot who had worked for Sid until he got his licence now ran his own charter business in Maryborough. He enviously watched Sid ferrying people to and from the island, and knowing Sid did not have a charter licence, reported him to the Department of Civil Aviation.

Federal police came and questioned Sid about a particular group of 11 people he had flown to Eurong to stay for a long weekend. He was quite open with them, and next thing there was a summons and a charge sheet with breaches of aviation rules to answer.

At first Sid took it all lightly because he believed he had done nothing wrong – until he spoke to a solicitor, who suggested he prepare himself properly and, if possible, get some witnesses to give evidence for him.

Sid asked the Maryborough travel agent who had booked the 11 people to stay at Eurong, and his friend, Bevan Whitaker, who now owned an air charter business in Maryborough, to come to court for him.

When Sid entered court there were several Civil Aviation officials from Brisbane, the Commonwealth Crown Solicitor, Federal police officers and the 11 passengers, all from Victoria.

Sid learned the Department had chartered two large aircraft to fly all these people to Maryborough, and if he were found guilty of the breaches he would not only be fined, and possibly grounded, but would have to pay the Department's costs of chartering the two planes.

The Department of Civil Aviation officials told the court that Sid only had a private pilot's licence and was not qualified to do charter work.

The Federal police officer said Sid had admitted flying the 11 people to Eurong.

The Maryborough travel agent in his turn responded it had been a quiet time of year, so Sid had been prepared to fly the group to the island and back at no cost just to get them there, and they had only paid for their accommodation and meals. He produced the accounts and a resort brochure to prove the sum they had paid tallied with the brochure cost of their rooms and meals.

If they didn't pay for the flight, as the travel agent testified, then Sid had not run an illegal charter.

A second charge was that Sid's Cherokee was not suitable for charter.

Bevan Whitaker told the magistrate that he operated Cherokee aircraft, identical to Sid's, for his charter business, and it was ideally suited.

The Commonwealth Crown Solicitor claimed this was not the meaning of the law. It meant the plane was not suitable because Sid was not qualified to use it for charter work.

Whitaker sharply responded "That's not how the law is written. If that is the meaning, then it is not worded properly."

The evidence took hours and was only completed at 4 pm, the time the court normally finished for the day. Sid was very worried, thinking if he lost the case the costs would also include paying for overnight accommodation in Maryborough for all the witnesses.

The magistrate, who must have understood this, said he would continue until the case was concluded. He retired to consider the evidence.

Two hours later he emerged to exonerate Sid completely. Then a surprising thing happened. While the Crown Solicitor fumed, the officials from the Department of Civil Aviation went over to shake Sid's hand.

They had known him for many years, some through examining him for his pilot's licences as he upgraded, and without exception admired him for overcoming the obstacle of his poor education to become a pilot.

The 11 passengers came to congratulate him too. They had enjoyed their stay at Eurong.

* * * *

As Christmas and Easter became busier each year, it was hard keeping food and fuel supplies up to the stream of people.

The worst part of the supply runs during the holidays was that they had to be done several times a week. The truck had to go along the surf beach even if it was high tide, and this meant ploughing through soft sand with waves surging up to the wheels.

If Sid had sent a driver and the truck hadn't returned by dark, Sid would be out on the beach looking for headlights in the distance, imagining it broken down with the sea washing over it. After a brief impatient wait he would get in his 4WD and go looking for it.

Stores orders would be telephoned through from Eurong and the suppliers in Maryborough would have the goods waiting for the truck to arrive.

Even then the shop, bowsers and kitchen would run out of some things. It was pandemonium if it was petrol, or milk or cartons of beer, until the truck got back.

* * * *

Having the only telephone in the area meant there was a long queue of holidaymakers waiting to use it every morning when the staff opened the shop, and it hardly diminished all day, because the calls took so long to put through.

Staff would have to wind the handle on the veteran phone to alert the operator in Maryborough exchange, give the number for the customer, then ask for a ring back price so they knew how much to charge. If the exchange was busy, this was a prolonged process, and kept one shop assistant fully occupied.

Incoming calls were signaled with two short and one long ring, the Morse code for the letter U, and as soon as one ring was heard, everyone had to be quiet while we listened to see if the number of succeeding rings meant the call was for us or for one of the Forestry folk on the party line.

As time went on the fencing wire telephone line that Sid and Johnny Lenthall had strung through the forest started to sag. Many a laden timber truck hurtling through the island would snag the line and drag it down, often for many kilometres, so all communication was cut off. Sid and his workers would have to set off to find the break, join it again and tie the line all the way back up to the insulators. Sometimes it took days.

It became increasingly difficult to rouse the mainland operator because so many twigs and branches had fallen across the single line, shorting it out.

Sid came up with the solution, when he got tired of waiting. He took the handle off the phone and put a connection on it, so when he couldn't raise the operator he would put an electric drill on to the connection that would turn the shaft so much faster, increasing the voltage.

As it deteriorated yet further, he attached a plug to it and would put it in a power socket. There were some very fast operator responses to 240 volts shooting down the line.

After Max Williams got zapped one time he was fixing the line and a shop assistant made an impatient call, Sid or the men made sure to take the plug with them when they had to go and do repairs on the line.

* * * *

There were changes all through the island in the late 1970's and early 1980's.

At both Happy Valley and Eurong more people began to take up the subdivision blocks to build houses mostly for holiday letting, though a few retirees or people who could earn a living, made the little townships home.

Sir Reginald Barnewall sold the resort at Orchid Beach in 1972 to a Brisbane consortium, and went on to develop an airstrip and charter flying business at Rainbow Beach, then gave commercial flying away and bought an avocado farm at Mount Tambourine in the Gold Coast hinterland.

Don Adams sold his airstrip at Scarness for subdivision and went into aircraft development. A new airport was developed by the Hervey Bay Council behind Urangan.

The ownership of Orchid Beach Resort was muddy for some years afterwards until in 1983 it was purchased by another consortium headed by a Brisbane car dealer, Keith Leach.

With expertise in promotion, Leach soon devised an annual fishing contest to attract guests to the by now deteriorating resort in the quiet month of May. The first competition in 1984, with big cash prizes, attracted about 200 entrants.

It was a great success. Numbers doubled the next year and continued to grow until a limit of 1500 entrants had to be put on the contest. It attracted the adverse attention of John Sinclair and F.I.D.O. and the positive interest of Toyota, who saw it as a potential advertising event for their 4WD vehicles

Graeme and Wendy Coutts-Smith and their two sons bought the Happy Valley store. Before long they demolished the original shop and built a splendid timber shop and restaurant with a home on top for themselves, and eight cabins for guests.

Some 20 km further north, close to the Cathedrals coloured sand cliffs, a Happy Valley holiday unit owner, Geoff Hannant and his wife, Norma were given a 30 year lease over some 25 hectares of land to make a camping park.

Island residents questioned how such a large area, which was named The Cathedrals Resort and Camping Park, could be granted to the Hannants without tenders being called.

When they began to build a shop on their lease, Graeme Coutts-Smith objected formally that this was not allowed under the lease conditions. The Queensland Government acted quickly to give the Hannants special approval.

Sid remained the constant at Eurong, and I joined him in 1979. We had known each other since 1969 when I was working as a journalist for the *Maryborough Chronicle* newspaper and became friendly with Johnny Stevenson, the linotype operator who was Sid's friend.

I had a hobby mushroom shed on land at Urangan in Hervey Bay and one day was busy mixing horse manure and straw to make mushroom compost when an E Type Jaguar turned in the gate.

Stevo had brought Sid to meet me. I was not in the least interested in Sid, but very interested in the car. "Can I take it for a drive?" I asked. Sid looked at me covered in muck and said "No".

The next time we met was when I wrote the story of the Reville accident of 1970 for the *Chronicle,* and watched a very sombre Sid bring Reville's *Island Queen* into Urangan jetty with the seven bodies aboard.

A year later I was camping on Fraser Island and fell off a motorbike badly burning my leg on the exhaust. I went to Eurong to ask Sid if he would fly me to the mainland so I could go to the doctor. He was just helping two ladies who had been staying at Eurong into his plane, and told me to sit in the front next to him.

We had hardly set off when I began to feel airsick. Sid saw my plight and asked one of the ladies sitting behind us to open a bag and pass it to me. She could not see me going green and the only bag she could see was Sid's briefcase with all his flying documents in it, next to his seat. So she opened it and passed it to me.

I learned later it had taken Sid weeks to have his documents replaced.

In December 1978 I left journalism and returned to Fraser Island to write in quiet seclusion. I offered to do the bookkeeping for Eurong in return for room and board.

At the time it seemed a good deal for me, for there were only about a dozen staff and the major item of bookkeeping appeared to be adding the price of the ice creams, cigarettes and other small items that they took from the shop, written carefully in a daily diary by the shopkeeper, and deducting it from their weekly pay.

The relationship between Sid and me developed some months later, and as my involvement in the resort grew, I was left with increasingly less time for writing. I persevered for a while, shutting myself in my room but was distracted by staff knocking on the door with one thing after another.

I hung a "Do Not Disturb" sign on the door but then the staff would hover outside the window, which was even more distracting. In any case Sid felt it did not apply to him and would come to collect me at meal times. I told him I would come out of the room when I could for my meals and he should not distract me.

Next day he came and sat quietly waiting, while I tried to ignore his presence. This did not suit, for after a few minutes of waiting for me to get to a point where I could take a break, he suddenly leapt to his feet and started banging on the wall.

I said "Go away." He kept on banging and said "I think we've got white ants." Still trying to write I said "I don't care," and he still thumping on the walls got cross and said "The whole building will fall on top of you, then you'll care."

I was warmly welcomed into the resort community by Kelly in particular for my unit was next to the take away bottle shop. Every afternoon that Sid was away, Kelly would appear and ask if I would like a beer. Then we'd sit and be sociable for a while, with me drinking maybe one can of beer to Kelly's half dozen.

As soon as Kelly heard Sid's plane he would thank me graciously for my company and depart while I went out to greet Sid. When we came back into the unit there would be six empty cans on the table in front of my chair and one in front of the chair in which Kelly had been sitting.

Kelly was not the only one who played upon my early naivety.

Whereas Kelly told fibs, quite expecting to be caught out, Victor Pyjamas would tell the most convincing lies and went to endless trouble, not only to concoct the stories, but to furnish supporting evidence.

He had no trouble convincing me he was very wealthy and was just helping Sid out for a couple of weeks before heading for Brisbane to take possession of a big motor launch he had bought. He showed me photographs and a list of specifications.

As Sid and I were going to Brisbane, I said I would like to see the new boat, and arranged with Victor that I would be on the Botanic Gardens bank of the Brisbane river at a certain time, when Victor would cruise past.

Sid told me not to waste my time, saying "Victor doesn't have a boat. Victor will never have a boat. He has made it up."

"But he has a photograph," I said.

"Anyone can take a photo of a boat," replied Sid.

"Victor told me he has a boat and I believe him."

So Sid came with me to the Botanic Gardens at the appointed time in pouring rain and we huddled for two hours in a bus shelter with a host of homeless men, who got to fighting over a flagon of port.

Victor never came by in his boat, and he never came back to Eurong.

Chapter 12

Always on the lookout for a bargain, early in 1979 Sid saw an advertisement in the *Maryborough Chronicle* for the sale of the wharf barracks at Urangan in Hervey Bay for removal.

Urangan had been a port for the export of sugar, and there was a long jetty for large boats to come in and load. But this trade had long since ended and the Urangan port closed. With no port and no workers there was no need for the barracks, where the wharfies had stayed while there was a ship to be loaded.

It was a large, well maintained, two storey weatherboard building, 30 m long by seven metres wide, the largest building in Hervey Bay. When Sid went to inspect it he found that inside were lots of small bedrooms. More interesting, from his perspective, was the interior framework of large hardwood timbers running from the roof to the foundations at each bedroom wall, which made it immensely strong.

He was certain he could find good use for it at Eurong, and being so large, it could be a focal point for the resort. He had always felt that a hotel, the first on the island, would be a draw card, and a necessary adjunct to a proper resort. A bar would take up most of the ground floor and upstairs, without the bedroom walls, could become a restaurant to replace the Island Inn, which was rapidly becoming far too small for all the day trippers.

A tender was put in to the Maryborough Harbours and Marine Department for a little more than $7,000, a big sum in 1979, and two months later Sid became owner of the building with conditions on the sale that it be removed quickly.

Before it could be dismantled, concrete foundations and floor had to be laid on which to rebuild it once it arrived at Eurong

Tons of gravel, sand, cement and mesh as well as the building itself had to be trucked in. While semi trailers could bring the materials from Maryborough to the barge point at Inskip Point, there was only one truck capable of carting so many big loads up the beach to Eurong – the Peterbilt.

After almost two and a half years standing idle in Maryborough, the truck was to come into its own again. The mechanic who had put the big truck into temporary retirement had died in the interim, and when Sid asked a friend and first class mechanic Alan Wylie to get the truck ready to roll after the long layoff, he couldn't find one of the gears. A new one had to be manufactured – then of course the original turned up where it had been left soaking in a bucket of oil.

Paddy Doran, of Melksham, Cullen and Doran was commissioned to rebuild the wooden tray back.

Sid knew the truck would have problems negotiating the Maryborough city centre streets before it got to the open road to Tin Can Bay and Rainbow Beach. When he had taken it through town to moth ball it after sand mining, he had had to shunt back and forth around all the corners, holding up the traffic.

When the work on it was nearly finished, he applied to the police for a special permit for Alan to drive the Peterbilt through Maryborough once more. The police said it would have to be through the city centre very early so as not to disrupt traffic.

Alan planned a 4.30 am start on a public holiday. He had reckoned without Paddy. Time meant nothing to him and he did not arrive with the timber to make the tray until 7.30 am on the planned day of departure. The timber had to be cut and secured. It was 10 am before the Peterbilt was ready to roll.

Alan should perhaps have deferred the trip, but he knew Sid would be waiting at Inskip Point to drive the Peterbilt up the surf beach to Eurong – and maybe in his anxiety he forgot what public holiday it was.

So he set off hoping that, in spite of the racket from the Peterbilt's huge engine and the sheer size of the truck, he could get through Maryborough comparatively unnoticed.

There was only one route he could take, through the city centre where the street corners were big enough to wind the Peterbilt around without a lot of backing up, and perhaps he thought Maryborough would be deserted on a public holiday anyway.

He certainly had not planned to be the unscheduled attraction in the middle of the city's Anzac Day procession.

All the spectators lining the streets gave the Peterbilt a big clap, firmly believing it was meant to be there.

Meanwhile Sid was waiting anxiously for its arrival at Inskip Point. He relaxed only when he heard the roar of its engine as it approached Rainbow Beach 11 km away.

* * * *

Everyone buckled in, drivers, cooks, shop assistants, Kelly and all to dig the foundations for the hotel by hand. They were far deeper and wider than was needed, as Sid planned for the day ahead when perhaps he could afford a much bigger, better building on the same spot. He often spoke afterwards of the foundations being capable of supporting a six storey building.

Alan Wylie, the Anzac Day star, lent a big concrete mixer.

Sid drove the Peterbilt up and down the beach at low tide nearly every day to cart in the gravel and cement. Everyone used to dread hearing the truck approaching, for it signaled plenty of back breaking work ahead.

It took hours to shovel a load of gravel off the Peterbilt and through the mixer. Word got around that there was a big building job going on at Eurong and plenty of fellows came and asked for jobs, and were put on, but most didn't last more than a day or two. Two who did stay were father and son, Graham and Steve Mather from Hervey Bay who remained for years afterwards, Graham as head barman and Steve as a tour driver.

There was relief for the gravel shovellers and a crisis for Sid when an axle in the Peterbilt broke while Sid was backing up a rise off the beach with a heavy load.

Sid had heard there was a second Peterbilt somewhere in Western Australia, so he phoned a few likely places and tracked it down, hoping it was not working and the owner could send a spare axle. But no, that Peterbilt was working too.

Next Sid phoned the Peterbilt manufacturers in the United States. Yes, they could send an axle but it would cost $US3000 plus shipping costs and take weeks to arrive.

Plan three was to have a replacement axle manufactured locally. Sid and Jimmy Schmidt removed the broken axle. (Actually at the first attempt they took out the wrong axle which wasn't a great help either with solving the problem on hand or creating a calm working atmosphere.)

Sid then took the pieces to Roy Rufus's engineering workshop in Maryborough and asked if he could make a new axle.

Roy had the steel tested to find out its composition and strength and then set about making a new one. It was a complicated job. Roy kept shaking his head and telling Sid how expensive it was going to be.

Sid kept weighing up the possible cost of Roy's custom made job with the $3000 for the American assembly line axle, but decided time was of the essence and Roy should go ahead, whatever the extra cost.

It was with a fair degree of anxiety that Sid waited for Roy's account. It came to $350. Sid tentatively asked if Roy had left a naught off the end. Roy hadn't, so Sid told him that while he was set up, he should make a second axle, in case another one broke.

* * * *

Meanwhile work continued on the foundations. Four of Sid's men in turn shoveled gravel, sand and cement into the mixer, while another employee Luigi operated the mixer, putting the right amount of water in, and tipping the concrete into the bucket of a front end loader, which sometimes Jimmy Schmidt, sometimes Sid drove to the front foundation trench and poured in.

Sid, driving the front end loader delivers a bucket load of concrete to Kelly shovelling it in the pub foundations.

At first there was just an elderly builder, Emil Fuchs and Kelly Page to level the concrete in the foundation formwork

As the front and side foundations, that Jimmy could tip directly into, were filled, Emil and Kelly used small planks of timber to scrape the mounds of wet concrete across the seven metre wide floor space into the rear foundation trenches.

Kelly and Emil shovelling concrete into the pub foundation formwork.

When Alan Wylie's wife, Carol and I saw the two of them struggling away, we hopped in to help. I remember losing my thongs when I stumbled into a trench and the concrete sucked them right off my feet as I clambered out.

The foundations filled, the floor then had to be poured, so the same routine was gone through for several more days, with Carol and I doing rough leveling of the interminable concrete deliveries and Kelly and Emil screeding it off smoothly.

Luigi, at the mixer, was lame and had real difficulty keeping up with his three year old son, Aaron, who wanted to be part of the action. To keep him out of harm's way, Luigi took to tying a rope lightly round his waist and the other end to a nearby banksia. Aaron played happily in the shade until we had two big areas of floor poured and screeded off to perfection.

Then Aaron announced he needed to go to the toilet. He stood up and unhesitatingly wriggled the rope over his bottom.

We watched in awful fascination as Luigi limped over to him, but was, of course too late to stop his son running the shortest route towards him, in a straight line over the still soft, but nicely smooth, concrete floor.

Each night after a section of the foundations or floor had been poured Sid used to sit up most of the night to keep Kelly, the expert troweller, awake and not consuming too many beers until the concrete had cured enough for a final smoothing off.

All this work took a long time and Sid kept receiving letters from the Department of Harbours and Marine saying he had overrun the agreed time limit to remove the wharf barracks and what was he going to do about it? Sid thought silence the best response.

Sid had problems too with the Maryborough City Council, which administered Eurong. He thought the plans he had to submit for building approval could be a simple matter of drawing the layout of the building as it stood in Hervey Bay.

He asked the builder, Dennis Crooks of Maryborough to draw the plans. Sid then presented them to the council building inspector. He gazed at them for some time, than asked "Who drew these?"

Sid replied "Crooksie, the builder."

"But," objected the inspector, "builders don't normally draw plans."

And resort owners don't normally strangle building inspectors," retorted Sid, "but there is always a first time."

This was obviously the wrong approach for the inspector simply instructed the girl at the front counter to give Sid a list of architects who would draw plans acceptable to the council and disappeared into his office.

There was a further delay until the chosen architect could find time to do the plans, while numerous tradesmen were waiting to start work and letters came regularly from the Department of Harbours and Marine about expired time limits.

At last the mail brought the long awaited building approval and work began again in earnest.

The building was numbered plank by plank, beam by beam, truss by truss, and dismantled.

A crane was hired to lift the heavy roof trusses down and on to Alan Wylie's semi trailer. All the material, except for the fibro roof, which was discarded, made two semi trailer loads. Alan brought each semi trailer load from Hervey Bay to Rainbow Beach. There all the long timbers had to be manhandled across to the Peterbilt and brought the rest of the way along the beach to Eurong. It took weeks to dismantle the building and months to resurrect.

All the previous buildings at Eurong had been built end on to the beach and the cyclonic winds.

This was to be such an important building however, that Sid wanted it to look its most impressive from the beach front so chose to put it lengthwise on to the beach, which made it more vulnerable to strong winds. However he was confident, with its immensely strong framework, it would be able to withstand a cyclonic blow.

With the work on rebuilding just begun, I had to leave Eurong to go to New Guinea to research the story of a medical missionary on Karkar Island for a book I was writing, and after two weeks Sid joined me in Madang.

We spent two further weeks traveling around the country together, Sid coming up with ideas for businesses for the tribes people everywhere, such as importing wheelbarrows to save the women having to carry all their shopping in the traditional bilums, woven bags hanging down their backs with the handles round their foreheads, or fibreglass water tanks to replace the dozens of rusted out iron tanks in the town dumps.

He also took careful notice of the design of some of the tropical resorts and hotels, and got the idea of adding an upper level verandah the full length of the rear of the proposed Eurong hotel, to give it construction strength as well as make a pleasant shaded outdoor eating area.

No-one had been able to get in touch with us during our travels in New Guinea, so when we got home and found the hotel still just a frame and the builders gone, it was an awful shock.

Soon after Sid had left Eurong, the Maryborough City Council building inspector had come on a routine visit, seen the size of the building just back from the beach front in a cyclone category one area and put a stop work order on it.

The builders had left to do another job in Maryborough until Sid could come home and either sort out the problem or not.

Sid went haring off to Maryborough to see the building inspector the very next day.

The building inspector explained that the building could not be re-assembled as it had been in Hervey Bay, where it had been protected from cyclones by Fraser Island. He wanted it to be made even stronger because at Eurong it would be exposed to the full brunt of cyclonic winds.

He suggested helpfully that Sid put big timber buttresses all around the outside of the building, so close together in fact that a plump person might well find access impossible.

Sid exploded that it would look stupid as well as being very expensive, and left. He was not mollified or the least bit amused when someone suggested his pub would look like a Gothic cathedral.

Sid said there was no way he was going to put up buttresses, went out to water his lawn and ponder the problem. He recalled seeing a railway bridge sometime somewhere with structural bracing that he thought could apply to the hotel now.

That night he devised an internal bracing method to give the hotel building added strength. As it had stood in Hervey Bay and as it was to be rebuilt at Eurong, the building had two parallel rows of big timber supports which ran from foundation to roof inside the building.

Sid worked out that if he attached steel brackets to the timber supports at floor and ceiling, both in the bar and the restaurant above, and got steel rods with turnbuckles which could be bolted into the brackets crosswise, he could brace the building from these supports if a cyclone came. In between times the rods and turnbuckles could be stored out of the way.

He drew a sketch of brackets, rods and turnbuckles and took them back to the building inspector, who did not ask who had drawn the sketch, but said he hadn't seen anything like it.

"Where did you get this idea?" he enquired.

Being a man of few words, Sid replied "Railway bridges."

"What do you mean?"

"I have seen railway bridges braced underneath like this."

"But this is not a railway bridge."

"It's the same principle."

"Well I've never heard of anything like this..."

"That's the trouble with you fellows. You read a couple of books and think you know everything…" Sid started to shout.

The building inspector said if Sid could get the bracing approved by an engineer, he would accept it.

With very little trouble Sid found an engineer who understood immediately what he was talking about, did a lot of stress calculations and assessed Sid's method of internal bracing as being in fact stronger than external buttresses.

* * * *

Work began again, but the lost time meant it was all systems go to finish the building before Christmas 1980 to earn money to pay for it from the holiday crowds.

The biggest task was getting the huge roof trusses on to the roof of the ten metre high building. They were made of double 6"x 2" hardwood and were enormously heavy. A crane had been needed to get them down from the building at Urangan, but there was no crane on Fraser Island to hoist them up.

A system of ropes and pulleys was devised and it took 10 men to haul them to the top of the building. It was an impressive feat. The original weatherboard walls were all nailed into place, with a new front of fine green coloured Tanilith pine. A large rear verandah was added with a tropical garden planted underneath.

Large concrete aprons were laid at the front and back of the building for outdoor areas where customers could sit in the sun.

The pub is finally complete.

A restaurant, decorated island style with sea grass matting, murals and hanging plants, was built upstairs, with a kitchen at one end. Once the restaurant was complete, it was opened for business and the old Island Inn was converted to three accommodation units.

Most of the downstairs was taken up with a bar, which extended the width of the building, and there were tables built around the vertical timbers in the body of the big room at one end and, at the opposite end, lounge chairs.

The floor was tiled, with Sid going over the work with a 20c coin in his hand, tapping the tiles to ensure they had all been well cemented in and weren't "drummy".

Sid went to ask Warren Hyne, then CEO of the big Maryborough timber company, Hyne and Sons, if he might donate some valuable lengths of timber from the unique island satinay trees to make a feature of the front of the bar. Warren said "Yes, as long as it doesn't stretch from here to Tiaro."

Sid took him almost literally, as long as the bar wasn't 25 km long, and instead of specifying the quantity to cover the seven metre long bar front that he had already worked out, he said he'd go and measure exactly how much he needed.

Then he went back to Eurong and measured all the inside walls as well as the bar, and that was the measurement he sent back to Warren Hyne.

When the generous gift of satinay arrived, it polished up to a deep red hue and gave a much admired warm appearance to what had been a fairly stark interior.

At one end of the downstairs area, beneath the kitchen were a freezer room, and two big cold rooms, one for food, one for beer and wine, and another open kitchen where steaks and grills could be served to people in a garden behind the hotel, grandly called the bistro.

When the council building inspector came for a final visit, he confessed "I did not expect it would turn out like this. I see I needn't have been so worried."

Chapter 13

While the building of the hotel was going on, the day trips and tours had to be kept running, and Sid was fortunate to have a young chap with personality plus come to ask for a bus driving job.

Steve Jensen had had his own tour business bringing people in a Ford Bronco from Noosa several days a week but was now getting married and wanted a job where he and his wife, May could be together. Sid already knew Steve well, as he had been a regular visitor to Eurong and had seen how he had kept his passengers entertained. But he didn't know May, so asked Steve to bring her to meet him.

Steve said May was a highly competent shop assistant, which was just what was needed, but when they arrived at Eurong Sid was very doubtful, for she was a shy seeming 19 year old who walked across the front lawn about ten paces behind Steve with her head down. But if Sid wanted Steve as a driver it looked as if he would have to employ May as well.

One big advantage was that the Jensens had their own caravan to live in, for accommodation for staff was in very short supply. A week after their wedding Sid had their caravan towed up the beach to the camping ground, and they started work.

Steve Jensen remembers it well. "Sid put me on as a tour bus driver, but we had to do all sorts of work if there was no driving. They call it multi skilling now. Anyway the day I started he told me to rub down some of the timber in the pub ready for painting," he says.

"There were a couple of us working away, when we heard Sid's plane take off. Immediately the other fellow, a chap called Luigi stopped work and said Sid was gone for the day we should both knock off until we heard the plane coming back. He cleared off to have a beer but I didn't. After all it was my first day.

"Anyway Sid must have suspected there was some skiving when he went to town, because he suddenly appeared in the pub doorway. He had landed his plane up the beach and walked back to the resort. He saw Luigi wasn't there.

"I didn't have to say a word. There was a little lad called Ross living with his grandparents at the resort, and he was at Sid's heels telling Sid exactly what had been going on and where Luigi was.

"Apparently word must have got to Luigi and he set off to try and hide for the next thing I heard was Ross calling out "There he goes Sid." It was the funniest introduction to a job I've ever had."

Steve's shy little wife, May proved to be a treasure. Two days after she had been shown the shop and had everything from how the phone worked, how accommodation bookings were written on large cardboard charts under the shop counter as well as all the other Eurong idiosyncrasies explained to her, May took over with great efficiency and never looked back.

May says "I was very shy at first, but soon got the hang of things and from then on I worked for Sid for 22 years apart from the times I left to have my two children."

* * * *

Our pride in achievement in building the hotel and restaurant was offset by a major disaster. One November night in 1980 soon after midnight, a knock on Sid's door heralded bad news.

A voice outside shouted "There's a fire down on the beach."

Sid tried to ignore it, thinking it was just a camp fire until the voice added "I think your plane is on fire."

For economy sake, Sid still turned off the power generator every night around 10.30 pm in the off-peak times when there were few people around. He shot out of bed and, after one look told him the Cherokee was indeed ablaze, he raced up to the generator shed to turn on the power, so the electric water pumps would start and he would have water to dowse the flames.

In his frantic haste Sid forgot he didn't wear pyjamas, which was no problem when he was racing in the dark up to the generator shed – but it was, when he had to run back with the resort lights on.

By time he got back to the beachfront, and started hosing the fire, it was too late for him to save the plane. He wouldn't give up, though spectators feared one of the wing tanks could blow up, Sid with it. When he finally dowsed the flames only half of one wing and the tail were left whole.

As, now dressed, he walked around the smouldering remains, a shattered man, he noticed a small petrol tin under the remaining piece of wing.

It had not been there when he parked the plane that afternoon.

The remains of Sid's Cherokee 6.

He telephoned the police immediately. A camper reported having heard a small explosion and seen a car drive away before he saw the flames leap up.

Car tracks could be seen in the sand around the plane and Sid stood guard over the wreckage for the rest of the night to preserve them, until the police could arrive on the first barge from the mainland. Before he could point them out to the police, they drove right up to the wreckage over the same area, obliterating them.

They found a piece of plastic hose melted on to the wing remnants and concluded that someone had been trying to siphon fuel from the plane, using a piece of chopped off resort garden hose. The combination of high octane aviation fuel, plastic hose and tin drum had set up static electricity in the fuel tank and caused the fire.

Enquiries revealed that late the evening before a group of young fellows had arrived at the resort and asked if they could buy petrol, as they had run out. But the resort had run out too until the next load of drums was brought in.

Others knew of the young men from the description and said they had seen them driving up and down the beach in an elderly Volkswagen.

By time these facts emerged and a phone call was made to Rainbow Beach to ask barge skippers to keep an eye out for lads with burned or singed hair, they could have long gone. Certainly they were never found.

The insurance money did not cover the cost of buying another Cherokee. Sid was grounded then for several years, depriving himself of his great pleasure in, and the convenience of, flying.

He chose to put the money his business earned back into improving the resort instead of buying another plane for some years.

It made life on the island that much harder. There were no quick trips to Maryborough anymore, just the long 320 km return drive via Rainbow Beach.

To make the journey, if he wasn't driving a truck, Sid acquired a Range Rover that had been rolled over on the island and written off. With his old panel beating skills not forgotten, he repaired it himself, and over the ensuing years traded up to a new Range Rover.

They were comfortable vehicles and made for a fast trip across the island to Ungowa in spite of the rough road if Sid had to meet the day trip and drive one of the buses. He had so much on his plate that he was always running late, and it got to be that when any of the island folk saw Sid coming in their rear vision mirrors they would automatically pull straight off the road to let him pass.

The plane burning was a major loss to the island too. The previous Christmas holidays alone, Sid had flown 12 sick and injured people to the mainland for treatment.

* * * *

A totally unanticipated hurdle with the proposed hotel then occurred.

Sid already held a liquor license at the take away bottle shop next to the grocery shop, and the law said one person could not hold two liquor licenses on the same property. This meant as the building neared completion I had to apply for a resort liquor license for the hotel.

A licensing inspector duly arrived to inspect the premises. He was given the grand tour, and said everything looked fine to him.

So it was with no hint of anything untoward, we took ourselves to Brisbane in mid November to the year's final sitting of the Liquor Licensing Court.

We told Graham Mather, the already appointed head barman, we would telephone when we had the license, and he could start serving the already purchased liquor.

We were incredulous when the judge asked the head of the Liquor Licensing Commission for his opinion on our application and this chap stood and said "I'm sorry Your Honour, but a resort license application requires a report from a senior inspector and unfortunately we only sent a junior inspector to Eurong. I therefore submit the application be postponed three months until a future hearing of this court."

We were horrified. If we missed the Christmas trade a lot of our debts, to the builders and the firms from which we had, prematurely it now seemed, bought quantities of liquor would remain unpaid, and Sid could be bankrupted, losing everything he had worked for, for so many hard years.

The judge asked me what I thought. I was too desperate to be tongue tied. I explained what a good building it was and how everything had been furnished and fitted in accordance with liquor licensing requirements.

More pertinently, I protested it wasn't our fault the Licensing Commission had sent the wrong inspector and pleaded that we needed the money from the Christmas trade to pay our bills.

The judge then turned to the Licensing Commission fellow and said "When can you send a senior inspector to Fraser Island?" The reply was "Not until maybe March or April next year."

We were in big trouble, for this was the final sitting of the Licensing Court for 1980, and no matter when the inspector came to Eurong, it would be too late for Christmas.

Then the judge said "I am ordering that a senior inspector be sent to Eurong within a week and I shall hold a special sitting of this court to hear this application again in two weeks."

If we got a tick from the senior inspector, we could still open for Christmas.

We dashed back to the island and made sure everything was as well presented as it could possibly be for the senior inspector's visit.

We had the builder, Dennis Crooks and a couple of his men standing by to make any minor corrections to the building that the inspector decided were needed.

The senior inspector, Ray Halloran duly arrived and from the outset came down hard. He explained that he wanted to inspect all the other resort buildings as well as the hotel. He started in the bar, expressed curiosity about the brackets and had it explained how Sid had devised this method of cyclone bracing.

He then went to the kitchen upstairs, where he looked at the stainless steel splash back behind the two big new stoves, and said there were not enough screws holding this splash back to the wall. Immediately Dennis Crooks stepped forward and installed a couple more. So it went on, with Dennis hastening to rectify every little thing.

We all moved on to the shop, which got a cursory nod, and above it to the two spacious two bedroom units, glamorously named Penthouses. Ray looked at them and said one of the bedrooms was too small. We had thought the bedrooms pleasantly large and airy, but at a signal from Sid we immediately picked up the double bed and took it out into the lounge, then the headboard, wardrobe and chest of drawers, swapping them for the dining table and chairs, couches and easy chairs.

Ray started to laugh, and told us we could put them all back. At the end of his inspection he told Sid and I he didn't anticipate any more problems as he felt we had done everything right.

Still we didn't have any faith in the process and it was with trepidation, and a solicitor to speak on our behalf if needed, that we went back to Brisbane for the special court sitting. This was make or break. The judge asked the Licensing Commission officer what its recommendation was after the senior inspector's visit, and the reply came "that the license be granted." The judge concurred with a smile to an obsequiously grateful me.

Eurong could now be truly called a resort and we were in the hotel business, before Christmas too.

Sid was in such a state of euphoria I led him to one of the best restaurants in Brisbane for a celebration lunch before he could remember he was too shy to go in such a place.

When we got back home everything was ready to go for the grand bar opening that evening.

A group of regular Eurong visitors, the Rovers Football Club and supporters from Maryborough, was in residence and happily took part in the ceremonial occasion.

The Rovers Football Club members and supporters pose outside the pub. One of their number, Peter Baker, helps Sid carry in the first keg.

When it was set up, Sid proudly drew the first beer.

The cyclone rods for Sid's bracing system were stored under the rear verandah of the hotel, ready to be brought out and bolted quickly into place if a cyclone threatened. And after all those decades of fierce cyclones, they were never needed.

Only once in February 1981, when Cyclone Cliff crossed the island, everyone stayed up in the pub all night ready to spring into action with the rods, but the winds never became strong enough to need them.

The conversion of the Island Inn into three holiday units had only just been completed by the Christmas holidays too. The painting of door and window frames was finished the day before the first guests arrived to occupy them, but the curtains on rods, had not been hung to give the paint time to dry.

As I showed the guests into the first one, I saw the curtains still hadn't been hung.

I explained the situation, and the man of the party stepped forward, took the curtains, said "Allow me," and hung them for me.

* * * *

The new hotel immediately attracted great interest. More than 90 people booked for our first Christmas lunch in the new restaurant, and everything was planned in great style.

"There was Santa Claus," says Steve Jensen. "One of the barmen, a Dutch chap called Floris Rotteveel, had a Santa suit, and even though he was a skinny little guy he wanted to be Santa and wouldn't let anyone else have the suit.

"May and I had just bought new Odysseys, four wheeler bikes for riding up and down the beach, and Floris asked May if he could borrow her Odyssey to make his grand entrance to the Christmas lunch. May said 'No.' She then went to the kitchen to help with the dinner preparation, and all the guests arrived and were standing on the front verandah with all their kids waiting for Santa.

"Suddenly we heard the sound of an Odyssey and May looked out and saw Floris riding her Odyssey up the path from the beach to the pub.

"She quietly asked Sid if she could be excused for a couple of minutes. He hadn't a clue what was going on. Next thing we look out of the window, and there is May beating up Santa Claus."

With events like this giving Eurong its unique character, it was little wonder word about the new hotel spread.

The first New Year's Eve saw it packed with people and hundreds more overflowing on to the lawns in front and behind.

As well as driving buses, Steve Jensen ***(right)*** was an excellent guitarist and singer and he sang himself hoarse.

He discovered there were so many different nationalities and out of state visitors among the crowd that the New Year had to be celebrated five times to suit all their time zones.

My only worry was that we would run out of toilet paper because I had forgotten to order a new carton. We might have just got over the problem had not one bright spark decided streamers were needed. Into the toilets everyone went, grabbed the toilet rolls and draped the precious paper over all the trees.

Four o'clock on New Year's Day saw all the visitors gone and the staff carefully undraping the paper and winding it back into crumpled rolls.

It was the most successful Christmas holiday period Eurong had had. May Jensen recalls "We were exceptionally busy in the shop and when the till was rung off one evening we found we had broken all records. We told Sid proudly it was the best day we'd ever had – and he gave each of the shop staff a bottle of champagne for working so hard."

* * * *

A few months later, and literally out of the blue, came Harry Geltch. He had an air charter business in Wyong, New South Wales. A friend who had stayed at Eurong on holiday had gone back to tell Harry there could be an opening for a charter pilot to do joy flights from the resort.

Harry came to investigate. Sid was away and Harry saw Max Williams to ask if he could come and operate a flying business from the resort. Max said it would be all right. When Harry questioned Max's authority, Max blithely told him he was the owner.

No-one said anything to Sid about Harry, perhaps because no-one expected him to reappear, so it was a total surprise when Sid answered the phone one day to hear a man say "It's Harry here. I've sold my business and house and I'll be up in a week."

So Harry flew in and fortunately for all proved a delightful fellow and a skilled pilot. His arrival must have been a shock to Max who kept his head down and said nothing.

Harry's joy flights became very popular. He would make a big fuss of his passengers. As they boarded his plane, he carefully brushed the sand off their shoes with a banister brush.

One lady returned from her flight a little puzzled. "He brushed my shoes, then he brushed my bottom," she reported of Harry, "but I hadn't been sitting in the sand."

Harry brushing feet.

Harry was also invaluable as Steve Jensen recalls. "After May and I had been at Eurong for a while, Sid put us in charge of the place while he and Angela were away.

"One time a waitress came to me and complained the chef, Ian had put the hard word on her. I didn't quite know how to handle this because Ian was a very touchy bloke.

Anyway I went to him and told him there was a nasty rumour circulating that he'd done this, and I wanted to hear his side of the story. Ian gave a different version of what had happened, so, nonplussed, I said I'd go and put an end to the rumour mongering.

"Next thing I hear Ian's motorbike and see him go roaring off down the beach. He was obviously making a quick escape. I was frantic, because I knew Sid would be upset if Ian left because he was such a good chef, and generally a good bloke. I raced for my 4WD to chase him.

"Harry Geltch said I'd never catch Ian in the car, so to hop in his plane and we'd chase him down the beach.

"We overtook Ian and landed in front of him and Harry said "Now handle him tactfully."

"So I said 'What the b…h… are you doing, running away ….?'

"Anyway I managed to persuade him to come back and when Sid arrived home that evening, there was Ian cooking dinner for the guests quite normally."

"It was years before anyone told Sid what had happened."

* * * *

It was inevitable the new hotel would attract rowdies from time to time. It was also apparent, in the absence of police that we would have to deal with the problem ourselves.

Stuart Crichton, a huge, former navy man from New Zealand, was our answer. He was given a test drawing beer when he applied for a bar job a few weeks before Easter. He flunked it, but the rest of the staff pleaded with Sid to employ him because of the protection his size would offer.

It used to give the smaller barmen, like Floris, and girls who served in the bar a comforting sense of security if a customer started to get out of hand, to be able to warn "Please don't make trouble because you're not big enough to handle it."

The customer usually would ignore the warning. Someone would run and ask Stuart to come quickly and faces would fall when he appeared. He was a gentle giant who never provoked a problem but if one arose concerning an unruly customer he would handle it. Diplomatically if possible; forcefully if not.

When Stuart went to the mainland on his first days off, Sid got a call from him "I'm just ringing to tell you I'm in the Hervey Bay watch house and I won't be back for a while."

Sid rang the police to find out what was happening. It emerged Stuart had gone into the police station with his first wages to part pay a $200 traffic fine. Because he was late paying in the first place and couldn't pay the whole sum, he was arrested. Sid was told Stuart was going to jail in Brisbane.

Sid told the police he would guarantee the money. But that wouldn't do.

"We'll pay when we're next in town." That offer was similarly refused.

"What can we do then?" Sid asked.

"Be here in two hours with the cash."

"But I can't get from Eurong to Hervey Bay in two hours," Sid replied.

"If you don't, Crichton will be on the train to Brisbane."

It seemed very drastic but there was no arguing with the law.

Sid grabbed $200 from the shop till and went looking for Harry Geltch to fly him to Hervey Bay. But there was no Harry. He was doing a joy flight round the island. Sid waited on tenterhooks as time began to run out.

At last Harry landed and was promptly bundled back into his plane by Sid with a shouted instruction to me to phone the police to say he was coming, and to ask if one of them would mind coming out to Hervey Bay airport to meet him. I hardly liked to ask, but surprisingly the police agreed.

When Stuart was released, he had a few more days off so stayed in town while Harry flew Sid back to the island.

On the way they ran into a squall. As a precaution Harry landed on the beach about five kilometres north of Eurong, where the plane bogged in soft sand. Sid jumped out to give the plane a push and once it was moving, Harry had to take off, leaving Sid to hike home in the pouring rain.

It was just as well Stuart had another couple of days off. It took that long for recollections of the walk to fade a little from Sid's mind.

* * * *

One day we were visited by the Maryborough organizer of the State Emergency Service, who asked Sid if he would help form a Fraser Island branch. Sid agreed and set about enrolling other useful members of resort staff, such as Stuart.

Sid gave him am S.E.S. application form, which he completed. In reply to one question about his qualifications Stuart wrote "Practitioner of nuclear and biological warfare."

When Sid queried this, Stuart insisted this is what he had been doing in the New Zealand navy. There followed a lengthy discussion on New Zealand's nuclear and biological warfare policy, but Stuart would not be dissuaded and his form was duly submitted as he had written it.

The S.E.S. must have had misgivings about their Fraser Island off-shoot for Stuart never received the promised boots and orange overalls provided for members. Neither, incidentally, did Sid, but we assumed the S.E.S. knew Sid would not wear the boots anyway.

* * * *

One of our Eurong neighbours, Snow Buffey became a regular visitor to the pub. He had been a Forestry Department worker on the island but was retired on a pension to a little beachfront house south of the resort, and the pub, with the now retired Kelly invariably ensconced in his corner of the bar, ***(right)*** was a relief to Snow's hitherto solitary life on the island.

He was about 1.6metres tall with a pointy pixie face topped by a peak cap. Small as he was, it did not take much beer to have an effect on Snow.

There was a wonderful tale of the time Snow and fellow forestry workers had gone to Maryborough. Snow drank too much beer and fell asleep in the pub. His mates, for a joke, carried him out to an alleyway behind one of the banks and propped him, still sleeping, against a wall. Then they had put a balaclava helmet over his head, and rung the police that the bank was being robbed....

Snow, front, with Eurong regular, electrician Alan Jones.

Another Snow story was about the time he had woken from an afternoon sleep and forgotten he was retired.

When he saw a Forestry Department 4WD on the beach on front of his home with the keys left in it, he assumed he must have left it there, so drove it behind his house for safe keeping.

When the two Forestry fellows, who had been fishing further down the beach, returned to find the vehicle gone, they telephoned the police to report it stolen. The police came to the island next day and eventually found the vehicle at Snow's.

Happily they didn't arrest Snow on either occasion, but he didn't take kindly to their interrogation of him.

One day two uniformed policemen were in the hotel. Snow, in his cups, approached them and gave them a piece of his mind.

The two policemen grabbed him under the arms and marched him between them all the way to his house his little legs well off the ground and waving wildly.

Next day Snow was back. "I can't have had as much to drink as I'd thought yesterday," he reported proudly to Sid "because I walked home in a straight line."

Chapter 14

With the new pub proving a big draw card to Eurong, Sid decided to keep on building. His next project was a swimming pool in front of the hotel.

Sid decided we would do the basic stuff ourselves, which involved digging the pool, building the walls and pouring the floor, only getting experts to add the finishing touches. Sid and his work gang of drivers, the cook, and Kelly dug the swimming pool with the front end loader, finishing it off neatly with shovels.

Then it was back to the Peterbilt to truck in gravel, sand, cement and concrete blocks and more concrete mixing.

The pool sides were constructed of concrete blocks, and then concrete mix was to be poured through the holes in the blocks so it penetrated right through, and ran out of the bottom of the walls and on to the floor, sealing it in one run. It had to be done in one long operation to avoid cracks and joins and make it leak proof. Work began at 4 am.

Alan Wylie's big cement mixer and another smaller one were kept going simultaneously and first Sid then driver, Jimmy Schmidt drove the loader, first to the big mixer to have a load of wet cement dumped in the bucket, reverse then forward to the pool, pour in, reverse then forward to the second mixer for cement, reverse, forward to the pool and so on ad infinitum.

Jimmy got so bored with the routine he went into a dream and gave us all a break for a laugh, when he tipped the bucket in the pool one time – and there was nothing in it.

Luigi and Max Williams were handed long sticks and it was their job to push the wet concrete through the holes in the blocks, and then shake the sticks so the mixture became uniformly solid.

The pool was poured without a join by 5 pm, 13 hours from the start.

The marble chip finish and tiling were added by recognized pool builders who did an excellent job.

The day came for filling the pool. We had expected clear sparkling water and looked forward to our first swim. The water was murky and not at all appealing however. A pool expert said that was normal and that we had to add chemicals in the right proportions, keep the filter switched on and vacuum the pool constantly. In two weeks we would have an inviting pool.

The hardest part was vacuuming. Sid arranged vacuum relays and as one staff member fell exhausted from pushing the cleaner around the pool floor on a long pipe, another would take over. At the end of a fortnight the pool was still murky.

Sid recalled the expert and he said he couldn't understand it. Then he watched one of the fellows vacuuming. "You do realize this is an electric vacuum and you haven't got it switched on, don't you," the pool man asked.

* * * *

Sid wanted lights around the pool and a good mate and electrician, Alan Jones came to install them. He brought help, his friend Dave. Dave had never visited Fraser Island before and his wife wasn't too keen on his coming without her. We were soon to find out why.

Dave dug a trench to put the cables in for the pool lights and work had progressed well by nightfall. Dave, Alan and a couple of resort fellows retired to the pub.

Late that night, after everyone else had gone and the generator had been switched off, they decided to take a swim in the new pool in the dark. There was some horseplay and one of the fellows pinched Dave's underpants.

Fun over, they set off back to their rooms – and Dave fell into the trench he had dug that very day, breaking several bones in a foot. When he returned to the mainland in a very sorry state, his wife stipulated he was never to visit Fraser Island again. She was less worried about the broken foot than about Dave's missing underwear.

That was not the only horseplay in the pool.

In spite of Sid's energetic arm waving the brumbies refused to give up their territory at Eurong.

One night Sid was awakened by loud knocking on the door. "Come quickly Sid, there's a horse in the pool," someone shouted.

Sure enough there was one of Eurong's seven mares thrashing around in the pool with the stallion, Silly, watching her anxiously from the edge.

The pool had been deliberately built the same depth throughout, deep enough so that if someone fell in when they were leaving the hotel, the water would cushion their fall, but not so deep that they couldn't get to their feet with head and shoulders above the water. So the mare was able to keep her back hooves on the bottom of the pool, as she threshed with her forelegs, but she looked exhausted.

Sid sent for help from staff and a couple of ropes. He lassoed the mare around its neck to pull it to one end of the pool. Then the bigger rope was thrown right across the pool behind the horse, with three men holding on to each end of it, ***(below).***

Everyone shouted at the horse then, and in fear, it reared up and managed to get its front hooves over the edge of the pool. The men on the big rope brought it along, hooked it under the horse's rear end and heaved it out of the water.

The horse rescuers were very pleased with themselves.

Then a voice piped up from the crowd of watchers which had gathered "That's nothing. I was in a hotel in Africa last year and they had a hippopotamus in their pool."

Horses aside the pool was a great success. At school holiday times it was packed with children while their parents had a beer.

The pub inside and out.

With the increasing influx of people to Eurong accommodation was soon in short supply. Every holiday period dozens of people had to be turned away.

Sid decided his next project would be 22 motel style units in a two storey building overlooking the pool and the surf beach.

He found the bureaucratic process of obtaining planning permission no longer rested solely with the Maryborough City Council building inspector, with whom Sid felt he now had a good working relationship, but a body of which he had never heard before, the Beach Protection Authority.

Two representatives, summoned by the council, duly arrived at Eurong and explained the new Beach Protection Act to Sid. It stated that people with surf beach front properties could not build within 15 metres of their front boundaries as an erosion prevention measure.

Sid argued that there was no erosion problem at Eurong. However the Beach Protection officers produced plans of the area showing there had been a dramatic change in the frontal dune pattern over the previous five years.

Sid could not understand this. He knew the dunes hadn't changed because he had been living at Eurong for 12 years through numerous cyclones, and visiting the area at least once a week for nine years before that.

Where did they get this strange misinformation, he enquired. The B.P.A. officers told him they had a volunteer helper at Eurong, who took daily readings of the sand movement on the foreshore and this helper had recorded a great change some years before.

All became clear. The volunteer, Sid knew, was a neighbour across the road, Charlie Sinclair. Charlie had an impressive pole with markings stuck in the beach in front of his house, which he checked every morning and evening.

Sid also knew dear old Charlie had a secret method of brewing the most potent beer imaginable. The beer was tremendously popular, as was Charlie, but now and again in the euphoria of having a houseful of visitors, Charlie would partake a little too freely.

Towards the end of one such evening when Charlie, ever aware of his responsibilities, went to take his beach reading, he fell against his pole and knocked it out of the ground.

He put it back in the hole but, under the circumstances, didn't worry overly about sinking it to its previous depth. The reading he took that night and ever after differed substantially from the readings he had taken up to that point.

Of course the B.P.A. in Brisbane knew nothing of this and in the light of the irrefutable evidence in their records that there was an erosion problem at Eurong, Sid had to set his new unit building 15 metres back from his front boundary. This meant building four units, two up and two down, less than had originally been planned.

Finding the front boundary was another thing. One of the front survey pegs was in a lagoon; one of the back ones in the middle of a shifting sand blow, presumably now buried under tonnes of sand.

Sid and the council Town Planner, who was charged with ensuring the Beach Protection Act was obeyed, could find neither.

A joint effort was made to work out the line of the front boundary. Sid and the Town Planner stood by the single front peg that was still visible.

I was sent to stand at the other side of the land, more than 100 metres away, behind a big clump of banksias trees, and take a line of sight over Charlie Sinclair's house which, Sid knew, had been built right on his front boundary in the pre B.P.A. days.

I was handed a long piece of conduit to hold in line with the front of Charlie's house over the tree tops so Sid and the Town Planner could see it. Conduit was all we had of suitable length. Conduit also bends and waves about, particularly if the person trying to hold it over the tree tops recognizes the futility of the exercise and gets the giggles. Thus was the front boundary of Sid's land established and the new units set out.

The precious turf where the building was to go was carefully dug up and transplanted elsewhere. Regretfully Sid also had to pull out a big clump of old banksias trees with one of his trucks and drag them into a big pile ready for burning. As it happened this was on the track which Snow Buffey used to take a short cut to the pub.

Everyone was working on the site next day when an anguished cry was heard. Looking up we saw a peaked cap almost at the top of the pile of trees. His way barred, Snow had set off to climb over and had become hopelessly entangled.

When he was freed, he rounded fiercely on Sid "If you don't want me in your pub, all you have to do is say so."

* * * *

The new units were to be built of split rough faced concrete blocks, to be sealed against water entering and painted white, with individual balconies overlooking the ocean at the front and a large wooden verandah at the back with stairways for access to the upper floor. The name chosen for the building was appropriately *Surfside.*

Remembering that Ray Halloran the Liquor Licensing inspector, on his visit six months before, had said one of the bedrooms in the Penthouse units was too small, Sid rang him to ask what the dimensions of the *Surfside* motel units had to be to meet Licensing standards.

Ray's reply was unexpected "Oh Sid, there is no size standard. We accept whatever the local council accepts. When are you going to realize you have a powerful political enemy who wants to stop you getting ahead?"

We discussed this at length, wondering what Sid had done to incur enmity in the corridors of power. He didn't know any politicians personally.

Nothing had changed from the pub building methods. Foundations had to be dug by hand. Sid had to drive the Peterbilt to collect the gravel and sand. It had to be shoveled off the Peterbilt into Alan Wylie's mixer, which seemed to have found a permanent home at Eurong.

When it came to the concrete blocks, a semi trailer owner, Phil Scougall would bring as many pallets of blocks as he could fit on from Maryborough and would meet Sid at Rainbow Beach. As neither had a hoist to lift the pallets from the semi trailer to the Peterbilt, all the blocks had to be passed from hand to hand between the two of them. When Sid arrived at Eurong the blocks had to be transferred from truck to site again by hand by a human chain.

One day on the way back to Eurong up the surf beach Sid stopped to pick up a couple of young men hitchhiking. They asked to be dropped at one of the big creeks south of Eurong, but Sid wouldn't hear of it. He brought them right back to the resort and before they knew it they were in the chain gang too, passing blocks.

At the end of each day Sid shouted a carton of beer for the workers and the two lads were included, and for dinner. Then we expected they would disappear with our thanks. Not so. There they were next morning to ask Sid if he was going down the beach for more blocks, and if he needed a hand. In all they helped for a fortnight and were to return for many a non-working holiday for years afterwards.

The chain gang lifting blocks for Surfside off the Peterbilt.

Sid supervised the building very carefully. He had to go to Rainbow Beach for materials every day but as soon as he returned, he would race over to inspect the day's progress. He would sight along new-laid rows of blocks and have the bricklayer pull them out and re-lay them if they weren't absolutely straight. It was a far cry from the first amenities building.

Walls were thoroughly scrutinized so that not a single run of mortar was left to set hard. He would climb up the scaffolding onto the roof to make sure the shavings from holes drilled for roof screws were swept off properly.

In addition to building to Sid's exacting standards, the workmen had to be careful not to damage the lawn surrounding the building. In most such projects the site is a mess. At Eurong not one cement bucket could be washed out on the precious grass; not one bit of waste material left lying where it fell.

Sid came for dinner quite worried one evening. He had overheard the tradesmen talking about him and the block layer had described him as a fanatic.

Sid was wondering whether this was a good or a bad thing. Fortunately perhaps for the block layer, it was decided under the circumstances it was a good thing.

Everyone was very proud when the units were completed. Sid and the builders were having a celebratory drink outside the pub the first night of the units being let, when they saw a man kick down a brand new door.

Sid didn't even have time to get out of his seat before all the builders had rushed over and grabbed him. He and his wife had had a fight and she'd locked him out. Subsequent efforts to recover the cost of a new door from him were a waste of time. He was never home at the address he'd given when booking in.

The pub, the pool and the Surfside units.

There was one more memorable incident in the early days of *Surfside.*

An elderly man went missing on the island. Six weeks after his sister reported he had not returned home, a police search found his car at Rainbow Beach. He had come to the island with a pushbike and a blue tent.

Police put out a general alert and every time anyone saw a blue tent they would go and investigate. But the man was not found and it was generally accepted he had died.

Periodically for weeks afterwards we would receive phone calls from the police saying someone had reported an odour on one of the bush tracks and asking us to we go and investigate to see if there was a body.

We were not keen on searching for bodies and became increasingly less so as time went on. But we duly investigated all reported smells with no result.

Then one day a terrible smell wafted over the resort grounds from the south.

No-one wanted to go and investigate. They just told Sid. He went and tracked the smell right to the back of the new *Surfside* units, where he found a departing guest had thrown a bag of decomposing fish bait out of his back door.

The missing man was never found.

* * * *

When a skilled mechanic Laurie Toy, Wally Toy's elder son, came to work for Sid and live at Eurong with his wife, Elaine and baby daughter, the next building needed at Eurong was a workshop.

Laurie did repairs and daily maintenance on the day tour buses checking and greasing them every lunchtime, while the passengers were having their buffet lunches, and kept the generator, and water pumps working well.

The new workshop, built of corrugated galvanized iron, was on the southern side of the camping ground, behind the staff cottages and over a rise so it was out of public view.

What Sid didn't know was that on the original township survey, a road had been marked in across the back of the leases to join the northern section of Eurong to the southern. It went nowhere, and never would, for the big sand blow ran between the two but it was an official road on paper.

Inadvertently Sid built one corner of his workshop on this paper road. When folk talked about it, as they did, no-one ever mentioned it was a road that didn't actually exist and went nowhere. Nor that the workshop, which grew in size with every telling, was built in such a way that it could easily be removed. Another story was added to the Melksham legend.

"There was no floor in the workshop at first, just loose sand, which made it very hard to get under the buses on a mechanic's trolley. I'd lie on the trolley then had to push hard with my feet to get the trolley to move. Then we got a concrete floor and the first time I lay on the trolley I gave it a really hard push with my feet, as I'd been used to, and I went careering back across the floor and crashed into the workshop wall," Laurie Toy says.

"One time I had to repaint one of the trucks bright orange. The workshop walls got painted orange too. I was told in no uncertain terms never to pick up a spray gun again."

Laurie says Sid was supportive of his staff to outsiders, often in unexpected and humorous ways.

"Sometimes when we had big numbers I had to drive the day trip," Toy recounts. "I was driving a Studebaker with the day trip one time and came over the hill to Lake Birrabeen. There was a VW in the middle of the track and the driver was an obstinate chap who wouldn't make way for the bus.

"I asked him nicely to back up and he refused. I showed him where he could pull off the road and he refused to move.

"I asked the day trippers what to do and they all shouted 'Drive over him.' He was embarrassed then and finally pulled over.

"When I got to Eurong there was this chap yelling at Sid about how I'd made him drive into the scrub. Some of the passengers came and told Sid what had happened.

"Sid turns to me and says 'You're fired.' The VW driver has a big grin thinking he's got me into trouble, and Sid says 'You know the customer is always right. You should have done what your passengers told you - and run over him.'"

* * * *

The original little subdivision at Eurong had been slow to develop, but the island began to attract more people wanting to live there.

Most of them were content to build holiday houses for rent, but a few others looked for business opportunities on the island.

One of the new landholders was Murray Reid, a Brisbane plant operator, who was to play an important role in the future of Eurong Beach Resort, and saved my bacon the first time we met.

One day when Sid was away in Maryborough, a trawler pulled close in shore and three men rowed a dinghy to the beach.

They bore a couple of kilo of prawns, and headed for the pub, where they soon persuaded barman Floris Rotteveel to swap the prawns for a few beers.

When they became increasingly inebriated and wanted more and more free beer, Rotteveel refused.

When they became angry he realized he had more trouble than he could handle and called on me to sort out the situation.

It was already beyond me, and with Rotteveel the only man on staff present at the resort, the fishermen set off on a rampage of destruction.

I phoned all the suppliers in Maryborough that I knew Sid was calling on, and left messages with all of them to get him to phone me back. Then I cowered behind the shop counter with the shop door locked, waiting for Sid's call.

When it came I told him what was happening and he said he'd get police and a plane from the Maryborough Flying Club and be at Eurong in half an hour.

That was too long to wait, so I ran over the sand blow to the southern section of the little township to see if there was anyone there could help me.

I came upon two men working on the roof of a new house, and told them the problem we had. One turned out to be Murray Reid; the other his friend Pat Wilson. Both of them unhesitatingly returned with me to the resort and when the fishermen threatened a fight, soon sorted the three of them out.

By time Sid arrived in the plane with two policemen the fishermen were back on their boat, licking their wounds and refused to come back to shore. Police were waiting for them when they returned to their home port of Mooloolaba and charged them, but before the case came to court, the three of them were involved in a dreadful car accident, and the matter was never pursued

Chapter 15

Fraser Island was an ideal place for army personnel on training exercises, and they were frequent visitors, some enterprising, some less so.

One contingent of army clerks who had a minimum exercise requirement of walking five kilometers a day craftily set up camp exactly two and a half kilometers south of the Eurong pub.

Far less enterprising was the army group on war games. All one morning five tonne trucks and Land Rovers roared north up the island's surf beach. One driver managed to run his truck into the rocks at Poyungan, smashing its front in.

Three young soldiers in a Land Rover came back to the Eurong shop to phone their base for a tow truck to be sent. Five minutes later they were back to report the fan belt in the Land Rover was broken.

The shop assistant offered to sell them just the right fan belt from the shop stock. They said they could not buy one as they had to rely on their own resources, but could they use the phone again to ask for a fan belt to be sent up with the tow truck.

Then they asked if they could camp in the resort camping ground until it arrived.

Next day an enormous tow truck arrived. The driver took it right into our camping ground, tearing up Sid's lawn to give the hapless trio their fan belt. It departed to Sid's angry shouts on its way to Poyungan – where it ran into the rocks and was wrecked.

Another little squad of soldiers arrived at the shop to phone for another tow truck.

Meanwhile the original three had discovered their replacement fan belt was the wrong size. Now there were three lots of stranded soldiers, two with wrecked trucks at Poyungan, one in our camping ground.

The Eurong three were not good at survival on their own. They turned up for their meals with the staff, all the while adamantly refusing Sid's offer to give them a fan belt as a cheaper alternative to feeding them.

Two days later another tow truck passed the resort heading north and over the next few days towed first the wrecked five tonne truck, then the tow truck back down the beach. But no-one brought a fan belt for the Eurong trio.

About a week later they made another call to base to ask if a helicopter could be sent to the island with a fan belt for them. Sid took the phone and insisted on his rights as a member of the tax paying public to give them the fan belt he had in stock.

A short time later there was a front page article in a national newspaper in which then Defence Minister Jim Killen said how greatly improved Australia's coastal defences were.

Sid had me write a reader's letter telling the story of the events at Eurong and commenting that we hoped no-one would want to invade through Fraser Island. The newspaper used it as a front page article – with a cartoon.

Poor Killen copped it again when there was a controversy as to whether Australia could afford a type of new fighter aircraft. Killen announced in the same paper that of course it could.

At that time the army had been owing money to Sid for petrol bought at Eurong for months. Again I wrote querying how could Killen say that when obviously the defence forces couldn't afford their petrol bill. A cheque arrived two days later.

* * * *

The partnership between the Toy family and Sid continued to operate day tours to Fraser Island from Hervey Bay for more than a decade. The Toys took care of bookings and getting visitors to the island on the *Island Queen* from the little concrete jetty at Urangan Boat Harbour to the Forestry Department's jetty at Ungowa, a trip of up to three hours each way at low tide.

Sid had his converted open air Studebaker buses waiting at Ungowa and took the visitors to the surf beach at Eurong for lunch with a stop in the rainforest at Central Station and a swim in the clear blue waters of Lake Birrabeen on the way back.

Wally Toy was a fiery little fellow, who firmly believed he was the senior partner, particularly after he bought a bigger and faster launch, the *Philanderer*.

Sid wasn't particularly worried about that, as long as the partnership worked and the people kept coming.

He took Wally's frequent outbursts in his stride and let Wally make many of the business decisions, though sometimes he was unhappy with them, particularly when Wally increased the prices for the tours beyond what Sid felt most people could afford.

After a meeting with Wally when the latter had laid down the law, Sid would muse, "I'm a lot more patient than most people realize," just in case there was anyone who did not recognize patience as one of Sid's virtues.

When a competitor Barry Murphy entered the Hervey Bay to Fraser Island day trip market in the late 1970's, cracks soon appeared in the Toy/Melksham business relationship. Murphy was an engaging and shrewd businessman, and set out to provide a day trip with the advantages of three fully enclosed ex RAAF buses, and a shorter sea crossing.

He had built a flat bottomed vessel called the *Islander*, which, if the tide was right, could land on Mackenzie's Beach to let its passengers off on a gangplank extending from its bow. If the tide was low, his passengers had to walk through water to get ashore, but whatever the tide, the sea trip was an hour less each way than the *Philanderer.*

Murphy's island tour was shorter, on the rough island tracks, from McKenzie's beach to Lake Mackenzie, another of Fraser's lovely freshwater lakes and to Central Station, where his folk had a picnic barbecue, and back.

Sid and the Toys believed their trip was better, going to the surf beach and having a sit down lunch at Eurong, but Murphy started getting good numbers of people. He had one big advantage. As owner of both vessel and buses, he kept all the income from his tours while Sid and Wally had to share theirs.

As passenger numbers began to drop, Sid privately blamed Wally for putting up prices and Wally blamed Sid's open buses. Wally, his son, Dennis and daughter-in-law Helen evidently felt it would be in their best interests to cut Sid out of the business.

Sid got wind something was in the air in mid 1980 when one of the Forestry workers at Ungowa reported to him that he'd seen Dennis Toy measuring two of his open buses.

Soon afterwards Wally phoned Sid insisting he come over to a meeting with him, Dennis and Helen at their house in Hervey Bay.

There was no preamble, no attempt to discuss the situation, but Wally plunged right in to tell Sid they would no longer want him to be involved in "their" day tours.

It was an ultimatum. Either Sid sell Wally his buses or Wally would buy other buses within two weeks. He said he would run a shorter trip on the island, similar to Murphy's trip, and would only run to Eurong one day a week, on a Thursday.

Sid was furious and concerned. His half of the day tour fares was his major source of regular income. Without the trip coming to Eurong daily or even at weekends, he would be limited as to how he could get people there to rent his accommodation, shop or camp at his camp ground. He also felt he had put all the hard yards into pioneering the island day tours, creating interest in the island, making roads, providing facilities and the like before the Toys came on the scene.

Amazingly for him he did not let his anger show, but went very quiet. He simply waited until Wally had finished dictating the terms of the new arrangement, reading them from a piece of paper he had prepared.

Even when Wally had finished, and gave Sid the paper to read, Sid still said nothing. He simply folded the paper, put it in his shirt pocket, and stood up preparing to leave.

Wally said "So that's it then. You'll sell us the buses?"

Sid simply replied "No."

"What are you going to do then?" Wally asked.

"I'm going to buy a boat and run the trips myself as I used to," Sid responded, got up and walked out.

It cannot have occurred to the Toys that Sid would take such a course. From thinking he had him over a barrel one minute, Wally suddenly realized he was going to have another competitor in the tour market.

In the face of this completely unforeseen but, for the Toys, disturbing reaction, the partnership continued, but certainly on Sid's part he no longer believed it would last.

He had other things to do with his income than buy a boat at this stage however. He saw the development of his infant resort at Eurong as a priority. He had borrowed money from the bank and was building the *Surfside* units.

* * * *

Over the next couple of years the number of day trip operators to Fraser Island increased. As long as the vehicles they used were registered, insured for passengers, and passed machinery inspection, there was no bar on their owners starting a tour, and several did, from Hervey Bay, Rainbow Beach, and the rapidly developing Sunshine Coast.

With access to the island limited and roads few and only wide enough for one vehicle, it followed that the tour operators often clashed as they scrambled for the same few beauty spots they could access in the time they had on the island.

There were arguments when two tour buses met on the narrow roads, particularly one stretch between Central Station and the turnoff to Lake McKenzie with a high bank on one side and a steep drop on the other. Here there was no possibility of one driver pulling off the road to let the other pass, and one had to back up as much as a kilometre. On one occasion when neither bus driver would back up, brush hooks were waved threateningly.

At the most popular places there was unseemly jostling as drivers tried to cook lunchtime steaks for their passengers on too few barbecues.

The Forestry Department, which by this time had been charged with managing tourism as well as the timber industry, stepped in to try and solve the problems. In 1982 they licensed the tour operators, limiting the number of people they could carry, where they could go on the island and the times they could be in a particular place.

* * * *

There was no limit set on the number of private 4WD vehicles that could come to Fraser Island however and as the number of visitors in their own vehicles grew, Fraser Island was caught short with a total lack of services and controls.

Most of the visitors camped wherever they chose along the surf beach fore dunes, which became ever more prone to erosion as four wheel drive vehicles were driven over them, wearing away the grass which bound the sand.

Access tracks were forged willy nilly into beauty spots and in some cases irresponsible drivers ruined the very things they had come to see. Trees were hacked down for firewood and some well vegetated areas were denuded of trees in a very short time.

Names were etched into the coloured sand cliffs. Fire became an increasing hazard as campers took up unregulated sites.

None of the visitors contributed to the government for management and they stretched the resources of private enterprise in their demand for the services they took for granted on the mainland.

There were still no public amenities, no police, no medical services, no public telephones, no water supply, no waste disposal and no facilities to maintain a healthy environment.

Conservationists started to call for government to manage the island properly. But there was no direct income for government to do it. An incredible tangle of bureaucracy needed to be cut through for anything to get done. Many government departments and authorities had involvement or interest in Fraser Island, but those interests often clashed.

A prime example was a rubbish dump on the beach about three kilometers south of the resort at Eurong, which had been started in a most haphazard way. From time to time civic minded groups conducted clean ups of the surf beach and one erected signs "Dump Litter Here" for volunteer rubbish collectors to leave the garbage bags they had filled for collection by a truck.

The sign south of Eurong was inadvertently left behind, so long afterwards every holidaymaker with rubbish to dispose of, obeyed the sign. The pile of refuse right on the beachfront grew and the Maryborough City Council, which administered Eurong and the southern section of Fraser Island, was almost continuously castigated for its apparent neglect.

Occasionally the council would pay for a loader to be brought from the mainland to clean up the mess, but it was obvious the dump could not remain. The council sought land behind Eurong township to establish a certainly less visible dump. The Lands Department had to investigate the suitability of the chosen site. When everything seemed to be moving forward the Water Resources Commission became involved and vetoed the site in case the water table behind Eurong from which the townsfolk drew their water became polluted.

Another site was selected. This time the Aboriginal and Islander Affairs Department became involved and gave the thumbs down as there was an Aboriginal midden of eugarie shells nearby.

For the Maryborough City Council, the tourism explosion was an administrative nightmare. Its experience was of a well ordered small city with an industrial base; its only island income, the rates from the few residents at Eurong.

Sid argued for the provision of a few basic public amenities on the grounds that his resort directly supported Maryborough with the business he brought to the city, but his argument fell on deaf ears and the council compounded his burden.

When every day scores of people driving past the resort on their way to and from Central Station and the lakes parked and galloped to the toilet block in Sid's camping ground, the council complained it was overloaded. Sid explained it was adequate for his campers, and suggested the solution would be for the council to build a public toilet nearby. The council responded it did not have the money.

After concern was expressed about the purity of the fresh water flowing out of the island dunes in countless creeks across the beach and from which beach campers drew their drinking water, the council tested the creeks. They found that some of the larger ones were contaminated, most likely by wildlife. Their solution was to erect warning notices.

The result was that Sid's resort was then deluged with people seeking good water.

Sid was always most careful where he located the spears he sank into the island water table to draw off the resort drinking water and had it regularly tested for purity.

But occupants of holiday homes and weekenders on minimum size residential blocks had problems locating their water spears a safe distance from their neighbours' septic trenches. There had been an outbreak of hepatitis at Happy Valley.

When the Maryborough City Council planned to allow the rezoning of a single family house on one such small parcel of land to accommodate 28 people at Eurong without doing anything about water supply or sewerage, Sid objected.

He was very fearful that if something similar happened at Eurong his business would suffer, as most visitors associated Eurong with his resort. The council stuck to its guns.

So Sid took his objection to the Local Government Court in March 1982 and won.

He accused the council of risking the water table because it had exercised no controls, thereby neglecting basic health safeguards on the island and having no town planning standards.

The court hearing, for all its serious import, had its lighter moments. Sid in the witness box was asked by the judge what he meant by the island water table. He gave a practical man's explanation with disarming simplicity.

"You have your hard topped table," he told the judge. "That is the rock base to Fraser Island. You put a bucket of sand on your table and that is the dunes. You sprinkle water on the sand and it filters through, then runs out on either side of the table. That is the island's natural water system.

"In the case of Fraser Island it can take up to five years for the rainwater falling in the centre to run out to the shore on either side so it is particularly pure. The water that is held in the dunes is the water table."

Sid was asked many more questions, and he knew the answers from experience. But the council's barrister protested continuously that Sid had no qualifications and should not be allowed to answer.

The judge disagreed. "I think this man can teach a lot of experts about Fraser Island," he ruled, adding "furthermore I look forward to his explanations."

Chapter 16

Later that same year, 1982, a situation arose which spurred Sid into getting a vessel of his own and becoming self sufficient.

Two Maryborough men, John Flynn and Ron Fielding, both welders, put a small barge, the *Fraser Trader* into service to run from Hervey Bay to Fraser Island. They had spent all their spare time over two years to build the barge in Flynn's backyard.

They asked Sid to come and look at it and told him they would run it to various points on Fraser's west coast depending on high tide to get over mudflats and into the creeks, including Wanggoolba Creek, giving access almost directly across the island to Eurong.

Sid was delighted because the *Fraser Trader* service would give him an alternative to having to bring supplies and materials the long way round from Maryborough to Rainbow Beach, with all its attendant problems, to get to Eurong.

But the *Fraser Trader* only ran for a few weeks. The ubiquitous Jack Pashley was the skipper and recounts that Flynn and Fielding crossed to the island on it one day early in the piece, but when they came back Flynn had had a few beers and tried to push Jack away from the wheel. Jack resisted and the situation became heated, with the result that Jack said he'd never skipper the barge for them again.

Flynn and Fielding fell out, and another skipper, Peter Young was asked to do one more trip to the island to take off people who had booked to come back and then to take the *Fraser Trader* to Maryborough to tie it up at the wharf there.

Flynn approached Sid to see if he would be interested in buying the *Fraser Trader.* Sid said he was, because he could see it would be the end of his transport problems, but Ron Fielding refused to sell. After two years building the barge, within weeks, all the hard work had been to no avail.

Every time Sid went to Maryborough on a shopping or business trip he would go and look at the *Fraser Trader* sitting idle in the river.

He and Flynn contacted each other many times to do a deal, but Fielding was obdurate. Sid thought Fielding would never come to an agreement with Flynn.

After many months, by which time Sid had weighed up all the pros of having a barge and come to the conclusion it was an essential adjunct to his resort business, if the resort were to grow, he had developed a far more ambitious plan, to bring a whole new concept to transport to Fraser Island. The *Fraser Trader* was too small for what he saw could develop.

Up to then barges to the west coast of Fraser Island from Hervey Bay had been small scale. First there was Kev Donnelly's small barge, the *Way-Lillie* which did not last long. The Toys had operated a small barge, which likewise did not last.

Then in 1976 Noel Mathiesen, son of an island original, Charlie, who skippered timber punts to the island in the early days of timber cutting, built a small barge *Wathumba II* and operated it from Urangan across the Straits.

He ran mainly to Urang Creek on the west coast across the island from the little surf beach front township of Happy Valley, which, at this time had more private houses than Eurong, and a small store.

The arrival of these barges at the island depended on high tides, so they could get over the rim of sand that ran for some 30 km along the island's west coast, and into the shallow creek mouths. If it were high tide at midnight, that's when the barges had to run, which was hardly conducive to tourism. But then previous barge owners had never really thought tourism would be a major factor in traffic to Fraser Island.

After all Hervey Bay was a very small seaside town with retirees from southern states bringing their caravans to the Bay for winter its only regular visitor clientele.

Instead barge owners saw their income coming from the few folk who had holiday cottages on Fraser Island. These customers had no alternative but to tailor their visits to whenever the barge could operate and accepted the service available.

Sid however had a totally different perception.

He had watched the growing popularity of 4WD vehicles and believed that if there was a good, fast, regular barge service, it would attract tourists in their own vehicles, who wished to drive themselves around the island.

He recognized the most important factors were that a barge should run at convenient times and to a regular schedule. He wanted a dual purpose ferry, attractive to passengers as well as able to carry vehicles. He would use it to bring his day tour passengers to Fraser Island, which would give him a regular income base.

He also wanted to minimize the time taken to cross the straits from Hervey Bay to Fraser Island so visitors would have more time to spend on the island, the purpose of their whole trip, instead of hours just getting there.

To achieve this Sid started to think about dredging a channel deep and wide enough for a barge to access Fraser's west coast at low tide.

It was a bold and expensive vision that Sid believed could not only develop into a good business, but would make life on Fraser Island so much easier as well as take tourism to Fraser into a whole new era. If he could bring his plan to fruition, Hervey Bay could develop as a major tourist gateway to Fraser Island.

He was to gamble everything he had worked for over the previous two decades on the new ferry concept working, for he had to mortgage the growing Eurong Beach resort to raise the funds for the new ferry and the dredging. If the gamble failed, he would be back to square one.

* * * *

In May 1982 he went looking in Brisbane and Moreton Bay at other ferries to get ideas. One evening he was at the Brisbane river side suburb of Bulimba waiting for the *Moreton Venture* to return from Moreton Island.

Dusk was falling but a last shaft of sunlight fell on the white painted *Moreton Venture* as she sailed downriver and she looked superb, if a lot bigger than the ferry that Sid had contemplated. When it berthed, he went on board and talked to its skipper/owner Nev Hawkins. Nev told him he had had it built at Index Engineering in Brisbane.

The very next day Sid was in the office of Ross McLean the head of Index Engineering to find out how much a similar barge would cost to have built. Ross told him the *Moreton Venture* carried 22 4WD vehicles on its open 33 metre long bottom deck.

A saloon deck was built above that, and on top of the saloon was the wheelhouse with an open area behind. It was capable of 11 knots. He said to build one similar would cost almost $500,000.

Although this was far larger, and much more expensive, than Sid had contemplated, he didn't hesitate for long. He and McLean straightaway worked out details of the new ferry that Sid envisaged.

With his typical foresight Sid wanted a specially strengthened centre aisle in the vehicle deck, for example, so it could carry the laden Peterbilt and other trucks when he began building again at Eurong, as he knew one day he would.

He wanted it to carry 250 passengers, so it could cater for his day trip as well as people in their own vehicles, and for their convenience, a shop as well as seating in the upper deck saloon, so they could buy snacks, drinks and souvenirs. More seats would be needed on the top deck around the outside of the wheelhouse.

The ANZ bank agreed to fund progress payments on the new ferry as it was being built, using the resort at Eurong as collateral, and within days Sid had signed up with Index to build the *Fraser Venture.* It was a huge financial gamble, bigger than any Sid had taken on before, but Sid had great faith in his vision and was confident he could make the ferry pay.

Sid was back in his Brisbane motel room after having just signed the contract with Ross McLean, when he got a telephone call from his accountant, Barry Keys to say Ron Fielding would now sell the *Fraser Trader.*

Sid felt he owed Fielding the courtesy of a personal visit to explain his situation and that he was no longer interested in the *Fraser Trader*, so made a time to call at his home.

When he arrived, it was obvious Fielding was expecting some hard bargaining, for he had with him a Maryborough businesswoman, Fay Lynch who announced she was going to do the negotiation on Fielding's behalf.

Sid said "I'm sorry but I don't want to buy the *Fraser Trader.* Your decision to sell came just hours too late. I have contracted to have a new, much bigger, ferry built."

Fielding looked stunned. He had obviously counted on a sale to Sid.

Fay Lynch immediately launched into a tirade, calling Sid a liar and that he had no such contract, and was just saying that to get Fielding down in price.

There was nothing Sid could say in the face of her outburst, to make anyone feel better, so he simply said to Fielding "I'm sorry, but I'm telling you the truth," and left the house with Fay still screaming invective after him.

She put the word all around Maryborough what a so and so Sid was, trying to take poor Ron Fielding down, making up this story he had another barge being built, and many people believed it for a while.

One Forestry worker in his cups in the Eurong pub one night said to as much to Sid. It ended up with him betting Sid $500 he didn't have a barge coming.

Months later Sid was at the ferry landing waiting for the *Fraser Venture* to arrive to take him to the mainland and this same Forestry chap was there waiting too. Sid said "See this," and pointed to the ferry. "You owe me $500." The Forestry worker replied "Oh, I say some stupid things when I'm drunk."

Two years later when Sid was having another barge built, this fellow, again a little inebriated, declared this wasn't true. Sid just replied "Double or nothing." Nothing more was said.

* * * *

Just a month after the *Fraser Venture* was commissioned and the first stories about it and Sid's plans were published in the *Maryborough Chronicle,* conservationist John Sinclair launched an extraordinary attack on Sid.

Since they had been on different sides during sand mining, Sinclair had sniped at Sid fairly consistently in the quarterly newsletter, *Moonbi,* which he wrote for his Fraser Island Defenders' Organisation members, and which he sent to newspapers, politicians and bureaucrats.

With Sid now looking as if he was taking a huge step forward, as he was, Sinclair got on to the attack. In the *Moonbi* of June 1983 he wrote a highly defamatory diatribe about Sid, claiming many of the things he had done on Fraser Island were illegal, and calling him a criminal.

His basis for this latter assertion was that Sid was not the licensee of the Eurong pub and Sinclair assumed he could not get a liquor licence because he was not, as the law required, "a fit and proper person". In fact had he done his homework, he would have found Sid already owned a liquor licence at the take away liquor store at Eurong.

While he had done nothing about Sinclair's newsletter before, this was an extraordinary outpouring of lies that Sid decided could not go unanswered. Sinclair refused to apologise in print and found himself and FIDO facing a defamation suit.

It took eight years before the case came to court so Sid's name was blackened just as he needed government support for his dredging proposal and for all those years after.

Sid may not have been well educated, but he was a hoarder and kept every bit of paper that had anything to do with his Fraser Island enterprises – and was able to prove that Sinclair was wrong in everything he had written. As for being a criminal, his only conviction had been for stealing petrol for his motorbike as a youngster.

When in July 1991 the case was finally heard in the Brisbane District Court, Sinclair had been abandoned by his legal help and did not even turn up to answer the case. Judge Pat Shanahan said the allegations Sinclair had made were baseless and grave and wounding. "It was terrible that untruths like this were published," he said.

He awarded Sid the highest damages for defamation in Queensland up to that time, $20,000 plus $7,200 interest and costs of $23,000.

The judge said the damages would have been even higher had Sinclair's newsletter been distributed to more than the 100 supporters it appeared were in FIDO. No-one thought to tell him that Sinclair had many newspapers and people of influence on his *Moonbi* mailing list, and had probably damaged Sid's name irreparably. Sinclair went bankrupt, and never paid the damages and costs awarded against him.

Many FIDO members resigned, and one who did, Mike West said "The bill is far in excess of what FIDO has. It is highly likely the group will be finished anyway. The only way it could continue is if Sid Melksham relieves us of that burden."

Sid did exactly that. He did not even attempt to pursue the members of FIDO for the damages, for he realized hardly any of them, if any at all, knew what would be appearing in *Moonbi* until it was put into their letterboxes.

He achieved his purpose of halting Sinclair's regular and reckless outpourings of calumny about him.

Chapter 17

It took seven months for Index Engineering to build the *Fraser Venture* on the banks of Doboy Creek off the Brisbane River.

In the meantime Sid worked on other aspects of his grand plan.

To cut down the time it took to reach Fraser Island, Sid decided he would run the *Fraser Venture* from River Heads, a narrow promontory on the north bank of the Mary River, which he had used 20 years earlier for cargo and passenger trips in the old *Lady Fraser*.

The sand mining company Dillinghams had built a barge ramp there, and on departure, their manager Ron Cross had told Sid he could have it.

He would operate the new ferry across to another former sand mining barge ramp on the west coast of Fraser Island at Buff Creek, south of the Forestry jetty at Ungowa. The crossing would take about an hour.

However if he could get the barge into the mouth of Wanggoolba Creek, on the island directly opposite River Heads, Sid estimated it would take the *Fraser Venture* a mere half an hour to make the crossing.

The biggest disadvantage was that Wanggoolba Creek, like all the other creeks on this stretch of the island's western shore, ran over a 600 m wide ledge of sand and mud to deep water in the Great Sandy Straits. This ledge was exposed at low tide. Vessel access could only be achieved at high tide – unless an all tide access channel was dredged into the creek mouth.

Every afternoon when he'd finished work for a few hours, the resort chef of the time, Ian Edgar, and Sid would go to the creek mouth to explore the possibilities.

They waded through the creek in water up to their waists. They ploughed through mud up to their knees. They borrowed a dinghy and at low tide plumbed the creek depths with Sid's version of a depth gauge, a big shiny socket tied to a tape measure.

They were plumbing the depths one afternoon when suddenly a big shark came by, mouth agape, and snatched the socket, breaking the tape. The pair of them looked at each other in horror: they'd been wading there just an hour earlier.

When Sid felt he knew all he needed to know to decide whether his plan was feasible, he called on an engineering firm from Hervey Bay and took its principal, Bob Gregg to the site, to draw up plans for a dredged channel, a barge landing and a good road to it.

Bob and his staff spent days studying tidal flows and heights and, taking those into consideration, plotted the channel to be dug 650m from the creek mouth across the sand flats to deep water.

It was to be 30m wide with a larger semi circular swing basin to be dredged at the island end of the channel, so the *Fraser Venture* could drive in to a ramp, offload, turn around, and drive out again. Finally the channel would have to be dredged deep enough so the *Fraser Venture* with its 1.4metre draught could get in easily even at the lowest tide.

The mouth of Wanggoolba Creek where Sid planned to make an all tide channel to run straight across 650 metres of tidal sand flats from the edge of the mangroves. A former timber cutters' track across a salt pan to their former log dump at the creek mouth is visible on the lower right of the photograph. Sid planned to make this track into a causeway, using material dredged from the creek bed.

Sid worked along with the engineers to help them take depth readings on the Wanggoolba Creek mouth and the sand ledge, so they could work out how much sand would have to be removed.

One important question was what Sid would do with all the sand. He explained he planned to pump it ashore to form the landing area, where his tour buses and any vehicles that used the barge could muster, and make a causeway across a salt pan to join in with a disused timber road.

The former timber truck drivers, who knew the island environment well, could drive across the salt pan with no fear of going off track and getting bogged, but tourists, to whom it was all a new experience, certainly couldn't. All this had to be incorporated into the engineering plans.

Only the Forestry Department, the big Maryborough timber companies or the multinational sand mining companies had ever undertaken work on this scale on Fraser Island before. It was a massive undertaking for a private individual even to contemplate.

Plans in hand Sid went to Brisbane to see what, if any, obstacles were in his way. He had absolutely no idea of what awaited him.

In fact he was confident of approval. In the wake of sand mining the Queensland Government had commissioned a study into the future management of Fraser Island. One of its recommendations was that a good all tide access should be made to the island's west coast. The site selected in the study was at Urang Creek across the island from Happy Valley, where Noel Mathiesen ran his barge service. However no work had been done there and in the intervening years, Eurong with Sid's resort had overtaken Happy Valley as the major centre on the island.

Sid's first call was to the Forestry Department, without an appointment of course, and while we were sitting waiting for someone to agree to see him, to his great good fortune a former Fraser Island Forester, Peter Kernowski happened by. All the Fraser Island folk, who'd battled conditions and put up with the primitive lifestyle in the 1960's and 70's, had developed great fellowship and Peter and Sid regarded each other with friendly respect.

Kernowski, now a very senior officer, took Sid into his office and asked what he wanted.

Sid told him and Kernowski said the first step Sid would have to take was to get tenure of the land onto which a barge landing could be built. He said if Sid could get the approvals he needed from all the other government departments involved, he would grant Sid a lease on a small parcel of land for the purpose.

Sid went straight round to the Lands Department, and after a long wait was given an audience by a friendly fellow who told him that seabed dredging had nothing to do with his department and he should go and see the Department of Harbours and Marine.

Next morning Sid walked along there, waited to see someone, and was eventually told that the seabed around Wanggoolba Creek mouth had recently been declared the Maroom Fish Habitat and it was highly unlikely he would ever be allowed to dredge a channel in a Fish Habitat, but in any case he would have to go and see someone at the Department of Primary Industries.

Anyone with more experience of dealing with government departments might have thought they were getting the run around. But Sid had no such experience and just kept going where he was sent.

At the Department of Primary Industries, he was eventually shown into the office of the Chief Inspector of Fisheries, Mr. Frank Olsen, who looked at the plans and then at Wanggoolba Creek on a map, and then told Sid he had no hope whatever of getting approval to dredge in a Fish Habitat.

I was worn out walking from department to department and this to me was the ultimate blow to Sid's hopes.

I excused myself and left Mr. Olsen's office in despair, expecting Sid to come too. But he was made of sterner stuff and stayed. I sat and waited in the reception area.

Sid was so convinced of the merit of what he was trying to achieve he told Mr. Olsen his whole vision for decent access to Fraser Island and what it could mean to the economic future of Hervey Bay if it came to fruition.

To get rid of Sid, who showed no move to leave, Mr. Olsen finally uttered the words which he thought would be the death knell to the grand scheme, which he probably thought was pie in the sky anyway – and he was not alone in that.

"The only way you will get approval is if you can convince the Government to pass a special Act of Parliament to excise a piece out of the Fish Habitat for you to dredge a channel," he said.

He suggested that if Sid could get the support of all the fishing organizations, professional and amateur in a vast region from Bundaberg to Rainbow Beach, it would go a long way to helping his case. He would also have to get letters of support from the local police, the coastguard, the air sea rescue organization, local government, the Forestry Department and whoever else had any official involvement

Sid's response was unexpected "Oh so I can do it." He came out of Olsen's office with a big smile and said to me "We just have to get an Act of Parliament passed and then we can do it." He had absolutely no idea of the magnitude of the task ahead. I just looked at his optimistic face in dismay and thought "You poor man. You haven't got a clue."

As Sid was to say many times "I just didn't have the education to know it couldn't be done." So he went ahead and did it.

He was fortunate in that Wanggoolba Creek mouth was not pristine.

Decades before it had been used as a log dump by timber cutters, who made a track across the tidal salt pan to the creek mouth and carted huge satinay and brush box logs there to be hoisted aboard punts and taken down the Mary River to the big Maryborough sawmills. Several huge logs had been left lying on the creek bank as a reminder of this early use of the area.

A couple of the later barges had made occasional forays into the creek mouth at high tide to offload vehicles. Sid himself had brought a truck on the first barge in the area, operated by former Harbours and Marine Department officer, Kev Donnelly – with disastrous results.

This former use of the creek mouth for timber and barging operations meant that the government was prepared to consider allowing it to be used again.

Sid, who had never addressed a meeting in his life, determinedly took his engineering plans to the monthly meetings of all the professional and amateur fishermen's' associations in the area to explain what he wanted to do and seek their approval.

Overcoming his shyness presented a real difficulty. Still he managed, his enthusiasm driving him.

Without exception the fishing groups gave the thumbs up to Sid's proposal, some even writing that the channel would be a good thing as a potential place to shelter in a storm safe from big seas and in the lee of the island.

But some admitted afterwards that it was such an ambitious plan, they hadn't really thought it could be done. That was their one fear, that it was too big for one man to achieve and it could be abandoned before it was finished. They had long known of Sid as a battler against the odds in the isolation and tough environment of Fraser Island and his exploits had become famous. But this was a huge scheme, bigger than any of them would have ever contemplated him tackling.

The police, air sea rescue and coastguard were totally supportive.

An all tide access to the west coast of Fraser would make all their jobs easier, when it came to evacuating the sick or injured, for they would be able to come in to the channel with their small vessels and pick up anyone needing to be taken back to the mainland for medical treatment at any time of day or night.

Sid submitted all the letters to Olsen. Several weeks passed and nothing more was heard.

A Queensland state election had been called for November 1983 and Sid asked the National Party candidate for Maryborough, Gilbert Alison if he could find out what was happening. Alison arranged for him to meet the Minister of Primary Industries, Mike Ahern to explain his plan.

Sid was very nervous in the Minister's office, but once the ice was broken he soon had his drawings spread all over Ahern's desk and was explaining the whole thing in detail. Ahern listened to Sid put his case, then asked the all important question "Are you seeking government funding?"

Sid had always assumed he would have to pay for the work, and was just grateful that he might be allowed to do it.

When he said "No," to Ahern he perhaps didn't realize it, but he had made a hugely favourable impression.

Many years afterwards a fellow minister in the government at the time said Sid was the only chap he knew who had come up with a major scheme like that and hadn't expected the government to pay for it.

But what Sid did expect, was that the channel and barge landing that he had conceived, planned and was going to pay for, would be for his exclusive commercial use.

Ahern told him he should get in touch with all other barge operators who might have used the channel in the past and get them to write in that they had no objection and no intention of using the creek for landing again.

Ahern then asked how Sid would feel about emergency service boats, government boats and private vessels using the proposed channel. Sid said he had would be happy to let them all use it. He just felt it wouldn't be fair for him to do all the work and pay for it, then another barge owner come in and use it.

Then Ahern instructed his department head, Gordon McCormack who had sat in on the meeting, to give Sid the help he needed. In turn McCormack called in the Chief Inspector of Fisheries, Brian Venz, who came to the island with two other officers and ploughed through the mud at the creek mouth, inspecting the whole area and researching the wildlife.

Venz then prepared a positive submission on the proposal for the Queensland Cabinet.

Cabinet, well aware that conservationists, especially John Sinclair, would be looking at the whole thing carefully, decided Sid would have to commission an independent environmental impact study so they could be assured the benefit of the proposed access would outweigh the habitat disturbance.

Sid went to Ted Coaldrake, a scientist of impressive qualifications, whom he had met during sand mining days and who already knew a great deal about the Fraser Island environment. Ted remembered Sid well and within a matter of days he and his scientific team were studying the Wanggoolba Creek mouth.

Their report was favourable. In particular it stated that the dredging would have no adverse effect on fisheries nor would it significantly interfere with mangroves, but it recommended conditions on the dredging, that it should only be done at certain tides for example.

Finally Sid had to ask other barge owners to write that they had no objection to him having exclusive use for the channel for his barge.

There were only a few men who had run barges to Fraser Island in this area before: Kev Donnelly, John Flynn and Ron Fielding, all gone from the barge business, and only one existing barge operator, Noel Mathiesen who worked from Hervey Bay to island landing points well north of Wanggoolba. Sid approached them and they all wrote that they had no objection to him having exclusive use of his channel and had no intention themselves of bringing a barge into Wanggoolba.

Sid presented all his paperwork to the head of the Department of Primary Industries. From that point on it was just a matter of waiting, something Sid wasn't very good at. But he had plenty to keep him occupied, bringing together the other elements of his plan.

The expected opposition from conservationist, John Sinclair was not slow to materialise. As soon as he heard of Sid's dredging plans he contacted various newspapers to announce that a flotilla of fishing boats would be organized to blockade the dredging if it were approved.

Sid had already obtained the fishing organisations' support and didn't take the threat seriously. In fact when journalists kept telephoning to ask if dredging had started and if the flotilla of boats had turned up yet, Sid jokingly advised his staff they would have to go out in boats and pretend to be the blockade to satisfy the media.

Chapter 18

Sid knew that the *Fraser Venture* would be finished well before the Wanggoolba Creek channel and barge landing would even be started. He planned in the meantime to run the new ferry from River Heads to Buff Creek, where the defunct sand mining companies had built a rough ramp for their barges to offload fuel and supplies.

The voyage from River Heads to Buff Creek would take an hour each way, considerably less than any other day trip operating out of Hervey Bay by launch, but when he got the Wanggoolba Creek ferry landing in operation the crossing would take a mere half hour.

Knowing it was the day trip income which was going to keep the *Fraser Venture* financially afloat, at least in the beginning, Sid set about planning big improvements to his island day trips. With the shorter time crossing the straits, Sid was able to extend the tour on the island.

Up to this time his buses had taken the day tour passengers across the island from the Forestry jetty at Ungowa to Eurong with time for a wander on the magnificent surf beach and stops for a walk in the rainforest at Central Station on the way across the island and a swim in Lake Birrabeen on the way back.

Now Sid planned to have the buses travel along the surf beach another 25 km northwards from Eurong to visit three big scenic attractions there, Eli Creek the largest freshwater creek on the eastern side of the island that poured millions of litres across the beach into the ocean every hour, the shipwreck of the *Maheno*, and the Cathedrals, high coloured sand cliffs, carved by the wind into turrets and spires.

Only too well aware of the problems of driving the surf beach, Sid worked out how he could juggle the timing of the beach leg so it could always be done at low, or on an outgoing tide.

Sometimes the beach run would be done after lunch; on other days the buses would come straight across the island, do the beach run, then back to Eurong for the passengers to have lunch and visit Central Station and Lake Birrabeen on the way back.

One big disadvantage was that Sid had to persuade his customers to go 11 km out of Hervey Bay to River Heads, where the *Fraser Venture* would operate from. The road to River Heads was unpaved, very hilly and in wet weather its clay content made it slippery.

Rival tour operator, Barry Murphy operated out of the little boat harbour at Urangan, at the southern end of Hervey Bay itself and readily accessible for passengers to drive themselves there. This is where the Toys operated the *Philanderer* from too, and it had become the established jump off point to Fraser Island.

But it led to a two to three hour long sea voyage to and from the island, and this was what Sid aimed to reduce, so visitors had the maximum possible time on the island, not getting there and back. But how to entice those potential customers from Hervey Bay to River Heads?

Sid pondered over his problem as he pondered over many of his problems, while he was hand watering his lawn at Eurong. In good time he worked it out.

He would bus his customers to River Heads as he had with his early day trippers. From that followed the idea that he would go one better than having them drive their own cars to the Urangan Boat Harbour, as the Toy and Murphy day trips did, but would pick them up from their motels and caravan parks in the bus.

But on good days his and the Toys' day trips were getting far more customers than one bus could carry. Then came the flash of inspiration. He would get a double decker bus, a rarity in Australia then. Not only would it carry a lot of people, but it would be a real novelty around Hervey Bay and he was sure youngsters would love to have a ride on it, and persuade their parents to go on Sid's trip.

He heard of six double deckers that had just been imported from England and flew down to Sydney to look at them. He came home, the purchase made of one, and an arrangement to have the bus delivered to Brisbane.

It wasn't a very appealing double decker, painted in the sombre maroon and fawn colours of its home city, Plymouth.

Sid had decided on a colour scheme for the *Fraser Venture*, white with two broad diagonal stripes, one blue and one orange, and had the double decker painted to match in Brisbane before it came to Hervey Bay. Sid was absolutely right about it being an attraction in its own right. As he and Max Williams took it from the painter's workshop in Brisbane, dozens of children began running along the footpath calling "Give us a ride, mister."

Getting it to Maryborough was a test of nerves. Max drove while Sid sat on the top deck judging the height of power lines, low bridges and overhanging tree branches ready to stamp on the floor for Max to stop if an overhead collision seemed imminent.

They set off along the freeway thinking it would be clear of obstacles, and came to a low bridge about a kilometer past the South Brisbane turn off. It looked as if it was just too low for the bus to go under. While Max stopped and Sid peered upwards, traffic began to pile up behind and there was hooting and hollering. The alternative to going under the bridge was to reverse against the traffic about a kilometer to a turn off. They decided to go ahead. Max inched forwards while Sid listened for a scraping sound. The bus made it under, but it was very close.

Sid hoped to get it to Maryborough the same day so it could be machinery inspected and then taken straight to Hervey Bay. From Gympie, with more than an hour's drive still to go, he telephoned the government machinery inspector, Bill Watson to ask if he would mind staying late to look at what Sid described as "a really interesting vehicle." He said no more but Bill's curiosity was aroused and he waited. When he saw the double decker lumbering along, he had a big smile, waved it over the inspection pit and clambered down to look underneath. "Press the footbrake," he instructed Max – and a big squirt of oil came out of a pressure release valve and hit Bill fair in the eye.

* * * *

To compete with Barry Murphy's trip, Sid believed his open Studebaker buses would no longer suffice.

"It was a great shame to part with the Studebakers, certainly from an economic viewpoint. They earned the money to buy the new buses.

"They hardly ever let me down and because their mechanics were so basic, I could do almost any work needed on them while the day trippers were having lunch," he says.

The big upgrade he was planning to the whole concept of Fraser Island day trips demanded closed in buses. There were very few buses available that were 4WD, but Sid heard of a tour operator in the Northern Territory who had 4WD buses to travel the desert tracks and got in touch with him. Luck smiled on Sid for the fellow had three buses for sale.

Sid caught the first plane to Alice Springs and bought all three buses on the spot. Getting them from Alice to Brisbane was quite a job. When he came home Sid got in touch with a Brisbane transport firm that ran supplies out to Alice and persuaded them to bring two of the buses on their big trucks as backload to Brisbane. The man he got the price from, $600 per bus, turned out to have no authority to give Sid a quote and while the transport company honoured the deal, they wanted a much bigger price to carry the third bus.

Instead Sid sent Max Williams to Alice Springs to drive the bus back, and gave him money for board, food and petrol for the trip.

Only a couple of days passed when there was a call from Max. He'd lost the money in the casino, could Sid send more. Sid knew any more money he sent to Max would probably go the same way so he sent the money in installments to the petrol stations on the route back to Brisbane, to give Max petrol and food. He was told he would have to sleep in the bus.

These buses were also painted in the new colour scheme. Coincidentally not long afterwards the Brisbane City Council decided on a very similar colour scheme for its new city express bus fleet, and quite a few people when they saw Sid's buses in Hervey Bay thought Brisbane City Council was taking over the town.

* * * *

All the time the *Fraser Venture* was being built Sid had had a multitude of other things to organize.

When he had been in partnership with the Toy family, they had done all the day trip bookings, and ticketing and visiting the agents in motels and caravan parks to collect the trip money every month.

Sid's staff could not handle bookings from Eurong with the phone system as it was, so before the *Fraser Venture* arrived, he asked a Hervey Bay travel agent, George Bezant if he would do the job on 10 per cent commission. George said he'd think about it and let Sid know later as he was on his way to a meeting. It must have suddenly dawned on George what the potential income from the day tour and vehicle bookings could bring him, for he rang Sid within half an hour to accept the job.

Sid needed staff on the mainland, in particular a driver for the double decker in Hervey Bay who could then come on the ferry and drive on the island section of the day tour as well. He asked Steve Jensen if he would do the job and May Jensen if she could set up and manage the shop on the *Fraser Venture*. Sid was sorry to lose them at Eurong but felt they would be ideal to help get the new operation off to a good start and they agreed.

"We had mixed feelings," says May. "We were excited about the new opportunity but I was very sad to leave Eurong. It had become our home, not just our workplace.

"This was very much due to Sid. He had this rough, tough exterior, but underneath was the kindest and most compassionate of men. I always thought of what he did for Kelly Page, letting him live at the resort when he was too old to work anymore. The staff was Kelly's family and the resort was his home.

"Sid was the same with Harry Geltch when he turned up to try and make a living doing joy flights. Sid gave him a room and all his meals all the time he was at Eurong and never took a penny from him – not even commission for the joy flights he got from our day trippers.

"He was very generous to us. I remember I went with Steve to Maryborough on the stores truck one day and somehow lost both our wage packets. They had probably fallen down between the truck cab and back on to the road. Sid found out and replaced both lots of wages. He didn't have to do that.

"Then when Steve and I were going on holidays to Tasmania one year Sid kept asking where we were going and how much it was going to cost us. When we went to say goodbye to everyone over a few drinks in the bar, Sid gave us an envelope and when we opened it later we found it held the full cost of our holiday.

"Another example of his kindness was when Steve and I left the island, I had to leave my washing machine behind for one of the stores truck drivers to bring it over to the mainland for me later. It was a long while coming and when it arrived it was broken because other staff had used it while I was gone.

"I cried and the driver who delivered it must have told Sid because a few days later when I got home from work on the *Fraser Venture*, the old washer had gone and a brand new, family size washing machine was in its place."

Laurie Toy decided he too would leave the island by Christmas as his wife, Elaine was pregnant with their second child, but he would continue to work for Sid on the mainland. Now the 4WD buses could be taken back and forth to the island on the *Fraser Venture*, he could maintain them on his property at River Heads.

It would also be more convenient to do any work needed on the double decker and the *Fraser Venture* itself, as well as being the ferry's relieving skipper.

Sid had a new workshop, high enough to house the double decker, built on Laurie's property at River Heads.

* * * *

There was a lot of work to be done on the island roads. To prevent the new paintwork on the buses getting scratched by small branches and twigs sticking out over the narrow sand tracks, these branches had to be cut back. Up to now this work had been done piecemeal by Sid himself and his employees using brush hooks if it looked like the occasional branch was going to smack into a Studebaker windscreen. But now 21 km of track had to be cut back on both sides to the height of the new buses.

Sid invented a machine, which everyone called the whipper snipper, to do the job faster.

The man who got the job of driving the whipper snipper was a long distance lorry driver, Harold James, who had started working for Sid just the day before.

Harold tells the story "I was told about Sid and a driving job on Fraser Island by Jimmy Schmidt, an old mate of mine. He said he'd ring him and there and then picked up the phone and said 'Ungowa 7U' and I thought what's this? It's a funny way to make a phone call.

"Anyway I got to meet Sid and he told me he'd just got a new ferry starting and had a big dredging job coming up. He'd need someone to drive his Peterbilt truck with sand to make roads, and in the meantime there'd be plenty of other driving jobs. That sounded all right, so I started working for him on December 18 1983.

"Next morning he took me to the workshop where the mechanic Laurie Toy was in the final stages of building the whipper snipper.

"He had taken the bucket off a front end loader and hooked a Studebaker motor, gear box and tail shaft assembly to the two arms. The tail shaft ran through a solid bearing mount to a metre diameter disc cut out of steel plate. Laurie was just bolting four 60 cm long slasher blades on to the disc at even spaces. Once the motor was started, these things flailed around very fast and would cut anything in their path.

"Sid told me I was to drive this along one side of the road across the island and back along the other side, lifting the slasher up and down on the loader arms, cutting back overgrown branches so they wouldn't scratch newly painted buses he'd just bought. He said if I started at lunchtime that day, Friday I'd be finished by Monday.

"It was 21 kilometres from Eurong across the island to Buff Creek with a turn off to Lake Birrabeen, so that meant I had to cut back 42 kilometres, one side of the road on the way there and the other on the way back.

"I got about 300 metres from Eurong and thought the job was some kind of test, the machine was such a terrible thing to drive.

"Debris from the trees kept flying back on to me. I had to go back to Eurong and Laurie built a mesh guard in front to protect me. I thought I was never going to last in this job, but off I went again. Debris kept coming through the holes in the mesh, so Laurie came up with the idea of replacing the disc and slasher blades with a metre diameter circular saw instead of the disc and slasher blades. It didn't work as fast as the flailing blades, but it stopped all the debris flying back.

"Sid's timing was out, just a little bit. It took me six days until Christmas Eve to clean up the road.

"Then another chap and I had to go out on Christmas morning to cut a few branches that had been too big for the whipper snipper, so the new buses could start on Boxing Day. A job like that today would take someone a month and it wouldn't be done half as well."

* * * *

Tree trimming had also to be done in Hervey Bay. The route for the double decker was set along the Esplanade with small diversions to pick up passengers at caravan parks and motels one street back. Then it would drive out to River Heads.

The bus was so tall that branches of the trees planted along the Esplanade bashed against its upper windows. Sid persuaded the Hervey Bay Council that as the bus was a registered vehicle it had to be given unimpeded passage along the roads. The Parks Curator obligingly cut back overhanging tree branches all along its route.

But sagging power lines were a problem too, as they crossed the Esplanade from tall power poles on one side of the street to the gutter line of low set houses on the other. The electricity authority denied there was a problem until Steve Jensen invited the authority engineer to come for a ride with him and sit in the top deck. Within a few 100 metres the engineer came down the stairs white faced – he'd seen power lines come too close to the front window for comfort – or safety. So the power lines all had to be hitched up.

Wires got crossed in more ways than one, and two weeks before the double decker was to begin its inaugural run, the Hervey Bay council hung up its Christmas bunting across the Esplanade, and whoever did the job forgot all about the double decker.

There followed a heated exchange of words between Sid and the mayor about who was going to take action against whom for obstructing the road or damaging council property if bunting was pulled down by the bus.

Good sense prevailed and the council's and Sid's staff worked together to raise the bunting.

Passengers dismount from the double decker at River Heads on its inaugural run.

The new colour co-ordinated island 4WD bus fleet.

Chapter 19

Sid frequently went to Doboy Creek in Brisbane to watch progress on the *Fraser Venture.* It seemed it was slow to take shape at first, but after two months there was a lot of steel on site; another month and a half and a formed hull had appeared.

Then things started to happen faster. The big lounge deck had been built elsewhere and next time he went to look, it had been swung on to the hull by crane. The vessel began to look huge.

At the shipyard Sid, second left, meets with the Fraser Venture builders, George Vaggelas, left who did the saloon shop fit out, Barry Flannigan, head of the steel fabrication works, and Cliff Fraser, the foreman.

Sid inspected every weld and had long discussions with the foreman on the job a laconic fellow named Cliff Fraser. After a few such visits I asked Cliff how he was getting along with Sid and he replied "He's great. He leaves us alone."

The heavy steel door is lifted on to the Fraser Venture.

As the barge progressed Sid told Ross McLean of the colour scheme he had chosen to have it painted, gleaming white with one broad blue stripe and one broad orange stripe running at an angle from its upper deck to its water line, the resort insignia of seagulls painted along the outside of the saloon on both sides, and its name in dark blue across the front with gold surrounds.

Ross protested "Barges don't have stripes and seagulls and gold lettering." Sid said "Mine is going to. I want the best looking ferry on the Queensland coast."

The shipyard foreman, Cliff Fraser had a shock too. A month before the *Fraser Venture's* completion date, Sid announced he was going to stay in Brisbane to watch all the finishing touches being made.

Sid rang Eurong every night to recount the day's events and it was apparent he was far from leaving the *Venture's* builders alone anymore. "I want everything to be right," he kept saying.

When next I went to see the *Venture* I asked Cliff how he was getting along with Sid now. His reply was a little different from before. "He's a bit excitable isn't he?" Cliff said.

Sid studied different types of engines for the new barge and decided on two M.A. N.s. When he went to talk to the supplier he asked for a price on not two but three motors.

By this time he needed a new generator at Eurong to cater for the growth of his resort and realized if he had it powered by the same motor as the Fraser Venture, essential spares kept on hand would fit all three.

While Sid's new barge and plans were the talk of Hervey Bay and regularly written about in the local *Maryborough Chronicle,* folk had no real idea just how big the *Fraser Venture* was going to be.

Sid decided to bring the vessel into Urangan Boat Harbour to have an open day on board before it went to work from River Heads.

He went to a meeting of the Hervey Bay Air Sea Rescue and offered the vessel to it to hold an evening function to raise funds. One of its members, Don Caswell held up his hand and said he would organize the event.

A local skipper with wide sea going experience called Harry Brutnall approached Sid for a job on the new ferry and, after checking out his qualifications, Sid employed him. He was to remain as its skipper for more than 20 years.

Finally on November 12 1983 the *Fraser Venture* was ready for its voyage home to Fraser Island, almost. The carpenters were still working in the wheelhouse and had to be ordered ashore so Sid and Harry Brutnall could catch the tide out of the Brisbane River into Moreton Bay, and be in time for television helicopters to fly over and film it under way.

The television crews had come aboard to a little launching party, taken one look at the distinctive stripes and seagulls and gone back to order the chopper. Even Ross McLean confessed he thought the colours were great and that he was using photos of the *Venture* for his shipbuilding promotions.

Sid said his farewells and a special thank you to Cliff Fraser. "I'll drop in and see you whenever I'm in Brisbane," Sid offered. "Good heavens, no," said Cliff and they both laughed.

Sid, Harry Brutnall and several other employees who wanted to come along for the voyage brought the *Fraser Venture* from Brisbane to Hervey Bay and it performed very well indeed, arriving much sooner than expected in spite of a storm en route.

There was a crowd waiting to meet it at Urangan Boat Harbour.

Bedecked in bunting, it dwarfed everything else there and when the ramp was lowered, there was a rush of people to go aboard and have a look around.

The Fraser Venture in Urangan Boat Harbour.

All day long crowds came to inspect the new ferry.

Wally Toy, who had stopped running the *Philanderer* some weeks before, and put it up for sale, came for a look and said to Sid "I remember you saying you would get a boat – but I never expected one like this."

Barry Murphy, who Sid had believed would be his competitor, had sold out, and the new owner of his business, John Webster came to look too. He introduced himself to Sid, but his dismay was evident as he said "I didn't know this was coming."

After a very successful day the Air Sea Rescue held an evening cruise with a barbecue on the bottom deck, a fashion parade then dancing on all the decks until the early hours.

All the tickets were sold and about 300 people, who had left their cruise booking until they had seen the *Venture,* were regretfully told they were too late.

The Eurong resort folk let their hair down at the evening fund raiser.

More than $3000 was raised, and the Air Sea Rescue decided to divide the money between the widows of three men who had lost their lives on a fishing trip to the northern tip of Fraser Island some weeks before.

Don Caswell, organizer of the evening, was a highly valued volunteer skipper with Air Sea Rescue and had undertaken a dangerous rescue attempt of the three fishermen. In spite of his and his crew's best efforts to reach the foundering vessel the fishermen drowned before they got there.

* * * *

Sid claimed in his ferry advertising that, living on the island, he hadn't heard about inflation. When he took vehicles to the island, three at a time on the deck of his little launch, *Lady Fraser,* in the 1960's he had charged $20 a vehicle there and back. He kept the fare on the *Fraser Venture* at $20 per vehicle return.

The new ferry made its first run on December 19 from River Heads to Buff Creek and back in the morning and a second run in the afternoon. With the Christmas holidays just having started, it was a success from the first day on, with full loads of vehicles.

On its first run into former sand mining ramp at Buff Creek, the Fraser Venture has a full deck.

As a community contribution Sid offered free ferry passage to all school groups going on his island tours, an encouragement to come and learn about the island environment.

This gesture enabled children to come, whose parents might not have otherwise been able to afford the trip.

The day trips began on Boxing Day, a week later. Now he had control of his day tours, Sid decided on many changes, not least the price, which he had felt had been increasing too rapidly before. This was now set at $20 per adult, including a chicken and salad lunch with champagne.

The Fraser Venture unloads at River Heads.

New colour brochures for the day tours had been designed – and Sid persuaded the wine company, from which he bought the champagne, to pay for them.

To top off the smart new look of the buses, Sid put his drivers in uniform of pale blue shirt with navy blue epaulettes with gold embroidery and navy shorts.

He also had a private radio network installed so he could keep in touch with the *Fraser Venture*, the buses and George Bezant's office from Eurong. This network could be extended to wherever Sid expanded his business.

Importantly Sid decided he would run the day trips every day, no matter how many people booked to go on them. Up to then the Toys and Barry Murphy had cancelled their day trips if they did not have a pay load of passengers. Often these cancellations were not advised to the caravan park and motel owners, who booked the trips for their customers, until just an hour before the day trip was to go. This led to a lot of bad feeling and unhappy people who had been looking forward to their day on the island.

By having a multipurpose vessel, which carried vehicles as well as people, Sid hoped any low numbers on one would be offset by good numbers on the other.

In any case he felt if he had to take a loss on any particular day, his new policy of absolute reliability would pay off in the longer term.

"Booking agents knew that if they booked on the *Fraser Venture Tours,* they would not have to tell their customers the tour was cancelled, and would not have to bear the brunt of their disappointment," says Sid. "It gave them confidence in booking."

He kept his word, even though one damp February day he only got four day trip passengers. He drove them around personally in his Range Rover.

* * * *

Sid and skipper, Harry Brutnall, in the Fraser Venture wheelhouse.

From that very first Christmas, the new ferry service proved a big advantage to the operation of the resort, with the stores truck easily managing daily runs to keep up with the demand for food supplies for the restaurant and shop, and fuel, gas and all the other things island holidaymakers wanted.

As all Sid's regular drivers were going to be needed on the new day trips, Paddy Doran was employed to drive the stores truck over the holiday period, and brought his mum to stay with him at Eurong.

It was steady work and Paddy felt he was entitled to the best treatment as well as his pay. He certainly didn't know he was expected to take second place to customers.

Every night the bistro behind the hotel was frantically busy. One night when the bistro cook, Geoff Smith was, as usual, swamped with orders, Paddy's mum appeared. Paddy, having just arrived at Eurong with a load of stores, wanted a big steak.

Geoff told Paddy's mum she would have to wait. She went to report back to Paddy. Next thing Paddy arrived on the scene, pushed his way to the front of the queue, took a swing at Geoff, and blacked his eye. He wasn't badly hurt but took himself off to his room to put a cold compress on his eye, with Paddy, full of remorse, going with him to offer sympathy and sorrow. Accountant Barry Keys' wife, Marie took over the cooking.

Geoff was a game little chap. Next day he went on the *Fraser Venture* to the mainland for treatment and came back with an eye patch and a toy parrot. He was back at work in the bistro that night, wearing a patch over the black eye and the parrot on one shoulder.

By the end of January the ferry had earned enough to cover the lease repayments on her for the next four months, which gave Sid a breathing space.

Once the rush was over, one of the first things brought to the island on the *Fraser Venture* was a second hand grader Sid had bought ***(below).*** This was to repair and maintain the roads his newly painted tour buses used across the island from Buff Creek to Eurong and the loop road to Lake Birrabeen. The very versatile Harold James was to drive it.

The grader came on the same trip as a brand spanking new Forestry Department machine, and staff waiting to board the ferry were greatly impressed thinking it was Sid's purchase. Then to their disappointment, Paddy Doran drove off the elderly grader. Still, as Sid said, it did the job.

To make sure Harold was taught the proper way to grade the sand and not damage the tree roots, Sid employed a retired Forestry grader driver, Frank Schikowski to teach him.

Every time Sid himself was driving inland he took a shovel with him to clear leaf or sand clogged drains, so rainwater would run off and not pond on the road.

He was forever shifting fallen branches off to the side. There was no wonder he cut a disheveled figure when he went to the mainland, after clearing the road on the way across the island.

He also cheekily put a sign on his land by the side of the road "This road is maintained by Sid Melksham for his customers and friends". He was asked to remove it by the District Forester, and Sid promised he would as soon as the Forestry did as much work on the road as he and his staff did.

All was not plain sailing with the *Fraser Venture.* Just a few months after starting operations, skipper Harry Brutnall ignored an unfamiliar warning bell and simply turned it off. One of the two big engines overheated and seized and had to be completely rebuilt. A mechanic from the engine suppliers came to do the rebuild with new pistons, liners and head, while the vessel kept going on one motor.

Laurie Toy was helping him when his wife, Elaine went into labour.

"I rang Laurie and he said he couldn't come to take me to the hospital until he'd fixed something crucial on the *Fraser Venture,*" says Elaine. "I walked up and down to try and hold the baby back until he came home. The doctor kept phoning and telling me to hurry up and get to the hospital. Laurie just made it in time before the baby arrived."

Chapter 20

The Queensland Parliament resumed sitting three months after the *Fraser Venture* began running, and word came that the proposal to excise the mouth of Wanggoolba Creek from the Fish habitat so Sid could dredge his ferry channel, was to be put before Parliament on March 7 1984.

A motion to that effect was put by the new Minister for Primary Industries, the Hon. N. J. Turner. He explained the Fish Habitat was 23,000 hectares in area, and that during the dredging only 3.7 hectares would be disturbed. This was the area for which he sought Parliamentary agreement to revoke from the Fish Habitat.

Turner stated that the proposed new channel and landing would improve the management and public enjoyment of Fraser Island and would increase the safety of all who visited, and pointed out the wide support such an all tide access to the island had from fishermen, tourism associations, local councils and emergency services.

There were only three opposition Labor Party speakers against the move, the most vocal being Pat Comben, who was to become Minister for Environment when Labor came into government in Queensland five and a half years later.

Comben had been taken to Fraser for his first and brief visit by John Sinclair, and under the protection of parliamentary privilege, questioned the environmental impact study, Sid's character, the letters of support Sid had received, the *Fraser Venture's* capability and whether the crossing would in fact be faster. This speech was very similar to what Sinclair had written about the proposal, claiming public interest, in his newsletter, *Moonbi* a few days before.

Comben did however add one comment of his own. In Ted Coaldrake's environmental impact study of Wanggoolba Creek mouth, he mentioned the sighting of an unidentified tern. Comben, claiming he was something of a birdwatcher, suggested this might be a rare fairy tern and Sid's dredging could disturb the nesting site of this rare bird.

Cold water was immediately poured on Comben's claim by another parliamentarian, a former school teacher, who interrupted to point out "Fairy terns only nest on coral atolls. We are talking about a sand flat here."

Not one to take criticism readily, and ill founded criticism at that, when he had worked so hard and had such a strong belief his proposed new barge service would bring immeasurable benefit to the region, Sid sent a cross letter to Comben afterwards putting his point of view and regretting Comben had made no effort to talk to him before his attack.

Sid's plan was defended strongly in Parliament by Mr. Turner and the members for Maryborough, Gil Alison and Hervey Bay, Lin Powell.

Voting on the motion went strictly along party lines and it was passed 44 to 23. Comben promised the Labor Party would be keeping a close watch on the development to see it complied, but nothing more was ever heard from that quarter.

Now Sid could get to work on dredging the 650m long channel into Wanggoolba Creek mouth and all the road building associated with it.

* * * *

With very little money, Sid's options as to the dredge he hired were very limited. They were expensive beasts and just getting them to a job was costly, with the dredge itself having to be towed to the site from its home base and long lengths of piping trucked in.

Sid naturally wanted to get the work started as soon as possible, and he hired a small sand dredge from the Sunshine Coast. In the event it proved far too small for the work involved, for in spite of the many samples of material taken from the bed of the proposed channel by the engineers, they had missed three bars of hard coffee rock across the proposed channel.

There are outcrops of coffee rock all around Fraser Island's shore. When dry it crumbles easily, but when underwater it is very hard – too hard for the cutter wheel on the small sand dredge to break through. It wasn't for want of trying, and the dredge operator worked hard to remove it – to no avail.

Abiding by conditions on the dredging, that it could only be done at low tide, work on the channel was done for six hours twice a day or night.

Sid had decided he could save costs by being on hand personally to help the dredge operator. Every day for the nine months the dredging took, Sid went to the creek with the dredge operator and spent most of his time thigh deep in mud shifting the pipeline and its swing anchors, or whatever else the operator needed doing. The job was bedeviled by a series of dredge breakdowns and Sid had to do repairs too.

It was hard just to walk in the mudflats, dragging each leg out of mud above the knees and he was having to manhandle drums of fuel, heavy sections of pipeline and digging out buried anchors and hauling them to their next holding point. It might have been cheaper, but Sid was to find it was tremendously hard on him physically and it needed all his willpower to keep going sometimes.

There were so many dredge breakdowns he was often in anguish with exhaustion and frustration. His hands were cut badly on the wire ropes and his feet on shells in the mud. Many of the cuts became infected so he could barely walk sometimes, but he drove himself day in and day out.

On top of that it was a bad winter with the coldest snap to hit Queensland in a quarter of a century, and the water felt freezing cold as he had to wade into it, especially at night. In the spring the sand flies came out in their millions.

The actual dredging and pumping the sand ashore was only part of the process. Large logs had to be placed around the area that was to be the barge landing to create a bund wall, and the sand pumped into it. Then as more and more slushy sand in enormous quantities came gushing ashore, a bulldozer had to be brought in to keep piling it up, so it didn't run into the surrounding salt pan.

Cousin Joe Cunningham's son, Tommy had asked Sid for a job and was set to work on an excavator, digging a deep channel in the dredged material, where the road and causeway were to be built, for the ever gushing sand to pour in to build it up above the tidal flats.

Sid had had the Peterbilt converted to a tip truck by Laurie Toy. The tip body rose almost vertical, and was an awesome sight. As Tommy filled the huge tip body with the sand and rock, Sid or Harold James would take it to tip on the road. In all they carted a total of 90,000 cubic metres of sand and rock from the channel to make the road.

With Sid supervising everything, Tommy would switch to a bulldozer to level the heaps ***(above),*** then Harold would drive the Peterbilt back and forth over the road to compact it.

"The truck was a dream to drive," says James. "But one day, working alone, I backed it up to the edge of the ferry landing, which was about four metres above the salt pan, and the edge fell in. The Peterbilt went backwards down the slope and I couldn't drive it out.

"I got the loader and tried to dig under the wheels on one side to straighten it up and bogged the loader. I ran to Central Station and got Kev Sloper one of the Forestry blokes to come with a six tonne truck.

"He got the loader up, then we attached two chains to the front of the Peterbilt, one to the truck, the other to the loader, then we both pulled and managed to get it back up the slope and on to flat ground."

The Forestry Department offered the help of its bulldozer and driver, Sandy Luck to improve a short section of the old road, where it joined the new section Sid had built, and left it to Sid to supervise. Sid seized a one and only opportunity and had the road widened, so two vehicles could pass without difficulty.

After six months the little dredge finally got all the sand cleared out of the channel, but it could not make an impression on the coffee rock ledges in the channel bed at all.

Tip trucks were hired to speed the job of shifting the huge quantities of sand and making the road.

Sid hired a big excavator to dig out the coffee rock, and had its very skilful operator walk the machine into the creek so the water was well over its tracks, to break up the rock *(below).*

The next stage was for the excavator to dig the rock and pile it up in the centre of the creek to make a temporary road for the excavator and trucks to work from.

Harold would back the Peterbilt, or one of the other drivers a dump truck, on this road out to the excavator to be loaded up with spoil to take ashore, ***(below)***. It made a big difference to the speed of the operation.

When the coffee rock was cleared the excavator then dug up the roadway it had made into the centre of the creek, and put the material into the trucks to cart away.

At the end of a day's work Sid, the dredge operator, excavator and truck drivers come ashore.

"Sid worked out this way of getting rid of the coffee rock ledges with an excavator. It taught me he was always planning ahead, and always had a plan in reserve if anything went wrong or if the first plan didn't work," says Harold. "It was a lesson that stands me in good stead even today."

* * * *

Dredging and road making was immensely hard work for everyone involved and the costs had blown out far beyond what Sid had expected. Sid was not amused when he heard a Maryborough bloke, Ken Eckert had had a small barge, the *Fraser II,* built and was telling all and sundry he was going to come into Wanggoolba Creek when the dredging was finished.

Sid immediately wrote to Eckert saying he was welcome to use the creek if he was prepared to pay half the costs. He asked Eckert to send his first $250,000. That was the last heard of Eckert's plan. Instead he ran the *Fraser II* from Urangan Boat Harbour to two other points on the island's west coast, Urang Creek and Moon Point.

Finally after almost nine months and with the Christmas holiday rush to the island starting, Sid decided the channel was deep enough for the *Fraser Venture* to come in.

On Boxing Day 1984, the peak day of the year for visitors to come to the island, Sid, friends and a few staff as could be spared from the resort, gathered with a crowd of curious islanders to watch the *Fraser Venture* come into Wanggoolba Creek for the first time.

It was a splendid summer morning, and as the *Fraser Venture* nosed her way into the channel, it could be seen she had a full load of vehicles and the decks were crowded with excited people, ***(below).*** When they saw Sid waiting they cheered and tooted their car horns in spontaneous salute.

All the work had been going on right to the last minute and the ramp ashore was just sand and sloppy sand at that.

It was planned that the vehicles would drive off first then buses would be backed on to the barge deck for the people to board, as they couldn't walk through the slop.

It was not a ceremonial occasion. No-one had time to make things pretty for everyone had worked all through the night. But a friend staying at Eurong, Alan Jones had the forethought to bring a toilet roll with him and before the *Fraser Venture* put her door down and vehicles started to stream off, he made a toilet paper ribbon from one mangrove tree to another across the way. As the first car breasted and broke it, there was a big cheer. And that was that, ***(below).***

Sid commented simply "It has been a massive undertaking. I cannot see how I will recoup the cost in my lifetime, but it will still be there to be used in 100 years.

"If I see something needs doing on this island I have never been one to sit back and expect others to do it. I do it myself and regard it as putting something back into the island which has been such an important part of my life since 1959."

Sid realized a concrete ramp at the head of the channel for vehicles to drive on and off the *Fraser Venture* would be quickly undermined by water seepage.

Instead of building a ramp, he obtained several big unwanted metal plates from an engineering workshop in Maryborough, and placed them in line for vehicles to drive on and off the *Fraser Venture* to the landing. If they became undermined, they could be lifted by crane and repositioned.

The metal plates to make a ramp at the Wanggoolba landing are lifted off the Fraser Venture, above, and put in place, below.

Only a few months later the newly dredged channel began to silt up, with the quite heavy outflow of water from Wanggoolba Creek bringing sand with it, and the sides collapsing. This was as expected with new channels.

A much bigger dredge owned by John McQuade of the Gold Coast came to work in Hervey Bay and when it had finished there, Sid hired it to clean out the creek and remove the remnants of coffee rock. A thoroughly professional outfit, there was no need for Sid to be on hand full time to help.

* * * *

The much loved Studebaker buses had been left at Ungowa, and now the Forestry Department asked Sid to get rid of them. He asked if it would be all right to bury them on the spot and the Forestry agreed.

Harold James was given the job on the front end loader of digging a big hole, then pushing the Studes into it and covering them over again with sand.

At the end of the day one of the day trip drivers was supposed to take Harold back to Eurong. The driver forgot and went without him.

"I was left in pitch dark to make my way home," James remembers.

"It was terrible. I couldn't see the road, and had to feel my way, tripping over tree roots, stumbling through soft sand, having branches hit my face. I heard rustling behind me but I couldn't see where I was going, so I couldn't run.

"Then I heard a car coming, and it was Sid come to pick me up. He'd gone and checked with the day trip driver to make sure I'd got back, and when he found I'd been left behind, came to get me. He was like that."

* * * *

Sid had worked out the *Fraser Venture* timetable in and out of Wanggoolba Creek around the different markets he expected to patronize the vessel, with the initial emphasis on the day trippers.

He knew from personal experience large numbers of them came to the island, but he had no idea how many vehicles would be booked. No-one did, because previous barge services to the island's west coast had been small and irregular.

As it was the vehicle service was an immediate success. The *Fraser Venture* began doing three return crossings a day with up to eight return runs during peak holiday times. The day tour and the vehicle deck were fully booked in peak seasons, and even in the off peak times, the vessel carried good loads. The Forestry Department immediately asked for special runs twice a week to get their workers to and from the island, so they could do away with the expensive Forestry launch.

From its beginning the *Fraser Venture* service into Wanggoolba Creek became the cornerstone of Sid's financial success and the ongoing development of his business. It was a tribute to his foresight – and endurance.

* * * *

The combination of the new ferry and its fast, scheduled run to Fraser Island represented such an immense leap into the future that it is hard now, decades later, to appreciate.

By making access to Fraser Island easy and running to a timetable one chap described as "impeccable", the *Fraser Venture* enabled Hervey Bay to develop as the gateway to the island. It was as if floodgates had opened with visitors pouring through to go to the island.

Over the next few years, as the number of people wanting to visit Fraser grew into the hundreds of thousands, this was largely responsible for the remarkable growth of Hervey Bay, transforming it from a seafront ribbon of small communities to an important tourist destination.

A new four wheel drive hire industry grew up to service those folk who wanted to drive themselves on the island.

Fraser became a "must see" on the major coach company circuit, and motels, hotels and hostels were built in Hervey Bay to accommodate the growing influx of tourists.

It was the beginning of a boom that has continued to gather momentum to this day.

Fraser Island businesses grew rapidly, none more so than Eurong resort.

Sid's day trips, offering so much more to see of the island than earlier trips, attracted many more passengers, and more buses had to be bought and new drivers employed.

To further his relationship with the day trip booking agents, Sid threw a grand party at a Hervey Bay restaurant and announced he would give a holiday prize with the agents having their names put in a draw. The winners of a trip to Singapore were John and Sally Bush, relative newcomers to Hervey Bay who had started a new type of tourism business, a backpacker hostel, an indicator of things to come.

More than 100 people were invited and Sid began to feel a little overwhelmed in his role as host. He thought, because he spent most of his time on the island, many guests wouldn't know who he was and he and they would be tongue tied.

As the guests arrived Sid found he was much better known than he had realised. Every second one remarked "Well that's the first time I've seen you in a suit, Sid."

The only worry Sid had as the party went on into the early hours was that some of the staff there wouldn't wake up in time for work the next morning. Not only did everyone scheduled for work turn up, but so did several who were on days off. They had obviously shared Sid's concern and were there to fill any gaps for their colleagues.

The party was such a success that Sid decided to hold one every year. They became a big feature of Hervey Bay with attendance numbers rising to more than 350 as the years went on and the city grew. It was not only the biggest and most important tourist networking function in the region but when, after the first few years, the superb smorgasbord dinner was prepared by Eurong's head chef, Trevor Henderson it became a showcase for Sid's resort too.

* * * *

The *Fraser Venture* made living on the island so much easier. Driving from Eurong to the mainland involved a mere half hour driving across the island, half an hour having a coffee sitting in a comfortable saloon cruising across the Great Sandy Straits, and half an hour driving from Riverheads to Maryborough. The struggle and problems of getting to the mainland became non existent.

With the new ferry, stores and fuel runs for all the island businesses were shorter and much safer with the trucks no longer having to run along the surf beach between Inskip Point and Eurong.

In November 1984 Sid's enterprise won him the Queensland Small Business Award for Outstanding Achievement.

His award was presented at a ceremony in Brisbane by then Foreign Minister, later Governor General, Bill Hayden, ***(below).***

When Bill asked him to respond, Sid, totally unprepared, nudged me into making his acceptance speech for him and I, equally unprepared, didn't do it very well at all.

Sid won again the following year, and although he knew in advance that if he won, a speech would be called for, he was too shy to say anything, so again I was nudged. But this time I was prepared so I didn't get caught twice with a silly grin on my face and an empty head.

By the following year, to his undoubted relief, Sid's business had grown too big to qualify.

* * * *

After the Paddy Doran stores delivery debacle the previous Christmas, it was small wonder that one of Sid's priorities was to properly organize getting supplies to Eurong.

By this time Murray Reid, the man who had stopped the rampaging fishermen two years before, had become a regular visitor to the house he built at Eurong for himself and his wife Vera as a holiday home.

He had bought an ex-army 6WD Acco truck to carry his building materials to the island from Brisbane, which Sid was quick to notice.

Sid asked Murray if he would consider coming to Eurong to live full time and contract to truck in all the resort supplies and any other trucking jobs that came up.

The Reids discussed it at length for it meant a total change in their lives. Murray was a crane operator/rigger and Vera managed a record store, but by then they had come to love Fraser Island and eventually agreed to Sid's proposal.

Murray, ***(right)*** contracted to Sid for the next 20 years, and became deeply involved in the resort, filling in as a day trip bus driver and barman whenever help was needed as well as transport.

"Carrying the stores on my Acco was quite a job on the rough roads," says Reid.

"I'd have drums of petrol on the bottom of the load, with sheets of board on top of them then cartons of drink and food for the shop and restaurant piled on top of them.

"Sometimes there'd be so much stuff ordered, that I had to leave the tail gate down and carry cartons on it roped down as best I could.

"Many a time as I was driving along on the island a 4WD would race up behind me flashing lights and the driver would give me a carton that had fallen off the truck, or tell me I'd dropped something on the road.

"The ideal when I got to the resort was to go to the shop first to unload, then the hotel, to take off the beer and kegs and finally the generator and bowsers to decant the fuel.

"But often as I approached the resort one of the workers would come running out waving his arms and tell me to go to the power plant first as it was on its last litre of fuel.

"So there I'd go unloading cartons to get to a drum of fuel, and out would go all the resort lights until I could get some fuel poured out of the drum into the tank. Then I'd have to load the cartons on again and head to the shop."

Quite often Sid would turn up to make sure Murray had brought a full load, so he got his money's worth. He soon learned Murray was more than fair, and if he had space left on his truck would go back to the soft drink factory on his own initiative and get more cartons of soft drink to fill it.

* * * *

Other new neighbours who came soon after the Reids were Nigel and Maureen Fremantle. Before long they came up with the idea of a taxi service for the island, then joined the Reids in starting up a tow truck business to recover the never ending series of vehicles in accidents, and take them back to the mainland.

There were many more habitual weekend and holiday time residents, a lively lot, and soon regular get togethers enlivened the limited social life on the island as never before.

These folk also took on many community responsibilities, such as membership of the State Emergency Service and they began an island branch of the Rural Fire Brigade ready to fight the always threatening bush fires.

There were no government funds to equip the fire brigade, so they organized annual Boxing Day cane toad races on the beach at Eurong. There were hamburger and drink stalls and hundreds of holidaymakers gathered to take part in what became an island institution.

For the races a circle was drawn in the sand and a heap of toads, collected the night before, would be dumped out of a sack in the middle of the circle. Bets would be taken as to which toad got to the rim of the circle first, for prizes of cartons of beer.

For identification the toads had numbers painted on their backs, and one day soon after the event, a resort guest approached Sid to remove a toad from her toilet. It was a hapless Number 4.

The toad races raised enough money to build a large shed, which became also a community meeting hall, and buy and equip a second hand fire engine.

There were annual pre-Christmas cricket matches with residents verses the Forestry staff, each side ringing in increasing numbers of players until the Forestry ended up with 54 in its team, most of them from the mainland.

There was great camaraderie as community, resort and Forestry folk all worked and played together to overcome the hardships of isolation, and it was the happiest of times.

Chapter 21

Once the dredging and road works at Wanggoolba Creek were completed, and with the *Fraser Venture* successful beyond all expectation, Sid started to look where to expand next.

On a European coach tour holiday the year before, he had worked out the distance between overnight stops and realized Eurong, now it was so much easier to reach, could be ideally positioned to cater for major coach companies which ran tours up the coast from Sydney to Cairns. When he got home he set about preparing a package of tours, meals and two nights' accommodation to take to major coach company groups. With the *Fraser Venture*, the new buses, and the *Surfside* units, he felt the time was right to make his approach for them to stay at Eurong.

He got an immediate response from AAT Kings, whose owner came to inspect the facilities. Within a short time AAT-Kings tour groups of mainly international visitors started coming to Eurong once a week.

The package worked well and as soon as it appeared in the AAT Kings brochure, other coach companies followed suit. Their overseas marketing helped put Fraser Island on the international map. The coach company business became a major source of year round income for Eurong. Fitting in all those who wanted to stay became a growing problem, and many coach companies were directed to stay at Hervey Bay and come to the island on day tours.

* * * *

Not all efforts to attract international tourists were successful. A trio of Japanese tour operators called on Sid to talk about bringing groups on day tours.

They didn't have time to actually go on a day tour so Sid obliged by driving them around the route himself in his Range Rover. At the end their spokesman asked if the day tour could be done in two hours not eight.

Sid said that wasn't physically possible, so the Japanese told him that they would not be bringing their groups to Fraser Island.

The 1970's fleet of Fraser Island 4 and 6WD buses, a mixture of trucks of all sorts, Studebaker, International and Toyota converted into open beach buses.

In 1983 the fleet was changed to 4WD buses colour coordinated with the new Fraser Venture ferry, below.

The Fraser Venture makes its first entrance into the Wanggoolba Creek landing with a full load of vehicles and passengers on Boxing Day 1984.

Sid gets ready to go to the mainland in his Cherokee 6 aircraft, which he parked on the beachfront at Eurong.

The Rainbow Venture was the second ferry Sid had built. From 1986 it operated between Inskip Point near Rainbow Beach and Hook Point, the southern tip of Fraser Island. It was to involve him in three "barge wars".

The iconic record making 4WD coach, the Australian Explorer was bought to begin day tours from the Sunshine Coast to Fraser Island's rainforest and lakes.

Palm studded Wanggoolba Creek at Central Station

The Fraser Venture was lengthened in 1991 and had a sun deck added to meet the growing demand for travel to Fraser Island from Hervey Bay.

Fraser Dawn was custom built in 1995 to handle the difficult wind and tide conditions at Moon Point. Sid, on the top deck, looks down to see how the new steering leg performs. Below: The Kingfisher Bay ferry.

The Islander, a 275 passenger catamaran, is introduced to the Hervey Bay whale watching fleet in 1992 and in its first season proves to be the most popular vessel operating.

Sid goes to Antarctica to learn more about humpback whales. Here he is bundled up against the -20degree temperature outside the historic Scott's hut with the American McMurdo Base in the background.

Jack Pashley in the tug with Sid and I in front of the Beechcraft Duke, which was sold when Sid began flying helicopters.

Sid did 1000 hours over 10 years flying his Bell Jetranger helicopter.

The impressive portico to Eurong Beach Resort's signature building.

The reception has the theme of timber paneling with green marbleised tops and brass inserts, which carried through the whole of the building

The lounge in Eurong Resort's main building with historic balustrade rails, brought to Australia as ballast in an English sailing ship.

The bar follows the same theme of timber, green tops and brass rails with decorative feature glass.

The free form pool front the main building with the Tradewinds apartments and units at the rear.

The Coral Sea apartments, Eurong Beach.

Lake Birrabeen, one of Fraser Island's unique lakes rimmed by a pure white sand beach, where many of Sid's day trip visitors stopped for a swim.

Discovery One passengers watch a humpback whale close in to the vessel. Below: A new look coach for the day tours from the Sunshine Coast in the early 2000's.

All ready for a tourism function, from the left, May Jensen, Hervey Bay office manager, Trevor Cecil, Islander whale cruise booking agent, Warren Mulrine, head chef at Eurong Beach, Angela, Sid, Terrina and Gerry Geltch of Air Fraser Island. Below: Olympic torchbearers, for the 2000 Sydney Games travel to Fraser Island on the Fraser Venture.

Sid is honoured by his home city of Maryborough by having a plaque with his name on it embedded into the historic wharf precinct foothpath in 2000. Here he is pictured receiving his commemorative certificate by Mayor Alan Brown, left, together with Cleone McRoberts and Peter Olds who were similarly honoured.

An aerial view of Eurong Beach Resort, 2001.

Sid flies in to his then Gold Coast home, Bartinon, after leaving Fraser Island in November 2002.

Sid and his son Bill with Sid's XK120 Jaguar.

Southern Cross II in Acapulco during Sid's voyages around North and Central America from 2002 – 2005.

Cruising under the Golden Gate, San Fransisco.

Masai warriors in Tanzania have never seen a beard like this one.

They politely explained that only "medium" attractions warranted eight hour tours and they did not feel Fraser Island was in this category. Curiously Sid asked what a medium attraction was and the spokesman replied "Paris."

He had no better result with 56 Taiwanese tourists sent by a Sydney travel agent to do a day tour. They would come in a coach from Brisbane for the day. It took 17 calls from Sydney and 5 return phone calls from Eurong to organize their island tour.

Could Sid please provide a tropical fruit platter for them for the *Fraser Venture* crossing? Could he also organize a plate of little cakes? Could he organize another fruit platter with lunch at Eurong? Could he organize a Chinese speaking member of staff to greet them, and thank them for traveling with us? Could he organize two small souvenirs to give to each of them?

Finally all the details were in place and Steve Jensen was to meet them at River Heads and be their main driver-guide for the day.

At 9.10 am Sid received a telephone call from Steve from the River Heads store.

"These Taiwanese people thought they were going to the Barrier Reef," he said.

"O.K. Steve. Tell them how great Fraser Island is, and they'll be happy to come here," Sid instructed.

A quarter of an hour later Steve phoned again "I have talked my head off and they really don't want to come to Fraser Island. They want to go to the Barrier Reef."

Sid recognized that if Steve had talked his head off no-one could have done better. He said "They are going to have to make their minds up because they have already held up the ferry and a lot of other people and it has to go."

Steve replied "The coach captain says they've already been on three day tours from Brisbane already thinking they were going to the Barrier Reef and have refused to go anywhere else. They got so angry with their interpreter, when she took them out west somewhere yesterday, that she resigned and the new interpreter is on her first day and doesn't know how to handle the situation. I don't think they are going to come to the island.

"The coach captain says even if they do come to the island now, with all the mucking around he can only take them back as far as Gympie before his regulation driving time finishes.

"They're going to have to stay in Gympie overnight or wait there for another driver to come from Brisbane to meet them."

The group did not come to Fraser Island. The *Fraser Venture* left without them 45 minutes late. The little cakes got eaten by the crew. The fruit was put out for the day trippers. The souvenirs were put back on the shop shelves. The Chinese speaking staff member went back to her duties in the bistro. Their coach turned around and took the group back to Gympie or Brisbane. We never found out what happened to the new interpreter, but the travel agent in Sydney who organized the tour never afterwards answered his phone.

* * * *

Another year round tourism market of backpackers was in its infancy in Australia. Young people had started to travel the world before settling down to careers, and Australia began to be targeted by them.

Over a few short years Fraser's scenic beauty encouraged many of the young people to put it on their Australian "must see" list along with Sydney, the Great Barrier Reef and the Red Centre.

Coach companies catering specifically for these backpackers started to run from Sydney along the east coast to Cairns and Hervey Bay became a useful break in the journey. Backpacker hostels offering budget accommodation proliferated, competing fiercely for custom at the local bus terminal.

Most of the youngsters wanted a more adventurous island experience than to go on a day tour, and four wheel drive vehicle hire businesses sprung up in the Bay.

The hostel owners cleverly worked out how they could earn more of the backpacker dollar than selling a cheap bed for the night. They bought camping gear, maps and food and hired the vehicles, on-selling the whole package at a good profit.

They put up to 11 youngsters in a long wheel base 4WD, and sent them on their way for a three night camping stopover on the island.

They booked them on the *Fraser Venture*, which now ran two morning and two afternoon return sailings, and soon there were so many backpacker vehicles that they could not all fit on the first sailing of the morning.

Hostel owners worked out between themselves that half would book them on the first sailing, the other half on the second. When they returned, those that had gone earlier would come back on the earlier afternoon sailing three days hence.

With the advent of the backpackers the number of bad vehicle accidents proliferated. Some were caused by recklessness; others simply because the young drivers had no experience of driving on sand roads and beaches.

It was recognized that police were needed on the island primarily to control driving behaviour and arrangements were made to have two officers stationed at Eurong, as the biggest tourist venue on the island, every Christmas to New Year period and Easter. A parcel of land was set aside for a police post but lack of funds meant a stalemate when it came to building.

A rescue helicopter for medical emergencies was available at Nambour, but by the time all the procedures had been gone through to call it out, a doctor had been alerted and it had flown to the island, several hours had often elapsed. There was an aerial ambulance at Bundaberg, but it could not land on Fraser Island.

Sid had agreed the Hervey Bay Air Sea Rescue organization could use the dredged channel into Wanggoolba Creek mouth to pick up medical emergency cases in their vessel, but to get there involved taking a dangerously ill or badly injured person across the island over the rough roads.

In an emergency this was an impossible situation. It was still left to island resort owners to handle the accidents.

"If the injured could be moved and Harry Geltch was available with his plane, he flew them out, sometimes at night with us bringing trucks and buses on to the beach to light up a strip with the headlights for him to take off," says Sid. "But most of the cases we were asked to deal with were very serious."

One emergency brought about a change in thinking. Two young men who were sitting on a vehicle roof rack were thrown off when the driver swerved to avoid a wave.

One man was so badly injured he could not be moved, so Sid alerted Maryborough hospital and a charter plane was organised to bring in a medical team. Murray Hawkings, an ambulance bearer with the team was also Superintendent of the volunteer St. Johns Ambulance Brigade.

He spoke to Sid briefly at the scene and proposed that, with Sid's help, St. John's could look at setting up a first aid post at Eurong during peak holiday periods.

Sid promised all help in fund raising to buy a caravan for the St. Johns Brigade, medical equipment and possibly an ex-army four wheel drive ambulance. I wrote to the Health Minister, Brian Austin asking for help to buy a second hand 4WD vehicle if Eurong resort also contributed. He did not reply.

The year before, the resort, through the efforts of tour driver Steve Jensen, had raised $3000 to provide a radio tower on a headland just south of Rainbow Beach to cover the Cooloola and Fraser Island coast for medical emergencies.

Murray Hawkings set about arousing the interest of Maryborough people in fund raising for an island first aid post. There were some great responses.

Les Smith a worker at the Maryborough TAFE College volunteered to do a sponsored swim from the mainland to the island. Sid offered the *Fraser Venture* to cruise alongside him so people could watch and with the Apex Club selling tickets and food on board, more than $700 was raised.

Two men, John Robertson a Gympie stud master and Kev Patroni, a Tin Can Bay forestry worker raised funds on a sponsored walk 320 kilometres around Fraser Island.

It took them a week and they got sunburned and very sore ankles from walking through soft sand. John said he nearly gave in after he was woken one night by a dingo licking his face.

The 12 Sunday morning golfers of the Craignish Country Club near Hervey Bay proved they had more than a one a week golf game in them and came up with the idea of hitting a golf ball in relay all the way up Fraser's surf beach from Eurong to the *Maheno* shipwreck, a distance of 32 km. They sold 50c tickets for guesses how many strokes it would take them using only a no.5 iron, with a donated grocery order for the winner.

Putting the factors involved such as lost and buried golf balls, wind, tide, creek crossings and such into a new fangled computer, they expected the golf marathon would take them 18 hours so they brought four support vehicles laden with food and drink to last them through the day and half the night. They also brought 160 golf balls. They completed the course in three hours 50 minutes and were back in the Eurong pub by lunchtime.

They had lost only six balls. Through ticket sales and donations from campers and day trippers they raised more than $500.

Others in Maryborough became involved and a committee to establish the St.John's post was formed. Sid and I were invited to the first committee meeting and were amazed at the wrangling that broke out. One doctor said that nothing less than a full time doctor and nursing sisters with the latest in equipment would suffice. He was talking $10,000s every year. We kept thinking of the modest sums raised so far. Sid intervened and said the good doctor's ideas, while ideal, were far too ambitious.

The doctor repeated nothing less would do. Sid responded "Right now we have nothing at all, except totally unqualified people, coping as best we can. A first aid post has to be better than that."

The issue of ambulance boundaries was raised. Eurong was in the Maryborough Hospital area which had its own ambulance service. A Queensland Ambulance Service superintendent based in Hervey Bay then pointed out that if we did manage to buy a four wheel drive ambulance, and it came on the *Fraser Venture* with an accident victim to River Heads, which came under his jurisdiction, he might not let it through en route to the Maryborough hospital.

Sid said seriously "I'll make sure I'm driving it then."

The committee was by-passed from then on. The St. John's Ambulance people made a direct approach to Sid and he agreed he would continue to raise money. By Easter 1984 a second hand caravan had been bought and the first aid post opened in the resort camping ground.

Over that Easter weekend the St. John volunteers treated 24 medical cases and organized the evacuation to the mainland of six more urgent ones.

These included a young lad with concussion after falling from a 4WD on the surf beach; two men with burned feet after a fuel leakage on their beached boat ignited; a girl hit in the face by a cricket bat and a man who cut himself with an axe while chopping wood.

For recognizing the need and starting up the post, the Maryborough St. John's Ambulance Brigade was awarded a special citation.

The St John's first aid post was to last at Eurong Beach Resort until September 1992, when ironically the number of cases it was handling was so great, it placed too big a drain on the St John's volunteers and donor resources. Appeals to the Queensland Government and local government for help with funding met with no result.

Chapter 22

No-one kept records so no-one knew how many people were coming to the island each year by that time, but the then island forester, Murray Keys, said that during the peak holiday weeks in early January 1984 his staff had counted between 1,000 and 1,500 people a day through Central Station, half on tours and half in private vehicles.

There was no equipment or programme for road maintenance to restore the sand roads after increasing numbers of vehicles of all sizes, in the hands of drivers unskilled in sand conditions, had been bogged and dug out. Only heavy rain washing loose sand into the holes they created made the roads reasonably trafficable again. The Forestry Department tried to repair the roads by putting truckloads of woodchip in the bigger holes, but as soon as it rained it was washed away. Sid bought woodchip for the roads too as it was all the Forestry would allow, short term though its effect was.

There was still only a single vehicle width road from Wanggoolba Creek to Eurong. One day trip driver, that Christmas, reported having to stop his bus, pull off, or wait for an oncoming small vehicle to back up to a place its driver could get off the road, 94 times between Central Station and Eurong.

Once again the Queensland Government through the Forestry Department sought to limit the number of tours to the island rather than private or hire vehicles.

In 1985 it placed a moratorium on the issue of any more tour licenses, and decreed that if licenses weren't being used to at least 50 per cent of their passenger capacity, they would be taken off the operator.

The moratorium gave the licenses a monetary value they had not had before, but several folk who had found operating a tour on Fraser was far harder than the dream job they had imagined, and were just sitting on their licenses, were now happy to sell them, rather than have the Forestry Department take them with no recompense. Seeing Sid as their best bet for a quick sale they came and offered their licences to him.

With his usual foresight that, as his business kept on growing, he would need more passenger numbers in the future than he had been originally been allotted, he bought a number of them of them.

One was a half share in an island day tour from Rainbow Beach called Sun Safaris.

The purchase of another tour, from Hervey Bay to Buff Creek and Dilli Village, brought Sid one of its owners as a new employee. Don Caswell was a well qualified skipper with experience in large coastal vessels. He was the chap who had held up his hand to offer to organise the introductory party night for the *Fraser Venture* as a fund raiser for the Hervey Bay Air Sea Rescue, and had done an excellent job.

By now Laurie Toy had more than enough work to keep him busy in the workshop, so Don took his place as relief skipper on the *Fraser Venture* for four days a fortnight. He was roped in as a driver for his other days' work.

"Sid started me off driving a gravel truck across the island to Eurong," says Don. "He said it'd teach me the route so I wouldn't get lost in the maze of tracks."

He graduated to driving the day tour buses and loved to tell his passengers about the old days on Fraser Island, when there was only one remedy if a timber cutter or Forestry worker was bitten by a venomous snake, and that was amputation. His audience would inevitably show their disbelief, so Don would hold up his hand, missing one finger after a boating accident, and say "It's true, look."

* * * *

The major problem with buses on Fraser Island was caused by them being driven in salt conditions along the surf beach. The bus bodies rusted out long before the motors and running gear wore out, because the buses were doing only a few kilometres each day.

To Sid the solution was to buy second hand buses with bodies in good condition from mainland owners, and put those bodies on the running gear of his 4WD island buses to replace the original rusting bodies. It was an economical way to build up and keep a good and good looking fleet of 4WD buses in operation, which enabled him to keep the prices for his tours down.

The workshop became one of very few in Australia licensed to convert conventional buses into 4WD buses.

Sid would regularly go on forays around mainland bus companies looking for buses he could buy to convert for the island.

In this era Sid invariably wore a peak cap, and one he hung on to was an increasingly tattered cap with a CAT badge on the front advertising Caterpillar motors and trucks. He was wearing it one time when he went to northern New South Wales looking for buses. No sooner did he walk through the door at one big bus company, than he was given the royal treatment.

A quick telephone call from the manager brought the company owner hurrying from home to give Sid a conducted tour of the works, show him the coach fleet, ply him with coffee and all, for about two hours.

Then the owner remarked "I'm surprised to see you here so quickly."

Sid, whose visit was purely on spec and with no forewarning, wondered what the fellow was talking about and said as much. It emerged the bus company had been bought just that morning for millions of dollars by the NSW Caterpillar motor importer and everyone had assumed Sid was he – all because of the old cap.

Telling the story when he got home, Sid said his only regret was that if he'd known what was going on and had played his cards right, he could have had the bus company deliver half a dozen buses straight to Hervey Bay for him.

More mechanics were needed to help Laurie Toy rebuild buses as well as maintain what became a steadily growing number of them as well as the *Fraser Venture.*

Toy says Sid was a "rare boss, who knew everything about his whole operation and how it should run. It made it very simple for us. If something went wrong and we weren't sure how to fix it, one phone call to Sid got an immediate answer. There was never any drama about getting anything organized. He knew exactly what to do and how to do it because of his experience. He got everyone working as a team."

As an example of teamwork, Laurie remembers one emergency when the main generator at Eurong died, which meant there was no water, no lights, no petrol bowsers working and the freezer and cold rooms had to stay closed so as not to lose the cold air.

"Sid was in Maryborough and the staff finally managed to get in touch with him early in the afternoon." Laurie describes. "He went straight around to electrical engineer, Graham Dix, and only just gave him time to throw some clothes in a bag before he had him on Fraser Island looking at the generator.

"They found it had burnt out, so set about starting the stand by plant which had stood idle for quite some time. They cleaned it up but as they tried to get it firing the starter motor flew apart.

"I was skippering the *Fraser Venture* on the way to River Heads when Sid radioed me to get a couple of spare starter motors I had in the workshop at home, over to Eurong quick smart.

"As soon as I landed it I shot off home leaving Elaine to tie up. We also did a Friday evening run, and she had to explain to boarding passengers they would have to wait for the skipper to get back.

"I got back, drove straight on board and took the ferry across to the island while one of the passengers, island taxi owner, Nigel Fremantle put the starter motors in his vehicle. When we landed we held all the other vehicles back, so Nigel could race off and across to Eurong."

Harold James takes up the story "The starter motors arrived at 8.15 pm. They didn't fit the generator. Sid, Graham Dix, resort mechanic Dave Muller and I set to work by torch and gas light to pull them apart and make one starter motor out of the two that Laurie had sent and the broken one.

"We found we needed to grind some of the motor casing. To do that we needed power. Dave raced to a neighbour to borrow a portable generator to fit on to his grinder. The portable generator broke down, so we had to fix that. Fortunately it was only carbon build up on a spark plug.

"After starting work on the generator at 5 pm we finally got it going at 5 am working through the night, with only a short meal break while we were waiting for the starter motors to arrive.

"Guests were great – wining and dining by candlelight as part of the great island experience.

"We were all too exhausted even to pat ourselves on the back."

After this incident Sid wanted a backup generator.

When he saw the local electricity board had one it had used in time gone by to light the little seaside township of Burrum Heads, he put in a bid for it. The electricity board gave it to him.

It weighed eight tons and was lifted on to Murray's Acco with a crane. However there was no crane at Eurong to lift it off. Sid came up with the solution of digging a hole in the sand with one sloping side for the truck to back into, so that its tray was level with the ground just outside the shed where the generator was to be housed. Then it was a comparatively simple matter of pulling the generator off the back of the truck and on rollers into the shed with another truck.

* * * *

For all their mutual respect, Laurie had some memorable set to's with Sid.

"We got bigger buses and I was backing one out of the workshop at my place in a hurry to get it to the ferry to go over to Fraser, and backed it into a tree. It was a fair whack, which took the back seat out," Toy says. "I had to phone to tell Sid and he gave me the sack. Next morning he phones and tells me I have to get the bus going again by the next day, when it was urgently needed. I think we managed to do it too.

"He never held a grudge. He'd shout and then it was soon over. I got fired another time one Thursday night and on Friday morning he phoned to ask if a bus was ready to go. I said 'You fired me yesterday,' and he replied 'That was yesterday.'

"There were some funny incidents. One day Sid came to the workshop and was shouting about something that had gone wrong as he approached. Tommy Cunningham was there using a grinder and sparks flew up and ignited the two way radio battery.

"Sid was just about inside the workshop when the battery blew up and showered the place with battery acid. There was absolute silence. Sid completely forgot what he'd been shouting about.

"There was another time he surprised me. Elaine and her friend Marilyn were fencing our place along the road, and a friend stopped to chat to them, then Sid came by in his Range Rover and stopped to chat too. A police car came along and the copper must have been looking to see if there had been an accident with all these people standing around on the road edge.

"Instead of watching where he was going he ran right into the back of the Range Rover. I expected Sid would explode but he simply walked over and asked the copper 'What did you do that for?'"

* * * *

Sid kept a careful eye, or at least ear, on his business. All the day tour drivers and ferry crews were well aware that when he was at Eurong or in his car he monitored the radio network, and there were frequent calls back and forth.

Mal Clonan recalls that one day when he was a new tour driver, he had radioed Eurong with the day tour numbers from the *Fraser Venture* wheelhouse so the kitchen staff could be told how many lunches were needed, and knowing Sid would be listening in, added that Sid's mother was on board.

"There was a pause," says Mal, "then Sid asked for confirmation. I told him she was in the wheelhouse with us. Next he asked whether his mother had a ticket.

"I wasn't sure what to do, but replied 'I didn't know your mother needed a ticket.'

"Sid came back 'Mal you have been working for me for several weeks and you know the cost of a tour.

"I was completely bamboozled, and after a lot of thought I asked 'Do you want me to charge your mother?'

"There was another long pause to let me stew and eventually Sid replied 'No, she can travel for free.'

"Sid's mum, listening to all this and enjoying my embarrassment simply laughed and said 'He's a bugger isn't he?' I was so relieved it was all a joke.

"But it wasn't the only one he had at my expense. Another time I was doing the day trip solo with a full complement of passengers in the bus. Our first stop was at Lake Birrabeen and getting there was all right but getting back up a long hill in very soft sand was very difficult.

"I unloaded all the passengers, deflated the tyres, put brush and debris in the wheel tracks and things still weren't looking good.

"Afraid we would break a front axle, I radioed Eurong to advise my situation and suggest a driver from the resort be on standby to bring another bus to pick up the passengers in case I couldn't get up the hill.

"It was a very weak signal from where I was. Sid answered and suggested all the things I had already done, then the radio reception got worse. I couldn't hear what he was saying so asked him to 'please repeat,' several times.

"Sid finally responded by saying 'You have a $100 a week pay rise. I bet you can hear that.' I was used to his humour by now and replied 'I copy the part about the pay rise, but what about the bus?'"

Mal also tells "When the day trip buses on their return across the island came within radio range of the *Fraser Venture,* the drivers would always call the skipper to let him know they were on their way and when to expect them.

"Knowing Sid was always listening and never wanted the scheduled sailings to run late, we drivers had a code. If we radioed through saying we were on time the skipper would know we were 15 minutes late. If we said we were 'on time, on time,' we were 10 minutes late. If we said we were 'on time, on time, on time,' we were actually on time."

Clonan adds "Sid always thought we were punctual drivers."

In that he was completely wrong. It took Sid no time at all to work out the code – and many other supposedly secret messages.

When Peter Young, one of the relieving skippers, was mooring the ferry at River Heads one day, he knocked the outboard motor off the dinghy that the crew used to get ashore and it sank.

"I hired a diver who eventually found the outboard, and I took it to Don Caswell's to repair. I asked him not to tell Sid and he promised he wouldn't. Three days later the outboard was fixed and back on the dinghy," says Young.

"When Sid was next on board the *Venture* he came to sit up in the wheelhouse as usual. He said "You found the outboard eh?' I still don't know how or when he found out. He'd never said a word about it before."

Skipper Harry Brutnall also tried to keep secret that one day he had dropped the ferry door on the dinghy and squashed it. He worked diligently to hammer the sides back in to shape, and thought he'd got away with it until the next time Sid was on board the *Venture* and asked to see the log book.

He turned unerringly to the date the accident happened and read aloud "Reduced freeboard on dinghy huh? I wondered how you were going to record that in the log."

* * * *

In early 1985 Sid was approached for help by Rex and Gloria Bacon, a middle aged couple who had moved to Hervey Bay from Victoria in pursuit of a more carefree lifestyle. They had bought a flat bottomed launch called *The Crab,* which they decked out very nicely to take passengers on leisurely cruises in the Great Sandy Straits. Unfortunately demand for their cruises was minimal and the Bacons were in dire financial straits.

They came to ask Sid if they could work with him in operating to Fraser Island, bringing passengers on a relaxed cruise in *The Crab* from Urangan Boat Harbour into the ferry channel at Wanggoolba Creek, then transferring them on to one of Sid's buses for a shorter tour of Fraser Island, visiting Central Station, Lake Birrabeen and Eurong but without a drive up the surf beach. It was very similar to the cruises and tours Sid and the Toy family had done before the advent of the *Fraser Venture.*

Sid felt very sorry for the Bacons, and agreed to their idea. The new cruise and tour began in May two or three days a week. But it was not a great success.

Visitors wanted to maximize their time on Fraser Island, not getting there, no matter how attractive the Bacons made their cruise with boom netting and Devonshire teas.

The Fraser Venture is put on the bank at Wanggoolba Creek to have work done while The Crab cruises past in the channel.

The Bacons persevered for about a year, for there was little other work they could get for *The Crab,* until another whole new tourism industry began in Hervey Bay, whale watching.

A couple who ran a charter fishing business, Brian and Jill Perry noticed their clients were far more excited when they saw humpback whales in Hervey Bay than at the fish they caught.

The Perry's thought maybe whale watching would be an added attraction between fishing trips, and put a classified advertisement in the *Maryborough Chronicle.* From such small beginnings do big businesses grow.

Within a few weeks every charter boat in Hervey Bay had switched from fishing to whale watching cruises and was packed with people.

Rex and Gloria Bacon joined the bandwagon.

They got good bookings for their first whale watch cruise, when sadly Rex had a fatal heart attack. Gloria went ahead with the cruise, and invited Sid and I. To our amazement when *The Crab* was well out to sea, Gloria asked us to come to the rear deck, while she poured Rex's ashes overboard. It was a cruel irony that after struggling for so long Rex did not survive to see his business become a success at last.

* * * *

One incident during this time was when the *Fraser Venture* needed some work to its propeller and was motored over to the bank of the Wanggoolba Creek channel to go high and dry when the tide ran out. A team of mechanics walked out on the sand flat to do the work and I went along too. After a while I got bored, so walked up on to the ferry, got myself a Mars bar from the saloon, went to the toilet and walked back down to the sand.

All the mechanics had stopped work and were looking at me. Sid said "Have you been on the ferry?" With the Mars bar in my hand I couldn't very well say "No." Then Sid said "Did you go to the toilet?" I knew I was in trouble, but didn't know why.

Sid said "Do you know how toilets work on vessels?" I said I hadn't even thought about it.

So he said "Well, do you know why you shouldn't flush the toilet on a train while it is standing in a station?"

I knew that and looked around. One of the mechanics was wet through.

So mainland staff did not miss out on Sid's 49th birthday party at Eurong, he had a second party for them in Hervey Bay. From the left rear are Laurie Toy, Russ Parker, Elaine Toy, Harry Geltch, Pam Williams, Max Williams, Julie Richardson and Harry Brutnell. Seated at the front are Angela, Sid, and Ron Coleman.

Sid gives a special hug to the marine girls, Elaine Toy and Julie Richardson, deckies on the Fraser Venture. Both worked on Sid's vessels for almost two decades.

Chapter 23

A management plan for Fraser Island had been drawn up by the Queensland Government in 1978, in the wake of sand mining and as tourists started to arrive in significant numbers, but few, if any of its initiatives had been implemented. Although some of the timber royalties were diverted to work on tourist areas, there wasn't enough money to do any major works.

By 1984 complaints about conditions on Fraser Island were coming from all quarters, government departments, business folk, conservationists, 4WD Associations and more. The island looked set to continue as a hot political issue. Queensland Premier, Sir Joh Bjelke Petersen announced that his department was going to investigate.

Sid immediately had me write to Sir Joh, welcoming any initiative that would lead to better management and offering his help.

Soon after he had a visit from Peter Ellis of the Premier's Department who wanted to know what Sid considered the greatest problems facing the island. They talked for several hours and Ellis said he had not realized the extent of the issues and hardly knew where to start listing them in his report to the premier.

At one point he asked if he could use the phone, and was told he would have to wait until Sid's staff had moved a tree that had fallen across the line, and restrung it.

Surprised he said "You don't have a Telecom phone? You didn't mention that was a problem." Sid replied there had been promises of a radio phone system for years, but we had begun to doubt we would ever get a good telephone service.

Ellis said the government was looking at establishing camping grounds along the beach to try to break holidaymakers of their uncontrolled camping habits and asked Sid who he thought would best manage them and tourism on the island generally.

Sid said "Without a doubt the Forestry Department."

While he never stopped complaining about the roads, he recognized maintaining them was beyond the departmental budget and he appreciated the genuine efforts the Forestry staff on the island was doing in all sorts of other areas.

Enlightened administration since the tourism boom began had led the Forestry to do a tremendous amount of work outside the normal parameters of its job of managing the state forests.

It had established camping grounds at Central Station and at Lake McKenzie and Lake Boemigen; developed walking tracks and produced a hand book for tour operators so that correct information would be given to the passengers they transported.

The northern section of Fraser Island from Sandy Cape to Indian Head had been managed by the National Park Service since 1971, but Sid knew little about how it was run simply because it was so far from Eurong. He was not surprised to learn however that the National Parks rangers were baulking at the idea they should clean toilets and empty rubbish bins.

Ellis pointed out the government received no direct income from Fraser Island to fund the measures spoken of, and put forward the idea that people coming to the island should pay for services. It was not a new suggestion. The 1978 management plan for Fraser Island had recommended that a fee be levied on private vehicles and day tour passengers. Again it hadn't been implemented, perhaps because it was felt it would be too politically unpopular. While recognizing a fee system was inevitable, Sid advised that the fees should not be so high as to deter visitors.

To get the ball rolling in improving island facilities, Sir Joh organised a one off loan of $2 million to the Forestry Department and National Parks Service to do an ambitious programme of capital works. A Fraser Island Recreation Board was set up to manage the island, comprised of senior Forestry and National Parks officers.

Plans were put in hand to build boardwalks along the banks of Wanggoolba and Eli Creeks to save them being further trampled. An information centre was to be built at Eurong, as were two toilet blocks in popular areas. More barbecues and shelter sheds would be built in the camping grounds at Central Station and Lake McKenzie.

Stretches of surf beach fore dunes were to be fenced to keep brumbies and campers out to allow dune grasses to regrow. Tree planting would be done in denuded areas.

Steep hills on selected roads would be boarded and rubbish collected.

New island forester, Mark Planck plotted the route for a new road to run parallel to the existing road from behind Eurong to within a couple of kilometres of Wanggoolba Creek barge landing, so that the roads could be one way and the problem of hold ups due to oncoming traffic ended. The new road was so desperately needed that it was the first priority and as soon as it was bulldozed through the bush, everyone started using it, in spite of Forestry pleas to give it time to settle.

In the dry seasons bogs and huge holes still developed but now there was twice the length of road to try and keep trafficable. Broken axles in the buses were such a major issue, that little Ross Williams, Max's grandson, knew all about them.

He was just five years old when Max took him to a Brisbane Motor Show. Everyone was admiring a new four wheel drive vehicle that had just come onto the market, when from underneath it came a voice "Granddad you should just see the axles on this. They wouldn't last five minutes on Fraser Island."

* * * *

In mid 1985, the Queensland Government gave notice that it was preparing special legislation so that every vehicle, except those of residents, coming on to Fraser Island had to have a permit, and an access fee had to be paid. There were to be camping fees for every site, even camping along the beaches and there was to be a per head levy for every passenger on the day trips.

There was an immediate furore. When it was forecast the access fee would be $40 per vehicle, the members of various 4WD clubs gathered in protest outside the Queensland Parliament.

When asked by the media to comment, Sid forthrightly declared $40 was too much to ask. "Charge $40 and you will close down Fraser Island," he declared in the Brisbane *Courier Mail* in February 1985.

"Nobody realizes how far reaching the effects will be: we spend more than $1million a year in Maryborough on supplies and more than that when we are building. Put in a $40 toll and I will be down to collect my dole."

Ever colourful in his imagery he even suggested beat-the-toll "rum runs" could well develop, with vehicles being ferried to Fraser Island after dark.

However the Government had played it crafty by allowing forecasts of a $40 vehicle fee to be bandied about so that when the actual fee was $10, it rather pulled the rug from under the protesters. To try and lessen the impact, Sid introduced half price $10 same day return fares for vehicles on the *Fraser Venture.*

The passenger levy on the tour operators was also a smaller than expected sum, $1 a head, and the tour operators' planned withholding of the money from the government in protest, didn't eventuate.

In frustration at the ongoing bad state of the roads leading to so many bus breakdowns, Sid even offered to pay an additional 50c per passenger levy from his tours to go towards employing a contractor to keep the most heavily used Wanggoolba-Eurong roads in better repair. This would have amounted to about $20,000 a year, a huge sum for the time, and as well as his own tours would have made things easier for many rival tours as well as the public in their own vehicles. But his good intentions backfired on him.

He was asked to go and see the then District Forester, Peter Lupus in Maryborough with his proposal, so did so. Lupus accepted Sid's offer, then added "Of course there is no guarantee the money will be spent on the roads. If we need a new vehicle, it might be spent on that."

Sid was so angry that, pounding hard on Lupus' desk, he withdrew his offer then marched out, with Lupus shouting after him "Don't you ever come in here again."

When some months later Lupus phoned to ask Sid to go and see him on another matter, Sid cheekily reminded him he was barred and said if Lupus wanted to see him he would have to come to the island - and pay a barge fare to do so.

He was still prepared to do his bit towards better roads however. He advocated the building of a bitumen road across the island as the only solution.

When a major road making firm, Boral, approached the Queensland government with a quotation to build a bitumen road from Wanggoolba landing to Eurong, repayable over 10 years, Sid was there to help reduce the cost to government.

He offered to bring all the truck loads of road making material over on the *Fraser Venture* at no charge.

The government however did not want a bitumen road, it was said, for fear two wheel drive cars would come on to the island and cause endless problems by driving off the road and on to the beach. Instead the government tried all sorts of other road hardening methods, such as laying strips of rubber on the road and putting sand over them. Of course the tyres of laden trucks and buses soon ripped up the rubber.

When the new Fraser Island access and camping levies were introduced in February 1986, there was an immediate and startling downturn in the number of people coming to the island. Businesses reported a massive 50 per cent decline in trade for Easter, one of Fraser's traditionally peak holiday periods. The following June school holiday period was one of the quietest for many years.

* * * *

Amid all the government induced kerfuffle and worries about the future of his business, Sid had his 50th birthday on August 5 1986, and marked this momentous occasion by shaving off Fraser Island's most famous and long lasting beard.

It was the first time his chin had been exposed to the elements for more than a quarter of a century. In an era when every other chap was clean shaven, Sid had grown the beard as a promotions gimmick for his new Fraser Island day trips. After that he never took to the idea of using a razor again. Indeed, as bushy bearded photographs of the time testify, it was with some difficulty that he could be persuaded to go to the barber to have the beard trimmed. His favourite saying on the subject was "I go to the barber every six months whether I need it or not." He always needed it.

So when he announced the beard was doomed on his birthday there was untold scepticism. Two Maryborough businessmen, Jimmy Stevenson who supplied the resort with fuel and Paddy Stephenson who supplied the gas, even had bets with each other for a casket ticket. Barber, Ken Owens of Hervey Bay got such a shock when Sid turned up before the customary six months was up, that he removed the beard for him as a birthday present. When Sid's mum rang to wish him happy birthday and he told her the beard was gone, she came to Eurong the next day to see what he looked like under all the hair, because she had forgotten.

Chapter 24

A huge improvement in the lives of Fraser Islanders – and visitors – came about in 1985 when Telecom brought modern communications, in the form of automatic trunk dialing, to Fraser.

It was only the size of the *Fraser Venture* and Sid's organization skills, that made it possible to get all the equipment needed to the chosen island sites for the radio towers.

A mammoth undertaking, it took a year from start to finish. It involved the building of four tall steel towers on the highest dunes on the island to beam radio signals to Hervey Bay. The Telecom crew had no concept of what was involved for them at the outset – but they soon learned. It is fair to say that without the help and local knowledge of Sid and his staff, quite apart from the use of the *Fraser Venture,* it might not have been achieved, and certainly not as efficiently as it was.

Huge quantities of material had to be shipped to the island then trucked to each of the four sites, gravel, sand and cement for tower foundations, tonnes of steel for the towers, fencing to make secure compounds at the base of each tower, fragile solar panels and huts full of $100,000's worth of sensitive electronic equipment.

In the beginning Telecom believed the only way to get, at the very least, the huts to the sites was by helicopter. An approach was made to the R.A.A.F. in Amberley who said it would be a useful exercise for them with their big Chinook helicopters. Then the RAAF bloke added "Of course if the loads get a bit of a sway up, they would be cut loose and dropped." So that was the end of that, and Telecom turned to Sid to do the job by barge and truck.

He contracted to deliver all the materials to the four sites, the most accessible behind Eurong, then, heading north, Bogimbah behind Happy Valley, the third near Lake Bowarrady and the fourth on the least accessible and highest dune, behind Orchid Beach.

All the materials would be trucked on the *Fraser Venture* to landing points on the island's calm water west coast.

To bring the materials for the Eurong tower, the tallest at 64.1m, was the most straightforward, for the barge landing at Wanggoolba Creek and the roads to the site were well in place and comparatively wide to allow the passage of Sid's day tour buses. The only problem was presented by the size of the telephone exchange hut of electronic gear. It was 4.5 m high, 6 m long and three metres wide. Mounted on the back of a truck, it reached up into the canopy of large tree branches growing across the track just above bus height.

Sid solved the problem by having the body taken off an ex army Acco truck and the hut lifted directly on to its chassis, which lowered the overall height by half a metre. Even so a Telecom worker had to sit on top of the hut ready to cut branches that would obstruct its progress as Harold James drove it gingerly along, ***(right).***

* * * *

For the Bogimbah tower, behind Happy Valley, the *Fraser Venture* carried its heaviest load yet of 130 tonnes with trucks of gravel, including the famous Peterbilt, cranes, cement agitator trucks and an excavator.

Early one morning at high tide the barge edged over the sand flats between mangroves into Urang Creek, ***(above)*** to offload alongside the wooden ramp Sid had made to get his loads of fuel ashore in the 1960's. Skipper Harry Brutnall said he felt like Humphrey Bogart on the *African Queen* winding the way through the mangroves.

Sid directs an excavator off the Fraser Venture at Urang Creek.

Sid dumps the load of gravel for the Bogimbah job and drives the Peterbilt back on board.

The Bogimbah site had been cleared beforehand by timber cutter Andy Postan on his bulldozer. There was a foretaste of things to come because his dozer broke down and he had a long walk home. He wasn't heard of for two days.

"We loaded the gravel from the Peterbilt on to smaller trucks and didn't do too badly driving all the trucks across the island, until we came to the steep hill where the tower was to be built on top." says Harold James.

"The biggest problem was the Acco truck with the hut. There were huge holes in the road, and one of the Acco wheels fell into a hole. The truck tipped and I thought the hut was gone. But I managed to drive the Acco out slowly and steadily. The whole thing was absolutely nerve wracking."

* * * *

The loads for the final two towers at Mt. Bowarrady and behind Orchid Beach had to be dropped on the notoriously soft and often narrow north western beach, with which Sid had plenty of experience in his Orchid Beach cartage days.

Sid decided his whole truck fleet and Murray Reid's Acco would take all the necessary equipment and materials to the Mount Bowarrady site on one *Fraser Venture* load, so as not to keep running the risk with the difficult beach landing.

Nothing was straightforward from the start. A long shallow, sloping beach meant that the *Venture* skipper, Harry Brutnall, could not pull right on to the beach to let the trucks drive off.

Picking his time between waves, the most experienced driver, Murray Reid led the way in his Acco, dropping into more than a metre of water off the barge door, then ploughing his way to shore to show the other drivers how it was to be done.

"I had about $100,000 worth of batteries on my Acco," Murray describes. "I drove gently off the barge door and the truck just kept on going down with me thinking 'Just how deep is this?' Water came over my boots in the cab. Then the truck came up and out and I got it safely on to hard sand.

"Tommy Cunningham had to drive off next with Sid's front end loader, which was coming with the trucks to get us out of trouble, and then I had to scramble back aboard for the truck with the exchange hut on it," Murray says.

"We'd chained the hut on the chassis and put lumps of timber between the springs and chassis so it wouldn't rock about. Then I drove that off the door, all too well aware that if the hut slipped forwards, it would have taken me and the truck cab off with it. But we got it on to the beach in one piece.

"Tommy set off ahead of the trucks with the loader to clear the track ahead. I followed with the hut but it started to rock and roll in the potholes, so Tommy had to smooth the road out in front, as well as clearing trees off the track. We didn't have chain saws so he had to push the trees over.

"When we got to the bottom of the long steep hill the tower was to be built on, I thought we'd never get the truck with the hut up it. We put galvanized iron either side of the hut to protect it if it hit trees. The track deviated, then made a sharp left hand turn. To get around that, we used a big tree on the corner to swivel the truck around, scraping along the iron."

It was about 16 km from the beach where the *Fraser Venture* landed to Mount Bowarrady.

The Telecom man in charge of the job, John Whiting, hadn't been on the Bowarrady road in anything bigger than a Toyota. He did not realize how many trees would have to be pushed over, branches lopped, and washouts filled before the trucks, especially the one with the hut on the back, could get through.

He looked at the map and estimated it would only take a couple of hours to get the materials and hut through from the beach to the top of the hill, but said if the worst came to the worst the men might have to camp overnight.

"That's the longest two hours I've ever worked," said one Telecom chap when, nine days later, the job was done.

* * * *

After the Mount Bowarrady experience Telecom supplied a D5 bulldozer for the next stage, to take the fourth hut and materials to a high dune at the back of Orchid Beach.

John Whiting looked at a map again and seeing the cross island track was about 12 km, and having learned from the earlier experience, announced it would take up to two days to get the materials to the site, once the trucks were ashore at Wathumba Creek.

He would not be dissuaded, but Sid had his cook load the truck drivers up with food and drink for four days. He knew the track would be largely overgrown, never having been used by large vehicles since the building of Orchid Beach resort had finished in the early 1970's. He too fell far short in his estimate how long the job would take.

On the evening of the fourth day Murray Reid and Tommy Cunningham arrived back at Eurong for more supplies and clean clothes for everyone and took off again early next morning. The entire trip to the top of the dune behind Orchid Beach took ten days.

Again the trucks with the gear had to be offloaded from the *Fraser Venture* door in deep water on the long shelving beach, but this was just the beginning of the problems.

The trucks then had to be driven across the notorious Wathumba Creek estuary, which has invisible soft sand bogs and yabby banks all through it.

Sid had prepared his drivers with chains, and instructed the trucks be chained together in a long line behind the bulldozer to drive up the beach and across the estuary, so that if a heavily laden truck got bogged, it could be pulled to safety.

It looked like a line of circus elephants, holding tails with trunks, making the crossing through water at times up to the truck axles.

Once the trucks got across the estuary and with the dozer clearing the track, they got about a quarter way across the island, when they were met by a couple of National Parks officers who viewed the bulldozer, blade down making a road across, with grave dismay, and forbad the convoy to go any further.

"The Telecom foreman, Bushy Lee produced a piece of paper which was a way leave pass entitling Telecom to go through," says Murray Reid.

Promises were exacted that the least amount of road widening would be done to let the trucks through, and the least number of branches lopped off trees to let the high load of the exchange hut pass. This meant the dozer had to make slow progress through the overgrown track ahead of the trucks and branches had to be individually lopped off the overhanging trees.

"The final hill was far steeper and scarier than even Bowarrady with a long stretch of very soft sand just after a sharp turn," Reid describes.

"We had the dozer go ahead and once it got on to the top ridge, we strung cables from it over the hut to the chassis to hold it upright, and climbed up, the poor old truck groaning. It took two days to get all the equipment to the top of this hill and unloaded.

"Coming down the hill again the Acco lost its brakes and tipped half over in the soft stuff. The dozer came and pulled me back and then I told the driver to keep the ropes on to guide me down."

* * * *

The daring young men who erected the towers, climbing along narrow steel struts at a great height were nicknamed the Eagles. They stayed at Eurong Beach.

The chief Eagle was Rod Hobson, who enjoyed Fraser Island so much that he returned years later to become a National Parks ranger. Another Eagle, James Luttrell, married one of the resort waitresses.

Each settlement on the island was connected in turn to automatic trunk dialing, and residents were given telephones just like people on the mainland were using.

The system brought great joy to us all, pushing buttons instead of winding a handle; being connected straight away with whomever one wanted to talk to instead of having to wait for an operator first to answer, and then make the connection.

At Eurong Sid bought a couple of "gold" phones for the public to use, instead of having to wait in a long queue for the process of a shop assistant winding the handle, giving the required number to the operator, speaking over an often crackly line, then having to wait until the operator rang back with a price. It was such a relief for the shop staff not to have to go through the rigmarole.

The euphoria about the new phones diminished fairly quickly when Sid discovered the gold phone in the pub worked like a poker machine. Customers put their money in, made a call, put the handset down and often got back more money than they'd put in.

Pranksters got into the act too. Murray Reid answered his phone the day it was installed to be told it was a test call and would he whistle into the handset. So he did until he was blue in the face and his neighbours nearly died laughing.

It took only a few months before there was an outcry throughout the whole island about the new phones. After a trial period when phone calls to Maryborough and Hervey Bay were charged at local call rates, it was announced they would be trunk calls and the only local calls the islanders would have from then on would be between each other.

* * * *

Driver, Harold James was to work for Sid for almost two decades, except for a year when his father was terminally ill and he went truck driving based in Wollongong to spend more time at home with his parents.

Harold will never forget one job to South Australia, during this period, when he took the wrong road through desert.

"It was a terrible track and I never thought I'd ever make it," he says. "But I did get through and when I emerged, there was a chap standing looking at me in astonishment. He said there'd never been a truck through this track for 25 years. It was entirely thanks to what I'd learned on Fraser Island that I made it."

Chapter 25

The *Fraser Venture* enabled Sid to develop another arm to his business, access by air. He himself was eager to start flying again but, after the destruction of his Cherokee 6 aircraft, was no longer prepared to leave a plane parked at the front of Eurong.

The airstrip that Don Adams had cleared in the 1960's just inland from Wanggoolba Creek mouth, had been used briefly until one of his planes was damaged on it, and afterwards only for the rescue of the badly injured after the Jack Reville bus accident of July 1970.

Sid applied for a lease on the airstrip and it was granted in February 1986. It was a very short boggy strip, with the road from the Wanggoolba Creek barge landing running through the western end of the lease. The first thing Sid had to do was remake the sand road around the edge of the lease. He then had the strip lengthened to 960 metres, its surface leveled, and drains dug to channels along either side.

The *Fraser Venture* and skipper Harry Brutnall made it possible for Sid to have it graveled at comparatively little cost. Sid found a gravel pit at River Heads and had Harry, multi skilled as all Sid's staff had to be, take the Peterbilt every night to the quarry to load and bring it back to River Heads every morning.

Harry would put the truck on the barge on the last run of the morning, drive it about half a kilometre to the strip, tip its load of gravel and then take it back on the first afternoon run to the mainland for the next day's load. In all Harry dumped more than 3,000 tonnes of gravel to give the strip a good thick base. Sid contracted a big Hervey Bay building and road making firm, Belleros, to grade and roll the strip.

Sid worked alongside the contractors, driving trucks and an excavator. A passenger on one of the day tour buses watched the work with interest as they drove past the strip then asked the driver "Isn't that man driving the excavator, the one with his photo on our brochure?"

"Yes," said the driver and added "Sid isn't like most resort owners who sit in an office."

"You can say that again," replied the passenger taking a second look at Sid, who was covered in gravel dust from head to toe.

Belleros left their roller for Sid to use whenever it rained until the strip was well compacted. It took months before Sid was satisfied but the strip was made the best by far on Fraser Island. It had cost comparatively little to put the airstrip in good order, and was a good example of how Sid's infrastructure was opening up possibilities for him – and others.

The strip was now long enough for reasonably large aircraft to land on it, including the Bundaberg Aerial Ambulance, which opened another avenue for the evacuation of sick and injured people from the island.

For his own use Sid bought a Cessna 337, known familiarly as a "push pull" with two engines and two propellers, one at either end of the fuselage. Before making the purchase Sid went to see Don Adams, who had had one. Don said it was an excellent trouble free aircraft in spite of its unusual appearance.

For its safety Sid then had a hangar built at the strip by a Brisbane industrial builder, Barry Gartshore with whom he had had a long friendship.

* * * *

Getting back into aircraft led Sid to buy a unit in Brisbane as a getaway place from the island on days off. He would land at Archerfield airport in Brisbane and decided he would have a hangar built for his Cessna there. He called on Barry Gartshore again, but before the hangar was complete, Barry told him he had been approached by a helicopter parts supplier to lease the hangar. Gartshore said if Sid agreed, he would build him another hangar for the Cessna. The same thing happened, this time with an aircraft propeller manufacturer.

Along came aerobatic pilot and wartime aircraft collector, Barry Hempell, who asked Sid to build a big concrete hangar for him to lease as a war plane museum.

Sid ended up over several years with six hangars at Archerfield, each with a tenant in occupation.

Opening day at the Archerfield Warbirds Museum that Sid built for aerobatic pilot and aircraft collector, Barry Hempell.

Sid did not have the Cessna for long before he saw a sleek twin engine Beechcraft Duke, a former Queensland Government aircraft, for sale, and bought it as a replacement. The Duke was such a beautiful and sophisticated aircraft that Sid did not want to land it on the gravel strip at Wanggoolba. Its propellers were low to the ground and he knew they would flick gravel back on to the fuselage, chipping it.

The Beechcraft Duke.

He asked Belleros, to bitumen the strip. Speed was the essence of the job. If Belleros' two big bitumen tankers took too long to get to the airstrip from their works in Hervey Bay, the hot bitumen would cool and solidify. Sid organized a special *Fraser Venture* crossing for Bellero's tankers and the job was done – without a hitch.

When the work was finished on what was Fraser Island's one and only bitumen airstrip, Sid chose his moment to bring the Beechcraft in for its first landing.

Other pilots to whom he had spoken, said he would never be able to land the fast aircraft on the comparatively short strip.

Sid proved them wrong. He waited until there was a strong south easterly head wind, then flying solo and with a light fuel load, he landed – and was able to pull up with no difficulty half way along the strip. From then on he knew it was safe to land in far from ideal conditions.

* * * *

As well as Sid becoming airborne again, Sunshine Coast and Gold Coast charter plane operators could bring passengers to join the day trips coming off the *Fraser Venture,* as well as resort guests to fly in and catch the buses to Eurong.

Eurong became a popular venue for Flying Clubs from around Queensland. The Queensland Aviation Club made it a tradition to fly in on Australia Day each year with up to 26 pilots and families ***(below).***

One Christmas three planeloads of passengers from a cruise liner in Brisbane were flown in to the strip on an excursion to Fraser Island. Sid's buses took them on a five hour tour of the rainforest and lakes with lunch at Eurong. One of the passengers, Vincent Dotolon told Sid he'd been delighted at the opportunity to see Fraser Island. "It is famous you know, even in Florida and it exceeded our expectations."

Word soon spread about the existence of a bitumen airstrip on Fraser Island, and one day I answered the phone to a chap from Holdsworthy Army base in NSW who asked if Sid would allow a Hercules transport plane to land on it.

I said I'd find out and he should ring me back. I went to ask Sid.

He said "Do you know what a Hercules aircraft is?"

I knew that. I said "It's a military transport plane."

He said "Do you know how heavy it is?"

Before I could make a blind stab at answering he said "You know when we went to New Guinea there was a big plane stuck on the Madang airstrip, that completely wrecked the strip because it was so heavy? That was a Hercules, so when the man rings back, you'd better tell him it can't land here."

The man however didn't ring back and as the day, he'd said the Hercules would fly in, drew ever closer, Sid said I'd better be prepared to stand on the strip and wave my arms to try and persuade the pilot of the 70 tonne plane to go away. It never came.

Queensland politicians took to arriving in fair numbers, now it was possible for their twin engine planes to land. The island was subject to multiple inspections.

The government aircraft flies in with Molly Robson, Minister for Environment in the second Goss Government.

The brightest spark was the Minister for Tourism in the first Peter Beattie government, Merri Rose. As Sid drove her around the island, I told her one of the funny stories involving our tour bus drivers and Murray Reid.

It was the habit of these fellows, when they met on the one way road, for one to pull off to one side, and those passing would hand signal to him how many more buses and trucks were directly behind them, so he would not pull on to the road again until all were past.

On this particular day Murray passing a bus, which had pulled off, signalled with two fingers raised that there were two more buses behind him. The driver knew exactly what he meant, but as Murray drew level with the bus he saw 40 passengers doing a two fingered salute back at him.

When Merri flew away, I saw two fingers appear in her aircraft window.

* * * *

When his son Bill finished school with no definite idea of what he wanted to do for a career, Sid suggested he learn to fly and think about becoming a commercial pilot.

"I warmed to the idea," says Bill, "and went to a crammer's college to study subjects I hadn't done at school so that I could qualify."

He passed his commercial flying exams, but became discouraged when he found it hard to get work, as so many other youngsters had the same ambitions.

"Dad suggested as a backstop and to give me an income, I work on the *Fraser Venture* as a deckhand and do the time needed to qualify as a skipper," he recounts.

There was method in Sid's proposal. He was confident Bill would not enjoy being a deckhand as much as flying, and would no longer have doubts about his career path. He was right.

After some months on the barge, Bill, ***(right)*** had decided he definitely preferred flying and when a central Queensland company flying night freight and bank documents advertised for a contractor, Sid bought a twin engine Piper Navajo for Bill to get the contract.

This work gave Bill the needed hours of flying experience to further his flying career, and he is now a pilot for Qantas.

At the same time as Bill was working on the *Fraser Venture,* Sid's daughter Monica, after years of traveling and trying her hand at business, came back under Sid's wing to work at the resort.

She worked her way up to become maitre d'hôte in the restaurant and in 1997 married a resort employee, Col Pryor. They have two children, a son Campbell, born in 2001 and a daughter Clancey, born in 2004, and have a farm near Childers.

The Pryor family: from the left, Clancey, Col, Campbell, Monica and Col's daughter, Murphy.

Chapter 26

Sid had long recognised that the Inskip Point barge services with their closer access to Fraser Island for the big populations of Brisbane the Sunshine Coast and southern states, had far more potential to bring visitors to Fraser Island than the *Fraser Venture* operating from Hervey Bay with its far less populated hinterland.

The owners of the *Tom Welsby* barge had taken it back to Brisbane in 1983, when Sid introduced the *Fraser Venture* and the *Tom Welsby* lost his custom.

It was many years later that Sid found Gordon Elmer had been leasing the *Tom Welsby* but keeping very quiet about it, so it appeared he had a competitor at Inskip Point. As far as Sid understood at the time with the *Tom Welsby* gone, Elmer was now running the only barge service at Inskip, and with three very small barges, the largest carrying eight vehicles, he believed it was inadequate to meet the custom that could be developed.

He also thought Elmer, at $35 return trip for a single vehicle, was charging too much for his barge service with its short one nautical mile sea crossing, and said many times "Elmer has the key to my business and he is keeping the door locked."

He was also very concerned that access and camping levies mooted by the Queensland Government would cause an ongoing loss of visitors to Fraser Island and his core business at Eurong, as indeed proved to be the case.

Finally Sid wanted to be in charge of every aspect of his business, with nothing left to the dictates and decisions of others, and he wanted to expand into the fast developing Sunshine Coast tour market.

Up to this time much of the growth of Sid's enterprise had been opportunistic. Now he began to develop the idea of creating a totally integrated tourism infrastructure, independent of anyone else and with one facet drawing from, and supporting the others.

In early 1985 Sid was back talking to Ross McLean at Index Engineering in Brisbane, to ask if he could build him another barge, with more vehicle spaces than the *Fraser Venture* and to a totally different design for the Inskip Point to Hook Point crossing.

Sid had experienced the difficulty backing off Elmer's single door Inskip Point barges in the soft beach conditions at either side of the crossing. It sometimes took an undue length of time to get all the vehicles on and off.

He asked McLean to build a double ended barge, so vehicles could drive on one end, and drive straight off the other, with no backing or shuffling, or having to turn the barge around as it neared land. This would speed the loading and unloading. It was to have four engines, one at each corner, and extra long ramps to give it good reach on to the sloping beaches at Inskip and Hook Points.

Sid planned, as with the *Fraser Venture*, that he would develop a day tour around the new barge, so he had it designed with a large saloon with a shop, a bar and seating to be set amidships, with the wheelhouse on top. The barge would have dual controls; one set on each side of the wheelhouse, so the skipper could switch from one to another and face the way the vessel was heading.

In May 1985 Sid signed the contract with Index to build the 34m long barge, to be named the *Rainbow Venture.* It was an altogether more complicated vessel, and a third again as expensive as the *Fraser Venture*, but his bank lent him the $660,000 taking another mortgage over the resort. Its completion date was set for late 1986.

Within two months of the signing of the contract, a bombshell fell on Sid's plans to start a new day tour from the rapidly developing Sunshine Coast to help make the *Rainbow Venture* pay. The Forestry Department in conjunction with the Department of Transport, announced there would be a moratorium on the issue of any more day tour licenses to Fraser Island.

It was too late now to cancel the contract with Index. Sid was not sure by how much vehicle use at Inskip Point would drop when the proposed access and camping levies were introduced, and how quickly it might build up again.

He was very concerned whether, without the income from a day tour, he would be able to keep up the payments on the money he had borrowed for the *Rainbow Venture*. Interest rates were soaring to 22 per cent.

He decided he would go and see the Minister for Transport, Don Lane and tell him what a bind the new moratorium had placed him in. Sid took with him his contract for the *Rainbow Venture,* signed before the unexpected moratorium. The Minister agreed the moratorium could be breached under these circumstances, and Sid could have a new permit to carry 1,000 people a month on day tours to Fraser from the Sunshine Coast.

This caused absolute dismay and anger among three of the existing six tour operators on the Sunshine Coast. They had naturally been very happy at the protection the moratorium had given their businesses. Now here was Sid who, on the face of it, had far more resources than any of them, being allowed to come into competition.

They went as a delegation to Don Lane, to ask him to reverse his decision. They were not the least mollified when Lane refused and explained the situation Sid had found himself in with the *Rainbow Venture.* From being friendly with Sid and calling in at Eurong so their passengers could patronize his shop, they no longer dealt with him. At quarterly meetings called by the Forestry Department to discuss tour issues, their animosity was made quite plain.

* * * *

As he had with the *Fraser Venture,* Sid spent a lot of time checking on the progress of the *Rainbow Venture* being built. He usually arrived at Index Engineering's Brisbane River shipyard after the builders had all gone home for the day, but he would get through the fence and give the vessel a thorough examination, then go back the following morning with a long list of questions and comments.

The shipbuilders were always waiting for him and Sid became very curious about how they knew he was coming. He asked one of the workers and was told Cliff Fraser, the foreman, had instructed all the men to let him know if they saw bare footprints in the yard from Sid's inspection the night before.

One day at the shipyard, Sid glanced around and saw Gordon Elmer peering through the wire fence. Elmer had not acknowledged Sid since he had switched his patronage to the *Tom Welsby* during sand mining days. Now Sid went up to him and invited him to look at his new barge and took him on a conducted tour.

It must have made Elmer heart sick.

In the light of the coming competition, Elmer had his nephew, Barry White, a steel fabricator in Maryborough, build a double ended barge for him to carry 12 vehicles in two rows across the deck. It had no saloon because Elmer was not seeking a vessel to serve day trippers, and with its high twin prows at each end and wheelhouse on a steel stem in the middle, it was soon nicknamed the wing nut ***(below)***. Elmer named it *Eliza Fraser II* and put it into service in August 1986, three months before the *Rainbow Venture* was completed.

The introduction of government levies on all Fraser Island visitors earlier in the year led to a massive drop in custom for all island businesses as Sid had feared. Elmer declared no more barges were needed at Inskip Point, and started to attack Sid in a war of words in the media.

Provocative challenges were uttered by both Sid and Elmer, foreshadowing a fierce price war. Sid, who believed Elmer was a very wealthy man and wanted to hide his own precarious financial position, suggested in a fit of bravado he would run for nothing if things got too heated.

Elmer was more circumspect and said there was no profit in that, but he would make sure Sid made nothing from his investment in the *Rainbow Venture.*

Sid was told that a very senior officer in the Department of Harbours and Marine was a close friend of Elmer's, and might put obstacles in his way.

He was to believe this could be true when he was put through the hoops by the Department before bringing the *Rainbow Venture* from Brisbane.

On completion of the vessel, Index Engineering, a very professional shipbuilder, had stability tests done and all the necessary work for it to pass survey to carry 28 vehicles and 200 passengers.

Once any vessel passed survey, the normal procedure was for the Department of Harbours and Marine to issue a temporary permit with a flag for it to go into service, until a formal survey certificate could be issued.

Knowing the *Rainbow Venture* had passed survey and wanting to take it to Inskip Point and get it working as soon as possible, Sid, all unsuspecting, went along to the Department office in Brisbane to collect the flag and temporary permit.

"No-one wanted to know me," he recalls. "I had expected the flag to be all ready for me to pick up, but I was given the run around like you wouldn't believe. I had arrived at the Department as soon as it opened and I sat there waiting for eight hours. I think no-one expected me to wait them out. Finally a few minutes before the Department office closed, the flag was ungraciously given to me, perhaps because they couldn't close the doors with me still in there and thought I'd refuse to leave without it."

The Rainbow Venture.

Sid had heard that Gordon Elmer's *Eliza Fraser II*, the first vessel of its size and type in Queensland had not had to have a stability test, a standard for all commercial vessels.

Angry at the way he'd been treated by the Department, Sid contacted several other vessel owners, including the owner of the little Noosa River ferry which ran on a wire from bank to bank, and in each case found they had had to have stability tests done on their vessels.

With this information he then wrote to the Department, asking why *Eliza Fraser II* hadn't had a stability test, and he got a reply signed by the Minister for Harbours and Marine, Martin Tenni, saying it was not needed because the vessel was a standard design. Sid filed the letter.

Elmer was charging $35 for a return vehicle crossing, which he dropped to $30 just the week before he knew the *Rainbow Venture* was due at the end of November 1986.

One of the reasons Sid had bought the *Rainbow Venture* was because he believed Elmer's prices, combined with the new $10 vehicle levies imposed on island visitors, were discouraging many people from coming to Fraser Island, and he charged $25, the same price as on the *Fraser Venture.*

The war that was waged in response was no holds barred.

Chapter 27

As skipper on the *Rainbow Venture* Sid employed Brian Clarke, the son of Jack Clarke, skipper of the *Tom Welsby* when it had worked at Inskip Point. He was an even tempered man, as was Don Caswell, who relieved him four days a fortnight for days off. Before long both men had been roused to anger by the tactics used by Elmer and his crews.

The Inskip Point barges worked directly off the beach. Most of the traffic coming to them was driven along the beach from Rainbow Beach township, because the 11 km former sand mining road to the Point was in a terrible state of repair with huge potholes and corrugation.

Inskip Point beach where the barges left to cross to Fraser Island.

Brian had to wait for custom on the beach in close proximity to Elmer's two and occasionally three small barges. Elmer always had his barges in pole position so the oncoming traffic came to them first. If Brian tried to get in the better position and get a share of traffic, Elmer and his skippers would go around him, back into the best spot.

The only time Sid spoke to Elmer during this period was when Elmer tried to tell him the *Rainbow Venture* should be 500m away from his barges, and Sid refused to have the *Venture* move so far away from the arriving traffic.

The *Rainbow Venture* was not as fast as Sid had hoped.

The skippers of Elmer's two small single door barges would drive them up alongside the *Rainbow Venture* when it was crossing the strait, and time and again cut closely across its bows, causing Brian Clarke to have to throw his engines from full ahead to full astern to avoid a collision.

"If there had been a collision, the *Rainbow Venture* would have run right over Elmer's much smaller barge. People's lives were being put in danger," Sid said.

Within a few weeks the Department of Harbours and Marine got so many complaints from passengers and observers, and witnessed for themselves this dangerous tactic of Elmer's barge skippers that they felt bound to take action before there was a major incident.

In an effort to ensure the barges travelled in a straight line, parallel with each other with no need to cross over, they designated a stretch of the Inskip Point beach as a barge landing area and allotted sections of it to the two barge operations.

In deference to Elmer's being at Inskip Point first, and in a gesture of appeasement, Sid gave Elmer the choice of position, and naturally Elmer chose to be closest to where the traffic approached the barges along the beach. If ever there was a time when peaceful co-existence could have begun, this was it. Instead things went from bad to worse.

The next tactic of Elmer's crew was to put a big mooring rope from the front of one of their barges right across the beach at chest height to a tree or their work utility vehicle purportedly as a land anchor, so that traffic could not get past to the *Rainbow Venture.* The Eurong chef, Ian Edgar came along the beach on his motorbike to drive on to the *Rainbow Venture* one day, didn't see the rope against the sand background until too late and was dragged from his bike by the rope across his throat.

Elmer's crew not only kept putting the rope across the beach but to make doubly sure drivers would not go past, one of their deckhands was stationed on the beach to stop vehicles and wave them on to one of the Elmer barges.

The young Greek man most often charged with this duty was Kosta Ladas. One day Sid, watching him running about most energetically, called "You are working hard for Gordon," and Ladas replied, "When I come and work for you, I will work hard too."

Don Caswell remembers that on the Thursday before the busy Easter long weekend, when the barges worked through the night, he was driving along the beach to relieve Brain Clarke the skipper on the *Rainbow Venture* at midnight.

"Kosta didn't recognize me in the dark and thought I was a customer. He just stood in front of my vehicle and wouldn't let me pass, so I drove on whichever of Elmer's barges he was waving me onto, and when he approached for me to pay him I sprayed him with a can of CRC I had in the glove box," Don says. "He thought it was paint and ran off screaming up to the wheelhouse. I backed off Elmer's barge and went on to the *Rainbow Venture*. I got to the wheelhouse and Sid's voice came over the radio 'What did you do on Elmer's barge?'

"I told him I'd sprayed Kosta with CRC and then it hit me – how did Sid know? I asked him where he was and he said 'I'm sitting in the car in the bushes watching what's going on.'"

The mechanic at Rainbow Beach who worked on Sid's buses, George Milham woke up one night to find two of Elmer's crew in his bedroom. They assaulted him – and Milham soon afterwards left Rainbow Beach.

On September 26 1987 skipper, Brian Clarke had just set off across the straits, when he heard two shots, which struck the *Rainbow Venture* amidships, mere centimetres above the roof of a vehicle on board, leaving big dents in the thick steel.

There were no police at Rainbow Beach, so Clarke called on the Harbours and Marine to investigate, showing them the damage when they arrived next day. After the event, with no witnesses as to who fired the shots, they said there was nothing they could do.

"Brian was quite fearful following the shooting, and so was I" says Don Caswell. "I was always looking over my shoulder in Rainbow Beach, particularly if I went out in an evening."

The barge war had become so heated by this time that the Harbours and Marine called a meeting in Tin Can Bay in October "to discuss the problems affecting the safe operation of the barges and to seek a solution acceptable to all parties."

Captain Arthur Diack, the manager of the Marine Board, said the existing situation was very serious and the many reported near collisions and the general atmosphere of confrontation was of deep concern to his officers, and posed a risk to public safety.

He stressed business competition must not involve breaches of the collision rules.

Gordon Elmer said there was a deliberate campaign to discredit his operation by malicious complaints – and then had to agree not all the complaints had been malicious and that they occurred on both sides.

The Harbours and Marine officers were overly optimistic if they thought they could end the conflict.

The *Rainbow Venture* saloon was broken into with beer and cigarettes stolen so often that Sid had the stock taken from the saloon shop and it served only to provide cups of coffee to passengers.

Throughout this period Sid kept his price below what Elmer was charging.

He believed had he not charged less he would not have had any customers at all with Elmer's advantages of position, his tactics with the rope across the beach, and him operating at least two barges and often three to Sid's one.

When Elmer dropped his prices, Sid would drop to stay lower. The prices spiraled downwards, and customers started to come back to the island. Both barge services had agents in Rainbow Beach township selling tickets for them, as well as on the barges, but Sid had the best agent, the owner of the Rainbow Beach service station where a huge majority of drivers called in to buy fuel before heading on to Fraser Island.

Come the Orchid Beach Fishing Competition in May, the *Rainbow Venture* crew saw Elmer's barges promoting that their customers would qualify for a 10c a litre fuel discount at Orchid Beach. Sid countered by offering his customers 10c a litre discount on fuel at Eurong.

Neither side gave an inch. Elmer declared in the *Maryborough Chronicle* that he was staying on not to make money but to make sure Sid didn't either. He said "I have never drunk, smoked or gambled. I can hold out here a long time."

* * * *

Within four months of the start of the *Rainbow Venture* at Inskip Point, Sid began to run day tours to Fraser Island from the south to supplement the earning capacity of the big ferry.

One of the earlier purchases Sid had made was a half share in a day tour from Rainbow Beach called *Sun Safaris.*

His partners, Paul and Sue Arthur ran the tour using a six seat Landrover. By time their wages for taking bookings, driving the vehicle and other expenses were taken out, there was no profit. By March 1987 the Arthurs wanted to go and live in Brisbane, so asked Sid to buy them out. With sole control Sid set about realizing the potential of *Sun Safaris* by using a 14 seat Toyota bus.

Max Williams, who had been working for Sid at Eurong since the 1960's, had the care of his young grandson, Ross. His wife Pam had been teaching Ross by correspondence, but they now felt Ross should go to school.

It was a good solution all round for Max and Pam to move from Eurong to Rainbow Beach and operate *Sun Safaris,* Pam taking bookings and doing the accounts, and Max driving.

A better tour business could be expected from the much larger and rapidly developing Sunshine Coast than Rainbow Beach, and Sid was anxious to begin operating there. He brought more trouble on himself when in April 1987, one month after he became sole owner of *Sun Safaris* and only five months after the *Rainbow Venture* began, he bought a bus to start running day tours from the Sunshine Coast.

To break into this market Sid had looked for an outstanding bus, and he found it, the *Australian Explorer.* A luxury 33 seater, this was the most famous 4WD coach in Australia and when it was put up for sale in Sydney, Sid just beat adventurer, Dick Smith and Red Centre tourism character, Bill King to its purchase. Driven by adventurer, Hans Tholstrup, the coach held three records. It was the first coach to cross Australia west to east direct over the desert from Perth to Alice Springs to Townsville, its route along oil rig shot lines, not roads.

It was the first coach to cross the Simpson Desert from Birdsville in Queensland to Poeppel Corner at the intersection of Queensland, South Australia and the Northern Territory then to New Crown Station in the Territory. Its third record was that it was the largest coach to reach the tip of Cape York Peninsula.

The first thing Sid did when he got the *Explorer* to his workshop was to have Laurie Toy remove all its complicated electronic systems, and bring its back to basics.

The tour was going to have to drive up the long surf beach or over rough forest tracks from Noosa to Rainbow Beach, cross to Fraser on the *Rainbow Venture* then up another 30 km of surf beach to Eurong, inland to Central Station and Lake Mackenzie and back every day, a distance of 450 kilometres. Sid knew the *Explorer's* complicated electronics systems would not work for long in such intensely salt conditions.

The *Australian Explorer's* yellow paint job had got a little tired, so Sid had a major paint company make up an outstanding acid yellow for it, which the paint company named "Sid's yellow."

A short time later Brisbane City Council decided to change the colour of its bus fleet – and chose "Sid's yellow". That was the second time the council had followed Sid's colour schemes.

* * * *

By serendipitous chance when Sid and I were in Noosa, looking for a tour booking office, we met John and Jan Graham, a couple who had had a Fraser Island tour but had sold it and were looking for other opportunities. They knew us well from their regular stops at Eurong, and when Sid told them he was going to start a day tour from the Sunshine Coast they put up their hands as managing agents. It was agreed there and then.

They found a booking office in Noosa's renowned Hastings Street, in which they could share space with a time share sales company.

The Grahams were very excited when they saw the *Australian Explorer*, but didn't know just how hard they were going to have to work initially to overcome the constant bad mouthing of the new *Fraser Explorer* tour and themselves to booking agents by the hostile competitors.

Graffiti was spray painted on the bus almost nightly, and John's first job in a morning would be to clean it off before setting off all the way down the Sunshine Coast, in a small courtesy bus, to bring passengers to the tour starting point in Noosa.

The Grahams were tough and determined people and they countered everything thrown at them, to the extent they eventually sold their house and moved on to an acreage block out of town so they could garage the buses safely behind high fences. Their perseverance paid off and in time they made the business a great success and continued to run it for almost two decades.

The *Australian Explorer* was an immediate winner with day trippers and from the start its seats were all filled, even if some of its passengers were a little confused about the records it held. One elderly chap was overheard explaining to his wife that the coach was the first to go around the world and the first to cross the Sahara.

* * * *

While the Grahams were battling rival tour operators on one front, it seemed barge war troubles would never end. Sid's two 14 seat Toyota buses were destroyed.

On his way back to Rainbow Beach from an island day tour late on the afternoon of April 28 1988, Max Williams got one badly bogged in soft sand trying to get up a track from the surf beach to the hardened road built by the sand miners behind the dunes.

He radioed Sid at Eurong, and in turn Sid rang Sam and Maureen Mitchell, who hired out 4WD's in Rainbow Beach, to ask if they would go and pick up Max's passengers. They did so and Max reported from the *Rainbow Venture* radio that the passengers were on their way, and so was he, leaving the bus safe, well above high tide.

Sid tried to get the island's tow truck operator Nigel Fremantle to go and recover the bus, but when he could not raise Nigel on the phone until late, he decided to leave the bus where it was overnight.

Few people drove the beach in the dark, it was so dangerous with washouts and creeks crossing the beach, and there was little point when the barges stopped running for the day, so Sid and Nigel agreed the bus would be safe until morning.

However another Rainbow Beach tour operator, Wendy Scheeres coming down the surf beach a short time after Max, also got bogged in the same place. She preferred to travel with Gordon Elmer's barge, and called the Rainbow Beach towing service, run by Rob Rye, a friend of Elmer's, to come and get her moving again. He did so and they returned on Elmer's barge.

When Nigel went at first light, before any traffic came from the Inskip Point barges, to recover Sid's Toyota he found it in a sad and sorry state. Its headlights had been smashed, a spike driven through its radiator and it had been dragged below high tide.

In the night, the sea had obviously come over its bonnet through its motor and into its open back, washing out its seat cushions.

In Sid's next mail came an anonymous sympathy card with a message in crabbed handwriting saying "In anticipation of many things to come."

To get *Sun Safari Tours* going again as quickly as possible, Sid bought a new Toyota cab and chassis and fixed the body from the wrecked Toyota on to it.

A second Toyota bus was used on the growing Hervey Bay day tour, and left at the Wanggoolba Creek landing every night. There was no room in the bus shed for it, so it was left alongside the shed.

One morning there was a radio call from the skipper of the *Fraser Venture,* when he arrived in the creek. The bus was a burned out shell.

Sid made a genuine effort to build good relationships in Rainbow Beach, but found it was a town divided into factions. There was no bridging the gap.

He joined in town approaches to government for better roads. He gave generous prizes to the annual Rainbow Beach fishing contest.

When the Gympie City Council won a government tender to repair the crumbling surface of the old sand mining road from Hook Point to Fourth Creek on the island with truckloads of gravel, Sid was there to help. He gave the council trucks free passage on the *Rainbow Venture* and sent one of his drivers with the Peterbilt to cart gravel at his own expense, so a longer section of the road could be repaired.

The Mayor of Gympie, Joan Dodt wrote in thanks, saying "It is not often that help of the magnitude given to us is offered freely with no strings attached."

While these things earned him the gratitude of some, it made no difference to others. After two years, it appeared there was no end in sight to the barge war.

Chapter 28

One of Sid's ongoing concerns was with the land he was using for a camping ground behind his 1.4 hectare freehold front block on the surf beachfront. He hoped in time to develop it with a new resort complex. The Forestry Department had given him an annually renewable occupation permit on the land.

In the early 1970's he had built three cottages on a crest overlooking the camping area, one for his own family, one for the Williams, and one for another staff family. Behind them he had a workshop for the maintenance of the tour buses.

With only an occupation permit, Sid felt that his ownership was insecure and building more permanent structures was too much of a risk.

In the mid 1970's he wrote to the Lands Department applying to freehold the camping ground, as in 1972 he had done with the front land purchased from Don Adams. He asked for another small parcel of land on the opposite side of the road to be included for a new camping area in due course.

Lands Commissioner Reg Stewart, on a routine visit to the island, called in to talk to Sid and he was encouraged to hope he would get the better tenure. A plan was drawn up incorporating the new land, but nothing else happened. For years nothing happened.

Every time Lands Commissioner Stewart came, about twice a year, Sid would ask how his application was going. Stewart would say it was progressing. Still nothing happened. On a visit in the early 1980's, Stewart suggested Sid withdraw his application for the time being.

Sid asked why and the Commissioner replied "Well maybe you should think of giving the Hannants time to get established."

Sid was nonplussed. Geoff and Norma Hannant had recently been granted a camping lease on the surf beachfront near The Cathedrals coloured sand cliffs, but what had it got to do with him? They were at least 50 km north of Eurong and he could not see the connection between them developing a camping ground and his wanting better tenure of his land.

With Sid pestering him for answers, Lands Commissioner Stewart finally hinted "There is an influential person in government who does not want you to get ahead."

This was the second time he had been told this, the first by the Liquor Licensing inspector. Sid began to put two and two together. It was easy then to work out who the influential person was, a Minister in the Bjelke Petersen government with local connections.

Sid did not know what to do with his information. He realized the Lands Commissioner and the Licensing inspector could both lose their jobs if he revealed what they had told him. But he was not going to give up.

Instead Sid went to the Lands Department in Brisbane to argue his case on its merits to a very senior public servant. He suggested Sid have a professional layout prepared of what he intended to do on the land.

Sid went home and employed Hervey Bay architect, Gavin Patterson, to draw up a plan of how he intended to develop the land with four large buildings, three of three storeys high, each to contain 30 accommodation units, around a large central building, which was to be the combined reception, bar, restaurant and conference facility. A huge free form swimming pool was drawn between the central building and one of the accommodation buildings. At the rear of the land were barbecues and a tennis court.

An area was marked on the plan across the main road for the new camping area to replace the one now to be filled with buildings. It was a most ambitious plan with buildings larger than any in Hervey Bay, let alone Fraser Island.

When Sid happily took his nicely bound plan, with artist's drawings of the buildings back to the Lands Department, the reception was not what he expected. Again it was suggested he be prepared to wait a few years more.

This time Sid voiced his suspicion as to who was holding him back, and had it confirmed. It seemed like stalemate had been reached, but Sid refused to accept it.

While his second barge, the *Rainbow Venture* was being built, Sid went to Brisbane frequently and took to calling in at the Lands Department to see the senior man, and ask how his application was going. One day he was told the man had died.

Sid realized he now had an opportunity to take what he knew to a higher level, and it would not jeopardize anyone's job. He asked for an appointment to see the Minister for Lands, Bill Glasson.

Well prepared, Sid told Glasson the whole situation, the work he had put in on Fraser Island from scratch, the length of time since he had made his application, and that he had been told he was deliberately being held back by a powerful person in government and named him. Angrily Glasson asked "Who told you that?" Sid named the public servant.

Glasson roared to his private secretary "Get him in here." Sid interceded quietly "If you can do that Mr. Glasson, you are a better man than most. He died."

The meeting settled down. Sid put his case and Glasson agreed that Sid should be given the opportunity to freehold the land.

The next step was to have the land properly surveyed, and application made to have paper roads closed, where they cut across the land. These roads had been drawn on the original survey of Eurong township. One ran across Sid's camping ground land to join the two halves of the township. It had never been formed because of the big sand blow in its way.

Residents, wanting to visit each other, trekked over the blow, or drove their vehicles along the beach, so as long as Sid agreed to pedestrian access across the land, there were no objections to the road closure.

Next Sid had to apply to the Maryborough City Council to rezone the land to Special Facilities – Tourist Resort. Sid, who by now had learned you sometimes had to call in experts if you were to make rapid headway, employed consultants, Cameron McNamara to prepare the documents for his case. He had to guarantee a good water supply and the setting up of a sewage disposal system, both to be monitored to quality standards, and ensure the stability of the land.

The Council approved Sid's development plans and concluded it would be of great economic benefit to Maryborough and the Wide Bay region without adversely affecting the recreational and environmental management of Fraser Island.

* * * *

These processes all took time, and when more months went by after he had obtained the approvals he needed and still nothing was heard from the Lands Department, Sid kept progressing with smaller projects.

The resort shop was by now far too small to meet the needs of the growing numbers of visitors in holiday times, so he started to build a larger resort shop on the front land by the main road to the beach.

When Lands Commissioner, Reg Stewart came to check the shop site, he said Sid was building on the road itself. Sid was perplexed, and pointed out his survey pegs. The Lands Commissioner said the pegs were not far enough away from the pegs marking the front of the house block across the road, which belonged to a wormer, Ray Wilson.

Sid guessed straight away there were some shenanigans, and asked the Lands Commissioner go and find the pegs at the back of Ray's block and measure from them. Sure enough Ray had attempted a bit of a land grab by moving his front pegs forwards by about 4 metres. Ray accepted he'd been caught out with a grin.

* * * *

Foundations for the new shop were laid but there they were to remain for years, for in mid 1987, a letter finally came from the Lands Department formally offering Sid a Special Lease on almost two hectares of land. It was made conditional upon Sid spending $2 million on the land within five years. There was no provision for a replacement camping area across the road.

It was not what Sid expected. He had expected freehold, but when he went to question this, he was told this was the necessary first step towards freehold. He had been given no earlier indication he would have to spend so much money so quickly, and was in no position to do so.

It was an enormous sum and Sid had no idea how he was going to raise it. He had already mortgaged the resort for a $660,000 loan to pay for the *Rainbow Venture.* The vessel was barely paying its way because of the fierce price war with Gordon Elmer, and interest rates were a massive 18% - 22%. He still had lease payments to meet on the *Fraser Venture* and the *Australian Explorer*.

It seemed extremely doubtful that Sid's existing business could bear the burden of a further large commitment.

Possibly Sid's "powerful political enemy" expected that would put the dampener on Sid's ambitions. If so, he was wrong. Sid never thought for one moment of backing away. In another huge gamble, he accepted the Lands Department offer. He then set about working out how he could raise $2million.

Bigger and better accommodation was urgently needed to satisfy the growing demands of the major coach line tour groups that came to Eurong. But Sid had been unable to start on it until he got the promised better tenure on the land.

Never knowing when that was likely to be granted after so many delays, he hadn't tried to save up ready for such a major project. He had always had plenty of other smaller projects to spend his income on as it was earned. Now it appeared he was going to have to move ahead with his new development more quickly than he had planned, or at this stage could afford.

He came up with the idea of time sharing apartments in the first of the proposed new buildings. Sid had learned of time share from a Noosa time share developer from whom he rented office space. Sid went to get more information from him.

He was also told there was a time share scheme operating at Tangalooma Resort on Moreton Island, and went to see how that worked. He found 30 or 40 sales people sitting under red umbrellas on a lawn which the day trippers had to pass to get to the resort from the launch landing.

All the day trippers were intercepted by the sales people and offered $50 vouchers to buy anything at the resort shop if they would go on a walking tour and see the time share units. He went on the tour and found Tangalooma had a collection of assorted buildings, in a situation not dissimilar to his own, with a brand new three storey building of timeshare units.

Sid had already decided the first three storey 30 unit accommodation building on his plan for Eurong, would have 24 motel style rooms on the first two levels, to accommodate coach groups, and six well appointed two bedroom suites on the top floor for letting to families. Now he decided he would time share these six top floor suites, giving him 300 weeks to sell at between $6750 and $9,750 and raising some $2.5 million.

This would pay for the first building and leave some money over to be spent on more buildings towards completing the development.

Sid had no real understanding of what was involved, the legalities, the ongoing administration, or the marketing of time share.

He asked advice from his accountant, Barry Keys, who organized the purchase of a company to handle the multiple ownership that time share required. Barry also steered him to a Brisbane firm of solicitors, who explained the legal aspects and would draw up the complicated documentation for timeshare sales and get it approved by government.

More comfortable with practicalities, Sid asked architect, Gavin Patterson, to draw detailed plans of the building, which he was to name *Korawinga*, after an early Forestry vessel which had plied to Fraser Island. Probably relieved that Sid had had proper plans drawn this time, the Maryborough City Council gave building approval within two months.

A copy of the building plan and approval was duly sent to the Lands Department, where officers, exhausted at trying to slow down this persistent and annoying fellow, sent him a Special Lease in September 1987. For the next few months, Sid went through all the necessary steps to start work on *Korawinga.*

He hired his cousin, Joe Cunningham, who by now had sold his island timber interest, and was doing land clearing on the mainland, to come and clear and level the chosen ridge of land. Joe came with his little bulldozer, ***(below)*** and soon had a ridge leveled and the excess sand piled into a hollow at the rear of the land.

Sid also applied for, and was granted, an occupation permit over a hectare of land by the side of the road into Eurong for a cement batching plant to make the big quantities of concrete needed for the building.

In August Sid organized to borrow $850,000 in stages from his bank's finance arm towards meeting the progress payments on the building, until the time share sales began.

Dennis Crooks, the Maryborough builder who had built the hotel and *Surfside* had gone to work for the government. However the architect, Gavin Patterson recommended a Hervey Bay builder, and in June 1988 the building of *Korawinga* began.

The builder sent his foreman to the island to supervise all the sub contractors he employed. But after only two weeks the builder got another job in Hervey Bay, and took his foreman back to the mainland, leaving the sub contractors to work unsupervised.

A very different scene from the earlier building at Eurong, with big equipment and contractors everywhere.

Soon after building started, Sid realized he wasn't getting what he had specified and was paying for.

The building was only up to the concrete pour of the ground floor, when Sid came back from the mainland on the *Fraser Venture* one day and saw a Wacka Packa, a machine for compacting earth, on board for delivery to Eurong.

Sid had told the concreting contractor that the only way to compact the fine island sand was to soak it thoroughly, pouring water on it for days on end. Now he saw his instruction was being ignored and the contractor intended to use the faster Wacka Packa method, but one that simply would not work on dry raw sand.

By time he arrived at Eurong he was fuming, and a major argument with the concreter followed. Sid took over watering all the sand between the foundations himself with quantities of water pumped up from the water table.

An aerial view of Eurong Beach Resort with the foundations for the Korawinga building at the left rear of the camping ground.

Only when he was satisfied the sand was compact enough, did he call the concreter back to pour the floor.

In the next stage block layers came to build the walls to the first floor. Sid had specified that the hollow concrete blocks have concrete slurry poured into each hole to give them added strength. When the block layers went home for the weekend, Sid went around the wall with a hammer and lightly tapped the walls. He found many of the blocks sounded hollow and obviously were not filled.

He phoned the builder, remarkable mainly for his absence, and had him come to inspect the walls. The builder had to agree with Sid.

To rectify the situation, he and his wife came to the island, and while he mixed up slurry, his wife poured bucketsful of it down inside the walls. It was hardly satisfactory, but better than nothing.

As well as driving an excavator to dump one tonne bags of cement into a hired concrete batching plant as needed, Sid took to making regular inspections of the building work.

The last straw was when, after a council building inspector had been to check on the quantity of steel rods being put in the concrete stairways of the building, Sid found the concreter removing half the rods before the concrete was poured.From then on Sid stayed full time on the job, even clambering on the roof.

"It didn't make me very popular," he acknowledges, "but I got the building I had specified and was paying for, a building I knew was so strong that it would long outlast me."

Many of the materials, 1350 tonne in all, were carted to Eurong by Harold James in Sid's GMC truck, and he remembers well the problems he had carrying the long roof trusses.

"The trusses were unloaded at Laurie Toy's place on the road to River Heads, and a crane was hired to lift them on to the GMC Sid had.

The roof trusses being trucked on the Fraser Venture.

"I didn't think we'd get them all on, but I knew Sid would have a fit if we had to get the crane back a second time, so I worked out how we could stack them," he says.

"By time they were all on, the load was 3.5m high by 3.8m wide and the length from the front of the truck to the end of the trusses was 18.8m long. I thought Sid would be really pleased with this effort but all he said was 'Don't tell anyone how you managed to bring such a heavy load, or the Forestry will never again do their share fixing up the road.'"

It took much longer than expected for the solicitors to finalise the essential documentation so Sid could start selling the timeshare units. When it was finally completed and prospectuses could be printed, Sid found to his complete surprise hardly anyone was interested in buying.

He thought Fraser Island so magnificent that people would want to return year after year, as indeed many did. But for most, Fraser Island represented a cheap, casual, open air holiday camping along the beach. None of them would forego this to spend money in advance on a timeshare unit.

Sid was so proud of his hard won achievements that he did not realise Eurong, though far ahead of anything on Fraser Island, was still very basic, and compared poorly with much more glamourous offerings on the Gold and Sunshine Coasts.

He did learn however that sometimes unscrupulous marketing elsewhere had led to time share losing its earlier appeal.

Finally he did not want to pay high commissions to a team of salespeople, such as Tangalooma had employed. Instead Sid relied on me and his shop staff to do the selling. We were highly skilled at selling ice creams and souvenir T shirts if a customer approached the cash register holding them, but selling time share was out of our league. Not that many people came even to make enquiries.

Chapter 29

In November 1988 in the *Gympie Times* newspaper, Gordon Elmer announced he had sold one of his barges out of the area, with a second one soon to go, and would sell the rest of his business and retire the following June.

He sent a single page handwritten letter to Sid saying he shouldn't go round telling people he was going to buy his, Elmer's business, but if he did want to buy it he should not deal directly with him, but through his solicitor, a Mr. Stanton in Gympie.

Sid was interested, but was already overcommitted financially through having to start the new resort building before he had really wanted to, so did not respond. In fact the two men had only communicated with each other once before, to have an argument about barge positioning, since the *Rainbow Venture* was built.

Sid believed the success of the time share scheme would be the solution to all his financial problems and give him the funds to buy Elmer's remaining barge and business. He became convinced that he had to get more people to look at the partially completed *Korawinga* units and the drawings for the completed resort, by offering incentives. He could not afford to offer $50 shopping vouchers as at Tangalooma or free weekend accommodation as he had learned other timeshare schemes did.

By this time the fare on the *Rainbow Venture* was a meagre $5 per vehicle while Elmer charged $10 and Sid knew the least costly incentive would be free barge passage.

Certainly Sid was fed up with the long drawn out barge war. A free barge would serve a dual purpose: attract more people to Fraser Island where they would inevitably visit Eurong for shop, bar and fuel supplies, when they could be invited to look at time share; and bring the price war to a head and hopefully end the ongoing danger to his crew, customers, barge and buses.

Sid began offering free passage on the *Rainbow Venture* in late December 1988. This was to earn him a fearsome reputation as a hard man to cross in business.

Few people knew the underlying purpose behind this move – to sell timeshare in part to raise the funds to buy Elmer out.

The free barge achieved Sid's desired result of attracting many more people to Fraser Island, but still there were no takers for time share.

When *Korawinga* was completed and furnished some months later, Sid renewed his efforts with an advertising campaign, but again it brought people only to look but not to buy.

* * * *

In the meantime the harassment at Inskip Point continued. In March 1989 the *Rainbow Venture* had to undergo its annual inspection by the Bundaberg Department of Harbours and Marine surveyor, David Mainwaring.

The vessel passed inspection and Mainwaring issued, as was standard practice, a temporary survey certificate to last until the Department could do the necessary paperwork for the final certificate. It generally took up to a month for the final certificate to be issued and the temporary certificate lasted for that month.

In this case the month was up on the Thursday before Good Friday, one of the busiest days of the year for barge traffic at Inskip Point. Sid had still not received the final survey certificate, but as the resort only got mail when he or Murray Reid went to pick it up from the Maryborough post office, he thought nothing of it.

Little did he suspect it wouldn't have been issued and he was being set up by elements within the Department of Harbours and Marine.

On Good Friday, when the new skipper of the *Rainbow Venture*, John Pearce arrived on the Inskip Point beach ready for the frantically busy day ahead, there were two Department of Harbours and Marine officers already waiting for him.

They had come especially, all the way from Mooloolaba on the Sunshine Coast, to try and stop the *Rainbow Venture* running, so Elmer would have all the income from the busiest day of the year.

They went on board the *Venture* and said that as the vessel did not have its final survey certificate, it could not start work. John Pearce called Sid at Eurong from the vessel on the radio to tell him the situation.

Sid explained over the radio to the officers that the vessel had passed survey, and the final survey certificate should have been sent to him by the Department.

He had done everything required by him to keep to the law. Any omission was completely the Department's fault. The two officers remained adamant the *Rainbow Venture* could not be moved.

Meanwhile queues of vehicles had started to line up to go to the island and Elmer had his barges running back and forth non stop.

Never one to give up, Sid looked up marine surveyor, David Mainwaring's home phone number in Bundaberg and rang him. Mainwaring was fortunately at home and was disgusted, when Sid told him the story.

"I'll go straight into the office and issue another temporary survey certificate to last you another month," he offered, "then I'll fax it to you."

When the certificate came through a short time later, Sid radioed John Pearce and told him he had it and was bringing it down to show the Harbours and Marine officers, so Pearce should bring the *Rainbow Venture* to the island to pick him up.

Pearce radioed back in anguish "These fellows won't let me. They say if I move the vessel, they will take my skipper's ticket, and I'll never be able to work as a skipper again."

Sid responded "Put them on the radio." When one of the officers spoke, Sid said the vessel would only be coming for him and would be in a private capacity. The officer refused to consider it.

Sid then an idea and phoned Sam Mitchell, the recent purchaser of the Rainbow Beach Information Centre, who booked tours for him, and asked if he faxed the certificate to him, would Mitchell take it to the *Rainbow Venture*.

In spite of having a shop full of people, Mitchell agreed, and the two Harbours and Marine officers had to concede defeat, but, Mitchell afterwards reported, suggested to him the certificate he bore could well be "a forgery." They were not however game to put that nasty little proposition to the test.

The *Rainbow Venture* loaded up and started work.

* * * *

The queue of vehicles waiting at Hook Point for the Rainbow Venture after the Easter 1989 weekend. A policeman on the very left of the photograph had to be called to duty to prevent queue jumping.

Sid was at a disadvantage in competing with Elmer in that with only the one barge, he no back up if things went wrong or work needed doing to the *Rainbow Venture*. He needed to be able to prove he could run a reliable service with just one vessel.

Don Caswell remembers well one night when the *Rainbow Venture* was in trouble. "Sid phoned me at home, and said the *Rainbow Venture* had gone aground while the skipper was taking it back to its mooring. He asked me to go and rescue it.

"I got to Inskip Point at 1.30 am. Max Williams met me and pointed to a light on the horizon. A deckie was waiting to take me out in a dinghy. The skipper on board was frantic.

"Sid kept calling on the radio to see if I'd arrived. I went onboard to the radio and tell him the vessel was very well aground. He was very quiet and thoughtful – as he is when things go badly wrong and gave me lots of suggestions as to methods I could use to try and free the barge. I told him not to call me on the radio anymore as I was going to be very busy.

"It was 4.30 am when I finally got the barge free. I called Eurong on the radio, not expecting an answer, but Sid responded immediately. He'd been sitting vigil all night."

Sid with the Rainbow Venture at Inskip Point.

When maintenance and painting was needed on the *Rainbow Venture* after two and a half years of continuous running, there was nothing for it but for Sid to take it out of service.

He chose the very quiet period before the Orchid Beach Fishing Competition in May 1989 to have it put on the slip in Maryborough.

He tried to hire another barge for the 10 days he anticipated the *Rainbow Venture* would be away, but there just wasn't one available.

When it left Inskip Point, Elmer made it known he would not carry Sid's day tour buses nor those of the other Sunshine Coast tour operators who had chosen to travel on the *Rainbow Venture.* Sid had to come up with a solution so he and the fellow tour operators who relied on him could keep running their tours.

Chris O'Grady and Mark Luscombe were two of these. Chris recalls "I started to go with Sid's barge soon after it arrived, because Elmer gave us tour operators a big lecture on what a bad bastard Sid was. I didn't like the things he said or the way he was going about things. He could have said thanks to us for all our support, but no, he just rubbished Sid.

"When the *Rainbow Venture* went on the slip, Elmer refused to carry my tour buses. But Sid wouldn't be beaten.

"He organized the *Snapper*, a charter fishing boat with a drop down front to come from Hervey Bay to Inskip Point to carry our passengers as well as his own.

"It could only carry passengers and no vehicles, so we left a bus on on Fraser Island, then our passengers were taken across on the *Snapper.* Sid kept us going by doing that. After the *Snapper* episode I knew Sid would always be able to work something out to keep us going in difficult circumstances".

O'Grady adds "Sid did a lot of things that we tour operators all benefited from, like fixing roads on the island. No-one else did anything like that. He deserved our support."

Another tour operator Mark Luscombe, who also had to use the *Snapper* says "I never thought to travel with any other barge operator than Sid after that. It wasn't ideal but it kept us going. I knew then Sid would do his best by me."

* * * *

The work on the *Rainbow Venture* on the Maryborough slipway had a lighter side, with Sid earning the gratitude of Kylie Minogue, and the crew of her first venture into movies. Already a television actress and pop singer, Kylie was making her first feature film, *"The Delinquents"* set in Maryborough in the 1950's.

One particular scene was of a mass of workers bicycling out of the gates of the big engineering works, Walkers Ltd. Cameras were set up ready for the bicycle exodus, and right then workers at the shipyard opposite the engineering works began to sandblast the *Rainbow Venture* hull for repainting.

Fortunately Sid was on hand keeping an eye on progress, for next thing an out of breath young man raced up to ask if a temporary halt could be called to the work on the ferry so the noise and dust didn't spoil the filming.

Although it was essential the work be done as fast as possible so the ferry could get back to Inskip Point, Sid had the workers stop. Next day the same young chap turned up to hand him a large envelope. Inside was a photograph of Kylie with a handwritten message how much she appreciated Sid's gesture.

On the night the *Rainbow Venture* was due to come off the slipway, the work on it complete, Sid was there to travel on it back to Inskip Point. But it got stuck on the slip.

In spite of the slip manager's and everyone else's best efforts to release the big vessel and let it slide back into the Mary River, it did not move.

Sid had skipper, Don Caswell put the motors on full power to try and create a wave to give it that bit more flotation. Nothing worked. The tide dropped; the opportunity was missed and it was another fortnight before another tide came high enough to try again.

During that fortnight the Orchid Beach Fishing competition took place, with hundreds of vehicles, most towing boats or trailers, heading to Fraser Island. Gordon Elmer could not believe his good fortune at having them all to himself.

When the next opportunity to get the *Rainbow Venture* off the slip occurred in the middle of the night two weeks later, slip owner Warren Hyne was there himself to watch, with two skin divers to go in the river to see if there was a blockage and a bulldozer to give the *Rainbow Venture* a big push down the slipway. It began to move and then slid quickly into the river. Hyne never sent Sid a bill for the slipping.

* * * *

Finally after eight months of running a free barge, Sid recognized the situation could not continue. His time share scheme was a total failure, and he had considerable loans to repay.

A conference with his bank financiers led to them strongly advising him to take up Elmer's offer to sell, and agreeing to lend the money to do so.

Mindful of Elmer's request he not deal with him directly, which he understood to be a face saving exercise, once he had made up his mind, Sid did not want any delay caused by dealing at third hand through a solicitor.

He went to his long time friend, Bevan Whitaker with the proposal they buy Elmer's barge business and Whitaker handle the negotiations with Elmer. Whitaker was happy to do so, for he had built a resort on Lady Elliott Island, and had been having problems finding a barge to make regular monthly stores and fuel deliveries to it.

He says "I had asked Sid several times over the years if he could bring one of his barges to Lady Elliott Island but it wasn't possible because they were being used full time on Fraser Island.

"I thought buying Elmer's business with two barges would be a good opportunity for me to get a reliable barge.

"We decided we would form a new barge company, and work out details of who would do what later, if my negotiations with Gordon Elmer were successful."

Elmer named his price and, once the bank agreed to finance the purchase in full, it was accepted without demur.

When it became apparent afterwards in Rainbow Beach that Sid was organizing the practical day to day operation of all the Inskip Point barges, Elmer claimed Whitaker had assured him Sid was not involved in the purchase. Whitaker was emphatic this was not the case, and he had given no such assurance, nor been asked to by Elmer.

The outcome was that the new company bought Elmer's business in September 1989, with his two barges, the 12 vehicle capacity *Eliza Fraser II* and the much smaller *Lady Fraser*, which in the event had not been sold earlier, and Elmer's landing area permits.

Sid was not at all surprised to receive a letter from the Department of Harbours and Marine telling him *Eliza Fraser II* had not been stability tested, and demanding that it should be before he could operate it.

He took great delight in sending a copy of the reply he had received three years earlier, when he complained Gordon Elmer hadn't had to have the vessel undergo stability testing. Signed by the then Minister for Harbours and Marine, Martin Tenni, it stated unequivocally that *Eliza Fraser II* did not need a stability test. The Harbours and Marine did not pursue the matter.

Barge fares now reverted to $25, the price Sid had charged when he introduced the *Rainbow Venture* three years before.

It was decided the double ended *Eliza Fraser II* would supplement the *Rainbow Venture* service at Inskip Point and the *Lady Fraser* would do the supply runs to Bev Whitaker's Lady Elliott Island resort. But the *Lady Fraser* was found to be so lightly constructed that it could not pass Harbours and Marine survey to go so far offshore. Sid immediately began to have plans drawn to have it lengthened and strengthened so it could become ocean going.

Bevan Whitaker, doing the administration of the new company, asked Sam and Maureen Mitchell at the Rainbow Beach Tourist Information Centre to manage the Inskip Point barges and offered Elmer's deckhand, Kosta Ladas a job.

Tour operator Mark Luscombe says "I was initially very concerned when Sid became the sole barge operator at Inskip Point that he could use the barges to make my life miserable. But he never did. His *Fraser Explorer Tours* from the Sunshine Coast was a direct competitor to my tours. But his buses appeared to receive no preferential treatment over our vehicles on the barges.

"Sid and I did have a few disagreements on various issues over the years. I remember one time Sid rang me because he had been told I had been saying his tour buses were not much good. We both argued and hung up on each other several times before it was over. I was worried about possible repercussions on the barges, but they never eventuated."

Over the years the hostility towards Sid by others of his rival Sunshine Coast tour operators had diminished when they saw he was prepared to give them mechanical help or accommodate their passengers if their buses broke down on the island.

They saw him too as being prepared to stand up to government on tour permit issues.

Sid asked a one time hostile fellow operator why the change in attitude and the man replied "We have realized you are the bastion between us and Government, and what is good for you is good for all of us."

Now the tour operators approached to ask if Sid and Whitaker would guarantee a reliable barge service, upon which their businesses depended, and give them a discount because they would be regular customers. In return they promised their loyalty should another barge come in to service at Inskip Point. This was agreed and when the operators asked for the agreement to be put in writing, Sid had his solicitors, Carswell and Co. in Hervey Bay, draw up a contract to this effect.

Once other regular users of the Inskip Point barges, island residents, professional fishermen and cartage contractors heard about the contracts offered to the tour operators, they came asking for discounts and contracts as well.

* * * *

At Eurong, the time share project was cancelled for lack of interest. In hindsight it was just as well because it could have demanded more administration than Sid's staff was capable of at that stage of resort development.

As soon as the *Korawinga* units were complete, five major Australian coach companies booked them out for two years ahead.

The Korawinga units completed.

As well as accommodation, their two night packages included ferry crossings, all meals and island tours giving Sid a very handsome income.

Sid's business went from strength to strength with this explosion in coach travel as well as the capacity patronage of the *Fraser Venture* from Hervey Bay, the rapid growth of his day trips and a steady build up of patronage on the Inskip Point barges.

* * * *

As soon as possible after the purchase of Elmer's business Sid set about having the *Lady Fraser* rebuilt so it could go to Lady Elliott Island to do supply runs for Bevan Whitaker's resort. Only a small portion of the original barge was useable. At Barry White's Maryborough shipyard Sid had the front cut off and a whole new, much enlarged front, built on, with a bigger door, stronger door wires and new motors.

Reconstruction took eight months to complete, and cost $400,000. The vessel was sandblasted and painted blue.

Sid discusses the rebuilding of the Lady Fraser with a whole new, much larger front, deck and door with shipwright, Barry White.

Don Caswell remembers well the night the *Lady Fraser* was to be taken off the Maryborough slipway at high tide and down to River Heads.

"There were Sid, Laurie Toy and Maurie Stone, a hydraulics engineer, as well as me to take it down the river and make sure everything was running properly. We had missed dinner, so Sid suggested we go to a roadhouse on the outskirts of Maryborough for something to eat before the *Lady Fraser* had to come off the slip at midnight.

"On the way Sid saw one of the resort cooks on days off coming out of a pub and heading for his car. Sid also saw a police car, so he did a bit of a swerve, and the police descended on him with the breathalyser. He blew into it and it recorded nil.

"Sid saw the cook starting his car so to keep the police distracted, he suggested they breathalyse me as I am going to be driving 'a big barge' down the river a bit later on. The police did, and again there was a nil reading.

"The cook has started to drive out of the pub car park, so then Sid suggested the police breathalyse Laurie as he was the engineer on the barge. They did. Nil. The cook was driving by, so Sid then said the police should test Maurie as he was the hydraulic engineer.

"They did so. Nil. By then the cook's car had disappeared over a hill."

With the *Lady Fraser* back in action Sid asked Don Caswell to go to Lady Elliott Island to check out where it would land with resort supplies.

Caswell came back shaking his head. "It is a narrow and very shallow channel cut through the coral reef." he reported. "It will be a tight squeeze for the *Lady Fraser* and it has to get in and out within two hours at the top of the tide. More than that and it will most likely hit bottom and get stuck. We can't risk it."

Sid found another vessel to run to Lady Elliott, owned by a former employee of his. By amicable accord Bevan Whitaker resigned as director of the barge company soon afterwards.

Sid now had no real plan what to do with the *Lady Fraser*. It was a very handsome vessel for carrying cargo or vehicles, but it was really superfluous to Sid's needs except to supplement his other barges for the few peak days each year.

Chapter 30

Encouraged by their successful campaign to have sand mining stopped on Fraser Island, conservationists led by John Sinclair moved on to have timber cutting halted and spoke of Fraser Island becoming totally protected and World Heritage listed.

They got nowhere, as expected, with Queensland's National Party led government but worked away on the A.L.P. Opposition. The A.L.P. shadow spokesman for the environment, Pat Comben was prepared to give Sinclair a good hearing – as evidenced by his acknowledging his first visit to Fraser Island had been with Sinclair and in Parliament in 1984 quoting information he had been given by Sinclair to try and stop Sid's dredging into the mouth of Wanggoolba Creek.

When it came to the state election of December 1989, the A.L.P. platform included a promise to hold an environmental inquiry into Fraser Island.

Within three months of the A.L.P. winning the election, the new Premier, Wayne Goss announced a Commission of Inquiry into the Conservation, Management and Use of Fraser Island would be held with Justice Tony Fitzgerald as its head.

Fitzgerald was possibly the most admired man in Queensland for his conduct of the earlier 1987-89 Inquiry into Official Corruption which brought about the downfall of Joh Bjelke Petersen as Premier, some of his ministers and senior police.

Impatient at delays before the Fraser Island Inquiry began, a group of radical activists moved on to the island in June 1990 to try and bring logging to a halt, and there they remained until May 1991 as a background to the inquiry proceedings.

They stood in front of bulldozers, glued themselves to logging machinery, interfered with the markings the Forestry Department put on the trees to be selectively logged, dug trenches across the roads used by the logging trucks and drove spikes into the trees making them too dangerous to send to the sawmills.

At one stage they invaded the home and logging camp of Fraser's last remaining timber contractor, Andy Postan disturbing and frightening him and his wife Helen in the middle of the night. More than a dozen protesters chained themselves to his equipment, super gluing their hands over locks, super gluing clasped hands together and super gluing themselves to the workshop doors. They had brought the media with them, and when the T.V. camera crew left, Andy and his workers were left to grind through the locks to release the protestors.

* * * *

At the end of August 1990, Tony Fitzgerald came to the island for a week to confer with interested people and see the island for himself. When he and his party came south of Happy Valley, Sid and I went to join the group. John Sinclair was already there. Fitzgerald proved adept at putting everyone at their ease, and soon brought out Sid's sense of humour, casting him in the role of big bad developer.

When the group stood on the high dune above beautiful Lake Wabby looking across at the dramatic bare sand blow dropping sheer into it, and Sinclair had finished extolling its beauty, Fitzgerald looked at Sid and asked "What would you do here Sid?" Sid played up brilliantly: "I'd put a cable car over the lake, from the top of the blow to where we are standing," he said. Sinclair, not on the same humourous wavelength as Fitzgerald and Sid, looked stricken.

At each scenic stop from then on, Fitzgerald always asked Sid what he would do, to see what he could come up with next and relieve the seriousness of the gathering. His best response was possibly at Red Lagoon, a reed filled lake off the beaten track that he had never seen before.

In the centre was a pole placed by the Forestry to measure water levels. "What would you do here, Sid?" came the usual question from Fitzgerald. "I'd hold speed boat races here," said Sid with a straight face. "In fact I've already started them. You see that pole in the middle, well on its other side it says 'Start' and 'Finish'."

During the inspection the group went to see the site for a big new resort, Kingfisher Bay, to be built on the west coast of Fraser Island just north of the derelict McKenzie's jetty where timber had been loaded on to punts in the 1920's.

The resort, to be built by Cosmos, a large Japanese development company, was on 67 hectares of land that had been made freehold many years before, when it was thought coal might be found under the peat bogs there. The site had a large flat area of low lying bogs encircled by high dunes.

When the proposed development had first been announced some years earlier by a man called Michael Hackett, he explained the bogs were to be transformed into lakes with units built around the edges on poles.

John Sinclair, who had objected to the development in the Local Government Court, but lost, was loud in his opposition to Kingfisher Bay, but by time Fitzgerald inspected the site, the developers had already built a massive timber wharf out to deep water in the Great Sandy Straits. Fitzgerald said that so much money having been committed to the project, there was no going back.

* * * *

Sid's role in the Fitzgerald Inquiry was not limited to lightening the sometimes heavy atmosphere with humour. He and I made a 21 page submission on island management issues. With the overriding purposes of the Inquiry, whether logging should be stopped, and World Heritage listing applied for, Sid was in a real dilemma. He felt sure that selective logging did not harm, indeed benefited, the forest. One major benefit was that firebreaks were maintained to protect the valuable trees.

He felt very strongly that the Forestry Department was the best to have in charge of the island because the men he dealt with on a daily basis on the island were immensely practical, energetic and capable. He recognised how important the timber industry was to the Maryborough economy.

But he also felt Fraser Island should have worldwide recognition as the special place it was, and be World Heritage listed.

His submission did not turn on these major issues, but when Fitzgerald's report was issued in May 1991, Sid was gratified to find the myriad practical suggestions he had made for improving island management were accepted entirely.

Fitzgerald recommended that logging be phased out and the whole of the Great Sandy Region, Fraser Island and Cooloola, be made a National Park and nominated for World Heritage Listing.

The Queensland Government followed these recommendations as far as Fraser Island was concerned, but not Cooloola, and the process towards applying to UNESCO for its nomination to World Heritage status began.

The last tree was cut on November 5 1991. All the Forestry Department staff left at the end of January 1992, and Sid and his staff were sorry to see them go. The fellowship between them and resort folk had been close and good natured.

The National Parks Service took over management of the whole island.

The last timber cutter, Andy Postan and his employees departed, leaving behind their "camp" to become a memorial to an important phase of Fraser's history. In January 1992 Sid's *Lady Fraser* barge brought a full load of Postan's logging machinery off the island.

Ironically just 10 days later two bush fires were caused by lightning strikes, one at the northern end of the island, the other around Dilli Village.

Postan had made a huge contribution in saving Fraser Island from devastating fires over the years, always being the first to be called on with his machinery to make firebreaks around the big blazes. Without his men and machinery, there was little the residents' Bush Fire Brigades, National Parks and Forestry Department fellows could do to stop the bush fires burning out thousands of hectares. The fires were so big that a massive pall of smoke hung over the island, Hervey Bay and even Maryborough. The Coast Guard had to put out a hazard warning to ships.

"We were working 15 hours straight before we got relief, day after day, back burning and fighting the fire against strong winds and were absolutely exhausted," described Murray Reid, First Officer of the Eurong Bush Fire Brigade. He added "It's pretty damn annoying when the greenies who spent so much time on the island to save the forests from logging couldn't even send one person to help us save them from fire."

The Queensland Government tried to minimise the adverse impacts of logging being halted after 128 years, not always successfully. Maryborough sawmills no longer needed as many employees, and six of them were employed by the National Parks Service as road workers on Fraser Island.

Unfortunately they did not have the skills to handle the equipment needed to keep the roads in good order, and the problems with the roads continued.

When the Government announced it would allocate a $1million towards improving the Wanggoolba to Eurong road, Sid pleaded publicly for the money not to be wasted.

"The Government knows hard surface roads are the only way to go through the open dry wallum country on either side of the rainforest and have been mucking about experimenting with rubber mats, wire mats and woodchip, none of which is working in any but the short term," he declared in an interview. "They should give up trying to reinvent the wheel. The most economical way to hard surface the roads is to do them properly from the start and that means bitumen.

"The roads through the rainforest would not need hard surfacing because the moisture content holds the roads firm. It is the dry sections at either end that deteriorate into great holes, bumps and dry bogs. I am sure the public would rather have the dry sections fixed up properly than keep having their money spent on futile experimentation."

Locky Fullerton, who was then responsible for the management of tourism operations on Fraser first for the Forestry Department then the National Parks, recalls one occasion when Sid lost patience with him and a man from the Department of Transport, when they were investigating ways to improve the roads other than bitumen.

"Sid felt that what we were doing was ludicrous and not worth pursuing. He made it clear he felt it was a waste of time," says Fullerton.

Sid pointed out that the sand miners had made a gravel road across the island from Buff Creek to Dilli Village, which was disused, but could provide a ready source of road base.

"In the past I have offered free barge cartage for materials, machinery and men if they were coming to make a decent road and would certainly be prepared to help again," he said.

Nothing however came of his plea.

The Government bought Andy Postan's big timber trucks and over the next few months put rubbish compactors on them to take rubbish off the island, as recommended by Fitzgerald.

They were so big and heavy, when filled from bins positioned along the surf beach and inland dumps, that steep sections of road had to be boarded for them to be driven up.

One of these roads was at Middle Rock, which immediately opened up the northern section of the island to everyone and effectively put an end to the National Park Service desire to keep it relatively tourist free.

Fitzgerald recommended that no more land be made available for development on Fraser Island and no more barge landing areas be established. As far as Sid was concerned these gave him a strong sense of business security.

Yet another management plan was drawn up for the whole Great Sandy Region to implement Fitzgerald's many recommendations, and again public input was sought. Sid felt it essential he be involved but it felt as if he was running on the same treadmill time and again, putting forward lengthy submissions.

In this period of intense government interest in Fraser Island a procession of politicians visited. Most of them called on Sid to get from the mouth of the most experienced island businessman his ideas what course future management should take.

Among them was the new Minister for Environment, Pat Comben, who had spoken out in Parliament about Sid's dredging plans in 1984 when in Opposition.

Now they met several times and developed a strong appreciation for each other's viewpoints. Comben to his surprise found Sid as committed to the island environment as he was, and was guest of honour at Sid's annual agents' party in July 1992.

When Comben resigned from Parliament for family health reasons after one term as one of the most dedicated Ministers of the first Goss government, Sid wrote a note of genuine regret.

Comben replied with a letter that Sid kept. In it Comben wrote "I will always appreciate the frank and open manner with which you approached all problems and challenges. Although we may have got off to a rocky start it became evident to me very quickly that you had the Island's future more clearly at heart than many others who claimed to speak for the Island.

"You have done a great job for tourism in the region and when you eventually move it will be a great loss to the industry."

Fraser Island was accorded World Heritage status a year later in December 1992 for its exceptional sand dune system, its rainforests growing in sand and its freshwater lakes. It was the 10th World Heritage site in Australia.

Chapter 31

Sid was philosophical about the proposed multimillion dollar Kingfisher Bay resort. He felt sure that he would lose his major coach company business to it for he wasn't in a financial position to do more towards his new resort plan for the time being, and while the *Korawinga* units were of high quality, the dining room and bar in the former Urangan wharf barracks were old country Queensland style, and guests had to walk 200 metres over the lawns to get between the two.

Sid prepared to move into new pastures rather than fight a battle he could not win to keep the coach company business.

When a Eurong neighbour Les Greensill, who had developed an island tour business around special interest and school groups decided to sell out in May 1991, Sid bought his business at auction. Its value was not in Greensill's three open backed Studebaker trucks, the last left on the island, but in his tour licences.

Because Greensill did irregular but wide ranging tours, his licences allowed him to go just about anywhere on the island at any time with three trucks full of passengers, compared with all other tour permits which regulated passenger numbers, times and routes. Sid realised such unlimited licenses would be of immense future potential.

In the meantime he expected his purchase of Greensill's business would bring him more school and safari group tours, and he believed this was an area in which the upmarket Kingfisher Bay resort would not be in the least interested.

To upgrade his facilities for these budget groups and to complete the Government's required expenditure of $2million on his special lease at Eurong, Sid built twelve timber cabins, on one corner of the land, well away from the new *Korawinga* units.

A covered dining area was erected in the midst of them and the small hut that was the original workers' accommodation, then shop, then linen store was transformed yet again into a camp kitchen for the use of the cooks that some of the regular safari groups brought with them.

When the cabins, ***(above)*** were complete Sid advised the Lands Department he had fulfilled the $2 million building condition on the special lease, and in 1992, the Queensland Government finally granted him a 99 year lease on the land. It wasn't the freehold he had been promised, but it was as good as he was going to get and indeed it was a secure enough tenure for him to move on with his resort planning.

New coach companies concentrating on 18 to 35 years olds had sprung up and they booked regular stopovers in the new cabins. But not all were worth the bargain rates they negotiated for their stays. Alcohol featured fairly prominently in their holidays, leading to some thoughtless behaviour. Sid had to tell one company it was no longer welcome after a series of incidents included its youthful patrons swinging on water pipes and breaking them; playing murder in the dining room, with falling victims dragging table cloths off tables with all the food and crockery; and putting invisible cling wrap over all the toilet seats.

The cabins also attracted special interest groups. One resort manager, Ken Bennett well remembers the group of artists who wanted to repay Sid and the staff for the great time they had had.

They decided they would leave a memento of their stay, so on their last day, when by chance Sid had had to go to Maryborough on business, the artists set about making a collage over the front of the pub. They strung a fishing net they had found on the beach from its upper balcony then worked into the net all the flotsam and jetsam they had picked up from the beach during their stay.

"They decorated the pub with all this rubbish," says Ken. "I thought I'd better get it down before Sid saw it, and hoped the group left before he got home. It was a near thing. I was waving them off at the front of the resort when I saw Sid driving in the back. I managed to get most of it down before he saw it, thank goodness."

* * * *

Sid's tours grew steadily and by 1991 his buses were carrying more than 30,000 day trip passengers a year from Hervey Bay, 20,000 from the Sunshine Coast and Rainbow Beach combined, and more than 13,000 on two and three night accommodated and safari tours.

Sid himself didn't drive his tours any longer, unless there was an emergency. Murray Reid remembers one day he got a call to race out quickly to Central Station to take over driving a bus load of day trippers.

Sid had been at the Wanggoolba Creek ferry landing ready to go to the mainland when the *Fraser Venture* arrived and he found he was short a driver, so he had to forego his mainland trip and drive a bus. He wasn't happy.

Reid got to Central Station just as Sid pulled up in the bus and let the people out. "Sid was always impressing on the drivers that they had to give a good commentary, so not wanting to repeat what Sid had already said, I asked him what he had told the people between Wanggoolba Creek landing and Central Station," Murray recounts.

"He said 'Nothing.' I asked if he'd introduced himself, and he said 'No.' So when all the people got back to the bus and I took over, I apologized and said Sid wasn't a regular driver, but was the resort gardener or something, and that he mumbled a lot.

"One of the passengers said 'He didn't mumble. He just didn't say anything.' I told the passenger 'You're very lucky.'"

* * * *

George Bezant's travel office in Hervey Bay continued to handle all the agents' day tour bookings and vehicle bookings on the *Fraser Venture* until one December day in 1989 Graeme Coutts-Smith, the owner of Happy Valley resort, telephoned Sid to ask if his stores truck was not welcome on the vessel. He complained that he had twice booked his truck on the ferry to have it turned away when it arrived at River Heads.

Sid immediately phoned George Bezant to find out what had happened, and it emerged a new girl had been employed to handle the ferry bookings among other things, but no-one had thought to tell her there was a limit on the vehicle bookings she could take. So she just kept on taking bookings until the *Fraser Venture* was well and truly overbooked.

Sid, who prided himself on the ferry service, was very upset and George Bezant responded defensively and perhaps too hastily that he would resign on Christmas Eve two weeks hence. Possibly Bezant felt he had Sid over a barrel with the holiday peak coming and Sid would ask him to continue.

Sid however took him at his word and approached Russ Parker, a tour driver who had been working for him since 1984, to ask if and his wife Polly would manage the *Fraser Venture*, with May Jensen doing the job on their days off.

Russ had been ready to give up driving over the rough island roads for health reasons and though managing the tour bookings was a big job, he felt he knew how the business operated well enough for he, Polly and May to be able to handle it.

And handle it they did for nine years with the utmost efficiency and by their good nature earned the friendship of all the agents. As the faces of the Hervey Bay arm of his business Sid could not have chosen better.

The work involved the Parkers for ten days and May for four days a fortnight taking phone calls from early morning to late evening from agents making bookings on behalf of their customers in motels, hotels and caravan parks, and finding out where they wanted to be picked up by the double decker and by now two more courtesy buses.

Polly was nominated by one agent for a Telecom business award for friendly and efficient telephone manner, and came second in the entire region, a very satisfying result.

Once they had the bookings, the Parkers then had to list all the passengers in order of pick up for the courtesy bus drivers, and make a second list by agent for the monthly accounts. These had to be personally taken to the agents and the money collected every month, as Sid insisted on Russ and Polly keeping close personal contact with the agents.

Russell had been a motorcycle policeman in Victoria before he had come to Hervey Bay in the early 1980's, and loved motorbikes but had never had one of his own. Sid bought one of Russell's choosing as a gift and to do his monthly rounds of the agents.

The Parkers worked from home and every morning the drivers would call in to pick up their passenger lists and Polly also found her kitchen invaded by drivers wanting an early morning cup of coffee before they went on their way. In the evenings the drivers would call in again to talk over any issues that had arisen during the day. "I was buying commercial size cans of coffee," Polly says.

Sid too was a coffee regular at the Parkers' house whenever he was in Hervey Bay and on one such day he saw both Russ and Polly writing page upon page of names. "How often do you have to do that?" he asked.

"Every day," Polly replied.

"Would a computer help?" Sid asked, in one leap overcoming his innate prejudice against computers, and his refusal to have one at Eurong. Once the Hervey Bay operation had given the lead, it was assumed that was a blanket change of heart and computers were quickly purchased for the rest of the business. Not before time.

* * * *

Another new business Sid moved into was whale watching in Hervey Bay. This industry had been started in the mid 1980's. He had been on one of the first whale watch cruises, and watched the growth of the industry with interest.

Humpbacks whales came into the Bay only between August and late October on their annual migration from breeding in Barrier Reef waters to their Antarctic feeding grounds. But those few short weeks brought thousands of visitors to Hervey Bay to watch the whales in ideal calm water conditions. Before long the National Parks Service stepped in to regulate whale watching and granted 20 licenses to existing operators, mainly the charter fishing boat owners.

Sid felt whale watching had far more potential if an upgraded fleet of more suitable vessels could be developed and he early realised how whale watching could be a useful adjunct to his Fraser Island enterprise, combining whale watching and island tour tickets at a small discount, each supporting the other.

John Webster, who had bought a Fraser Island tour business just before Sid introduced the *Fraser Venture* in 1983, had turned to whale watching during the winter months. He now wanted to sell his business with its Fraser Island and whale watching licenses, his three buses and his boat. Sid bought it lock stock and barrel in July 1991.

The launch Sid had bought from Webster, the *Islander*, was in poor shape, but Sid didn't intend to keep it long. He gave Webster's elderly buses to staff who asked for them to make into mobile homes for holidays.

Again it had been the licenses were what Sid was after. It was an ideal purchase for him. As well as giving him entry into whale watching, he could now carry as many passengers on island tours as all the other tour operators' combined and guaranteed his tours could continue to grow well into the future.

Webster's Fraser Island tour driver, Graham Stocks seemed to come with the purchase. The day after Sid became the new owner of Webster's business, Graham just turned up ready to go to work.

He had been a one time councillor on the Hervey Bay City Council and a couple of times had spoken out against Sid's business efforts, suggesting for instance when Sid began tours from the Sunshine Coast that he would be channelling his tour passengers through there at the expense of Hervey Bay. These hostile little forays, made obviously in his employer, John Webster's interest, were not mentioned by either man and Stocksie was simply kept on.

On one of his early driving days on an unfamiliar route, he was running about 10 minutes late driving through Eurong and Sid admonished him "You've got to keep up with the other buses, because you can't hold up the ferry."

"Well I haven't got a watch," Stocksie complained. "You'll have to give me a pay rise so I can buy one."

He didn't get a pay rise, but Sid took the watch off his own wrist and handed it to Graham. It was a $9 plastic one Sid had taken from the stock in the shop just the day before when his own watch had stopped.

Stocksie proved to be one of the most knowledgeable of Sid's tour drivers about the island's natural history, and remained with Sid until he retired – and then willingly came out of retirement when asked to lead special interest groups.

When Sid bought John Webster's business it was only a week or so to go before the whale watching season began. Sid did not have time to do anything other than operate the whale watching business as Webster had. He employed Webster as skipper and his deckhand/cruise hostess, Robyn Bostock for the season.

He asked Hervey Bay real estate and travel agent, Trevor Cecil to manage the whale watch bookings for him.

Sid's entry into whale watching was readily accepted by the other vessel owners.

One of the original commercial whale watch operators, Eddy May says "We were having problems with the Queensland Government and its permit system. When Sid came into whale watching the other operators felt it would benefit them having Sid on side as his influence on Fraser Island was well known."

Whale watching increasingly made the Urangan Boat Harbour a focal point for tourists, and the government called tenders for it to be developed. New finger jetties were installed for the whale watch fleet and a mass of private boats. A big resort complex and a terminal with shop spaces for rent were built on its fringes.

Sid took up one of the shops as a ticketing and sales office for his ever expanding business and more staff was needed to man it.

It was long overdue and Polly Parker was glad to have her kitchen back to herself instead of a home from home for Sid's mainland staff.

Whereas other shop lessees, including Kingfisher Bay and Top Tours, another island tour operator, leased large spaces in the new terminal and made walk-in booking offices in them, Sid rented a small space but put his counter right at the front of it.

This made it more immediately visible and more conducive to people stopping by to pick up brochures without having to walk inside and be engaged in a sales pitch.

He had his staff sell other holiday products too so his shop took on the appearance of an all purpose tourist information centre. Even in such simple things Sid put in a lot of thought to increase custom.

* * * *

The *Lady Fraser* barge had been left idle, apart from a few days work in peak seasons, since she had been extended and refitted the previous year.

Then Michael Hackett at Kingfisher Bay advertised for a barge to carry construction materials for the new resort.

Sid was not enamoured of Hackett. He had brought a party to Eurong Beach for dinner one evening, and the chef told Sid that soon after they had left, Hackett had telephoned offering him a job. He was obviously studying Sid's operations carefully, for next he bought the lease on the Noosa booking office Jan and John Graham, Sid's *Fraser Explorer* tour managers, were renting and gave them notice to quit.

The Grahams were never-say-die people, and straightaway went and found another shop in Hastings Street and opened up for business directly opposite.

But when Hackett advertised for a barge to charter and Sid had the *Lady Fraser* sitting idle, it seemed logical to try and recoup what it had cost him.

A contract was drawn up, with Hackett signing to make weekly payments for the charter, and in mid 1991 the *Lady Fraser* began carrying big trucks laden with building materials to Kingfisher Bay two and three times a day through the week.

The Lady Fraser with construction trucks onboard with the Fraser Venture in the background.

* * * *

At Eurong, Sid was building more as he could afford it. With Kingfisher Bay resort now beginning to take shape, he put his new accommodation buildings on the back burner for the time being until it became clear where his priorities would lie.

Instead at long last, he completed the urgently needed new shop and eight units above it that had for years been just a foundation.

No matter what happened at Kingfisher Bay, custom for the shop would always come from the surf beach campers and the vehicles driving through Eurong, now more than ever the cross roads of Fraser Island.

The shop was very large and catered for all holidaymaker needs, from a big grocery section at one end and a large selection of souvenirs at the other. Walls were taken up with shelves of 4WD vehicle parts, camping, and fishing gear. It helped make Eurong Beach the major supply centre on Fraser Island.

Lines of customers wait in the new shop during the Christmas holidays.

Representatives of Streets ice cream told Sid that he sold more ice creams than any other retail outlet in Queensland. They took photographs of the store, and Sid chuckled imagining them showing the photographs to other shopkeepers round the state to urge them to match the performance, without them knowing he had up to 20 bus loads of people pulling up at the shop at least once and often twice a day.

The shop had the only in-house telephones with outside lines, as well as the business radio, so became the hub of the entire resort with accommodation bookings and daily tour numbers being taken there and all the supply ordering done.

Its manager was a chap who had begun working at Eurong as a kitchen hand in the bistro some years earlier.

Ian Hagart's intelligence and earlier business experience were quickly recognised and he was soon transferred to the shop. Ian was to remain at Eurong for 12 years, marry an apprentice chef, Kim and have three children.

When Ian looked for a business opportunity for himself, hiring out two or three 4WD cars from the resort, Sid lent him some of the money to get started. He saw Ian's business as complementing the resort infrastructure but did not want to go into vehicle hire himself.

* * * *

By mid 1991, the *Fraser Venture* was running short of space for the increasing number of 4WD hire vehicles wanting to travel on it to the island. Russ and Polly Parker kept asking Sid "When are you going to buy another ferry?"

Sid decided to increase the size of the *Venture* rather than buy another vessel. He planned for it to be cut it in two across its vehicle deck, so a 12 metre long box section of hull and deck could be inserted into it. This would enable it to carry eight more vehicles.

To cater for the extra passengers in vehicles and his growing day trip numbers, he designed an open "sun" deck to project out from the saloon with bench seating. The work was to cost $500,000 – more than the *Fraser Venture* had cost to build eight years before. This was an important undertaking, not only for Sid's business, for the *Fraser Venture* was the major element in the growth of Hervey Bay tourism based on Fraser Island, and enlarging the vessel enabled the Bay's tourism industry to keep up with the demand for island access.

Sid went to Maryborough shipbuilder Barry White with the plans. To minimise the time the *Fraser Venture* would be out of service on the Maryborough slip while the work was being done, Sid instructed Barry to have the box section of hull and deck fabricated beforehand, so that when the vessel arrived, it could be cut in two, the pieces pulled apart on the slip and the new section welded in as speedily as possible.

The *Rainbow Venture* would be brought from Inskip Point to take over the *Fraser Venture* run between River Heads and Wanggoolba Creek and the Inskip Point run would be left to the little *Eliza Fraser II.*

The date chosen for this big job was after the October 1991 school holidays in the traditionally very quiet traffic period before Christmas.

Kosta Ladas, the one time Elmer deckhand, had by this time been trained to qualify as skipper of the *Rainbow Venture,* and it was arranged he go with it on the Wanggoolba Creek-River Heads run. He first wanted to go to Greece to visit his family and to take his young son, as insurance, he said, that Greek authorities would not keep him there to do the compulsory National Service he had avoided by coming to Australia. Sid gifted him $1,000 so the child could go, and away they went for six weeks.

Everything was organised but then everything changed. Ian Dean, the former head skipper for Gordon Elmer, announced he had acquired a $500,000 barge *Perseverance* and was bringing it to Inskip Point.

Chapter 32

When Sid learned Ian Dean was bringing a barge to Inskip Point to compete with his barges, he says his first thought was "Oh no, here we go again."

Sid believed Dean, as his earlier rival Gordon Elmer's head skipper, was the instigator of many of the Elmer "barge war" tactics, certainly crossing sharply across the *Rainbow Venture* bows, which would have caused collisions had the *Rainbow Venture* crew not taken emergency avoiding action time and again. He was fearful of his passengers, crew and barges being put in danger again.

He thought of cancelling the work lengthening the *Fraser Venture* so the *Rainbow Venture* could remain at Inskip, but when he saw Dean's barge he decided to go ahead with the original plan. It was a small cattle barge that had been running to an island off the Victorian coast, with high sides and a door suitable for loading off a jetty or high ramp. It could carry only eight vehicles and no large vehicles such as buses or trucks or even boats could fit through its very narrow door.

When it came to loading vehicles off the long sloping beach at Inskip Point, it was totally unsuitable, as Dean's son Tony acknowledged, for vehicles had to drive through the sea to get to it. Nobody wanted to put their vehicles in salt water. Tony Dean adds that the *Perseverance* rolled around a lot at sea. Before it began operating from Inskip Point, it lost a propeller. Next day the crew on the *Eliza Fraser II* found one of its propellers was missing, and the *Perseverance* was operable again.

Ian Dean started talking tough. In the media, which relished another barge war, he declared he was going to start operating without having a Harbours and Marine landing spot, even if he got arrested.

At Inskip Point the area allotted to barge landing had been changed by the Harbours Corporation in August 1991. As more people came to camp at Inskip Point and swim in front of their tent sites, it was too dangerous for the barges to operate there.

They were moved further west along Inskip Point to a specially designated area, at the end of the beach access track.

Four individual landing permits within the area were worked out by compass degrees, and three were allotted to the Melksham barges for which rent was charged annually. The most easterly was very exposed to wind and tide so only two of the three were useable but these were the best landing positions for traffic access. Dean was allotted the fourth, most westerly landing place.

He announced he was going to charge only $25 a return crossing, compared with Sid's price now of $30. Sid dropped his price to match. Soon after Dean began operating on October 19, the argy bargy between the crews began, and day after day the log books record he drove the *Perseverance* at dangerously close quarters to Sid's barges.

Early in November Dean told Sid's crew he was going to blow up one of Sid's barges. It may have been an idle threat made in the heat of the moment, but Sid thought it was a distinct possibility after the destruction of his buses and the shooting in the previous "barge war", so had one or other of his crew sleeping on the *Eliza Fraser II* every night. The log book of the time calls them watchdogs.

When Sid's crew learned Dean was charging $20 a short time later, Sid again matched his price.

Dean complained to the Harbours Corporation the westernmost landing area allotted to him was unusable. Sid was reluctantly forced by the Corporation to cede to Dean 20 metres of one of his landing areas to join on to his area. Reports on a meeting to discuss the issue mention how totally uncooperative Sid was.

Sid says he would have co-existed peacefully with any other competitor, but with Dean's earlier tactics and now threatening to blow up his barge, and again endangering his barges by cutting across the bows, he found the situation totally unacceptable. There is no doubt he did not want Dean as a competitor working right alongside him.

* * * *

When Sid told the Sunshine Coast tour operators, some of whom by now were running two and three buses daily, that the *Rainbow Venture* was going to Wanggoolba Creek to replace the *Fraser Venture* for several weeks, leaving only the *Eliza Fraser II*, they were very unhappy.

Their day tours to Fraser were a minimum of 12 hours long and they didn't want hold ups getting to and from the island adding to that. With the *Eliza Fraser II* only able to carry 12 standard vehicles they anticipated long delays for their buses. They said they could handle a week here and there while the *Rainbow Venture* was away but not a long period, as was now likely.

To prevent Dean getting a leg in with his regular customers and more so to keep faith that he would provide a good reliable service, Sid stopped charging for what turned out to be seven weeks while the *Rainbow Venture* was away. In this normally very quiet time of year Sid did not expect many customers other than his regulars.

At a tour operators' meeting in late November 1991 it was obvious the free barge had kept the Sunshine Coast operators on side, for they came to thank Sid and one of them, Rob Moffat light heartedly commented "You'll be giving us free cartons of beer next." Everyone laughed but this joke was to have amazing repercussions.

Word soon spread the barge war was on again. The media loved a good stoush, and took the obvious course of portraying Sid as the Goliath and Dean as the underdog. A bad media performer at any time, Sid's anger at the way he was portrayed when he had worked so hard to provide a good service, led him to handle provocative media questioning badly.

One reporter in particular appeared to set out to make Sid angry as a deliberate tactic to get him to make outlandish statements. He was harassed trying to solve problems with the lengthening of the *Fraser Venture*, and the last thing he could cope with was goading from the reporter. It took two interviews before Sid realised what he was about and when the reporter rang him a third time, Sid kept a rein on his temper and answered most politely.

When the reporter asked offensively "Which politicians do you know?" Sid began to list all the politicians he had heard of. When he started with Bob Hawke and Joh Bjelke Petersen, the reporter hung up on him and never bothered him again. He realised Sid had woken up to his tactics, but by then the damage was done.

Sid learned a harsh lesson by being too open, and trusted some journalists out for a headline with too much information.

Sid told the joke about the beer but one journalist out for stirring a good controversy reported it as Sid's intention. This appeared as a headline "Free fares, free beer likely."

It was one of the traditionally quietest times of the year, November to mid December when very few barge customers were expected, but the publicity was so great that visitors, who would not have thought of going to Fraser at that time, began flocking for the free barge. They must have been greatly disappointed when they were not given free beer as well.

The free barge lasted seven weeks, with the Trade Practices Commission being alerted by Dean and asking Sid to please explain. He did so, that it was a temporary measure only while the *Eliza Fraser II* was providing an admittedly inadequate service. In its reply the TPC said it would be taking no further action, but Sid had better learn about the competition law.

Sid had to spend almost all of this time in Maryborough supervising the lengthening of the *Fraser Venture.*

"If you are there you get a much better job and a faster job. When workers know you are around the place if anything is wrong, they put it right. If you are not there they cover it up if they can. That's true of any job in any industry," says Sid.

"In this case I found the shipbuilder had made the decking plate on the box section to be inserted into the ferry of thinner steel than the original decking. If I had made them rebuild the box section it would have taken months, and it was not acceptable with the Christmas holidays coming.

"The problem could be fixed a different way and so I did that, insisting the box section have a lot more bracing to compensate for the lesser plate thickness."

The Fraser Venture is cut in two and the halves moved apart on the Maryborough slipway.

The prefabricated box section of deck is delivered to the site.

The box section is lifted into place.

The new deck and sun deck are welded on to the back of the original ferry.

All the new sections are put in place and the Fraser Venture is ready for painting.

The *Fraser Venture* was completed and put back into service to Wanggoolba Creek on December 21.

The lengthening of the Fraser Venture did not come before time and it was soon carrying capacity crowds again.

The *Rainbow Venture* arrived back at Inskip Point on December 23 and the fare went back to $20.

Dean never did fare well. The *Perseverance* broke down at times, leaving customers stranded on the island, until one of Sid's barges brought them back.

Then on January 13 1992 Cyclone Betsy passed a short distance seaward of Fraser Island. Holidaymakers packed up and left en masse. Big seas were pushed by high winds into the Inskip Point strait. The *Perseverance* could not handle the rough seas, and Dean had to tie it up.

Some years before, Sid had been asked by the State Emergency Service if, in the event of a cyclone, he would keep the *Fraser* and *Rainbow Ventures* running to evacuate the island. Now he did so, although hardly anyone came on to the island. It was a notable demonstration that Sid took his responsibilities seriously – and how seaworthy his barges were and how dependable the service he offered.

When, towards the end of January, the Department of Harbours and Marine, wrote to Dean asking him to pay the annual rent for his landing area, a sum of about $100 and, more financially significant perhaps, also send proof he had third party insurance on the barge, which would have cost at least $7000, Dean threw in the towel. He sent neither, but a Departmental note made at the time says he contacted the Department to say he was not going to run the *Perseverance* any longer on the grounds that the landing place allotted to him was no good.

However Dean continued to pretend he had a landing area lease and just before Easter, he telephoned Sid and asked if he wanted to buy it. Sid agreed, for in bad weather conditions he needed the 20m landing area he had been made to give to Dean. A contract for the sale of the landing lease was drawn up and signed and Sid paid $10,000 for it. It was not until many years later that Sid learned that Dean had never properly acquired the landing area so had nothing to sell, and he had been cheated.

At the meeting to discuss their agreement Dean said he had no intention of ever going into the barge business again, and a fairly standard clause was put into the contract by Sid's solicitors that he would not do so for seven years. He soon began an ice works in Rainbow Beach. Tony Dean says the *Perseverance* had steering and hydraulic problems, and eventually it was towed from the area.

* * * *

The growth of interest in Fraser Island gave Sid a reputation far beyond its shores as the pioneer of tourism.

Reporter Charles Wooley came to interview Sid for a national television programme *Sixty Minutes.* At first when asked to do an interview Sid declined.

Wooley was not only charming but persistent and finally extracted from Sid an agreement he could do a story about him. He was however totally unprepared for how shy Sid was. He answered Wooley's questions quite naturally if a little grudgingly, until the camera was turned on, then he froze.

Steve Jensen remembers witnessing the first painful attempt to get Sid to talk.

"I remember Wooley asked Sid if he went fishing, expecting that anyone who lived on the beachfront of Fraser Island would be a keen fisherman and this would break the ice. Sid looked at Wooley as if he were mad and replied 'To go fishing I'd have to buy a rod and tackle, take time off work, buy bait and then there would be no guarantee I would catch anything. It's far cheaper for me to buy fish from the shop.' Then he went quiet again."

Exasperated Wooley finally asked Sid, on film "You really don't want us here, do you?" To which he gave a heartfelt one word answer "No."

"You wish we would go away, don't you?" Wooley persisted. "Actually I wouldn't mind you being here so much if you hadn't brought that camera with you," Sid replied.

Later in the pub Wooley was still bewildered: "We have never had anyone we've been doing a feature on not welcome us with open arms," he told a host of highly amused resort staff who knew how shy Sid was. He was only willing to be filmed reading one of his collection of *Truck and Bus* magazines, which he searched assiduously for bargains.

With no other option, Wooley did his story about how he couldn't get Sid to talk and used me to fill in as best I could telling some of the tales about Sid's early exploits while he just sat next to me saying absolutely nothing.

When he was not being interviewed, he was his usual self. Between takes the camera and sound crew complained about the weight of the equipment they were having to lug around the island.

"This is antiquated gear," they confided in Sid. "The latest gear is much lighter, but Kerry Packer won't buy it for us."

"Does that old gear still get good results?" Sid inquired.

"Oh yes," they acknowledged.

"In that case there's no need to buy new gear is there?" Sid responded.

Steve Jensen was at the barge landing when Sid drove Wooley and the film crew back to the *Fraser Venture* to go to the mainland.

"Wooley stood on the top deck and shouted 'Goodbye Sid.'" Steve describes. "He was clever enough to have had his cameraman wait on shore and get ready to film Sid, expecting him to finally break his silence to reply. And Sid spoke. He called back 'Goodbye Charles. Don't hurry back.'

"Wooley made his story around Sid not speaking, unlike other folk who never stops talking about themselves for the programme, and it was an hilarious segment when it came out."

Stories about how he pioneered tourism to Fraser Island even appeared in American media, with one such story emphasising how he used to go barefoot and describing my greatest contribution as persuading him to wear shoes.

May Jensen says "I remember when he first got shoes. He had been on holiday overseas and he'd had to wear shoes. When he came home he tried to go barefoot again. I saw him hopping along.

"His feet had softened up and the sand was too hot. But he persevered and we never saw the shoes again for years."

Laurie Toy too has a shoe story to tell. "I remember when Sid first got shoes. He hadn't worn shoes since I'd known him, but this day Tommy Cunningham and I were working under a bus when we saw these sparkling white Reeboks appear in our line of sight. Of course we didn't know it was Sid until we heard him give his usual greeting 'How's it going then?' We got such a surprise we both shot up and banged our heads underneath the bus. He said he wouldn't come into the workshop because he didn't want to get his shoes dirty. I said that was a good idea."

* * * *

Just when everything was going smoothly, there came a major hiccup. Michael Hackett, for no reason known to Sid, stopped paying the weekly accounts for the charter of the *Lady Fraser* taking construction materials to Kingfisher Bay resort in April 1992. Sid and I had planned a month's overseas holiday, and before we left in May Sid phoned Hackett asking him please to catch up the five weeks and many thousands of dollars owing.

When we returned, no further payments had been made. They were now nine weeks overdue, and it was becoming a worry for the costs of the fuel and wages for the *Lady Fraser* were high. Sid immediately phoned Hackett, who instead of offering an apology or explanation, made some sneering response.

This was not a good move, and the conversation concluded with Sid giving Hackett a week to catch up or he would stop the barge running and Hackett saying "You wouldn't be game to do that."

The week went to the following Wednesday. On the Tuesday Sid rang Hackett to give him a final opportunity to pay the money owing and again Hackett made a contemptuous remark. Come the deadline of Wednesday lunchtime and no payment, Sid radioed the skipper on the *Lady Fraser* at River Heads and told him he wasn't going to Kingfisher any more.

"But I have a full load of trucks on board," the skipper protested. "Back them off," Sid ordered, "I'm sorry but Hackett won't tell me what's going on and I can't keep running if I don't know whether I'll ever get paid."

A few weeks later he did get paid the $50,000 owing, the day before the issue went to court. It took months before Hackett could get another barge.

After that Sid would not deal with Kingfisher Bay for some years, until Hackett had long gone and new executives made every effort to heal the breach.

The *Lady Fraser* worked the July school holidays at Inskip Point and was then tied up, idle again. Only two months passed before a Proserpine businessman, John Bowman contacted Sid to ask if he had a barge for sale, suitable for cargo trips to the Whitsunday Islands. He offered a very good price, which Sid accepted and away sailed the *Lady Fraser*. It is still working in the Whitsundays.

Chapter 33

For almost a year since he had begun whale watching cruises in Hervey Bay, Sid had been looking for a vessel to replace the old *Islander* he had bought from John Webster. With the 1992 winter whale watch season fast approaching a fellow whale watch boat owner, Eddie May told him of two vessels for sale in Cairns.

A week later Eddie reported that Michael Hackett of Kingfisher Bay had beaten Sid to the punch. A short time later it emerged Hackett had indeed bought one of the Cairns boats – but it wasn't the one Sid had thought the more suitable for whale watching.

Off he went to Cairns with mechanic, Laurie Toy to inspect the *Calypso Lady.* A large 30m catamaran with decks on two levels, seating for 276 passengers in two large saloons, one with a bar and galley, and open areas all the way round so whales could be viewed wherever they appeared, it was ideal.

It had originally been built for tourism entrepreneur Keith Williams to transport people to his Hamilton Island development. Now it belonged to a Japanese company.

Sid tried hard to make an appointment with the company representative, to talk terms face to face. The man would only negotiate at arm's length, and it looked as if it was going to take a while to come to agreement so Sid sent Laurie home.

No-one was more surprised than Sid when the $1.2 million price tag was suddenly slashed the very next day, and he got the vessel at the bargain price he had begun negotiations with.

Sid was joined in Cairns by his son Bill, Laurie Toy and his wife Elaine and additional crew to motor the *Calypso Lady* back to Hervey Bay. It was not the island hopping holiday cruise the crew had hoped they would get.

For a start Sid didn't want to waste any time getting the vessel home to tidy it up ready for the whale season just weeks away, so he only allowed one island stop and as soon as the vessel was fuelled up, on they went.

Then Bill came down with chicken pox. Finally the weather turned bad and nearly everyone got sea sick – except Elaine who cheerfully worked her passage by cooking up huge plates of bacon and eggs for each watch.

* * * *

Once the vessel was in Hervey Bay, Sid had it taken out of the water to give it thorough overhaul, a new paint job, white with a blue and an orange stripe across its hull to match the *Fraser Venture,* and extend its exhaust pipes from the waterline to high over the vessel so engine fumes would upset neither passengers nor whales.

Sid on board the new Islander.

The new *Islander,* with Don Caswell an enthusiastic skipper and Elaine Toy as head hostess, was to become the most popular whale watch vessel in the fleet in its first season and remained so for the decade Sid operated it.

The majority of its passengers took advantage of the small discount to book Fraser Island tours as well and the winter months became the busiest three month period of the year for Sid's business.

The Islander goes whale watching with a capacity crowd of passengers.

Sid sold the original elderly *Islander* he had bought from John Webster to a Cairns chap who wanted to start cruises for backpackers, and there was great confusion when he applied to the Ships Registrar in Canberra to have the two names swapped. The forms were filled in; the money paid for the two name changes *Calypso Lady* for *Islander* and vice versa. It wasn't until Sid came to sell the *Islander* ten years later that he found it was still registered as *Calypso Lady*. It appeared the name swap had been put in the too hard basket and left there.

* * * *

As ever when he became involved in a new venture, Sid set out to learn as much about it as possible.

This learning process, he decided, would take us to Antarctica, the summer home and feeding grounds of the humpback whales, in February 1992, long before it became a tourist destination.

I was extremely fearful about the voyage, and the essential reading list we were given beforehand did nothing to make me feel happier with such book titles as *Blizzard and Fire, The Abominable Snow Woman, Voyage into Danger* and *The Worst Journey in the World.*

Sid got deeply involved in one book about whaling in Antarctica in the 1950's, and every few minutes would chuckle and pass the book over for me to read about horrendous seas, minus 57 degree temperatures, 135 knot winds and the like. The worst bit was when the whaling ship hit an ice berg.

We had to buy an incredible array of clothing from non slip gum boots to thermal underwear, thick woolly trousers, waterproof trousers, woolly jackets and parkas all to be worn at the same time. All my clobber was navy and red. Sid hated shopping and as soon as he got something that fitted he said "That'll do." As a result his colour scheme was khaki, purple, magenta, navy and olive green.

Off we went on a 6,900 tonne expedition vessel, *Frontier Spirit* which had a specially strengthened hull to break through light ice and was one of only two small ships, the other a former Russian ice breaker, going to Antarctica. It took a week to reach Antarctica from Bluff in New Zealand through the Southern Ocean, with shore forays at Snares, Enderby and Campbell Islands, two weeks travelling around the Ross Sea and Ross Ice Shelf region, Franklin Island, Cape Hallett and Cape Adare, where there were humpback, minke and killer whales in big numbers, and one week to return via Macquarie Island to Hobart, Tasmania.

The ship left Antarctica just in time as the pack ice started to form into fast ice, but it headed into a tremendous storm in the Southern Ocean with winds so strong they reached the maximum Beaufort 12, and then blew the wind measuring instruments off the ship. Waves of 22 metres crashed over the ship, and its captain had to hold station for 16 hours, just keeping the bow into the wind.

"I was very well aware that if the ship went down, we were too far from anywhere for help to get to us," Sid recounts.

The material gathered on the Antarctica experience gave an added dimension to the *Islander* whale watch cruises, with photographs and information for the skipper to relay to the passengers.

* * * *

Before the previous whale watch season the Hervey Bay vessel owners had decided to work together on an advertising campaign and to pay for a light plane to fly over the bay every morning whale spotting.

Come the end of the season several of them defaulted on paying their share, so Sid offered the *Islander* for a fund raising cruise and his crew volunteered their time to make up the shortfall. Eddy May and the chairman of the Fraser Coast Tourism Board, a bright spark called Ken Bennett held up their hands as cruise organisers.

The day before we set off to Antarctica, Ken Bennett announced that the cruise would take the form of a gambling night. Sid said "You'd better wait until I get home and find out exactly what you're planning."

But the day we got back Sid found that Ken Bennett, Eddy May and all had indeed waited for his return before holding the gambling night on the *Islander,* but not long enough for him to have any say at all, because all the tickets had already been sold. In the event it was a great night, all perfectly legal with no money changing hands for gambling, just play money for donated prizes and the debt was cleared.

* * * *

The *Islander* soon earned a reputation as a particularly whale friendly vessel with curious humpbacks coming right up to it to watch the passengers watching them. One whale dived so close to the bow, the barnacles on its tail scraped paint off the vessel; another actually swam through the tunnel between the catamaran pontoons. A whole pod came up alongside the vessel and "blew" spraying a line up of passengers on the deck. The people were amused – until the awful odour hit them.

"A mother whale recognisable year to year by the markings on her tail would always come up to us with her new calf," recounts Elaine Toy. "She would lie alongside the Islander and go to sleep letting the calf play around the boat, as if to say 'I'm tired; you look after the calf for a while.'"

The most amazing story Elaine tells was when a blind woman went on a whale watch cruise. "To give her a feel for the atmosphere I took her down the steps to the dive platform at sea level on the back of the *Islander.* The woman held out her hand – and a whale rose from the sea and touched it gently with its nose."

Other whale watch licensees began to upgrade their vessels to compete, so the whale fleet developed rapidly into one which, together with the close encounters with the whales, earned Hervey Bay recognition as the best place in Australia for whale watching.

Chapter 34

Sid's flying career took a new turn. Influenced by Australian adventurer Dick Smith who with his wife, Pip were guests at Eurong Beach resort, Sid decided to sell his Beechcraft Duke and learn to fly a helicopter.

In June 1993 he bought a small two seat Robinson 22 to learn on and employed a young pilot instructor, Darryl Jessop to come to Eurong to teach him and his son, Bill.

The minimum requirement for a fixed wing aircraft pilot to become qualified in a helicopter was 40 hours and both passed their exams in this time frame. I too expressed an interest in learning to fly a helicopter, and off I went with Darryl one morning for an hour's instruction. When we got back Sid was waiting anxiously to find out how I'd done.

After a few lessons, I suggested to Darryl that I fly around the whole island. Sid was kept waiting for about two hours, sure something awful had happened. He was not happy when he learned what we had done, and suggested we'd been on some kind of sightseeing joy flight. The very next time we flew north we saw a pod of humpback whales cruising just off the surf beach. Darryl said "Let's go back and get my camera."

We landed only 15 minutes after we had taken off. Sid was waiting again. Darryl told him we'd come back for a camera. Sid said to me "That's it. Out you get. You aren't taking this seriously at all."

Darryl suggested I get a particular book, a basic helicopter flying for very raw beginners instead of gazing in total incomprehension at Sid's more technical tomes. When Sid went off to Brisbane to take his exam I said "Don't forget my book." Sid returned in triumph having passed his exam – but without the book.

I put on a bit of a turn and Sid said "Well there are two books for beginners, and you can choose for yourself when you next go to Brisbane. I thought I knew which one you'd want but I wasn't sure," and then he muttered just loud enough for me to hear "It had lots of pictures of a helicopter with a smile on its face…"

Above: Sid and I in the Robinson 22 helicopter; Sid flying while I am relegated to watching. Below: Sid with his new Jetranger.

Once he had his helicopter license, Sid sold the small Robinson 22 helicopter and, as recommended by Dick Smith, bought a new five seat Bell Jetranger, which he kept for the remainder of his flying years. Dick had told Sid of the reliability of his Bell on flights to Antarctica and around Australia.

Dick owned the *Australian Geographic* magazine at this time and had its logo on his helicopter. He suggested Sid put a logo on the side of his helicopter that would ensure him a cooperative reception from folk wherever he landed. Sid thought for just a moment and came up with an idea for a logo that would fill the bill: "Australian Taxation Department".

* * * *

By this time Harry Geltch had retired from flying and once it became known there was a helicopter based at Eurong the calls on Sid to fly emergency medical cases to the mainland began again.

One, involving driver Harold James was a near thing. Sid was away from the resort briefly when Harold had a heart attack. An intensive care nurse, Margaret Cassidy happened to be at her holiday home at Eurong and was called on to help. She in turn called the National Parks officer on duty, Rod Hobson to bring oxygen quickly.

She told Harold's wife, Sharon that he had perhaps only 90 minutes to live, too little time to call in the rescue helicopter from the Sunshine Coast. An urgent call was put out over the radio to Sid in his car and he came racing home to get the helicopter started. Harold was carried over to it and lifted inside.

Rod Hobson went along to sit with him in the back seat and hold the oxygen mask to his mouth. Sid flew directly to Hervey Bay hospital and landed on the helicopter pad close to the entrance.

Out came a wards man shouting at Sid, asking who he thought he was to land there, and ordering him to take off straightaway as the pad was for emergency use only. Hobson told him there was an emergency, and he'd better get medical staff alerted. He added in no uncertain terms "If you were taken ill on Fraser Island, you'd be damn glad Sid Melksham was there."

* * * *

It was not long after Harry Geltch retired however that Sid persuaded Harry's son, Gerry to operate joy flights out of Eurong.

Gerry was a former baker who had been encouraged to learn to fly by his father and Sid. After many years flying in and around Eurong and building up a good business, Gerry was to describe Sid as the person who had the most influence on his life, apart from his wife Terrina.

Outgoing and energetic, Gerry soon developed a bigger business than Harry had ever attempted, with three planes flying in daily from Hervey Bay to Happy Valley and the Cathedrals as well as Eurong, though the latter, being the biggest centre by far on the eastern side of the island, soon became the focal point of his operation.

He says "Sid taught me a lot about business and understanding people, and gave me a lot of help. I certainly wouldn't have been anywhere near as successful without him."

Sid saw joy flights as an added attraction to his resort and tours, and as with Harry, refused to take any commission from Gerry.

"I started to do joy flights for passengers on Top Tours as well, and asked Sid if I could use his airstrip at Wangoolba for some of them." Gerry describes. "I expected him to say no because Top Tours was a competitor of his and thought he would want to limit the joy flights to his own tour passengers. But he said yes straight away."

Gerry repaid by offering flights to and from Hervey Bay if ever Sid needed. For all their mutual good will Gerry remembers he got a couple of roastings.

"Sid employed an Aboriginal chap called Steve to talk to his day trip passengers about the history of the island, bush medicine and such, but Steve often missed the courtesy bus in Hervey Bay and I'd get a call from Sid asking if I would fly him over," says Gerry. "One day I was waiting for Steve to show up at the airport and he didn't arrive. Eventually I had to go to Eurong without him.

"Sid was sitting outside the shop waiting for Steve, and when he saw me without him he asked very crossly why I hadn't brought him. I explained I had waited for an hour. Sid was about to give me another blast then paused and said 'What you're saying is don't shoot the messenger eh?'

"I replied 'Yep.'

"Calm as anything Sid said 'Well what are you doing standing here then? Off you go.'"

"Another time," Gerry remembers, "everyone was very excited because Sid, Harold James and another driver were to fly to Melbourne to pick up two new buses Sid had bought and drive them back. Sid and the second driver were already on the mainland but Harold had to be flown off the island to meet them at Hervey Bay airport.

"A huge storm rolled in on the island and my pilot Shane couldn't take off from Eurong with Harold. Sid was fretting as time was running away for them to drive down to Brisbane to catch their flight to Melbourne," Gerry describes. "He kept saying 'Where are they?'

"I was in contact with Shane and was up to date with the storm conditions and explained they were too severe for the plane to take off.

"'Well do something about it," Sid says, all stressed out.

"'What?' I asked.

"'Shoot yourself,' was his tongue in cheek solution.

"So I rang Shane and told him as soon as the storm passed to get straight over to Hervey Bay or I'd have to shoot myself.

"Luckily the storm went over and all turned out well and they made their flights to Melbourne...phew."

Gerry saw another side to Sid one Easter when his flying business nearly came tumbling around his ears. Two of his aircraft were damaged within an hour on the beach at Happy Valley.

"One of our pilots was acting the goat," Gerry describes. "He was by himself in the plane trying to do things the plane was not meant to do. Ultimately he landed it hard on the beach and flipped it on to its back. I was out of town when I got the news, so I directed another aircraft and pilot to go and inspect the damage and phone me back.

"The second pilot had a girl friend at Happy Valley, and she was waiting for him so he opted to land where she was instead of the hard sand landing area. He hit a wash out and snapped the nose wheel off the plane, which dived into the beach bending its propeller.

"Terrina and I were devastated at the destruction of two of our aircraft.

"We wondered if we could ever recover from this massive financial blow.

"Sid helped me get them both planes off the island and to our hangar in Hervey Bay.

"I was in the hangar next day trying to organise the rebuilding of one of the aircraft when Sid walked in, put his hand on my shoulder, and asked how I was going as we looked at the mess. Then he pulled out his cheque book and said 'Here's an open cheque. It's all yours. Spend whatever you need to get back on your feet.'

"I was absolutely overwhelmed that someone with Sid's stature and reputation could have so much compassion. I thanked him for the offer but declined. I told him 'If I can't rebuild myself I don't deserve to be in business.'

"He nodded and said he understood where I was coming from. This incident taught me a lot about Sid."

Chapter 35

The upmarket new Kingfisher Bay resort opened in 1993 and, as expected, made big inroads into the coach line business that Eurong Beach had enjoyed since the mid 1980's. However a massive advertising budget of $5million for each of Kingfisher's first two years of operation focused a great deal of attention again on Fraser Island.

There was significant spin off to Eurong Beach's benefit as its rooms were less expensive than those at the new resort, and its surf beach location was favoured by those who knew the island. There was a massive upsurge in new groups seeking to come to the island. Very quickly accommodation at Eurong was again in short supply.

Michael Hackett at Kingfisher still tried to poach Sid's key staff. He was successful with one man who was particularly valuable, head mechanic Laurie Toy.

Laurie was capable of both repairing and maintaining Sid's ever growing bus fleet, and the vessels, the three ferries and the whale watch catamaran, and trained the other mechanics working for Sid to be as flexible and multi skilled as he was. Sid delegated a great deal of responsibility to Laurie, but was always ready to draw on his own problem solving skills to give advice.

Now Laurie was enticed to Kingfisher with the promise he wouldn't have to crawl under buses and into barge engine rooms any longer, but would have a white collar job in charge of the new resort's workshop.

Sid had to find new premises, for obviously he could no longer use the workshop he had built at Laurie's property. He left it there for Laurie even though he was no longer working for him, and in return Laurie let Sid's mechanics use it until Sid found a new property.

After searching Hervey Bay for an industrial block to build a workshop on he found there was nothing of the right size. Not being one to wring his hands and wonder what to do, Sid realised if he had a problem finding suitable land, so would other folk.

He turned the problem into a business opportunity by buying a much bigger than needed two hectare block of vacant industrial land in Hervey Bay on the main road leading to River Heads and almost opposite the airport. He had a big new workshop with five bus bays and ample secure parking built on the rear quarter of it, saving the land fronting the main road for future industrial buildings that might need public exposure.

He found Laurie well nigh irreplaceable, however, and a little over a year later welcomed him back. Laurie's white collar job in charge of a team of mechanics at Kingfisher Bay had gradually devolved into a one man show with Laurie doing as much blue collar work as he'd ever done, but without a boss who knew as much about motors as Sid did and on whose account he could immediately get any parts he needed.

By the 1990's Sid owned the largest fleet of 4WD buses in Australia, as well as three new double decker courtesy buses running around Hervey Bay to replace the original English one.

The scene at River Heads with two of the new double deckers bringing day trip passengers to the Fraser Venture.

A team of five mechanics plus trade assistants was needed to keep them and the vessels in running order. His workshop also became an authorised repairer of M.A.N. motors and took on the repair and maintenance of all the trucks the National Parks used on Fraser Island.

"At times Sid demanded a lot," says Laurie Toy. "He pushed the goal higher all the time. There was always a goal. I always respected him a lot for his vision. I was just a cog, but I wanted to help him fulfil his plans because I could. He was a very fair employer. The more you did, the better you got paid."

One time when Sid was overseas, one of the engines in the *Fraser Venture* seized. As soon as he learned what had happened, Laurie rang the engine supplier in Brisbane, explained the situation and asked if they had another engine on hand. They did and he set off straight away in the workshop utility to pick it up.

The *Fraser Venture* got back to River Heads on one engine where Sid's whole team of mechanics were lined up to go aboard, cut a hole in the deck and pull the seized engine out while Laurie was gone. He arrived back at River Heads with the new engine just before midnight, and the mechanics and barge crew worked through the night under his direction, installing it and re-welding the deck.

The *Fraser Venture* missed its first morning run, but made up for it after the second run. This was the only time, during Sid's ownership, that a crossing was missed.

Laurie says he had no qualms about going to Brisbane and spending some $9,000 of Sid's money on a new engine in Sid's absence.

"I'd been working for Sid for so long that I got to think the way he thought. It was something that had to be done, so do it now and keep the *Fraser Venture* going. That was one of the good things about Sid. Anything the vessels or buses needed, they got, so if he wasn't there I was quite confident getting it anyway."

No-one contacted Sid overseas to tell him about the new motor, but he was told when he got home and asked, as he always did "What is the worst thing that happened while I was away?"

By this time, the crisis was over and as was pointed out "There was nothing you could have done if we had told you while you were away, except worry."

"Next day Sid came straight to the workshop to thank us," Laurie recalls.

The engine that came out of the *Fraser Venture* was rebuilt and kept as a spare either for the ferry or the resort generator. When Sid first bought the ferry and made contact with M.A.N which supplied the motors, he bought a new generator set with the same model motor for the resort. This forethought meant the motors and parts were interchangeable, and now one entire motor was always on hand if it were needed in emergency.

* * * *

In the mid 1990's Sid was to increase his vessel fleet by two more ferries running to the west coast of Fraser, at the behest of business rivals Top Tours and Kingfisher Bay Resort.

A couple who had run a very successful bus business in Sydney, Helmut and Helga Delfs came to Hervey Bay to retire in 1989, but before long bought a Fraser Island day tour business called Top Tours, as Helmut says "to provide jobs for my sons, Rick and Stephen."

Top Tours 4WD buses used Ken Eckert's barge the *Fraser II* to cross the Great Sandy Straits from Urangan Boat Harbour to Moon Point then went across the island to Happy Valley and north along the surf beach. Before long Helmut also bought the *Fraser II.*

He and Rick skippered the barge and Stephen worked for the family business as the mechanic. Top Tours became Sid's biggest competitor for the Fraser Island tour market from Hervey Bay.

"I found the Moon Point beach was a shocking place to land the *Fraser II* barge. It was exposed to strong north westerly winds and strong tidal currents," says Helmut. "A couple of times we stranded the barge there. One time we had *Fraser II* stuck fast on the beach at Moon Point in a gale force northerly wind when it was time to take our buses and passengers off the island.

"I rang Sid and told him my problem and he said to send my buses and passengers down to his landing at Wanggoolba Creek and he would put on a special trip on the *Fraser Venture* to take them back to Hervey Bay. Our tour bus arrived got there about 9 pm. Sid had the *Fraser Venture* waiting to get them back to Hervey Bay. I really appreciated that."

Delfs complained to the Queensland Government about the landing problems at Moon Point and a grant of $400,000 was made towards a barge landing, but this was nowhere near what a good all weather landing would cost.

The ideal position for a landing was just south of Moon Point in more sheltered conditions, but the beach did not extend beyond the point and it would have meant building a jetty through mangrove flats to get to shore.

Estimates put the cost of a jetty at more than $1million.

Nothing was done, no-one being willing to put up the rest of the money needed, especially when it would not guarantee exclusive use.

* * * *

In mid 1992, Graeme and Wendy Coutts-Smith retired, selling their boutique Happy Valley Resort to a Bribie Island real estate agent, John Boyd, his wife Gail, son Shane and daughter Julie.

The Boyds, recognising the value Sid's day tours added to his resort business at Eurong, went on to buy Top Tours from the Delfs in 1994. Helmut Delfs continued to own and operate the *Fraser II* to Moon Point to take their buses to and from the island.

Just a few months later, in late 1994, Michael Hackett pulled the rug from under the Boyd's tours.

He offered a two year contract to Helmut Delfs to take the *Fraser II* to carry supply trucks and guest vehicles to Kingfisher Bay resort from River Heads. Delfs jumped at the opportunity to get away from Moon Point, but his departure meant Top Tours had no means of getting their buses and passengers to Fraser Island.

This was not their only problem. The National Parks conditions on their tour licences meant they could only operate on the road from Moon Point to Happy Valley then north along the surf beach. The closure of Boyd's tour business stared them in the face.

In desperation John and Shane Boyd approached Sid, whom they hardly knew, to ask if he would help them out by letting them use his tour licences and travel on the *Fraser Venture* until they could buy another barge. Sid agreed straight away.

"If he had not agreed we could not have conducted our tours until I could organise barge transport to Moon Point," says Shane Boyd. "It was essential for our tour business that we ran daily to keep faith with the booking agents."

Within weeks, their search for a suitable barge unsuccessful, the Boyds came back to ask if Sid would build them a barge, an amazing expression of confidence in a business rival.

"I had no qualms about dealing with Sid, although he was a direct competitor in the Hervey Bay market for tours to Fraser Island," says Shane. "I never saw competition between us as an issue. I saw Sid as an experienced ferry operator whose knowledge would stand me in good stead."

Sid not only agreed to build a ferry, he set out to give the Boyds the best ferry and service he could.

To save the time involved in having a new ferry built, he cast around and found a barge for sale in Moreton Bay.

It was the *Fraser Dawn III,* the small steel barge Gordon Elmer had sold in the mid 1980's. Later owners had lengthened it by 12 metres and strengthened it, so it would now carry 16 vehicles, but its superstructure comprised only a small wheelhouse.

Sid bought it and stripped it back to its hull. Over the next five months he had it transformed into yet another very good-looking ferry, with an impressive superstructure. A passenger lounge in a large saloon deck was built above a newly strengthened vehicle deck and the wheelhouse was mounted above that.

The new paint scheme was white with horizontal navy and orange stripes along the hull then at an angle across the saloon deck.

But appearance was only part of the transformation. More importantly Sid made the *Fraser Dawn* suitable for operating into the long sloping beach at Moon Point, by having an extra long door with heavy duty cables and winches substituted for its original inadequate door.

He also had a steering leg built on the back with a large propeller able to be turned 360 degrees, so its skipper could hold it firm on the beach no matter the wind and tide. Its small motors were replaced with two new 6 cylinder motors.

The Fraser Dawn ready to go to work for Sid's rival, Top Tours.

Ken Eckert, the original owner of *Fraser II,* came to ask for a job on the new ferry. Sid was glad to have him, knowing that his long experience with the *Fraser II* at the difficult Moon Point beach would make him well able to handle the custom built *Fraser Dawn. Dawn* began operating in July 1995 with Sid and the Boyd's signing a five year contract.

"After the problems we had experienced earlier I now felt we could conduct our tours and grow our business with confidence," says Shane Boyd.

"It was of great comfort to me. I could sleep at night because of the reliability of service that the contract with Sid guaranteed to our tours business.

"I realised that Sid could potentially have made it hard for our tour business and that our access to Fraser Island was dependent on his barge service. But he never did. He always operated the *Fraser Dawn* as if he was a third party, not a tour competitor."

Once the *Fraser Dawn* proved itself capable of operating at Moon Point in poor weather conditions, Sid told the regional manager of the National Parks Service, Locky Fullerton that the government's $400,000 was no longer needed for a barge landing there. Once they heard about this, Fraser Island folk quickly seized the opportunity to ask for the money to be spent on other much needed facilities on the island. A toilet block was built with it at Middle Rock.

Over the next seven years there were only two or three days when the *Dawn* couldn't operate to Moon Point, in conditions so extreme that would have been dangerous to try and off load vehicles and passengers.

* * * *

Eighteen months later Helmut Delf's contract to operate his barge *Fraser II* to Kingfisher Bay resort came to an end. The growing resort had found Delfs' barge too small.

By this time Michael Hackett no longer had a connection to Kingfisher Bay and in January 1997, Gary Smith, the head of its new management company, called tenders for the supply of a new barge service. Sid had met Gary Smith on several occasions and the two formed a relationship of mutual respect, very different from Hackett's attitude.

Sid had no qualms then in tendering, after a phone call to Ross McLean of Index Engineering to ask if he was still in the barge building business. In fact the *Rainbow Venture* was the last barge Index had built ten years before, but McLean was soon to call back to say if Sid wanted another barge, he could get his old team back.

At the end of the tender period, Gary Smith was to tell Sid his tender had not been accepted and truck owner, Bob Byrnes, who had been carting supplies to Kingfisher Bay since its opening, had been successful.

It was only a matter of weeks before Smith contacted Sid again, this time to say Byrnes had withdrawn his tender and ask would Sid supply a barge.

He asked for a 16 vehicle barge and hinted the *Fraser Dawn* would be ideal, but Sid suggested instead that he have a new barge built for Kingfisher Bay. The problem Smith foresaw was that Helmut Delfs might not be prepared to continue with the *Fraser II* for the time it took for a new barge to be built. Delfs however said he would.

In discussion with Gary Smith, Sid baulked at building a new barge to carry only 16 vehicles.

"In two years time it might not be big enough if your business grows as I expect," he told Smith, "then my barge will be too small and you won't want it. What I propose is to have a barge built to the same plan as *Fraser Venture* before I lengthened it. It will take 22 vehicles and 200 passengers."

Smith wanted a charter agreement, whereby Kingfisher Bay paid for the barge as a whole, no matter how many vehicles and passengers it carried on each run. He did not want to pay for a more expensive 22 space barge.

Sid, faced yet again with the *Fraser Venture* having more traffic than it could handle, said he would take the remaining six spaces for the *Fraser Venture* overflow until such time as Kingfisher Bay needed them, at which time Kingfisher would pay a higher charter rate.

It was a most logical arrangement which suited both parties admirably – Sid because he then got a five year charter agreement with Kingfisher and Smith because he knew the barge would enable his business to grow. Immediately Smith booked the full barge for all future peak holiday seasons.

Smith also wanted Sid to handle all the ticketing on the barge and send him the income from ticket sales each week.

Sid went ahead contracting with Index Engineering to build their third ferry for him.

Even though he had persuaded Gary Smith to have a 22 space barge to cater for future needs, Sid had learned from his own experience that an even bigger ferry might be needed eventually.

In the building of the *Kingfisher Bay* ferry he had Index make joints in all the pipe work running the length of the vehicle deck, so that if need be in the future, it too could be cut and lengthened as the *Fraser Venture* had been, but much more easily.

The old team is back together, Cliff Fraser, left, Sid and Barry Flannigan, to build the Kingfisher Bay ferry.

Sid offered the job of skipper of the new *Kingfisher Bay* ferry to Ross Williams, the grandson of Max Williams. Ross had spent his early childhood at Eurong, and then gone to Rainbow Beach when Max took on driving Sid's *Sun Safari* tour.

When he finished school Ross became first a deckhand then a skipper on Sid's Inskip Point ferries. His employment actually meant that three generations of the Williams had worked for Sid, Max, his daughters Robyn and Rikki preparing buffet lunches for day trippers in the Island Inn days and now Ross.

In the contract Gary Smith had insisted on a starting date for the new ferry, so with only a couple of days to go when it was launched, it had to be brought up to Hervey Bay in spite of bad weather. It was only an hour into its voyage when rough seas caused a major problem.

A succession of big waves smashed the steel latch holding the top of the barge door in place, leaving one side loose and swaying. A catastrophe seemed likely.

The latch on the other side would inevitably have given way under the weight of the door. The door would then have dropped, been washed under the barge and torn off, perhaps taking the front of the barge with it.

Quick thinking and some astonishing work saved the day. While Ross held the wheel, Sid, Laurie Toy, Murray Reid and other men who had gone along for the ride raced down to the vehicle deck where the workshop ute was parked. They chained the swaying top of the door to the ute, and reversed the vehicle back, pulling the door in to place. They tied the ute to the back of the vessel with wire rope, so it would not budge, then wired and chained up the door tight up to the stanchion. When they got it to Hervey Bay a team of Index shipbuilders raced up to make repairs.

The *Kingfisher Bay* ferry was there to start work on the contracted day ***(below).***

* * * *

The addition of two more barges to Sid's fleet meant greater responsibility for Don Caswell, who had become Sid's marine right hand and Laurie Toy and his team of mechanics.

All relied on Sid's knowledge and experience.

"Sid's mechanical knowledge was so extensive that he could come up with the most inventive and practical solutions to problems, things other people never thought of," says Caswell. "They would go by the book, but Sid never read books, he just thought things through and sorted everything out.

"He was greatly respected for his knowledge. Every person who worked on the vessels could appreciate that he could run them himself if he wanted to and knew every part. He could sum up a problem situation so fast and he would nearly always be right.

"If he was contemplating some new marine project he would always do his homework. He would bounce his ideas off me, asking me what I thought. Then he'd come back a couple of days later and discuss it again.

"It was great to have him around when one of the barges was on the slip just to walk along and see that everything was being done properly. He had an amazing eye for detail.

"He had this presence, whether roaring or quiet, that ensured all his marine staff did the job asked of them whether they thought they could or not.

"He showed in many ways the faith he had in us, and it gave us great pride in our work. Newcomers on staff might ask 'Who's this bloke that throws his weight around?' but the ones who knew him longer knew he had a soft side to him.

"He was very fair to everyone. If you did the right thing by him he always did the right thing by you, often in little unexpected ways. For instance I had a fuel pump problem in a little utility I owned, so took it to Brisbane to the repairers. When I went to pick it up they said Sid had told them to charge it to his account.

"He is the most humble man I have ever met. He never ever skites about what he has achieved."

* * * *

However Sid now owning another new barge, albeit chartered to Kingfisher Bay, was to have fateful consequences for him.

To many interested parties it meant Sid had a monopoly on barge services to Fraser Island, and in effect totally controlled the main means of access to the island. Some were not comfortable that a man with his fierce reputation should be in such a position.

One such was the new Mayor of Hervey Bay, Bill Brennan, who saw Sid as a tall poppy ripe for the lopping.

Chapter 36

All unwittingly some months earlier Sid had upset the Hervey Bay City Council and this still rankled. The Fitzgerald Commission of Inquiry into Fraser Island had recommended in 1991 that the island come under the local government administration of a single council, instead of Hervey Bay City Council administering the area from Happy Valley north, including Happy Valley and Orchid Beach and Maryborough City Council the southern section including Eurong.

Following the recommendations, the Queensland A.L.P. Government appointed Commissioner Greg Hoffman to study the situation and report back. Hoffman had done similar work and been the guiding light behind the amalgamation of other local government areas, Ipswich and Moreton in south east Queensland for example.

Hervey Bay City Council was confident it would soon be taking over the whole island, and its mayor, Fred Kleinschmidt made noises about being able to take water from one of Fraser's big west coast creeks to supplement the inadequate city water supply. He also mooted that under his progressive council, Happy Valley and Eurong would become much larger townships and give Hervey Bay a much bigger income from rates.

Many Eurong residents, Sid included, were aghast. Sid fully realised that the growth of Eurong would bring him business benefits on his barges and at his shop and pub, but overriding that, he knew that larger townships would have major impacts far beyond their boundaries. Demands for facilities would pour in on a larger scale from more people, and large areas of forest would inevitably be urbanised instead of being left natural.

The idea to extract fresh creek water from Fraser had been suggested before, and been vetoed as affecting the water composition of the Fish Habitat, as well as an essential pumping station being an eyesore.

Sid found fellow residents at Eurong agreed with him wholeheartedly.

All of them were independent minded individuals, able to cope with the comparatively primitive conditions, which is why they had chosen the island their home in the first place. When Commissioner Hoffman came to Eurong to meet the residents and get their opinions he found they all wanted to stay with Maryborough.

The early days of Sid's disagreements with Maryborough City Council officers had long gone and been forgotten. Under Mayor Alan Brown, Maryborough Council had taken a genuine interest in Fraser Island, and held meetings with the residents on matters of mutual interest. It had a small income from rates on island properties and was prepared to plough this back into residents' needs at Eurong.

When he met with Commissioner Hoffman, Sid was particularly vehement and typically blunt. "We don't want to be amalgamated in one big council, like that idiot did with Ipswich and Moreton," he said. Hoffman had a pained look "I was responsible for that amalgamation," he said.

Sid tried to cover his tracks "I didn't mean Ipswich," he said casting about mentally for somewhere as far away as possible. "I meant that place near Perth," he floundered.

"That was me as well," Hoffman responded.

The outcome was, not surprisingly, that Hoffman recommended the whole of Fraser Island be administered by Hervey Bay City Council. Before it could be written into law, and never one to take a set back as a final decision, Sid asked for an appointment for a deputation from Eurong to meet the Minister for Local Government, Di McCauley to lodge a protest.

While Hoffman had been cogitating, the Goss Labor Government lost power to a National Party Government led by Rob Borbidge in February 1996. This undoubtedly worked in the Eurong deputation's favour, for the National Party had no great loyalty to its predecessor's actions or commissioners.

Minister McCauley agreed to meet a deputation of four in a motel lounge in Gympie. Sid and I went with Murray Reid and Nigel Fremantle. When we put our case, Mrs. McCauley said she had never met people who so liked their local council, and on the spot agreed Maryborough council could retain its Fraser Island interests. This was confirmed by the Cabinet in December 1996.

Maryborough Council was perhaps not overjoyed at having to continue to administer part of the controversial island, but its members were delighted at the vote of confidence. Hervey Bay Council was angry at the snub, and saw Sid as the catalyst.

* * * *

Now just months later, Hervey Bay Council planned to redevelop River Heads. The rough road from Hervey Bay to River Heads that existed when Sid's double decker first began to take tourists to the *Fraser Venture* landing had been bitumen sealed with an Australian Government grant for tourist roads in 1985. But nothing had been done with the rough little landing area at the end of it.

The council elected in March 1997 with Bill Brennan as the new Mayor decided the River Heads landing gave Hervey Bay a bad look to the thousands of tourists bound for Fraser Island.

Plans were drawn up to develop the area with two distinct bitumen parking areas, one for ferry traffic and the second for local amateur fishermen to leave their cars and boat trailers, after launching their small boats from one of the three ramps there.

The firm which won the tender to do the redevelopment was Bellero's Constructions, which had earlier bitumen sealed Sid's airstrip on Fraser Island. It seemed logical to their CEO, Bob Goodwin to show the River Heads plans to Sid.

He saw straight away the area for the ferry traffic was far too small, and he was upset that he had not been consulted. He went to see first the Hervey Bay council engineer, Ras Hird to ask for the plan to be redrawn and when he met with refusal, went to Mayor Brennan. He pointed out that the space for the barge traffic would not allow for a large truck to turn to reverse on to the *Fraser Venture* or the *Kingfisher Bay* ferry that he was having built.

He got a hostile reception, which left Sid nonplussed. He could not understand why his pointing out the problem barge traffic faced would not be received in the spirit of helpfulness with which it had been offered.

Typically he reacted with anger, especially when Brennan questioned who he thought he was to feel he had the right to have input.

Brennan had a similar fiery temperament, but whereas Sid soon got over his flare ups, Brennan didn't.

It appeared there was going to be no easy solution and Brennan, for whatever reason, had Sid in his sights.

* * * *

When the council wanted to increase the charge it had put on Sid's using the River Heads barge ramp, from a mere $60 a month to $300 a month, Sid saw red. It would have been a simple matter for him to make the new charge an add-on cost to his barge fares, but Sid felt again he was being singled out for adverse attention and refused to pay on principle.

His argument against having to pay the greater fee was that he was the owner of the barge ramp. He claimed, in good faith, that it had been given to him by Dillingham's manager, Ron Cross when sand mining ceased in 1976.

As far as he was aware River Heads was historically a naval reserve that had never been used as such. There was no paperwork on the ramp. Dillingham's had apparently built it without need to apply for tenure for no-one was much interested in the then scrubby little promontory in the early 1970's.

Now it was a different story for not only was the *Fraser Venture* attracting thousands of people, but the sealing of the River Heads road had led to residential subdivisions being developed along much of its route.

With neither Sid nor Mayor Brennan giving an inch Sid approached a couple of Queensland Government Ministers, when they visited Hervey Bay, Vaughan Johnson, Minister for Transport who was rudely brusque and Premier Rob Borbidge. When he was Opposition leader on a visit to Fraser Island, Borbidge had shown great bonhomie to Sid. Now he didn't want to be bothered to listen to him.

Sid was prepared to go to court to fight for his rights, and former Dillinghams manager, Ron Cross came from Brisbane to support his ramp ownership but Sid withdrew his claim, when the council agreed to redraw the River Heads redevelopment plans in a pre court mediation meeting and waive the unpaid ramp fees while Sid agreed to pay the new fees from then on.

The final, sensible, outcome was a new plan with big enough areas for barge traffic, bus parking and boat owners with landscaping between them, toilets and shelter sheds and a new wider barge ramp.

When the development was completed, Sid had to agree it was ideal. It seemed harmony might be restored.

A one and only occasion when four of Sid's barges, from the left, the Kingfisher Bay, the Fraser Venture, the Fraser Dawn and the Rainbow Venture are at the newly developed River Heads.

Then another factor came into play. The Queensland Parks and Wildlife Service had been issuing access and camping permits for a fee to all private vehicle owners going to Fraser Island since 1985.

The money was collected and permits issued both in National Parks offices and by agents in conveniently placed businesses to island access points, who were paid ten per cent commission.

It soon became evident that a significant percentage of island visitors were not bothering to get permits and pay the fees. By this time the fees had risen to $30 per vehicle to go to Fraser Island and $7.50 a night for a camp site.

The money raised was to go directly to improving island facilities and with the high level of avoidance, much planned work was not done and the tour operators in particular, who were paying their increased fees, felt the burden on them was unfair.

Sid was upset that by this time, between island passenger levies and whale watching fees, he was paying the QPWS more than $400,000 a year and the only improvement he wanted was to the island roads and they were in as deplorable a condition as they ever were.

The Fitzgerald Inquiry into island management in 1991 had recommended the logical course that the permits be issued and fees collected by the barge operators. By 1997 this was one operator, Sid.

Sid had been pushing for National Parks permits to be sold on the barges since the Fitzgerald recommendation to put a stop to the fee avoidance. He was finally asked by the National Parks Service to undertake the job.

A contract was drawn up with more stringent conditions than on any other agent, notably that Sid had to police the permits. His staff had to check every vehicle driver going on the barges at River Heads and Inskip Point to see if he had an access permit, and if not, sell him one.

Unless the driver said he was going into private accommodation or Hannant's private camping ground, then they had to sell them a camping permit as well. If the driver refused to purchase the requisite permits and pay the fees, he had to be reported to the National Parks at Eurong, where rangers would be waiting for him.

Sid agreed, working out that the only way of ensuring every vehicle going on the barges had a permit was to start a system of combined tickets, one for the barge and one for the permits.

This involved computerising the ticketing system with a specially designed programme, and setting up sales points at River Heads and on the beach by the barge landing area at Inskip Point.

The lack of shop or office facilities at both places led him to buy two kombi type vans, which he fitted out to make them suitable as mobile ticket offices. Solar panels were installed on the roofs to power the computers, windows cut out of one side to sell tickets through, with an awning over to shelter the customers and the ticket seller.

Knowing the vans would be carrying not only barge fare money but large sums of government money, Sid had safes installed and a most sophisticated alarm system fitted to the vans. This required a sequence of switches to be pressed before turning the key to start the motor.

Should a thief get in the one at River Heads and drive off with it, the van motor would start all right, but would cut out after a measured distance to the River Heads store and sirens would sound. The storekeeper would then ring the police. A thief would be unable to restart the motor without knowing where a secret switch was located.

For the van at Inskip Point, the alarm sirens would go off within seconds as there were barge crews on hand until the van left.

It was expensive to buy and set up the vans and employ staff to man them. Sid asked the QPWS for 15% commission compared with other agents, who were paid 10% but did not have the responsibility of policing the permits nor setting up a sales point.

Sid was also well aware that having a QPWS licence to issue permits, along with the barge tickets, could help safeguard his position as the sole ferry operator to Fraser Island.

All was ready and the new combined ticket system began in September 1997 to coincide with the introduction of the new ferry to Kingfisher Bay resort, and the beginning of the school holidays. It was a hectic time and the system had teething problems when the computer purchased by Sid and the printer purchased by the QPWS were found to be incompatible. It took a week to sort out, and from then on the system ran well – but the controversy just began.

* * * *

Up to this time the business people who hired out four wheel drive vehicles around Hervey Bay would book spaces for their vehicles on the *Fraser Venture* and write out the barge tickets for their customers. They took 10 per cent commission, and in some cases this added up to a considerable sum over a year. Now with all the ticketing being done in the vans at River Heads, they were no longer required to write the tickets and lost their commission.

Sid had for a long time felt the 4WD hire owners were getting "money for jam", taking commission for writing tickets for themselves.

When a couple of them approached him to ask him to reinstate their commission and claimed their businesses would be unprofitable without it, he suggested that they should look within their own businesses to increase their profitability and not at his. He suggested they perhaps increase their hire rates.

Their response was that their situation was so competitive that they could not afford to do this.

The commission loss caused tremendous bad feeling among three or four of the 4WD hire owners to the point where they considered buying their own barge and running in opposition to the *Fraser Venture*.

They asked Gary Smith if they could land a barge at the Kingfisher Bay resort jetty and he refused. They could have run to Moon Point, as the *Fraser Dawn* did, but later said they were afraid their customers would drive straight up the island's dangerous north western beach, instead of across the island then up the surf beach. They could have landed at the old sand mining ramp at Buff Creek, where the *Fraser Venture* had landed for its first year of operation, but they said this was too long a journey.

Mayor Brennan soon heard about the controversy and offered his encouragement to the 4WD hirers, and advised Helmut Delfs not to be in a hurry to find work away from the area for his now redundant *Fraser II.*

But not all 4WD hire owners and the backpacker hostel owners who gave them their custom joined in the proposal to buy their own barge. Some doubted their highly competitive 4WD hire industry would be able to work together for very long and felt preference would be given to their competitors' vehicles on a barge owned by some of their number.

And when it came down to it, they were happy with the *Fraser Venture* service and appreciated being able to have free passage on it when they had to travel to Fraser Island to recover vehicles that had broken down or been damaged, and if they had to stay overnight, accommodation at Eurong Beach Resort.

John Bush who owned one of the largest hostels, Beaches Backpackers says "I heard about some of the 4WD hirers proposing to get their own barge. The hirer who supplied vehicles for my hostel came and asked me if I would stay with him if they got their own barge.

"I told him I would not and preferred to stay with the proven and reliable *Fraser Venture* service.

"I believe this was responsible for him losing interest in the project as I supplied at least half of his total hire business. I knew all the 4WD hire businesses and I did not believe they would or could provide their own reliable barge service to match that of the *Fraser Venture*."

Sid got wind of the vehicle hire owners' plan to introduce another barge, and was concerned that, if it went ahead, there would be many empty deck spaces to be filled on the *Fraser Venture.*

Just a few years before he had spent $500,000 lengthening the *Fraser Venture* so the 4WD hirers could continue to grow their businesses.

The logical course for him, he felt, was to start up a 4WD hire business of his own in Hervey Bay to fill the *Fraser Venture* if need be. He had room on the frontage of his workshop land to build a hire vehicle depot and his team of mechanics was on the spot to do maintenance and repairs. Having the position close to Hervey Bay airport could bring customers to his doorstep, and he put up a small advertising sign of his intention, to create early awareness.

But Sid was reluctant to enter the 4WD hire market. He had seen how badly the hire vehicles were treated in the rugged wilderness and up the surf beach on Fraser Island. Breakdowns and accidents were daily occurrences.

Sid decided to wait and see what the 4WD hirers did. In the end they did nothing. They later claimed the possibility of Sid's entry into the 4WD hire market had put them off buying a barge.

Whether this was just a cop out can be judged by the fact they accepted Kingfisher Bay and Shane Boyd of Top Tours subsequently starting up 4WD hire businesses without strong reaction.

* * * *

But Mayor Bill Brennan took on Sid again over his ticket van being parked by the ferry ramp at the newly developed River Heads landing area. At his urging the council applied a bylaw about unlicensed mobile vendors to the ticket van.

Sid, who had not seen his van as a mobile vendor, was not given the opportunity to apply for a licence. He was simply told the van was not permitted.

He moved the ticket and permit selling operation on to the *Fraser Venture.* It wasn't as convenient, and it meant the ticket sellers, Russ Parker and "Pommie John" Rosser, had three idle hours at Wanggoolba Creek in the middle of each day. Never one to miss an opportunity Sid soon had "Pommie John" bringing his motorbike to the island and spending the spare time riding up and down the airstrip, spraying the edges for encroaching weeds.

Brennan in his view had taken on Melksham twice and won, and could not resist trumpeting his victories to a public meeting of Hervey Bay ratepayers at Orchid Beach.

In his euphoria he claimed, for some reason best known to himself, that Sid was not a man of his word among other things. This was reported in the *Maryborough Chronicle.* Sid was highly indignant.

Being able to commit so little to paper, his word was his bond, and recognised as such by the many business people with whom he had dealt over the decades. Now it appeared to him that Brennan was trying to undermine his whole reputation.

Sid was advised that he had a case for defamation against Brennan and had his solicitor, Peter Pagliarino of Carswell and Co. write to Brennan seeking an apology. Brennan did not want to lose face and refused. When a writ was issued, the coin changed.

He agreed to a brief public apology, and approached Sid to ask him to drop the action, saying he had no money for a court case. Sid did not let him off the hook immediately, replying "You have a very nice house though."

When Sid did drop the writ just a couple of days later, there was an amazing turn about. Brennan offered to have a kiosk built at River Heads where the tickets and permits could be sold, which Sid could rent for a minimal fee. He then took to flying to Eurong on occasion to have breakfast meetings with Sid to discuss all sorts of issues.

However Brennan, to his great distress, only served his first three year term then lost the next election.

* * * *

With his focus on collecting as much money in access fees for the QPWS so that much needed work could be done on Fraser Island, Sid did not realise that he had upset two small shop owners, in Hervey Bay who also sold National Park permits.

They resented his higher commission rate and when they found people going to Fraser Island bypassed their businesses to buy their permits with their ferry tickets, they lost income, and not only their commission. They were both operating on such slender profit margins that they counted on selling other goods to the customers going into their shops to buy permits.

They complained to the Queensland Parks and Wildlife Service.

Anxious to do the right thing by them, albeit one owed more than $150,000 in unpaid permit fees, the QPWS insisted that if anyone enquired of Sid's staff, they had to be told of all the options to get permits, not just at his River Heads kiosk.

Over the ensuing months Mrs. Hannant at the Cathedrals Resort complained that she was getting no customers. Sid's system was so efficient that the customers she used to get, who had not paid camping levies, and were confronted on the island by rangers asking for a punitive higher fee, were no longer coming to stay with her.

One man who owned the little convenience store at River Heads warned his customers that if he did not regain the volume of permit sales he had earlier enjoyed, he would have to close his shop. The River Heads residents were naturally upset at the prospective loss of their convenience store.

Then the store owner and another Hervey Bay permit agent got their heads together and told the QPWS that one of them had telephoned Sid's Hervey Bay office, pretending to be a barge customer and asked where he could get a permit while the second man listened in. They said a new member of Sid's staff had told the "customer" he could only get a permit in the ticket booth at River Heads. They claimed he had asked if he could get them anywhere else, and was told "No."

One of the two men ashamedly told Sid later that he had lied about this incident, and that it had never occurred. But the damage was done.

In June 1998 the QPWS ended its contract for the permit issue from Sid. When he pressed for the reason, the complaints from the other agents were sent to him, and a report on the problems of the first week of operation.

Until then, busy with building at Eurong, Sid had had no idea of the effect his permit sales had had.

No-one had been to talk to him about it, and he had just tried to do the most efficient job he could.

More significant, in Sid's opinion, was a letter the QPWS had sent to a government economist in which it had asked, before contracting Sid to sell the permits, what his likely commission would be.

The economist had replied that he expected Sid would sell up to $80,000 of permits a year and earn commission of up to $14,000. This was apparently based on the existing income from permit sales, with perhaps an allowance for some minor avoidance. This level of commission for Sid was obviously acceptable to the QPWS.

However fee avoidance was obviously far greater than the QPWS had realized and, from September 1 1997 to June 30 1998, Sid's staff collected more than $660,000 in permit fees and earned commission of some $80,000. Sid believed this was the crux of his permit sales cancellation.

He was earning far more than QPWS had estimated, although this apparently huge sum was barely enough to cover wages for four men to sell the tickets week about and the set up costs of the vans for River Heads and Inskip Point.

There was no implication Sid or his ticket staff had acted dishonestly in handling the National Parks fees. Sid toyed briefly with the idea of buying the River Heads store for his daughter, Monica, to run and asked if he could sell permits there. A director of the National Parks Service, Bill Fisher replied that he could, but at a lesser commission. In the event Monica was not interested in the store and Sid did not go ahead with the purchase.

"The stupid so and so's in National Parks should have recognised how much more money they were getting," Sid said. "And there's no way they can stop fee avoidance unless it is tied to barge ticket sales."

The National Parks certainly tried in the short term, by having their island rangers stand on the surf beach at Eurong stopping all the vehicles and sending the vast majority of drivers without permits into their information centre to buy them. But this push lasted only a matter of weeks. They later rented half the ticket hut at River Heads and had an employee sit there selling the permits, but she was easily bypassed if people did not want to pay.

What Sid also never realised was that his curbing the avoidance over those nine months had earned him the enmity of all the island visitors, who had been avoiding paying their access and camping levies, and as the figures showed, they were legion.

The men in the ticket van at Inskip Point, in particular, reported verbal abuse from many of the barge customers, when they insisted they purchase National Park permits as well as barge tickets.

These people were happy to see the honour system come back into effect. As well as affecting their pockets the regular visitors also saw the system as a strengthening of Sid's grip on access to the island.

Chapter 37

Over the previous decade, problems had developed on Fraser Island with visitors wanting to approach the wildlife, first the wild horses, then the dingoes.

Visitors began to tempt the brumbies with food morsels, semi taming them to the point where they would march into houses and tents and stick their heads through open vehicle windows hoping for handouts.

On one occasion a brumby walked into the Eurong Resort shop, ambled over to the bread rack and took a loaf, tearing off the plastic and eating it then and there. Another went into a house in Happy Valley and kicked out a wall.

The horses frightened many people when they approached for titbits, very much so when they took to biting the hands that didn't feed them. It became a major issue.

On a visit to England years before to meet my family, Sid had seen how wild ponies in the New Forest had been left alone by people because of the notices warning of heavy fines on anyone who approached them. These ponies ignored people totally – as had the Fraser Island brumbies before visitors made the first approach.

Sid suggested that meaningful fines be imposed on island visitors who attempted to feed the brumbies, mostly for a photo opportunity.

The National Parks Service would have none of it, but as the problem grew, it quietly decided the brumbies should be shot. They were not native to the island, but descendants of horses brought in the late 1800's by a chap who bred them for remounts for the British Army in India.

Sid wasn't keen on the brumbies. The Eurong herd of eight horses constantly damaged his lawn, but he thought shooting them a drastic solution.

He took matters into his own hands and persuaded a district farmer and a long time friend since schooldays, Stu Whittaker to come and round up the little Eurong mob, and take them back to his property on the banks of the Mary River outside Maryborough.

There he had sandy river flats so the brumbies' hooves splayed from always walking on sand would not be damaged.

The Eurong brumbies are rounded up into a holding pen and trucked to a farm property outside Maryborough. A foal is taken separately so she doesn't get trampled in the truck with the adult horses.

One mare escaped the round up – and she disappeared mysteriously a week or so later, evidently a victim of the official removal programme.

With the horses gone, visitors turned their attention to the dingoes. They had been hardly visible up to this time, except for red eyes in the bush looking out at the Eurong evening barbecues.

But they did scavenge around visitors' beach camps where food was left out, or for fish remains on the beach.

Then the same thing happened: people took to feeding the dingoes ***(below).*** In fact they grew to rely on being fed, and would craftily wait on the beach looking cute near the water's edge, where the cars drove along.

Like the brumbies before them, they lost their fear of people. Then came numerous reports of them nipping and biting.

Among island visitors to Eurong Beach at this time was Steve Irwin, the "crocodile hunter". When Sid saw him he remarked helpfully "There aren't any crocodiles on Fraser you know." Steve swiftly responded "You haven't seen what's in the bath in my room."

When Sid repeated Steve's witty response to the staff over dinner that night, the housemaids took him seriously. They refused to go in to Steve's room to service it for the rest of his stay. He didn't complain.

Steve had actually come to film the island dingoes, by now getting a bad reputation for biting.

One early dingo incident at Eurong Beach was nationally publicized. A couple with a seven year old boy were dining and drinking in the paved bistro area behind the Eurong hotel.

A dingo was seen in the trees beyond the area, and the boy set off to chase it. Three times staff members went to his parents to ask them to stop the boy and warn that dingoes were wild animals and should be left alone.

Each time the father called the boy, but when the boy went back to torment the dingo, he did nothing more about it. The inevitable happened. When the lad hid behind a tree and jumped out at the dingo as it walked past, in fear it turned and bit him on the back of his leg.

Appropriate treatment was given to the lad's bite, but when the family returned to the mainland, the mother contacted *Woman's Day* magazine, and told the story, likening the incident to the dingo taking baby Azaria Chamberlain at Ayers Rock camp ground some years before.

A magazine reporter contacted Eurong and was told about the boy's behaviour and the repeated warnings given to the parents and their ignoring them. The reporter revealed the father was a veterinary surgeon. Sid's response was that he most certainly should have known better and would probably have taken more action to stop his son tormenting a little dog in his surgery.

Both sides of the story were published, and the readers' letters which appeared the following week showed absolutely no sympathy for the family but a lot for the dingo, which had been shot by a National Parks ranger. The parents then sued Sid. His insurer, Suncorp chose to settle with them for $7,000 rather than, as Sid wanted, defend the matter in court.

Again Sid suggested to National Parks that meaningful fines be imposed on people feeding dingoes, but the fines threatened were very small, and like warning pamphlets had little effect. Biting dingoes became an ever growing problem, until a nine year old boy was killed by a pack of them near Indian Head in April 2001.

Only then were substantial fines imposed for feeding the dingoes, and strong action taken by rangers to ensure campers' food was not readily available to the animals. Rangers would go into campers' tents, even in their absence, to check no food had been left out and if they found so much as a piece of pumpkin or watermelon left on a table, the fines would be levied.

It was too late. Many of the dingoes had become reliant on visitors to feed them, and had lost all fear of people. Over ensuing years more and more dingoes, believed to be the purest strain of the animals in Australia, were shot by rangers after snapping at visitors until only an estimated 100 were left.

* * * *

In 1996 Keith Leach, the former owner of Orchid Beach Resort, approached Sid to ask if he could hold the annual Orchid Beach Fishing Contest at Eurong Beach Resort. The Queensland Government had purchased Orchid Beach Resort from Leach to close down as being inappropriate in a National Park.

Keith Leach was a tough negotiator, and negotiations for the sale went on for a long time. A one time Minister for Lands had told Sid years before that Leach had to be allowed to "leave with dignity" and the price of dignity it emerged was $6million.

This caused a furore for the purchase did not mean the northern end of Fraser went back to a natural condition. Land deals over the years had already led to a big subdivision being developed inland from Orchid Beach Resort. Many questions were asked why such a big price had been paid for a small resort when it did not achieve the desired aim. They were never answered.

However after the purchase and the bulldozing of most of the resort buildings, the Queensland Parks and Wildlife Service gave Leach only until 1995 to continue the Orchid Beach Fishing Contest, which had been the subject of ongoing complaints by conservationist, John Sinclair.

There was no love lost between Leach and Sid after a couple of minor differences but Leach was desperate for a venue for what was a big income earner for him.

Entries in the contest had been limited to 1500 and there was a goodly fee attached to being an entrant, as well as spin offs from alcohol and food sales. Leach had attracted a large number of sponsors who put on displays at the contest and in return provided a handsome raft of prizes. Since the late 1980's the major sponsor was Toyota and the main prize a Toyota 4WD vehicle.

Sid agreed the contest could be held at Eurong Beach. Leach wanted the contest fish weigh in, prize presentation and entertainment each evening held on the resort land at the back of *Korawinga*. But Sid was too worried hundreds of feet nightly would wear away his precious hand planted lawn and offered instead the industrial compound about half a kilometre behind the resort. Leach was not happy, but it really was his only option and he accepted it.

He asked Sid to accommodate and supply meals for the contest sponsors, for which they would pay, and for free accommodation for his own staff. Sid agreed to this.

Leach said initially he wanted to handle the liquor sales. Sid demurred because he saw it as the only good income earner for his business from the event. It was decided Sid could operate the bar in the entertainment area.

Sid was also to run buses along the beach for the contestants to bring them to the fish weigh in and take them back after the entertainment ended. And very importantly, Sid asked Leach to make a public address request to contestants not to drive or park on the resort lawns.

When Leach's advance staff came to tell Sid what was expected of him, it appeared the sponsors had to be treated like gods. It was evident that, together with the day to day running of Eurong Beach and his day tours, Sid's staff would be fully occupied looking after them. In particular the restaurant would have to be kept open for very long hours for them to dine after the nightly prize presentation. With so much on his plate, Sid gave the potentially high profit liquor bar back to Leach to run.

When the contest began Sid did his bit at public relations. He had acquired one of the first 4WD Toyotas to be brought to Australia in the mid 1950's. It had been bought by Fraser Island timber cutter, Joe Cunningham who had converted it to a tray back, long before Toyota thought about producing any other than passenger 4WD's. Sid got its previous island owners, Joe, Andy Postan, Trevor Gallehawk and Ray Downes together to pose with it for a television shot ***(below).***

The television cameraman asked if Sid would drive the old Toyota on to the lawn in front of the pub to put it next to the new Toyota being offered as the main prize in the fishing contest.

Sid willingly agreed. Australian Test wicket-keeper Ian Healy who was the celebrity guest at the contest slyly protested "You don't seem to mind **them** parking on your front lawn Sid."

There was no financial spin from the fishing contest off to the resort itself, as Sid had hoped, for the fishermen camped along the beach dunes, fished all day, bussed to the weigh-in in the evening, ate and drank in the compound there, and caught the buses straight back to their camp sites.

From Toyota's viewpoint the contest at Eurong was not a success. It did not attract the contestants with boats who had launched them in the lee of Waddy Point while the contest was based at Orchid Beach. It was these boaties who had plenty of disposable income and were most likely to buy new 4WD's.

Toyota attributed about a third of its new 4WD sales in Queensland to its exposure at the Orchid Beach Fishing Contest.

At Eurong the boaties simply did not come because there was nowhere to launch their boats except 30 km south at Hook Point and it was too far for them to drive up and down the surf beach in the winter dark each night to the weigh-in.

There must have been some heavy behind the scenes discussion between Leach and the Toyota executives for the outcome was that Leach bowed out, selling the fishing contest rights to Toyota for $80,000.

When in due course Sid billed the sponsors for their meals and accommodation he learned they had already paid Leach. The sum amounted to $15,000 and when Leach refused to pass the money on to Sid, it looked as if legal action was the only way he might get paid. Toyota stepped in quickly and paid the sum rather than have the fishing contest under its auspices get off to a bad start.

After long negotiations between Toyota executives and the Queensland Government, the fishing contest was allowed to return to Orchid Beach with a myriad environmental conditions to try and appease John Sinclair and his conservation group, and since then has continued on to great success.

Chapter 38

By the mid 1990's Eurong Beach Resort was bursting at the seams. It was not uncommon for the restaurant and bistro area to serve up to 800 meals a day. Rooms were booked out months ahead for peak seasons.

It was well and truly time for Sid to realise his resort vision. He had consistently made improvements at Eurong over the years but other priorities, taking opportunities as they arose, and clearing his debts, meant the big resort development building programme he had envisaged was put on the back burner for nearly ten years.

Now he started to plan to bring the resort to fruition, beginning with a new restaurant and conference centre to be positioned on a corner in the road, facing the ocean and the traffic heading inland from the surf beach.

Waiting for me to arrive on a delayed flight into Brisbane airport some years before, Sid had gone for a wander around the domestic terminal. When I arrived I got a very quick greeting before being hurried down a long passage to the end of the terminal wing. There was a 12 sided arrival complex with a centre garden.

"This," Sid declared "is the shape our main building is going to be. From the outside not only does every angle look like a frontage, but with the walls curving away it doesn't look anything like as big as it is."

As this building was to be positioned in front of the *Korawinga* units and with two new accommodation buildings set back from it on natural rises in the land at either side, he did not want it to have an obvious front and back. A multi sided building would have no unpleasing aspect.

Sid was in his element as he sat down with pencil and paper night after night working out how the new building should be. Initially he sketched the building with a garden in its centre core, like the Brisbane terminal, with a restaurant, a conference centre, a lounge bar, a reception area, kitchen, storage and an office in sections around it.

Flying over the Brisbane suburbs one day he noticed an octagonal building. As soon as he'd landed he drove off to see what it was, and what he could learn from it. It was a wedding reception complex and its service areas, like kitchens and storerooms were in its central core. Sid recognized this would be more practical than a garden, and would reduce the size of the building.

Another time when he went to look at a new design in 4WD coaches in Perth, he came back more impressed by the dusky pink and dark green foyers of the hotel he stayed in than the coaches.

Sid designed a grand entrance to his signature building, with eight large pillars holding up a peak roofed portico over a raised entrance.

Glass doors opened from either side, on the right to the reception desk; on the left to the lounge bar, then to the restaurant.

On the outer perimeter of the building were undercover walkways, the roof supported by smaller pillars. Windows and full length doors opened into the interior all the way round the walk way.

The restaurant had to seat 250 people to cater for the numbers expected to dine at any one mealtime. The octagonal shape of the building with well placed service stations and planters meant that diners would never appear to be sitting in too intimidating a space.

There were no walls between the lounge bar and the restaurant to allow easy passage between the two for customers, but again planters were to be used to mark the division between the two.

The conference room was a similar size to the restaurant, and was separated from it by concertina doors so that it could be used as a separate area or, with the doors pulled back, be used for overflow dining.

To break up the huge expanse of ceiling and point to Fraser Island as a source of so much beautiful timber for more than a century, Sid wanted exposed timber beams.

The floor of the central service areas would not be part of the main concrete slab, but would be timber and a space would be dug out underneath to enable the mass of piping, wiring and plumbing to be installed and to give easy access for future repair and maintenance.

When he had his rough designs to his satisfaction he took them to Hervey Bay building designer, Greg Pershouse, who had done work for him in the past and understood him well. The resulting detailed plans were just what Sid wanted.

He did not call for tenders. He had been well satisfied with the Hervey Bay firm, Bellero Constructions which had bitumen sealed the airstrip at Wanggoolba some years before and went straight to talk to the company head, Paul Bellero and CEO Bob Goodwin. In October 1997 contracts were signed for Belleros to build the new restaurant and conference complex. Work began in November.

Paul Bellero knew of Sid's fiery temperament and chose Paul Baldwin to head the project. Baldwin was ideal with his calm and diplomatic nature and he and Sid hit it off extremely well from the start. It was just as well for Sid was on site almost all day every day.

Project manager, Paul Baldwin and Sid go over the building plans.

The huge building was to cover more than half an acre.

The reinforced concrete slab floor, (***above***), covered 1700 metres with the centre core a timber floor of another 185 square metres for service areas.

In all 580 cubic metres of concrete were poured with 28 tonnes of reinforcing steel and 10 tonnes of reinforcing mesh. For the walls 15,500 concrete blocks weighing 240 tonnes were trucked in.

The biggest single job involved in the building was making the huge laminated roof and support beams, the largest, 17.3 m long with many just a fraction shorter. There were 48 main frame beams and 90 secondary beams.

Again Sid did not call tenders. He knew what he wanted; who was capable of the mammoth job and he had a good memory for past loyalties and good service. The contract to make the beams of local spotted gum went to Maryborough timber firm, Hyne and Sons.

During the initial planning John Schwabe, Hyne's design engineer had to go into hospital for shoulder reconstruction. Warren Hyne suggested John take his mobile phone to hospital with him to he could talk to Sid about the project from his hospital bed. And he did – many times.

The manufacture of the beams took 12 men working full time for three months. Then came the job of getting them to Eurong.

Murray Reid had bought a big prime mover in readiness to haul these enormous amounts of material to Eurong and could carry the huge beams six at a time.

Sid stressed to Murray that the beams should not be marked in any way – reminiscent of the same instruction given to Sid by Sir Reg Barnewall when he was building Orchid Beach and wanted undamaged satinay trunks as roof supports.

There was no way Murray could transport the longest of the beams on the one way track from the Wanggoolba landing to Eurong as it wound between huge trees in the forest. There was a better chance on the straighter road built parallel to the original old road by the Forestry Department in the latter years of its island regime.

Sid put in a special request to Locky Fullerton, manager of the Department of Environment in Maryborough. "Can Murray drive the wrong way on the one way road?" Locky gave his consent and more. He organized for a National Parks chap to drive ahead of the load to wave oncoming vehicles to the side of the road to let Murray's truck through.

The day chosen for the first trip had a conveniently timed high tide so the sea would be well up the ramps at River Heads and Wanggoolba Creek and Murray wouldn't have steep inclines to contend with getting his laden truck on and off the *Fraser Venture.*

The first six of the great beams, carefully wrapped in plastic were picked up at Hyne and Sons factory in Maryborough and transported on an extendable trailer to River Heads.

Murray took over the job hitching his new 6 wheel drive Kaiser prime mover on to the trailer, and inching his way on to the *Fraser Venture*. Off again on the island and he was ready for the drive across.

Sid turned up to shepherd the load as well as keeping an eagle eye on the beams. On the one and only tight corner, no matter how much shunting Murray did, one set of semi trailer wheels was going to ride high into a soft sand bog. Sid had brought a shovel and set to, digging away some of the bank.

Murray tries to get the long beams around a tight corner through the forest, while Sid digs away.

Sid had thought of everything and organized for a crane to follow the trailer in case of problems, but there wasn't one. The great beams arrived without a scratch ***(below).***

The journey was repeated for succeeding loads of beams and again and again for the huge loads of roof trusses.

Once on site the beams were put together using a special system of hidden steel dowels glued into the beam ends. This method was used both to join the beams together to support the huge roof and to anchor the supporting beams to the concrete foundations.

"The job of mounting the beams and supports on the dowels in the floor required a high degree of skill and coordination, but it was done perfectly," says John Schwabe.

The beams are accurately mounted on the concrete floor using a laser.

Roof bearers are secured on top of the beams.

The prominent entrance starts to take shape.

Villaboard and plasterboard for internal walls weighing 34 tonnes were trucked in next. Suspended ceiling material was another 18 tonnes as well as 2000 square metres of ceramic floor, kitchen and restroom wall tiles. The floor tiles were dusky pink in the main and were laid in pie shaped sections on the floor with dividing strips of dark green tiles to break up the vast size.

In all Murray Reid was kept busy for a year carting everything from sand and cement to furnishings and kitchen equipment for the new building as well as his normal work of bringing in stores and fuel for the resort.

Murray was not alone in his endeavours. His wife Vera who had formerly driven a one tonne Toyota tray back with small loads to supplement the big stores runs was quickly initiated into big truck driving to do her share.

One day Vera was going to the mainland and called in to the shop at Eurong to pick up the mail to take to town. Her hair, makeup and clothes were, as always, immaculate and she caught the eye of a couple of male customers.

Then she walked out of the shop, climbed up into the cab of an eight tonne truck and drove off. One goggle eyed bloke said to his mate "That's the best looking truckie I have ever seen in my life."

While work was progressing, Sid had the sand track past the resort straightened, graveled, bitumen sealed, and kerb and channeled.

The Maryborough City Council came to the party with a third of the cost.

Sid drives the compactor to make sure the base for the road is properly hard.

Getting the hot bitumen to the resort was a major project on its own. It had been a rush to get hot bitumen from Hervey Bay, across the straits on the *Fraser Venture* to seal the Wanggoolba airstrip. For this job the hot bitumen had to be brought from Hervey Bay in a tanker all the way across the straits and across the island as well before it cooled.

The bitumen is poured on the road.

To everyone's delight a school marching band happened to be on the island just a couple of days after the bitumening was done, and when the youngsters heard about the new hard road they came to take advantage of it to have a practice ***(below)***. It made for an unexpected road launching ceremony.

At last, after many years, and with a big crane on site, the *Maheno* anchor found a home in a small garden by the side of the new footpath, and was put in place by Sid and Col Pryor ***(below)***.

Many of the tradesmen Sid used on the building as sub contractors were local men who had done many previous jobs for him. The painter, Gordon Pavey, for example, had first worked for Sid at Eurong in 1978. Tiler, Peter Laban was a second generation tradesman working for Sid. His father had laid the tile floor in the original Eurong pub.

Together with the Bellero team there were 40 workmen on site much of the time.

When the roof went on, the building looked massive ***(below).***

As the interior of the building progressed Sid added many refinements. To break up the floor area in the bar area he adapted the idea of a raised lounge from a Gold Coast restaurant. To work out the shape and size of the raised section, he got a length of string and set it out in a wide curve from one corner.

When accountant Barry Keys saw this he offered to give Sid, as balustrade, the original balcony panels from the Maryborough courthouse, which had come out from England as sailing ship ballast. When they were replaced on the courthouse, Barry bought them but had never had a use for them.

Unfortunately there weren't quite enough panels to surround the raised lounge. The solution to fill in the spaces with glass panels featuring Fraser Island wildlife came after a long gestation period.

Some years before Sid and I had bought a bowl by Hervey Bay glass artist Ron Dellar and kept a collector's eye out for Ron's work ever since. When we saw a glass table top of Ron's with whales moulded in, we realized he could do large flat pieces as well as smaller artworks. A visit to his studio led to a commission to do glass panels of dingos, whales, sea eagles, goannas and turtles to fill the balustrade gaps.

Sid's next question: Could Ron do feature windows of island scenes to break up the wall area above the concertina doors between restaurant and conference centre? He could and did, but not all went smoothly for Ron.

He and his wife Alison were lifting one of the glass windows representing palm shaded Wanggoolba Creek out of the kiln, when Ron dropped his end and the window smashed.

It meant Ron had to start the laborious task of recreating the window from scratch. When Alison phoned Sid to give the news that the window would be late in coming she said "I was so sorry for Ron - but I was also very relieved it wasn't me who had dropped my end."

One of the feature panels representing Fraser Island scenes made by glass artist, Ron Dellar.

A big surprise for everyone was when a heavy parcel was delivered to Sid from Ron. It was glass door handles in the shape of Fraser Island that he had ordered for the two pair of main doors into the complex, and kept very quiet about. No-one had realized how creative Sid was. They made a great entry statement.

Receptionist Raine Foster shows off the glass door handles.

Spotted gum shiplap timber was added to all the white painted interior walls to windowsill height to give contrast and painted lattice panels were installed inside and out to tie the building in with the lattice features on the *Korawinga* units.

The bar and the reception desk all designed by Sid were timber with green marbleized tops, and brass fittings. The end result was absolutely stunning.

Nothing escaped Sid's attention, not even the more mundane details. When it came to working out what equipment was needed for the new kitchen, chef Karl White was given the job of looking through catalogues. His choices made, Karl stood by in the bare space that was to be the kitchen reading out the measurements, while Sid on hands and knees on the floor chalked out where everything was to go and what space it would take up.

It came to the stove Karl wanted and Sid chalked out its space on the floor then looked up and asked "How much is this stove going to cost?" Karl responded "$34,800." Sid didn't say Karl couldn't have it. He simply rubbed out its chalk mark.

Before the building was finished Sid had a huge free form swimming pool built alongside the restaurant, with a spa in one corner and a waterfall along one side.

The pool building gets underway.

Murray Reid was sent a long way into the country to buy and bring back a truckload of big rocks to make the waterfall.

But Sid was a little remiss in his instructions to the pool builders, who were not waterfall builders. When they asked for a sketch of the waterfall as Sid envisioned it, he went one better and tore a photograph of some famous falls out of a magazine.

Completely overwhelmed, but believing Sid wanted it high, the builders wasted the big rocks as back supports and poured a straight concrete wall in front of them.

The building of the pool and spa is almost complete.

When it is finished, the pool is soon put to good use.

Murray Reid recalls that throughout this year of carting building material as well as stores, he took only two days off, and no sooner was he out of the area than he got a phone call from Sid asking where an urgently needed compressor was for the pool construction. "That was the only thing I forgot in that whole construction," he says wryly.

While the development was going on the mechanics at Sid's workshop never knew what was going to be asked of them. Accustomed to maintaining the tour buses and ferries, their job description blew out completely. After having the sand track that passed for a road around the resort bitumen sealed, as befitting the new development taking shape, Sid then wanted street lights. He drew up his design by hand on the back of an old envelope, and took it to head mechanic, Laurie Toy with the request machinist, Arnie Pannasch make half a dozen.

Laurie pointed out Arnie was working to a tight schedule on the rebuilding of the *Australian Explorer* coach.

"But it won't take Arnie long to turn out a few street lights," said Sid. "And can he put arms on them for banners? Then get them powder coated dark green and get them over to the resort as soon as possible."

The street lights arrived and a big switching on ceremony was held, with all the staff sitting on the lawn to watch.

One of the street lights on the road to the main resort building.

But that was only the beginning for the workshop fellows. One of the Maryborough council conditions for the new restaurant was that the kitchen grease trap have a tall vent pipe. The only place for the grease trap was by the side of the main entrance, and there was no way Sid was going to have an obvious vent pipe by the front of his building.

Back he went to the workshop with a drawing on another tatty envelope.

"Get Arnie to make a seven metre long tapered pipe like this," he said to Laurie Toy, "and weld lugs at the top and 1.5 metres from the bottom, and get it powder coated to match the street lights. He'll have to make it in two lengths so it will fit in the powder coater's room."

"What about the *Australian Explorer*?" asked Toy.

"He's got to keep going with that," said Sid.

The vent pipe duly arrived, was put in position over the concrete grease trap, which was hidden under garden rocks. With an Australian flag flying from it, no-one knew the vent pipe was anything other than a flag pole.

The next idea Sid took to the workshop was more in the mechanics' line of work.

A new powerhouse and generators were needed to cope with the bigger power load at the resort.

Sid asked the mechanics to convert the newly purchased generator motors from standard radiator fan cooling to a marine heat exchanger system.

"Why?" asked Laurie.

"Not only will they be quieter, but by running pipes from the new engines to a heat exchanger, the hot water being expelled can run into the pool spa to heat it. This heated water will run over into the pool and heat it as well," Sid explained.

Becoming accustomed to Sid's unusual requests, the next one had the mechanics' minds boggling. He turned up at the workshop with a tracing of a 20cm long Fraser Island map.

"Can Arnie just make me a cookie cutter this shape and size with a good solid little handle on it?' Sid asked.

Job done, Sid took the cookie cutter to Curly Tatnell at the Maryborough terracotta tile factory, where the tiles were being made for the front entry and walkway around the restaurant.

He asked Tatnell if, before the tiles were fired, he could imprint the island map into about 30 of them. When the tiles were laid and the ones with the Fraser Island imprint randomly placed, everyone walking in would suddenly catch sight of one, pause and say "Look at that."

The next time Sid went to the workshop it was to ask for Arnie to make stands for signs about dress code for the restaurant.

Finally when all else was done, back he went with yet another drawing, this one of a bus shelter for outside the new centre.

It was simple beyond belief, two A Frames with a seat between and a roof over, to tie in with the two A Frame cottages which still stood through many refurbishments since the day they were first built 30 years before.

It was such a masterpiece of simplicity that one day Sid caught a man photographing, then measuring it. He turned out to be the council engineer from a north Queensland council who asked if he could pinch the design for the bus stops in his region.

The new restaurant and bar was opened on September 1 1998 with a trial dinner for the staff. Unheralded and unsung on the second night 40 people were booked for dinner and staff rostered accordingly.

But the Fraser Island telegraph had been working and more than 100 additional diners walked in. Urgent calls were made around the resort getting off duty waiters, bar staff and kitchen hands back to work.

The new restaurant quickly became very popular at every mealtime.

Up to now the shop had been the hub of the resort, under the long time management of Ian Hagart. Now Ian and the administration were transferred to the new building.

Belleros entered the building in the 1999 Queensland Master Builders Wide Bay Regional Building awards and as well as winning three section prizes it won the top award as Project of the Year.

Chapter 39

Construction at Eurong Beach did not end with the restaurant/conference complex. Six months before its completion Sid was so pleased with the way the building was progressing, and happy to be so involved in the practicalities of his development, that he decided to continue straight on with stage two of the new construction, a three storey 30 unit accommodation building to a four star standard.

Sid named this building *Tradewinds* after the little trawler he had owned in the 1960's for carrying blocks to Orchid Beach.

It was another huge building, with a concrete floor area of 2400 square metres with three accommodation floors and a basement tucked into the slope of the land to house resort and public laundries.

Each of the first two accommodation floors comprised 12 four person units and on the top floor were six two bedroom suites, to the same pattern as the earlier *Korawinga* building. The walls contained 31,000 blocks and the roof covered 820 square metres.

Working on *Tradewinds* in conjunction with the restaurant/conference complex meant that as tradesmen finished their part in the first building, they moved straight on to the units.

The Tradewinds accommodation building stands to the right of the main centre.

Sid was back to his old tricks. The roofers came back one Monday morning to have him tell them they hadn't cleaned off all the filings, which would cause rust, where holes were drilled for screws to secure the roofing to his satisfaction.

During the weekend he had clambered up the scaffolding on to the roof and inspected it thoroughly, in spite of him being 62 years old and having a damaged knee, probably from all those early years of lifting petrol drums on it.

Tour driver Mal Clonan quietly observed these things, and years later when he started his own business, building storage sheds on the Sunshine Coast, he happily told Sid he had followed his example and when the builders were away, he had climbed up onto the roof – and found filings.

Tradewinds was completed in mid December 1998, ready for the Christmas holidays.

The surrounding area was landscaped with terraces up the hills, planted with salt resistant plants, a tennis court and gazebos with barbecues.

* * * *

Sid was bringing day tours from Hervey Bay, the Sunshine Coast and Rainbow Beach in growing numbers. He had broadened the scope of his tours, offering more select day tours in smaller buses as well as the large ones and, because of his early foresight in buying additional licences as they came on the market, he could take people to many more places on the island than his business rivals.

Sid's eco tour from Noosa in the rainforest.

With all the extra accommodation at Eurong Beach, Sid now organized additional tours to fill the rooms. He began stopover tours of two and three days.

The response was immediate and he had to buy several new buses, bringing the size of his fleet to more than 40 buses, to carry the numbers booking on the overnight tours, which gave a good overview of the island as far north as Indian Head.

All meals in the new restaurant were included in the stopover package and after dinner most of the passengers went to the old pub and let their hair down with karaoke and other entertainment.

One of the new buses for tours from Hervey Bay pauses at the Maheno wreck. Custom built it had a steep cutaway back for it to drive on and off the Fraser Venture without scraping the rear.

Two new buses to carry 80 people were bought for the Sunshine Coast tours, and the rebuilt *Australian Explorer* was added to the Rainbow Beach fleet.

Its driver was a cheerful young fellow, Darryl Roper, the grandson of Eurong neighbor, Les Roper.

Sid said he'd give Darryl $200 if he didn't stake one of the big *Australian Explorer* tyres for a year on the tree roots sticking up in the island roads. Promptly at the end of the year Darryl fronted up to ask for his $200 and got it.

* * * *

For the first time, Sid employed people to travel throughout New South Wales and south east Queensland marketing and promoting Eurong Beach, his tours, and whale watching to travel agents.

One was the very humorous Ken Bennett, formerly chairman of the regional tourism board.

He says that when he returned to Eurong to report on his trips, Sid would scrutinise his expenses carefully.

Says Ken "Sid had very little experience of rising motel prices, and often said I should look for cheaper overnight accommodation. I was going to Sydney on one trip and Sid said to me 'At least you should be able to get a $30 a night room in a motel down there.'

"Late one night in Sydney, I got a telephone call from Sid, who asked 'What are you doing?'"

I replied 'Still looking for a $30 a night motel room.'"

When Ken moved on, the marketing was taken over by the energetic Eddy May who had sold his whale watching business and approached Sid for a job.

"Working for Sid was certainly different," says Eddy. "I was never asked for long reports of what was or wasn't happening. Instead a phone call from time to time for an update was sufficient. I could ring Sid at any time, get serious consideration of what I had to offer and be given an answer there and then.

"Sid had a total understanding of what was needed in his business, rather amazing in such a diverse concern and would act, not needlessly stuff around, which is often the case in businesses of this size.

"I also knew I was being appreciated for my efforts. I am convinced this applied to the rest of the staff also. Perhaps the best tribute that can be paid Sid was that so many of the staff were due for long service leave. His stable workforce worked wonders in earning confidence from the agents we dealt with."

* * * *

After a break of three months while approval for the next building was obtained, the builders came back to Eurong in March 1999 to start stage three.

This was another accommodation building with 12 four person units on the ground floor and 12 luxury two bedroom apartments on the first and second floors. Called *Coral Sea* after another vessel in the island's history, it faced the conference centre across the swimming pool.

It was not completed until February 2000 because, while it was under construction, smaller projects were slotted in. The need for more staff accommodation was pressing, and a 24 unit building for staff interrupted progress on *Coral Sea*.

The Coral Sea units and flagpole.

Sid planned next for a café/bakery, which not only baked all the bread and rolls for the restaurant but bread, pies and cakes for passing customers. He called it "Ferrari's" because, he claimed, he had the financial choice of buying a Ferrari car or building a bakery and the latter won. Fortunately perhaps the famous car manufacturer never heard of the Eurong Beach bakery.

Sid seemed to have an unerring instinct for what would work well. On the first day the bakery opened, the two bakers and café assistants made and sold $700 of goods. They enthused about how unexpectedly busy it was. Word spread quickly as ever on Fraser Island and on the second day their business doubled.

The new bakery.

Then it was Good Friday with masses of people and their business doubled again.

Happiest with the new bakery though were the day tour drivers, for they no longer had to bring trays of bread from a mainland bakery with them every day, carrying them on to the *Fraser Venture* then, once on the island from the ferry, on to the 4WD buses, and at Eurong, from the buses to the shop and restaurant.

* * * *

The next thing Sid wanted to address was the need for a doctor on the island, a need which had grown as the numbers of tourists grew. St. John's Ambulance Brigade had long left the island, so the job of looking after the sick and injured had devolved back on Sid and his staff.

Sid had by now organized for staff to take first aid courses, but some of the injuries were beyond their skills.

One particularly awful case was of a girl in a party of backpackers who had a fair bit to drink and thought she could imitate Fijian firewalkers. The burns on her feet were so bad that what remained of her toes were fused together after she walked through a camp fire.

A new National Parks head ranger on the island, Max Haste complained long and loud in the media about the demands on the rangers to look after accident victims and control bad behaviour. It wasn't their responsibility he maintained. This did not impress Sid who, with his staff, had been bearing the brunt of calls for help for decades.

They were still called on, especially at night when the National Park headquarters just a short way up the surf beach was in total darkness.

However Sid did recognize that Haste's complaint might be much more effective in spurring government action about the continuing awful situation on Fraser Island.

Sure enough there began to be talk of having a rescue helicopter stationed in Hervey Bay. It had long been established that the majority of call outs for the Sunshine Coast rescue helicopter were coming from Fraser.

Then one day a phalanx of senior police officers arrived at Eurong. Their brief was to investigate where a new police station might be best sited.

At a sit down meeting Sid told them that Eurong was the best place as it was centrally located to where most of the tourists stayed, either camping along the beach, or inland at the National Park camp grounds at Central Station and Lake McKenzie.

He also said that with the need for services such as water and power supply to be available, the logical site was in the National Parks headquarters compound just up the beach from the resort, where these services were already in place.

After so many years of having to bear the brunt of emergency medical assistance at last it looked as if the burden was going to be lifted. Knowing the mills of government grind slowly and it was likely to be more years before anything happened, Sid in the meantime was prepared, as a community contribution, to build a surgery to offer rent free to encourage a doctor to open a practice at Eurong.

The only logical place for the surgery was on the main road frontage between the café and the A Frame cottages. But when the plans went in, the Beach Protection Authority became involved as they now controlled land up to 100 metres back from the beach.

Although the shop, the pub, several accommodation buildings, and other buildings were between the proposed surgery and the beach frontage, the B.P.A. indicated it would take at least a year for it to get around to making a decision on the plans.

And there unfortunately Sid's gesture came to a halt, defeated by bureaucracy, for by that time the builders would have moved back to the mainland.

* * * *

Still determined to do something, Sid tried another tack. Most accidents involved young backpackers.

Some of the young drivers were downright reckless but others just unable to cope with driving conditions very different from any they had experienced.

The backpackers also had a bad reputation for loud partying at night in the island camp grounds.

The idea was floated that backpacker hostels and 4WD hire companies be licensed to do tag-a-long tours of up to four vehicles, with a guide made responsible for the driving and behaviour of the group.

However Locky Fullerton, regional manager of the Queensland Parks and Wildlife Service said he couldn't introduce new licenses because of the moratorium on tour licenses which was still in place.

One Hervey Bay hostel owner, David Jacobs, like Sid, had long been concerned about the backpackers' safety.

"Some of the accidents had been horrific and resulted in multiple deaths," he declares. "I wanted one of my vehicles with an experienced driver to lead the other vehicles in tag along fashion and look after the backpackers. But I was told by National Parks I would need a tour permit to do that and couldn't have one."

"After making my views known at a tour operators' meeting I was approached by Sid and we began to talk about what we could do. He offered to let me use one of his permits to achieve my goal. He was very helpful and we went together to see Locky Fullerton, who gave us written approval to run tag alongs on Sid's licence.

"From then on my backpackers had no more accidents.

"I found Sid to be a man of his word. We never had a written agreement, and I ran my tours on his permits for three years, until he sold out.

"Sid was ahead of his time."

A similar approach came from a second hostel owner, Tony Miller, and Sid agreed to let him too run a tour using his licence.

Chapter 40

Restless with the resort expansion completed as far as it could be until the massive extra day to day workload generated by the new development and its immediate popularity could be absorbed by the staff, and new people trained, Sid looked around for new challenges.

In 1992 he had bought a house on the Gold Coast, as a getaway from the island, and watched its vibrant tourism scene with interest.

A Gold Coast marine architect, Stuart Ballantyne introduced Sid to the concept of a new type of vessel, an American designed SWATH, which comprised a spacious hull built on hydraulic legs on two submarine pontoons. Once it was underway a switch raised the hull, so it rose out of the water and the wave action had no effect on its stability, a perfect vessel for landlubbers to cruise in.

Sid and I went to see a SWATH called *Navotek* in Hawaii, (***below)*** and were invited by its owner on a lunch cruise. It was most impressive. As soon as it left harbour, its hull rose on legs while its pontoons remained below water. Waves of more than two metres flowed beneath the hull, and the cruise along the Honolulu coast was so smooth that a Japanese wedding was held on one deck; hula dance lessons on another. Not one person was sea sick.

Sid became interested in introducing a SWATH into Australia, and began to research the possibilities.

As always when he was faced with a problem or opportunity, he worried at it, examining every aspect sometimes for weeks until he came to a decision. It was a long and arduous process, but he never did anything without going through it. He found he could have a SWATH built in Queensland and got a quotation from a reputable shipyard.

Before he committed to such an expensive vessel Sid wanted at least two strings to his bow.

He felt a good basis would be for it in Hervey Bay for the winter whale watch season in addition to the highly successful *Islander.*

The Hervey Bay whale watch season lasted only three months however and the SWATH could not be allowed to sit idle for the remainder of the year. As a second string, Sid thought of introducing summer time lunch and dinner cruises along the Gold Coast sea front. A SWATH's seaworthiness and stability meant it could be taken into the open ocean even in moderately rough conditions so passengers could get an unparalleled view of the Gold Coast's high rise skyline, in the evenings with the setting sun as a backdrop.

He believed the cruises would work well, but it meant setting up a whole new infrastructure on the Gold Coast and he recognized how much work this would take, as well as the element of risk in the new venture. To make the SWATH viable as a Gold Coast dinner vessel Sid determined it had to be a minimum of 35m long to enable it to carry a sufficiently large number of passengers.

The National Parks whale watch permits for Hervey Bay at that time limited the vessels used to 30 metres, though the rule has since been relaxed. Sid approached the Queensland Parks and Wildlife Service to ask if this condition could be waived, and the answer was a flat 'No."

In spite of what the SWATH would have meant in the terms of the Queensland economy in its building phase, as well as putting the state in the forefront of marine technology, the QPWS would not budge.

Sid asked then if he could do whale watching cruises from the Gold Coast in the SWATH. Again the answer from the QPWS was an adamant "No." These refusals were the determining factor, and Sid shelved the idea of a SWATH.

He was sick and tired of butting his head against a bureaucratic brick wall.

It was only a few years later when whale watching on the Gold Coast was flourishing without being licensed, that Sid learned the QPWS control on whale watching in Queensland was far more limited than it had pretended.

* * * *

Sid still felt he could expand his whale watching business and began to search for another vessel. He went to Adelaide to look at a Wave Piercer catamaran for sale there, but it wasn't suitable.

He heard of another Wave Piercer for sale in Townsville, so chartered Gerry Geltch to fly us up there to look at it. Gerry's wife, Terrina came along for the flight. The vessel was too well worn to be of interest, so, with time to spare, the four of us took a day off, hired a couple of open top mini mokes and went to Magnetic Island.

Gerry says "This is where I realised Sid has a totally different personality away from the resort. There he is very focused, serious and often stressed. On Magnetic Island he was like a big kid, hanging out of the moke, honking the horn, racing our moke, just having a ball. I'd never seen him like it before.

"Another incident on that trip showed me another side to his character that I had not expected. As we were walking through the mall in Townsville, an Aboriginal chap singled out Sid and asked ''Hey bro, you got a smoke?'

"Many folks would have ignored the man and just kept on walking, but Sid stopped, turned to the guy and replied 'Sorry mate. I don't smoke.' Then the two of them had a chat before we all toddled on our way."

* * * *

Unsuccessful in his searches for another whale watch vessel, in April 2000 Sid purchased an entire whale watch business from rival, Mimi McPherson and her father, Sydney businessman Peter Gow.

The purchase included a 25m catamaran *Discovery I.* Sid changed the look of the vessel by painting the hull red, like the expedition ships he had seen on his voyage to Antarctica in the early 1990s.

"Mimi got a lot of publicity as the younger sister of international model, Elle McPherson and had given Hervey Bay a strong recognition factor for whale watching," says Sid.

To compensate for the loss of Mimi's celebrity factor, Sid urged fellow whale watch operators to work together to uphold the name Hervey Bay had earned of being the prime place in Australia for whale watching.

He suggested they take an active role in the campaign, spearheaded by Greenpeace and the Australian Government, to stop Japanese whaling in the Southern Ocean.

He pointed out that not only was this a crucial battle, but Hervey Bay could gain attention from "a mouse that roared" type of campaign, with the angle that whale watching was much more profitable than whale slaughter.

Nowhere, he said, was there a better example than Hervey Bay of how whale watching had helped transform a community from a small city to a significant tourist destination in its own right with a bright economic future.

Sid's annual booking agents' party attracted around 350 business people involved in tourism and had become the biggest event of its kind in Hervey Bay. Now he sought to use the party to try and get the whole of the Bay tourism industry involved in a *Save the Whales* campaign. He contacted Greenpeace headquarters in Sydney and the Australian Department of Environment to ask if they would send speakers to the party.

Both responded with enthusiasm, Greenpeace by sending its new CEO, Peter Mullins and the Department of Environment, its deputy secretary, Howard Bamsey.

They had been seeking support from the Australian whale watching industry for some time, but had met with little result. The two men spoke about how the industry could present a commercial alternative to whaling.

Their ongoing fear was that the Japanese government would eventually win support at the annual meetings of the International Whaling Commission for the renewed hunting of whales. Each year the Japanese government was garnering more backing, particularly from the small South Pacific island nations, to which it gave considerable financial aid.

Early the following year the Australian Department of Environment contacted Sid to ask him to speak at a conference in Samoa called the Regional Forum and Workshop for a South Pacific Whale Sanctuary.

It would be attended by 19 Ministers of Environment from the South Pacific nations. Far too shy to go himself, Sid nominated Eddy May, who had been involved in the whale watch industry since it began in Hervey Bay.

"I gave a speech in which detailed the economic benefits of whale watching for Hervey Bay and how this industry could play a part in the South Pacific," Eddy describes.

* * * *

The expansion of Sid's business, with so many facets, put a lot of pressure on his staff, especially when the new GST tax was introduced in July 2000.

The Hervey Bay office expanded to a staff of seven to take all the bookings and handle the accounting for the day and overnight tours, the *Fraser Venture*, the *Kingfisher Bay* ferry, the *Fraser Dawn*, the *Islander* and *Discovery 1*.

They were a highly capable team led by former bank accountant Adrian Davie and May Jensen, and their efficiency and good nature were undoubtedly responsible for Sid's tours continuing to lead the field.

At Eurong the accounting for all the arms of the business from the Sunshine Coast to Hervey Bay was pulled together and it took a great deal of learning and ongoing hard work to cope with the new GST demands.

* * * *

There were some enlivening moments amid the hard work.

The Olympic Games in Sydney in September 2000 were preceded by the Olympic flame being carried by runners around Australia.

Fraser Island was selected as one of the places of particular importance, and Sid was asked if he would put the *Fraser Venture* at the disposal of the organising committee to carry the flame to and from the island, with ten runners taking it across to Eurong, then some way along the surf beach. Of course he agreed, and it was a momentous day as the *Fraser Venture* arrived at Wanggoolba Creek landing, escorted by police and coastguard launches.

Some of the best photographs of the Australia wide event were taken as the runners in their white and blue uniforms, holding their elegant torches aloft, ran abreast along the beach with the surf rolling in dramatically behind them.

There were crowds to greet them as they ran on and off the *Fraser Venture* at River Heads.

The Olympic torch bearers are swamped by enthusiastic schoolchildren as they arrive back at River Heads.

* * * *

To commemorate the millennium, Maryborough decided to restore its historic port precinct, where once sailing ships carrying thousands of immigrants pulled in to its wharves, and to honour some of its remarkable sons, living and dead, by putting bronze plaques in the footpath outside the former Customs House.

Sid was chosen as one to be honoured together with scientists, sportsmen, scholars, artists, businessmen and industrialists, and at the end of the year he and his fellows were invited to a celebration dinner then, each carrying a lantern, went to stand by their plaque while their achievements were read out.

It was a delightful occasion and Sid felt particularly pleased to be selected and have his contribution to the city recognised. Four generations of his family gathered for the event.

With Sid was his 85 year old mother, his daughter and son in law, Monica and Col Pryor and their new baby son, Campbell.

Sid and his mother stand by the plaque honouring him in Maryborough's historic port precinct.

Sid was naturally proud of what he had achieved and the way he overcame the problems of isolation to create the business infrastructure that he did, and to have his achievement recognised.

He had set the standard which the other Fraser Island businesses followed, many of them being given incalculable help by him.

It is impossible for a newcomer now to know what the isolation was like on Fraser in the early days, because Sid's lifetime's work changed the face of the island, and those who came after, followed in his footsteps.

He helped the tourism growth of the surrounding region, not only by providing facilities, but by his policy of buying everything he needed locally, from weekly stores to building materials, which enabled many other regional businesses to grow with him.

He never forgot the help some of the Maryborough people gave him in the early years, when he was mostly scratching for a dollar, and remained intensely loyal to the city.

"I got most of my supplies for the first little shop at Eurong from a wholesaler called Wally Minter," Sid gives as an example. "I got behind in paying him and owed him $2,000. I went to see him, told him I couldn't pay it there and then, but would he let me have more supplies as long as I paid for them as I went and I would pay the $2000 as soon as I could. Wally agreed straight away."

As Eurong Beach grew so did the size of the purchases from Maryborough and Hervey Bay until it was in the multimillions each year.

* * * *

Sid still had ideas for more resort expansion, to redevelop his freehold land with a figure 8 shaped building with lots more accommodation and shops, but acknowledged time had run away from him.

"I could have done much more," he said at the time, "if I had had a bit of money to get started and had I not been held back by government. I wish I were 40."

By now he had achieved much of what he had envisioned, and felt to press on would involve him in more and more bureaucratic entanglement and delay and there was no joy in that.

He was 64, and earlier in the year had purchased the iconic Gold Coast mansion *Bartinon* with retirement in view. In the latter months of 2000 he decided to call it a day.

Over the preceding years he had considered approaches to buy the business, but none had matched up to his expectation of its worth. Now he decided to make a determined effort to sell it in its entirety.

When the news got around that Sid was going to sell out and retire, people were incredulous. They could not imagine Fraser Island without him, nor him without Fraser Island.

After a long interview for a double page article in the Brisbane *Courier Mail,* headed "Last of the Barefoot Tycoons", Walkley Award winning journalist, David Bentley wrote "Sid has had enough of sand and rust. He prefers to spend his leisure time at his gold Coast mansion, formerly the abode of Sir Justin Hickey.

"He dreams of sailing the world in a luxury yacht. He looks forward to taking his red and black XK120 Jaguar out of mothballs, cruising Tedder Avenue in Southport and having fun…though he's not sure what other people mean by fun."

He quotes Sid as revealing "Fun to me is being able to achieve things and see that I'm doing something worthwhile.

"I'm never happier than when I'm developing something. It made me happy to have these big ferries built, organise the engines, watch them taking shape and being launched.

"When we built the conference centre and unit buildings at Eurong that was a very happy three years. I loved doing road works, and building the airstrip.

"I could see that I was achieving something. Figures on a piece of paper mean nothing to me."

Bentley commented "It is hard to imagine Fraser Island without Sid in his trademark baseball cap and shorts. His imprint is everywhere. Love him or hate him Sid is the last of the old style Queensland entrepreneurs – men who built empires with bare hands, knew every nut and bolt and spare part in their operation, understood what jobs needed to be done and how to do them."

* * * *

There was plenty of interest in buying Sid's business shown by a wide variety of people, but the complexity of the Eurong infrastructure was beyond most who had specialised in just one aspect of such a business, ferries, or whale watching or tours or an hotel, or a shop.

Sid and I had managed because we had grown with it, absorbing one new thing at a time, and because, while Sid was the only one capable of setting the direction and pulling things together at a strategic level, we had a nucleus of reliable, intelligent and extremely loyal long term staff to whom much of the day to day organisation could safely be delegated.

Offers came in to buy one or other aspect of the business, but Sid insisted it be kept as a whole, as he had envisioned and developed it. This put it outside the reach of all but the corporate world.

Interest came from several major players nationally as well as internationally.

Then came an event which quashed all hope of a quick sale.

Chapter 41

Sid made a mistake in believing all his long term staff were loyal. In particular one of the most trusted employees, Kosta Ladas, head skipper of his Inskip Point ferries, had ambitions to operate his own barge service there.

A very personable man, with Mediterranean charm, Ladas had begun working as a deckhand for Sid in 1989. He had been trained to qualify as a skipper and then put in charge of the Inskip Point barge operations.

However for six years from the mid 1990's Kosta admits he sought investors while keenly observing Sid's operation, collecting information, making contacts with Sid's most regular customers and useful agencies, like four wheel drive hire companies.

It emerged he had been undermining Sid's service for years, even while reaping enormous benefit from Sid's operation, apart from his regular livelihood. For several months each autumn hundreds of American youngsters on a Young Ambassador programme called People to People took Sid's tours between Noosa and Rainbow Beach. Ladas and his wife had a restaurant in Rainbow Beach and Sid asked if they would supply the young peoples' lunches, a very profitable supplement to their restaurant business.

Sid also allowed Ladas to keep any money he charged for making out of hours crossings for people who needed to return to the mainland urgently.

Ladas says in 1996-7 he began talking to Ray Maher, a Brisbane electrical contractor with a holiday house at Eurong, about starting a new barge at Inskip Point, but they did not have enough capital. They made a concerted effort to find a third investor in 1999 and in early 2000 found Eric Hume, a Maryborough man with a holiday house at Happy Valley.

From then on Ladas acknowledges he kept a careful count of how many vehicles went over to Fraser Island on Sid's Inskip Point barges, even on his days off and when he left Sid's employ, getting deckhands to keep count for him.

He admits he copied Sid's barge price lists from log books over the years and, as he was responsible for ordering fuel for Sid's barges, copied Sid's fuel invoices.

In December 2000 Ladas and his two backers, brought the *Manta Ray* a new $1.3million, larger and much faster barge to Inskip Point to compete with the *Rainbow Venture* and *Eliza Fraser*. The competition which followed was like a couple of workhorses trying to keep up with a racehorse. It emerged Ladas had a ten per cent stake in the new barge and his backers Ray Maher and Eric Hume had 45 per cent each. Ladas bruited it around that Hume had recently retired after selling a mining equipment business for $40 million.

Barge war number three began – with many of the same players there had been before. Ladas and Ian Dean had worked for Gordon Elmer and were involved in the intimidatory tactics he had employed when Sid introduced the *Rainbow Venture* in 1986. Dean had employed like tactics on his own behalf with Ladas watching, and now Ladas was in the fray with Dean's son, Tony, working for him as relief skipper. Gordon Elmer was one of the first people to turn up for a ride on the *Manta Ray.*

* * * *

Sid had had no inkling that a new barge was coming to Rainbow Beach until one mid November day in 2000 he and I were heading off the island for a few days break on the Gold Coast. We had just boarded the *Rainbow Venture,* when Sid got a phone call from resort manager Ian Hagart.

Ian said "I've just been told another barge is coming in to Inskip Point and Kosta Ladas and Ray Maher might be involved." His informant was a friend with a holiday house at Eurong who had just come up from Brisbane. He had been to a barbecue at which a senior officer of the Department of Harbours and Marine had told him about the new barge and asked how he thought Sid would take it.

Ladas had given a month's notice just two weeks before, but he was actually skippering the *Rainbow Venture* this day. There and then Sid went up to the wheelhouse to ask him what he knew of the new barge.

"Nothing. I have heard nothing," Ladas replied.

"What are you going to be doing when you leave then?" Sid asked.

"I might go and work for a car dealer in Gympie or take a break. I don't know," Ladas replied.

Sid was not convinced and when he arrived at the Gold Coast he telephoned Ray Maher, whom he knew slightly. Maher acknowledged he was involved in a new barge and when Sid asked if they could meet, agreed and a time was set for the next day in Brisbane. Maher had Hume, the second partner in the barge venture with him. Sid did not know Hume at all.

The conversation was brief and wary.

I said the new barge could not have come at a worse time for us with the sale of the resort in prospect. Sid fished in many different ways to find out if Ladas was involved. Sid was worried Ladas could damage his business, or take advantage of his position in many ways in the remaining two weeks of his employment. He was later to learn Ladas had been doing this for years. At the meeting however, Maher and Hume denied Ladas was involved with them.

Sid then asked about their new barge, called the *Manta Ray* and they told him the crucial fact that it would do 11 knots, which was faster than the *Rainbow Venture* or *Eliza Fraser*. This was important because it meant the *Manta Ray* could get across to Fraser Island and back to pick up any customers waiting on the Inskip Point beach ahead of the others.

Maher also informed us they intended to charge $55 per vehicle for a return crossing. He claimed Sid could not compete by dropping the price he was charging, recently increased to $70, by more than 15 per cent, that is to $59.50.

Maher said he had this information from the Australian Competition and Consumer Commission and told us his son worked for the ACCC.

Hume who to that point had said nothing suddenly piped up "Money means nothing to me Sid."

It was obvious from this that they intended a price war. After that there was little else to say and Sid and I left. On the drive back to the Gold Coast Sid worried away at the possibility Ladas was involved in the new operation.

"He knows our Inskip Point barge business intimately," Sid said. "He's lived at Rainbow Beach for years and knows all the locals and he knows all the dirty tricks Elmer and Dean played.

But then we've had a good relationship for 11 years and I gave him the opportunity to come up from deckhand to be lead skipper, so that should mean something to him and things shouldn't get out of hand as they did before."

* * * *

We did not know if it were true that we would not be able to compete on price, the thing that all customers are most interested in, but Maher had said he had this information direct from the ACCC. Sid telephoned John Richards a partner in our long time solicitors, Carswell and Co to ask if what Maher said was true.

We had had a brief correspondence with the Trade Practices Commission, the forerunner of the ACCC during the Dean barge period, and we wanted to clarify our whole situation so we did not breach ACCC law.

Richards arranged for us to meet with a barrister who specialized in trade practices law, Peter Davis and we met in his chambers in Brisbane a week or so later.

At the meeting Davis spoke to us for a full hour, but I found it hard to come to grips with many aspects of what he was telling us. I found his explanation of the trade practices law hard to grasp. The law appeared straightforward but had many underlying complexities.

Davis also spoke as if we had a greater understanding of the law than in fact we had. I left the chambers mystified except over the most straightforward points, that Maher had not been truthful and we could in fact charge up to $10 less than any competition as long as we did not try to drive them out of business; we could not run for nothing, and we could do fuel discounting at Eurong as an added incentive to customers to use our barge service.

It appeared Sid was equally as perplexed, for he asked Davis more than once to clarify what we could and could not do in the face of what we knew was going to be a tough competitor, with a newer, bigger and faster barge.

Solicitor John Richards accompanied us to the meeting. On the way out in the lift, Sid said he was baffled and asked Richards to write us a letter setting out what Davis had told us.

He did so in a brief one page letter, which Sid took as his behavioural reference point.

Sid went to see Ross Williams, the skipper of the *Kingfisher Bay* ferry to ask if he would transfer back to Rainbow Beach to operate the *Rainbow Venture* and be head skipper of the operation there.

"I asked Ross because he was a most capable and intelligent skipper, able to think for himself. I felt I needed someone of his calibre to look after the practical side of our business," says Sid. "Ross also knew Ladas, having worked as his deckhand for some years until he became a skipper in his own right, and I knew he would not be intimidated by him if he were to operate the *Manta Ray*.

"I knew it was a big thing to ask Ross to go back to Rainbow Beach. He had a house at River Heads and his wife Sue had a job in Hervey Bay. So as not to disadvantage them financially, I said Sue could have a job as a deckhand.

"Ross agreed to go to Rainbow Beach, and we discussed the guidelines of how he should conduct the operation on my behalf. I showed the solicitor's letter to Ross and explained the situation to him. I told him *Manta Ray* was going to begin a new price war by charging $55 and we could compete on price and charge less. I said if the *Manta Ray* undercut or dropped its price then Ross could offer $5 to $10 less but only if he had definite proof that price cutting was going on."

* * * *

Sid was concerned that when a price war began, as seemed likely, his 60 or so regular customers who had contracts for discount prices could find themselves disadvantaged. He asked solicitor John Richards to amend the contract, so that these regular users would continue to have discounted fares in proportion to whatever the fares fell to.

Richards asked us to fax to him a copy of the contract we had been using, originally drawn up by his firm, made the amendment and faxed it back. Sid then sent the contract to his Rainbow Beach managers, Sam and Maureen Mitchell to distribute to the regular customers.

* * * *

Once Ladas finished working for Sid, he made no further secret of the fact he was going to skipper the *Manta Ray*.

Ross Williams was concerned that Ladas' behaviour while he had been Sid's head skipper could have repercussions.

"I had lived with my grandparents, Sid's tour managers Max and Pam Williams at Rainbow Beach for many years and when I finished school, worked for Sid as a deckhand from 1992 then as a skipper at Inskip Point until 1997," Ross explains.

"Ladas was the skipper in charge of the Inskip Point barges and my boss. I knew Ladas deliberately kept people waiting. Sid had a policy that the standard waiting time was 10 to 15 minutes with private vehicles before his barges left Inskip Point to go to the island, whether they had a good load or not."

"This waiting time did not apply to the tour operators. We had to go as fast as we could for them because they had such a full day. But Ladas ignored Sid's instructions. He had a very casual attitude to his job and was well known by me and our regular clients for sleeping in the wheelhouse in the middle of the day. He would tie the *Rainbow Venture* up and let the smaller *Eliza Fraser* do all the work while he drank coffee, read the paper and slept. This went on for ages.

"When I was his deckhand people would come and complain 'How much longer do we have to wait?' because they were all trying to catch the low tide to drive up the beach. Some would say 'We have been sitting here for 40 minutes, when are we going?' I would have to go to Ladas and say 'When are we going? Let's go.'"

The one time Sid tackled Ladas about keeping people waiting was when he got the only complaint directed to him. Locky Fullerton, regional head of the Queensland Parks and Wildlife Service telephoned to say he had been kept waiting for an hour. But Sid did not realise this was Kosta's regular pattern of behaviour, for he came up with a ready excuse.

Some of the Sunshine Coast tour operators were unhappy at being kept waiting by Ladas in the years he worked for Sid.

"I didn't complain to Sid though because I thought sometimes Ladas was just saving fuel by waiting until he got a full load of vehicles on his deck before he set off," says Mark Luscombe.

"I used to tell Kosta the tour operators deserved better," says Ross Williams. "They came every day. It made no difference.

"A couple of time I told Sid and he said I had to do what Kosta told me because he was my boss. Sid had so much trust in him. He was so loyal to Ladas, then got taken down."

After he left Rainbow Beach to skipper the *Kingfisher Bay* barge from River Heads in 1997, Ross would return frequently to see his grandparents, and go to Inskip Point to chat with his former colleagues.

"Some months before the *Manta Ray* arrived the deckhands told me that Kosta had been getting all the ticket books and writing his personal mobile phone number on the back of the return tickets. I thought it was very strange. It had never happened before. I could not understand why he used his phone number and not the number of Sam and Maureen Mitchell, who were managing the Inskip Point barges for Sid. When Ladas' phone number appeared as the *Manta Ray's* advertised phone number it all made sense."

The skipper on Sid's *Eliza Fraser* barge, Neil Grono says "From about a year before *Manta Ray* arrived Ladas asked deckhands to keep count of the number of vehicles Sid's barges were carrying. Each day he would ask them and record the information. I could not work out why he was doing that, but as he was head skipper I just went along with what he was doing.

He says Ladas had a man he claimed was a friend interested in vessels go on board Sid's barges to look at the engine rooms. "When *Manta Ray* first appeared I recalled this incident and wondered if the 'friend' had something to do with designing the *Manta Ray*. Ladas had never asked me to let anyone look at the engine room before."

Grono also tells that Ladas, while working for Sid, kept people waiting longer than normal. "He wouldn't go over and get people waiting to come off the island. I always had customers complaining about him. They would say 'He'll take you over but not come and get you.' Some of our regular customers, tour operators included, nicknamed Ladas 'Captain Chaos' because ran the operation in a disorganised way and made them wait unnecessarily long periods."

* * * *

When the *Manta Ray* arrived on December 21 2000, with Ladas proudly at the helm, there was almost instant conflict, with deckhands from it and the *Rainbow Venture* waving at approaching customers to entice them on to their respective vessels.

On the one hand there were signs stating that the *Rainbow Venture* and *Eliza Fraser* were $45, and on the other, pamphlets were handed out to everyone approaching Inskip Point that the *Manta Ray* owners were battlers out to break Sid's monopoly and his high barge fares.

"Because the propaganda was directed at him, I had an idea Sid should let me handle the situation," says Ross Williams. "But he said he wasn't going to run away and hide. He was so very well known a public figure on Fraser Island and people loved him or hated him.

"Kosta was a real bullshit artist, very persuasive and plausible but then you got to know him and you'd think 'Hang on…that's not right.'"

Ross says "The day before the *Manta Ray* arrived I spoke to Kosta, trying to agree on some basic ground rules. We agreed that deckhands should not sell tickets nor solicit customers on the beach or the road to the beach. But from the very beginning that didn't happen.

"Not only were the *Manta Ray* deckies on the beach waving their arms directing cars, they were also shouting out things like 'Don't go with them. They'll keep you waiting for hours.' It seemed very obvious Kosta had been deliberately keeping Sid's customers waiting so he could use it against him now.

"Within a day or two I found Ladas was undercutting on price by charging several customers $40.

"I also believed Ladas had made an arrangement with 4WD hire companies in Brisbane and elsewhere to only charge their vehicle hirers $40 return, because I saw hire vehicles waiting for him. I approached the drivers and saw they had been given special vouchers.

"I soon found out the staff at the Rainbow Beach service station, where nearly all drivers call in to fill up before going to Fraser Island, were promoting the *Manta Ray*, telling their customers that with our barges they had to pay a passenger fare as well as a vehicle fare which made us dearer.

"Anne Rye, the wife of Rob Rye who ran the Rainbow Beach taxi and towing service, was managing the service station, and it was well known the Ryes didn't like Sid.

"On the second day our deckhand Chris Butt told me a vehicle had arrived at the barges with a prepaid ticket for *Manta Ray* and the driver told him he had bought his ticket along the road to the beach.

So I walked across the beach to the road and just past a bend where he could not be seen by the barge crews, I saw Ladas' son, Paul selling tickets to vehicles before the occupants could see there was more than one barge. He was very surprised to see me and ran back to the *Manta Ray*.

"More people were further up the road handing out pamphlets, which I later found were promoting the *Manta Ray* owners as battlers, although Eric Hume certainly wasn't a battler. Kostas told me Hume was a multi millionaire. You'd see people in their cars reading the flyers. It was an eye opener to me, the effect of the flyer.

"I believe Ladas started undercutting prices straight away. I had had signs made up advertising our price of $45, and when customers approached the barges I would see Debbie Lang, Ladas' deckhand, talk to them then look up at Ladas who would come out of the wheelhouse and they would hand signal prices to each other. I could see them holding up their fingers. Ladas tried to hide his hand signals by turning sideways but I could still see him.

"When I tackled him about undercutting Ladas at first denied it, then when I said I had seen it for myself one day, he offered to give me the money he had taken from particular vehicle drivers.

"I soon found he was also undercutting the $40 return fares Sid had been charging his contract customers. I found out from some of the residents that he was offering $30 for a return trip. He was doing special deals for both Fraser Island and Rainbow Beach residents and others. Some of our regulars stayed with us; some went with Ladas. Others changed each time about. Sid had contracts with about 60 regular customers, but some of them changed to the *Manta Ray* and Sid did not attempt to enforce the contracts.

"I soon learned that instead of contracts, Ladas issued people with discount cards which they produced to get the cheaper rate he offered.

"I saw one of these discount cards and it had a number in the 900's on it, indicating Ladas was offering discount fares on a very large scale.

"One Orchid Beach resident, a builder was approached by Ladas but vehemently told him he would never travel with him. I asked the builder why and he said when Ladas was skippering the *Rainbow Venture,* he always made him drive through deep water to get to it.

"I heard Ladas gave discounts to three or more vehicles travelling together but from what I saw of occupants of vehicles milling around and talking to each other before going on the *Manta Ray,* Ladas encouraged people who were not in fact travelling together, to form groups while on the beach so they could get a discount.

"I noticed too several people drove by and shouted at us that we had made them wait for long periods in the past. I answered that it was not us, but him, pointing to Ladas in the *Manta Ray* wheelhouse, but most people don't know a skipper; they just know a barge."

Chapter 42

Ross Williams's main concern, as a skipper, was about the marine tactics employed by Ladas.

"From the beginning, Kosta on the *Manta Ray* ignored Sid's allotted beach landing areas, and came jostling right between the *Rainbow Venture* and *Eliza Fraser* and when his and one of our barges were crossing the straits together Ladas reverted to the old tactic from Elmer days of overtaking, then cutting across the bow of Sid's barge," Ross describes.

"On the second day we came close to collision," Ross says. "On the *Rainbow Venture* we were less than a barge length away from colliding at speed. Kosta wanted to get a better position on the beach at Hook Point on the island so he could get in, drop off his vehicles and get out fast to beat us back to Inskip Point.

"I had to go hard starboard then hard astern otherwise we would have collided. Passengers came up to me and one asked 'Does that guy know what he's doing?' and others said 'That man's crazy. What's going on?'

"I went to see Ladas about it and he tried to make a joke of it. Then he saw I was serious so tried to play it down. It warranted reporting to Harbours and Marine. Mike Saunders from the Department came and had a good talk to me. While he was there Ladas came very close again.

"I told Saunders we could end up in a situation we could not get out of, and he agreed. He said he didn't want to take sides but said he would try and get Ladas to behave and stay a safe distance away. But Ladas was vying for position and prepared to push us around. Never before while he was working for Sid had there been this kind of reckless behaviour."

Eliza Fraser skipper Neil Grono says "When Kosta first brought Manta Ray to Inskip Point his whole attitude to the way he operated a barge changed. He became fiercely competitive and very aggressive. He manoeuvred the *Manta Ray* into positions too close to our barges.

"There were many close incidents which were prohibited under Marine safety rules. As much as possible I tried to keep out of his way."

After a second near collision as Ladas drove *Manta Ray* between Sid's barges nearly hitting the *Eliza Fraser,* Sid appealed to Eric Hume in a note by fax to ask Ladas to keep out of his landing areas in the hopes this would achieve a safe separation between vessels. Hume acknowledges that he spoke to Ladas about the fax, but Ladas says both agreed they should do nothing about it.

* * * *

As soon as the ACCC office in Brisbane re-opened after the Christmas holiday the third partner in *Manta Ray,* Ray Maher went to complain about Sid undercutting prices. An investigation was begun.

After daily reports of dangerous incidents from Ross, Sid took legal action to have the *Manta Ray* stay out of the landing areas allotted to him many years before by the Department of Harbours and Marine. These areas were on occupation permits and Sid was charged rent for them.

A few years earlier a good bitumen road had been built to the Inskip Point beach just short of the barging area. Sid's landing places were closest to the end of the road and now there was a competitive situation again this gave Sid's barges an advantage. Ladas refused to acknowledge Sid's rights to his landing areas, pleading ignorance of them although he had been working at Inskip Point since 1985, and for Sid between 1989 and 2000.

In the Supreme Court on January 25 2001 Sid sought an injunction to stop Ladas coming in to his landing areas. The judge ordered Ladas to keep outside Sid's landing areas and said he could use another allotted area, and the parties should try and reach a compromise. Another hearing was set for a few weeks hence.

Ladas acknowledges "Our barrister told me to stay away from Sid's areas, otherwise I would go to jail.

* * * *

There were other events away from the beach battleground.

Within a couple of weeks of the *Manta Ray* arriving, someone entered Sid's Rainbow Beach workshop where the tour buses were garaged and put sand in the *Australian Explorer's* fuel tank.

Its motor blew up while it was being driven up the beach next morning with a full load of passengers. No-one had thought to change the workshop locks, but now they were changed immediately.

While driving past the *Manta Ray* in a tour bus Max Williams told Debbie Lang, Ladas' deckhand, to stop running down Sid's barges or face legal consequences.

"That night her husband came to have it out with Max," says Ross Williams. "I was waiting for him on the street and I talked him into quietening down."

Sid became concerned for Max's safety. He asked the Mitchells to take on Max and Pam's duties and quickly arranged for Max to take early retirement. At the end of January Max and Pam left Rainbow Beach to go and live on the Gold Coast in a unit Sid bought for them.

* * * *

Faced with not being able to take the fight right up to Sid's barges in his landing areas Ladas came up with a new strategy – to move out of the established barge landing area altogether and operate from the beach in front of the National Park camping ground at Inskip Point.

Ross Williams explains "The road from Rainbow Beach down Inskip Point paralleled the beach for its last two kilometres and between the road and the beach the National Parks had developed a camping ground.

"Ladas's deckhands would go and stand on the road and wave drivers through the camping ground to the beach, so they never even saw our barges in the designated barge landing area at the end of the road. They diverted all the barge traffic off the bitumen road and sent it straight to their barge.

"When we got no traffic at all, I saw what was going on so I took the *Rainbow Venture* to the beach in front of the camping ground a few times. But I never stayed long.

"There were usually people walking or swimming and children playing on this beach and I thought having the barges and vehicles there created a serious safety risk to them.

"I knew that in 1996 a woman sunbathing on this beach was run over by a 4WD and killed.

"This is why the barges were moved into their own area further along from the camping ground in the first place. But by going back there Ladas could divert traffic and get an advantage over us."

Ladas records in the *Manta Ray* log book that the first time he went to the front beach on January 26, he had to leave after two hours due to "campers complaining about barge traffic going through the camping area."

When Williams took the *Rainbow Venture* to the front beach to compete directly with the *Manta Ray*, the *Manta Ray* partners applied to the Supreme Court to have him stopped.

"The National Parks officers at Rainbow Beach went out of their way to help the Kosta," says Ross Williams. "They fenced off a track through the camping ground for vehicles to go directly to the *Manta Ray*. They put signs to both barge areas, but with the sign to the *Manta Ray* placed so it was readable to oncoming drivers while the sign to Sid's barges was not. Only when Sid protested to the National Parks regional manager was the signage changed."

On February 19 the situation with the *Manta Ray* landing on the beach on front of the camping ground had become so serious that three senior government officers, Locky Fullerton from the Queensland Parks and Wildlife Service, Doug Courtenay regional manager of the Department of Natural Resources, and John Parnis from Queensland Transport held a meeting with Sid and Ladas on the beach.

The three officers all agreed it was too dangerous to the public for *Manta Ray* to keep operating from the front beach. Courtenay told Kosta to move *Manta Ray* back to the proper barge landing area.

Kosta complained he could not land in the area allotted to him in the designated barge area at certain tides. Sid agreed to concede 60m of his landing area for Ladas to use, and in a further compromise offered that in abnormal tides his barges would move further down the beach to allow the *Manta Ray* to land.

This compromise was taken back to the Supreme Court on February 22, and added to the original court order. Locky Fullerton, then wrote to Ray Maher stopping the *Manta Ray* from operating from the front beach "in considering the issue of public safety" and restricting it to its allotted landing area.

But Kosta protested to the National Parks officers at Rainbow Beach that he couldn't operate there and after Easter the *Manta Ray* was allowed to go back to the beach in front of the camping ground.

Sid says "I was very surprised he was allowed to go back there. I believe he could operate perfectly well in the landing area allotted to him. He was just determined to go back to the camping ground beach, regardless of the safety issues."

Sid accused Locky Fullerton to his face of dereliction of his duty of care to the public by allowing the *Manta Ray* to go back in front of the camping ground. Fullerton evidently felt Sid was simply trying to stop Ladas getting a commercial advantage, for his response was that Sid was charging less. He said he bore no responsibility for any incident that happened below high tide mark.

* * * *

In early March Ross Williams told Sid that he had applied for a job on big oil tankers operating around Australia and South East Asia months before, and had just now been offered a job. He offered to forego the opportunity to work on the tankers and stay to help Sid at Rainbow Beach. Sid, though upset at losing his right hand man at Inskip Point, would not deny Ross his chance for a big step up in his career.

But Sid's Rainbow Beach operation was not to be left rudderless. He had two other skippers on the Rainbow Beach barges, one a long time employee, the other a newcomer, but he was concerned neither would be able to counter Ladas's tactics. Unexpectedly a telephone call came from Rick Delfs, the elder son of Helmut Delfs who had skippered the *Fraser II* barge in Hervey Bay. Sid had become friendly with Rick and knew him for a capable no nonsense skipper with a likeable personality. When Helmut sold the *Fraser II,* Rick had gone to work in Brisbane. Now Rick was ringing to ask Sid if he had a job. Did he ever!

Rick had hoped to work back in Hervey Bay, but made no demur when Sid asked him to go to Rainbow Beach.

Before he began working on the barges there, Rick tried to work out what was happening for himself.

He found the Rainbow Beach service station was actively promoting the *Manta Ray.*

He says "When I went to pay for my petrol the counter assistant handed me a leaflet and said 'If you go on the *Manta Ray* you can go for the same price as the other barge, but if you take one of these leaflets and produce it on the *Manta Ray* you can get a discount.'"

Delfs found the service station staff would ring Ladas and tell him when vehicles had just left and were heading to Inskip Point. "Because of this, Ladas would know that vehicles were coming and how many. Even if the *Manta Ray* had begun its crossing, Ladas would turn it round and return to collect those vehicles, so we didn't have a chance to get them. A couple of times I asked what he was doing and he replied 'Shell rang me, I've got vehicles coming.'" Delfs says.

"One of the most annoying aspects of the service station support was the apparently intentional, inaccurate and negative information that was given about our barges. I was told they said they were dearer and that customers would be kept waiting.

"It was a big advantage that the *Manta Ray* was bigger and faster than the *Rainbow Venture* and *Eliza Fraser*. Ladas could leave the beach and make the crossing and be back on the beach at Inskip before us.

"He also hired another small barge, and once he had sold tickets to drivers, he would offload all the vehicles he had on the *Manta Ray* on to it and send it over to the island, so he could stay on the beach and continue touting for custom.

"Another advantage was that he always knew what our movements were. We skippers on the *Rainbow Venture* and *Eliza Fraser* talked to each other on our private radio channel. Ladas should not have been able to listen in but he did.

"I believe he had a scanner enabling him to do that, for one time I commented over our radio about a sign advertising some very low price on the second barge Ladas hired and next thing Ladas ordered its skipper to remove it."

Delfs also became concerned about Ladas cutting off Sid's barges.

"He was very aggressive and always trying to be that one step ahead. There were quite a few times when he narrowly missed colliding. I would just back off and let him go," Delfs says.

Delfs found Ladas was operating wherever suited him at any time, sometimes next to Sid's landing areas, sometimes from the beach in front of the National Parks camping ground.

"When the *Manta Ray* was using the camping ground beach some of our customers told me somebody was up the road diverting them through the camping ground and when they asked if they could continue down to our barges the person told them our barges weren't running that day, which wasn't true.

"When the *Manta Ray* had a full load, Ladas would blow on its horn and the deckhand would run back to get on board for the crossing. Then we'd get a few customers until the Manta Ray came back and the traffic was diverted again. This went on from early morning until late afternoon. It was very depressing."

Like Ross Williams, Delfs felt using the camping ground beach involved some very serious safety issues.

"I took the *Rainbow Venture* to this beach one time. It was just too dangerous to stay. A barge door could easily have come down on a swimmer. Ladas worked there most of the time. He didn't care as long as he was getting customers," he says.

"It was apparent the National Parks personnel favoured Ladas. They would always wait for him when they were coming or going to the island. We would see them waiting up the track and when *Manta Ray* arrived they would emerge and drive on to it.

"We had passengers tell us that when they went to the National Parks office in Rainbow Beach for their island permits they were told to travel with *Manta Ray*."

* * * *

Sometime between January and May two young women working for the ACCC visited the area and spoke to Ladas and others of his supporters in Rainbow Beach. They drove on to Fraser Island and actually passed Eurong Beach, but did not call in to see Sid. He heard of their visit and wrote asking for a meeting, but got no response.

* * * *

Early in 2001 Sid engaged a former travel consultant and Brisbane business man, Tony Newton to promote and organise the sale of the resort.

Weeks were taken up supplying him with the material he sought, booklets of all the assets with photographs and explanations, financial information, tour, ferry and whale watch passenger numbers over the last five years and more.

Within a short period and with a very clever advertisement looking for someone to step into Sid's thongs, Newton attracted a number of purchasers. Sid met with them and showed them around the resort and mainland operations. After weeks of assessment, he felt three had the financial wherewithal to buy the business.

Over the next few months Sid and I were occupied in frequent negotiations with, and updating our figures to, all three.

Sid acknowledges now he should have been more involved in the barge war to meet the competition of an on the spot owner-operator as Ladas was, with the ability to make decisions about fares to each individual customer and pursue a calculated course of conduct.

But he had to juggle this with the other demands the business made on him, and particularly the sale, which had priority. He set policy but then had to leave much of the responsibility for the day to day conduct of his barges at Inskip Point first to Ross Williams, then Rick Delfs.

Income from the Rainbow Beach barges diminished as the crews dropped prices and Sid was concerned it would affect the sale of his business. But the skippers assured Sid they had no alternative but to meet Ladas' undercutting as they learned of it, if they were to get customers.

Delfs reported to Sid that whenever Ladas was working next to the *Rainbow Venture* and *Eliza Fraser,* he consistently dropped his prices below the $45 Sid had set in the beginning. After four months with first Ross Williams then Delfs phoning him every day with instances of price cutting, Sid decided to drop his standard fare to $30.

"Ladas was fairly determined to try and stop us finding out what he was charging. When he was doing his hand signals with his deckhand he would turn his back to us or do the signals close to his chest," says Delfs.

* * * *

The ACCC investigation led to a sizeable package arriving at Eurong Beach in late May 2001.

It contained a mass of documents demanding the answers to more 1000 questions, from Sid, and officers of the private companies operating the entire business infrastructure, Sid and I.

The ACCC also demanded we send them a vast quantity of records going back 15 years. As with most businesses, once records were more than seven years old and beyond the interest of the Taxation Office many had been discarded. The ACCC found this highly suspicious. Those that had been kept had been moved three times in the 15 year period as new offices and stores were built, and all the early records had once been submerged when storm water ran through the room they were stored in. Finding all the documents the ACCC required was a major task.

One of the ACCC questions, incredibly, asked Sid to justify his having stopped giving the People to People tours lunch business to Ladas and his wife, even though they had sold their restaurant and the lunches were made by its new owner.

The ACCC wanted all the responses made in one month – the same month as end of year business and GST accounts for the Taxation Office had to be completed. Prospective purchasers were also seeking the end of financial year information as soon as possible.

It was an almost impossible task to satisfy all these demands properly on a complex and widespread business. A month's extension was sought from the ACCC. No response came, and I worked 16 hour days one after another to do all my normal work and fulfil ACCC demands, until I reached the point of exhaustion.

The extension was granted just before the original date set by the ACCC for the supply of the information, by which time the work had been done. It seemed a quite calculated attempt to harass and deny me a proper opportunity to make a considered response.

Sid personally found it impossible to answer the complex questions directed specifically to him apart from the private companies which ran different sides of the business. He simply wrote one or two word answers.

He did his best but this obviously aroused the ire of the ACCC which wrote back to say he had to do better and should get legal help.

Again he asked for a meeting at which he could verbally answer the questions but this request was ignored.

Chapter 43

The landing permits Sid held at Inskip Point expired on September 21 2001 and the National Parks made it known that they would not be reissued. From then on it would be open slather for places for all the barges to land.

Ladas did not wait that long. In August he brought the *Manta Ray* back, jostling for position, and again began the dangerously close quarter manoeuvring, obviously confident that with only six weeks to go no-one would be able to stop him.

"He totally disregarded the instruction not to come within 35 metres of another barge given to all the skippers by the Marine Transport Authority, after one close call," says Rick Delfs, for whom this was his first experience of the close quarter tactics Ladas had used when the *Manta Ray* first arrived.

"He also disregarded the safety rule that required overtaking vessels to give way. He would overtake one of our barges then cross over closely in front. If he had done anything like this in Brisbane where I had just come from he would have been barred as a skipper for life. In Rainbow Beach there was no-one to stop him."

In January, just seven months before, when Sid had obtained the Supreme Court injunction to have Ladas keep out of his landing areas, his barrister had warned Ladas that if he disobeyed the injunction he would go to jail.

With only six weeks to go before Sid's permits ran out Ladas totally disregarded this warning. Once he could go anywhere in the barge landing area that he liked, Ladas was confident he could win the battle of the barges. He did not want to wait until it was legally safe to do so.

In the event Ladas had judged the situation correctly that he could behave with impunity. After daily complaints again from his crews of Ladas' aggressive behaviour including an actual collision, and encroaching into his landing areas, Sid engaged a surveyor to take accurate readings so there was no mistake.

They went to Inskip Point early one morning, to find Ladas landing the *Manta Ray* well inside his area.

Sid asked his solicitor, Peter Pagliarino of Carswell and Co. to go back to court with the evidence he had gathered that Ladas had broken the injunction.

By time the matter came before the court, it was October 29. The crucial date of September 21 when Sid's landing permits expired had passed and the *Manta Ray* could now legally go into Sid's former landing areas. Judge Martin Moynihan perhaps felt the issue was no longer relevant.

The *Manta Ray* legal team cleverly clouded the hearing using Sid's earlier concession to let the *Manta Ray* into a specified portion of his landing area. Judge Moynihan's finding was in *Manta Ray* favour.

Sid appealed, and won the appeal. Three judges sent the case back to Judge Moynihan for reconsideration. He did absolutely nothing about it. Sid was totally disenchanted with the judge's inaction.

As skipper Neil Grono put it "Kosta thinks he can get away with anything – and he can."

* * * *

Sure of himself now Ladas gave a bit of a public hurry up to the Australian Competition and Consumer Commission, complaining in a newspaper article it was taking a long time to take action against Sid for price cutting.

It was distressing to see the income from the Rainbow Beach barges diminishing, but the skippers assured Sid they had to drop prices to get customers. Sid insisted his skippers never resort to intimidation or unsafe tactics.

Ladas had no such concerns. At the peak Christmas season on December 30 2001, he and two of his friends put *Eliza Fraser* skipper, Danny Rivers out of action for one of the busiest weeks of the year.

A log book note signed by Danny and *Eliza Fraser* deckhand Bill Fyfe describes "After talking on radio, Kosta and a big passenger boarded the *Eliza Fraser* and entered the wheelhouse saying verbal abuse then Kosta tackled Danny and threw him against the wheel while the big passenger held Bill on his back in the wheelhouse. The passenger returned twice to assault us again."

Rivers called for help over the barge radio and Sam Mitchell heard his calls and alerted the police. Rivers had to take a week off work because of the pain and bruising on his back.

When the police arrived and Danny told them what had happened, Ladas produced witnesses who said the assault never took place.

"I believe Ladas was trying to stop us running the *Eliza Fraser II* during this busy period. But we were able to bring a relief skipper in for the week Danny was on sick leave," says Sid.

* * * *

After many meetings with the three corporations which had expressed an interest in buying Eurong Beach resort and its associated businesses, ferries, whale watching vessels and tours, a purchase price was agreed with Kingfisher Bay Resort in December 1991. The price was to remain confidential, but when news of the sale reached the media, speculation ran riot.

A confirmation letter was signed in January 1992 and the takeover date was set at April 1992. With only two months to go Sid felt he could relax the reins he had held for so many decades, and leave the operation of the business to the very capable team of long term management staff, particularly Ian Hagart at the resort, Adrian Davie and May Jensen at Hervey Bay, Jan and John Graham at Noosa and Sam and Maureen Mitchell and the skippers at Rainbow Beach.

Psychologically he had had enough, and it was a natural reaction to move on mentally to look for possible future interests away from Fraser Island.

But it left Rick Delfs feeling isolated at Inskip Point, he says, although he could still phone Sid whenever he wished. And he did, to report Ladas' price undercutting was continuing. Sid dropped the price again, this time to $20 in an attempt to hold the line.

April came with a request from Gary Smith of Kingfisher Bay Resort to have another few weeks to complete the purchase. By this time Sid and I were spending more time at the Gold Coast house returning to Fraser Island only to catch up on essential work and satisfy the Kingfisher Bay accountants' demands for detailed financial information.

With the completion of the purchase again in view, Sid and I booked a three week holiday in China.

Then the ACCC reared its head again after months of silence, summoning Sid and I to a formal interrogation in mid May 2002. A solicitor and barrister accompanied us but were not allowed to take any part in the proceedings, nor even sit nearby for support. In turn each of us had to take a solitary seat facing a table of seven ACCC personnel including a Commissioner and a legal team headed by Water Soffranoff Q.C.

Neither of us gave a good account of ourselves answering questions spanning 16 years of running a very busy business in hands on fashion.

Both of us were suffering the after effects of injections before the visit to China, and worse, on our way into the interrogation Sid had received a telephone call from Eurong that the *Australian Explorer* bus had again been sabotaged by having sand put in its petrol tank and the motor had caught on fire while it was taking day trippers up the beach.

The bus had required some work on it the night before and been taken to the firm in Rainbow Beach that did mechanical work for Sid's buses and barges. It had been left outside the firm's workshop that night, the first time it had not been locked away since it was first sabotaged in similar fashion 18 months before.

We were both devastated by this bad news and came away from the ACCC interrogation feeling idiots at not handling better Sofranoff's aggressive questioning about incidents that had happened up to 16 years earlier, and which we hardly remembered.

We caused a minor panic to the ACCC team. It had been impressed upon Sid and me that until we had both been questioned separately we had not to tell each other what questions we had been asked.

Come lunchtime everyone took off ignoring us, so we went to a nearby sandwich shop. Then someone at the ACCC must have realised we had disappeared together and came looking for us. They found us in the sandwich queue chatting with the Commissioner, who, like us, had not been told lunch was provided.

* * * *

With the pressure on to get the *Australian Explorer* bus back to work as soon as possible, Sid by phone organised its tow to the Hervey Bay workshop for a motor replacement and asked Laurie Toy to take photographs and get the police to come and look at the bus. Toy later reported the police had not bothered to come.

The Rainbow Beach police were much more diligent – but not on Sid's behalf. The bitumen road from Rainbow Beach to Inskip Point was just wide enough for two vehicles to pass, but was punctuated by traffic calming islands and at the end, just before the Inskip Point beach, a small roundabout.

For months driver Harold James, who drove a special tour three times a week from Rainbow Beach to Fraser Island, had been complaining that he could not get the tour bus around the roundabout the correct way on his way back to Rainbow Beach He repeatedly asked Sam and Maureen Mitchell to see if they could get the council to rectify the problem.

The Mitchells phoned and wrote to the council several times, but nothing was done. It was not only Harold who had problems but other day tour operators and truck drivers. All adopted the only course of waiting until the road was completely clear then driving the wrong way around the roundabout.

But it was Harold that the Rainbow Beach police were waiting to book one day. Harold was indignant. He knew Sid would pay his fine under the circumstances but with Sid's backing he wanted to fight the matter in court on principle.

He did – and won when the magistrate was presented with the evidence of all the attempts to have the council improve the roundabout, and the fact that it had been improved just two weeks after Harold had been booked.

* * * *

We had only been back from China a day or so, when a Gold Coast shipbroker phoned Sid to say a 105ft motor yacht *Southern Cross II* was for sale in Mexico. Sid who read boat books as assiduously as he had formerly read truck and bus books, wanted a motor yacht to spend some of his time on once the all consuming island business was sold, and then use to do upmarket whale watching back in Hervey Bay. He had been watching the price progress of several motor yachts for months, waiting for opportune moments to make an offer for one.

Southern Cross II had been built in Brisbane in 1983 for Alan Bond to use as his home afloat and hospitality vessel during the America's Cup challenge in Newport, Rhode Island. It was an excellent ocean going vessel, and Sid was immediately interested. In spite of my protests that I hadn't even finished doing the laundry after the trip to China we were off again within the week to Ensenada, Mexico to look at it.

The current owner of *Southern Cross II* was a San Francisco computer software designer who did well out of the dot.com boom, took early retirement, bought the vessel in Australia and set off in it across the Pacific. They got as far as Fiji when the boom crashed, his shares plummeted and he had to fly home and go back to work, leaving his crew to continue the long journey to America, where he put the vessel up for sale.

Southern Cross II was everything Sid had expected and he made the purchase during the week in Mexico, leaving the vessel in the care of its existing crew until we could return in September, when Kingfisher Bay had advised the long-drawn-out sale would finally be completed.

* * * *

In August Rick Delfs had had enough of the daily battle at Inskip Point with no let up. When his wife was offered a job as an accountant in Toowoomba, he came and told Sid that he had to leave.

He talks about one day just before he left when he was taking the *Rainbow Venture* round to Inskip Point in the early morning to start work and came upon both the *Manta Ray* and *Eliza Fraser* stuck on a sand bar.

"It was a busy Saturday in the tailor season," he recounts. "I could see vehicles lined up on the beach waiting for the barges. The *Eliza Fraser* was well and truly stuck but I worked hard and managed to pull the *Manta Ray* off the bar.

"As soon as it was free Ladas raced ahead of me to get to the beach first and got all the vehicles. By time I got there he had got them all loaded. I wasn't pleased and wished I hadn't helped him when he did that.

"But you have to help in such circumstances. It is the done thing on the water. It was so depressing because he was lapping us all morning."

When Delfs left, another skipper turned up fortuitously, a former employee, Peter King.

Now Neil Grono who had worked as Sid's second skipper at Inskip Point since 1996 was put in charge – a thankless and stressful job, but Grono took it on uncomplainingly.

* * * *

In early September there was yet another delay in the purchase of Sid's business being finalised, but a definite date was set for the handover to Kingfisher in early November.

Sid offered to teach Kingfisher Bay management what was involved in his and my roles in the business, and this process began as well as compiling the multitude of documents relating to the ownership and operation of the whole infrastructure, from staff wage entitlements, vessel survey certificates, bus registrations, liquor licences, radio licences, tour permits, whale watching permits, certificates to operate shops at the resort and on the ferries, kitchen hygiene certificates, all the council building approvals and much much more right down to the post office mail box rental agreement. These had to be included in the contract of sale, with the necessary transfer papers all signed, sealed and delivered.

There were a couple of problems. Sid discovered that the workshop in the middle of the nonexistent road at Eurong didn't have a council approval certificate and the registration papers for the *Islander* were still in the name of *Calypso Lady*, but both were rapidly sorted out.

* * * *

In mid September our solicitor Peter Pagliarino got in touch with Sid with a demand from the ACCC that we increase our prices on the Inskip Point ferries to $34 and Sid agreed provided the ACCC applied the same price to the *Manta Ray.*

Peter gave no indication he had received a second letter from the ACCC at the same time.

The next day the ACCC issued a press release to say they had found Sid and I had a case to answer primarily for predatory pricing and had filed proceedings against us in the Federal Court.

Once we had to charge the same fares, the *Manta Ray* and its hired second barge got twice as much traffic as the *Rainbow Venture* and *Eliza Fraser* combined.

"To my mind this demonstrates that the cheaper fare we'd charged earlier was the only reason we had been able to survive by maintaining a reasonable percentage of vehicles in the light of the *Manta Ray* being a newer faster barge and Ladas' tactics," Sid says.

But with only a few weeks to go before we left the island, he had to accept the situation. There was too much else to do packing up after a working lifetime at Eurong.

The next seven weeks were fraught as the immense job of stocktaking was begun, staff entitlements worked out and the details of handover agreed. More than 250 cartons of documents from the business had to be packed and trucked off the island to storage. Sombre farewells were made to the people who had become dear friends as well as employees, and to the army of local business people who had given their support to the business in so many ways over so many years.

Finally on November 8 Sid and I got in the helicopter and flew away, circling over the resort that had been our home for so long, while all the resort employees gathered on the road in front of the conference centre and waved to us for our final departure.

* * * *

We were told later by Gary Smith of Kingfisher Bay, the barge war intensified immediately, with Ladas crashing the *Manta Ray* into the *Rainbow Venture* badly damaging its superstructure two days later and shouting out to customers coming on to the Inskip Point beach "Don't travel with them. They're Japanese," until Smith had to threaten legal action to make him stop.

Smith increased the fare on the *Rainbow Venture* and *Eliza Fraser* to $65. *Manta Ray* prices went up the same day to $60, so Smith dropped back $5 to match.

There had been rumblings for years that the National Parks Service would like to raise revenue from the barge operations, but Sid believed his operating barges before Fraser Island became a National Park could have been a stumbling block.

In any case no move was ever made to put charges on the barge operations. With Sid now gone, the way was clear, and the National Parks didn't waste any time.

Just a few days after our departure an advertisement was placed by the Queensland Government in the Brisbane *Courier Mail* newspaper calling for expressions of interest for four barges to operate at Inskip Point. Interested applicants should respond within three weeks and include offers of the fees they would be willing to pay for licences.

In the event two licences were granted each to Kingfisher Bay and the *Manta Ray* consortium, maintaining the status quo, but enabling the National Parks to get a piece of the action.

"No wonder National Parks wanted to get rid of me," says Sid.

Within a short time the *Manta Ray* owners ordered a second large barge to be built in Chile, and learning of this, Garry Smith had a new larger and faster barge built also, selling the little *Eliza Fraser II* to a new life as a river ferry.

When Ladas purchased a small information centre at the Rainbow Beach service station, Kingfisher bought the lease on the service station drive way and petrol pumps with direct access to most barge customers to counter any further promotion of the *Manta Ray* and ticket sales. *Manta Ray* directors began working with a Gympie service station to offer discount petrol for customers buying their barge tickets there.

It was all very expensive, and for most of the time at Inskip Point the traffic warranted only one barge not two and certainly not four. Barge fares climbed steadily upwards.

Chapter 44

Scores of folk warned that Sid would not know what to do with himself away from Eurong for it had been his life's work, but after two frantic weeks on the Gold Coast finalising the enormous business stock take, we left Australia to go and live aboard *Southern Cross II* in the southern Californian city of San Diego with Don Caswell as its captain.

If Sid missed Eurong, he never said as much. The last year, with the psychological up and downs of believing we were leaving, and then having to stay on a few more weeks at a time, had been emotionally draining. When the time came to go he was more than ready.

We were away from Australia, except for one month in every six, for the next two and a half years in America, cruising from San Diego to Glacier Bay in Alaska on the American west coast, then south through Mexico and Costa Rica through the Panama Canal and as far north as Boston on the east coast.

In his absence in the United States in September 2004, Sid was, to a standing ovation, awarded the Fraser Coast tourism award for the most outstanding contribution by an individual.

When he saw the 300 guests rise to their feet to acclaim the award, the guest of honour, the then Federal Minister for Transport and Member for Wide Bay, Warren Truss raced over to Russ Parker who was accepting it on Sid's behalf to offer his congratulations.

Truss from the podium at numerous earlier events, such as the opening of the Hervey Bay Airport, had frequently made flattering mention of Sid being present, and welcomed him specifically.

Much of the time on our voyages, particularly in the wilds of coastal Canada and Alaska we had no communication with the outside world at all, but when we returned to civilisation there would be anxious emails from Peter Pagliarino, our solicitor, about the ACCC and courts becoming increasingly irate at the delays our absence was creating.

On one such occasion Pagliarino emailed half a dozen affidavits the ACCC had collected, for a response from us.

One was from Warren Truss who had put in a singularly unpleasant submission about Sid personally to the ACCC, which he is probably unaware Sid saw. It concluded however with a grudging acknowledgement that no-one else could have done as much for Fraser Island.

"I don't know why Truss had ever bothered to recognise me in public, or pretend he was glad to see me if that's what he thought of me," Sid said, otherwise unworried. "If I hadn't been as I am, I'd have got nothing done. I'd still be puttering up and down the river in the *Rio Marie*."

* * * *

We always gave good notice of our return Australia, when nothing would happen on the ACCC front, but the minute we returned to *Southern Cross II*, the flood of emailed demands would begin again. This pattern was repeated so regularly we felt it could hardly be coincidental.

At times a barrister would have to go to the Federal court to seek delays in our producing material as we were out of the country. It was evident that the court was getting increasingly exasperated.

In 2005 Sid decided we would return to Australia. He had kept one Hervey Bay whale watching permit from the sale of his business to Kingfisher Bay and planned to go back into luxury whale watching in *Southern Cross II*, by now fitted out with a bow thruster, two new motors and a completely refurbished interior.

Sid and the crew would bring *Southern Cross II* across the Pacific Ocean, a three month journey beginning in April when the weather for such a momentous voyage was at its best, while I, far from being even a half way good sailor, chose to fly home.

What an incredible situation I flew in to. The ACCC had been extraordinarily active and Peter Pagliarino presented me with affidavits from all sorts of people who had anything bad to say about Sid's business conduct, as well as formal reports from public servants about vessel licences and permits at Inskip Point.

There were even affidavits from Shane Boyd and Gary Smith who had nothing bad to say, but the fact we owned the barges they used was to be held against us. In all there were 41 affidavits, all requiring an answer on every point raised.

I asked barrister David Jackson Q.C. to handle our case, and he involved other barristers in his chambers, Peter Davis and Rowan Jackson.

* * * *

Some of the ACCC witnesses made incredible claims. Rob Rye, the Rainbow Beach 4WD vehicle hire and tow truck operator, said that Sid had started up a 4WD hire business in Rainbow Beach and a tow truck business on Fraser Island deliberately to send him broke. He claimed his income had been $450,000 a year before Sid had done this and had then dropped to $20,000 a year.

Sid never had a 4WD hire business in Rainbow Beach. Certainly one was started in competition with Rye but it was begun by a couple we hardly knew. Neither did Sid have a tow truck business on Fraser Island or anywhere else.

I phoned Nigel Fremantle, a part owner of the Fraser Island Towing Service who was happy to swear an affidavit that Sid had had absolutely nothing to do with his business and that in the first year, he had made $22,000, hardly the inroad into Rye's business that he claimed.

* * * *

Another chap who had run unlicensed tours to Fraser Island for a time in the 1990's with three Landrovers had been forced by the National Parks Service to either buy an existing tour permit or close down. He leased a small permit which allowed him to carry only six people a day. Now he claimed Sid had ruined his business. He also came up with the story that Sid had tried to inveigle him into using his tour permits and get him to stay with his passengers at Eurong Beach resort. In fact the man had been barred from the resort by Sid.

His claims were easily countered by my finding letters from three schoolgirls who had been staying at the resort about this fellow harassing them at a night time beach bonfire.

This same chap was later to confront Sid in Rainbow Beach to say ACCC personnel had told him Sid was going to have to pay him a lot of money as compensation. Sid did not know what to make of this at all, but it certainly explained some of the extraordinary claims the ACCC had gathered.

If some of these witnesses believed they were going to get money, they might as well be in for a pound as a penny.

Six affidavits came from men who claimed they had been given six packs of beer aboard one of Sid's barges 15 years before. How the ACCC had found these six fellows can only be guessed at, for the free beer began as a joke by a tour operator and was always a joke.

To our certain knowledge beer had never been given to passengers as an incentive to travel on our barges. It was our word, our skippers' word, and the word of other tour bus operators who had travelled daily on Sid's *Rainbow Venture* against those of the six men and Kosta Ladas.

In his affidavit he swore that during the Elmer barge war of 1986 to 1989, Sid had told him he was giving customers free beer and that Don Caswell, when skippering the *Rainbow Venture,* had told him the same thing. Yet the free beer joke was not made until a tour operators' meeting in November 1991.

Don Caswell said in his response that this was "simply not true" and added "At no time while I worked for Sid as skipper of the *Rainbow Venture* was I instructed by Sid or anybody else to give free beer to customers or potential customers.

"If this was to occur I as master of the vessel would have been informed and if anyone in my crew was doing it I would have known about it and seen it for myself. I never saw any such activity and I am quite certain it did not happen when I was on board as master of the vessel."

My telling barrister Rowan Jackson that Ladas was lying about this to rebounded on me, for when I told him, for example, that Ladas had frequently boasted that his partner Eric Hume was a multimillionaire, Jackson said "But you have already said Ladas was a liar. Why did you believe him about this?"

Others who had fallen foul of Sid's temper displays at various times or were jealous of his success had a say too, and there were some remarkable twists and turns in their presentation of some events.

Many were straightforward to counter. Some were not. Issues which had had nothing to do with ACCC competition policy all of a sudden were presented as such.

With the apparent plan of going to the ACCC to complain about Sid before the *Manta Ray* even began operation, Ladas himself had kept a day to day log of every little thing, everything our skippers had said and done over the almost two year barge war and now made an affidavit of more than 300 pages.

Then there were the newspaper reports over the years with Sid adopting the "don't mess with me" attitude that he made so much his public persona in times of what he saw as unfair questioning. He was too easy to rouse to anger when commonsense flew out the window and fair game for an aggressive journalist.

I had to set about countering this mass of affidavits while Sid was coming across the Pacific in *Southern Cross II*, but in some cases I knew nothing about the claims. I had certainly been present at many incidents the ACCC witnesses described and could put my interpretation on them as different from the way they had been presented, but in fact my presence as a witness was mentioned by very few people.

Owners with Ladas of the *Manta Ray*, Ray Maher and Eric Hume, in giving their version of the initial and only meeting with Sid and I, when we had first heard of the *Manta Ray's* impending arrival, acknowledged I was there and then they claimed that after Sid and I had walked away from the meeting, Sid had left me by our car to walk back to threaten them.

To my clear recollection he had done no such thing, but they, and others, had to come up with reasons why I had not been aware of something they claimed Sid had said or done.

I found it extremely hard and tedious work writing my responses to this vast outpouring from the ACCC witnesses, having to go through the multitude of cartons of our records to find essential paperwork to counter some of the claims. As well I had to get all the log books off all the barges between 1986 and November 2002, and go through them page by page to be able to respond to allegations of marine incidents about which I had known nothing.

* * * *

When Sid arrived back in Australia in mid June, his time was divided between reading the ACCC affidavits, and getting the *Southern Cross II* into survey so it could operate as a commercial whale watching vessel, then taking it to Hervey Bay and beginning the operation.

He was given a front page welcome back by the *Maryborough Chronicle,* whose editor, Nancy Bates said that any story about Sid was an amazing circulation booster. The headline read "Sid's back in Bondy's posh boat."

* * * *

Barristers David Jackson Q.C. and Rowan Jackson realising our solicitor Peter Pagliarino could not possibly complete the preparation of affidavits from Sid, me and our witnesses in the short time frame now set by the court, decided that Rowan would act as devil's advocate and go through the answers Sid and I were making to prepare our case.

This too was an arduous process which fell mostly upon me for after one attempt to cross question Sid as he would be questioned in court by the ACCC barrister, Rowan didn't want to repeat the experience. "I thought he was going to throw me through the window," Rowan said from his 22nd storey office.

It was demoralizing to us to have Rowan say that many of the reasons we were relying upon to explain our conduct were irrelevant to the ACCC action. He said intimidation of our crews or reckless marine behaviour was not a matter for this action, and should have been dealt with by Department of Harbours and Marine officers, none of whom were stationed at Inskip Point, and whose instructions to Ladas were ignored as soon as they had left after their rare visits.

Rowan repeatedly said that whatever Ladas or others had done in the way of discounting or undercutting fares was not of interest. It wasn't them that the ACCC was taking action against. When we put to him that we had been fighting for the survival of our Inskip Point barge business, he said that was something the court would have to decide.

Rowan repeated several times the ACCC was ruthless and had infinite funds to pursue the case, and having spent so much money on it, he felt no matter how much evidence we produced to counter their witness statements, they would not now back away.

Apart from the stress of daily interrogation, our legal costs began to mount.

We asked the legal team what was the anticipated cost of the case being brought to completion.

We were told that it was likely the case would take five weeks before the Federal Court and could cost $1.8 million in our legal fees alone, apart from any fines if we were found to have acted wrongly by trying "to eliminate or substantially damage" our Inskip Point barge competitors.

Facing these kinds of legal costs, any victory would have been a Pyrrhic victory. Apart from the costs, it could have been that once all the documents were presented, the case would possibly not be heard for at least another 12 months.

We did not want it to overshadow our lives for that length of time now we had put the pressures of Fraser Island behind us.

Sid's business reputation had always been dear to him, but he was gone from Fraser Island now, and he took a more pragmatic view of the situation. He wasn't going to let the case cost him more than it need.

Chapter 45

At a meeting with barristers David Jackson, Rowan Jackson and Peter Davis and solicitor Peter Pagliarino on August 11 2005, Sid and I asked David Jackson if he thought the ACCC might be prepared to settle the case without going to court. We said we would like to settle this matter, if it was possible.

Peter Davis said he had put this idea of a settlement to the ACCC barrister two months earlier and "got a lukewarm response."

Peter Pagliarino suddenly announced he thought the ACCC would agree to a settlement. He said he had received a letter from the ACCC three years before with an offer to meet Sid and me to discuss a settlement.

This was the first Sid and I had heard of this. We were devastated to think Pagliarino had not told us of it before, and given us the opportunity to end the matter so much earlier.

Dealing with the issues since our return from America alone had cost four months of my time and two months of Sid's time in dealing with the affidavits presented by the ACCC, as well as Pagliarino's legal fees over the entire period since we had left Fraser Island more than two and a half years before.

Four days later on August 15, Sid and I called at Pagliarino's office in Hervey Bay as arranged to start getting affidavits from people for our defence. Straightaway I asked Peter what the letter from the ACCC with an offer to meet and discuss a settlement agreement had actually said. Pagliarino rose from his desk and looked through two binders in front of him. He opened one and found the letter. He pulled out one page from the binder and held it towards me, but did not pass it over.

I only had time to see the ACCC heading and the date 16 September 2002, and a second page still in the binder which looked to have several dot pointed paragraphs, before he quickly put the page back in the binder and closed it.

I said "Were we away then? No we weren't, we were still in business at Eurong. We didn't leave until November 2002."

I asked Pagliarino why he had not shown us this letter when he received it. He did not answer but still on his feet, he shouted "You would not have wanted to settle. Sack me, sack me."

We felt strongly that Pagliarino had acted very badly towards us and that he should have shown us the letter and given us the opportunity to meet with the ACCC with a view to settlement at that early stage.

Since September 2002 the ACCC had obviously spent many $100,000's in taking affidavits from so many witnesses, one as far away as Melbourne and going through so many of our records. We recognised any settlement now was going to have to cover their costs.

I realised we needed advice before we took action against Pagliarino or sacked him as he suggested for withholding the letter at the time and for refusing to let us read it even now.

It put us in a very difficult position as Federal Court hearing dates were set for some two weeks hence and Pagliarino was well on the way to completing affidavits from our Inskip Point barge crews and other witnesses for our defence.

We had also arranged to see several other potential witnesses that day with him so he could take further affidavits. We continued with our plans as we had two witnesses coming to Pagliarino's office within minutes and had appointments made with four other witnesses later in the day.

With all the witnesses Pagliarino asked Sid and I to be present and actually do the questioning of them, as he said we knew more about events than he did. He asked me to type up their responses on my laptop as he could not type or use a computer, and give them to him to put in legal form.

Sid and I left Hervey Bay the next day to go to the Sunshine Coast to see other potential witnesses, and at Pagliarino's request took their evidence by ourselves then we drove home to the Gold Coast.

Once back home, Sid telephoned barrister, Rowan Jackson for advice on the matter of Pagliarino withholding this important letter to settle from us. I told him our belief the only reason he would have deliberately withheld the letter, was so he could make significant fees from what he knew would be a big case.

He had already been paid $128,000. Rowan said it sounded as if we had lost trust in Pagliarino, but it would be a difficult and expensive process to bring another solicitor up to scratch in the short time left to us.

Next day Rowan phoned back to make an appointment for a conference with our whole legal team on this issue, and the general handling of the case.

At this conference on August 31, barrister David Jackson recommended we get another solicitor to look at the facts of the letter being withheld and establish whether there was such a conflict of interest, that Carswell and Co and Pagliarino, in particular, should no longer act for us.

Following the meeting we went with John Richards, one of the partners in Carswell and Co and Peter Pagliarino to their Brisbane office.

I said we were very unhappy at finding out about this letter offering to meet with a view to settlement at this stage.

Peter said "I did not show you the letter because you would not have settled the matter. Sid said how angry he was with Kosta and the ACCC."

I replied "It was not for you to make that decision. You should have told us about the letter and told us what the implications were, and let us decide. I do not know whether we would have agreed to a settlement then or not, but I believe we would certainly have gone to a meeting with the ACCC to see what the situation was. Sid had sought meetings with the ACCC several times earlier, but been ignored. "

Richards joined in "There you are. You do not know whether you would have settled."

Peter added "It is only recently that you have raised the subject of settlement."

I replied "That is because we did not know an out of court settlement was possible. It was not until we raised this issue of a settlement with barrister David Jackson, that we even knew it was possible to seek such a thing. Certainly I believe under our circumstances at the time we would have been anxious to settle and put the whole matter behind us. By September 2002 we had a contractual agreement with Kingfisher Bay to sell our business to them.

"We had already bought *Southern Cross II* in Mexico with a view to spending time in the U.S. We would not have wanted these retirement plans disrupted by this case, as they have been."

No-one had ever explained to us just how much work would be required. If the facts of what was involved for us had been explained by Pagliarino at the time the settlement offer was made, as Rowan Jackson explained them three years later, I am confident Sid would have entered into meaningful discussion with the ACCC.

I mooted the possibility of taking action against Carswell's over this issue. John Richards said he would have to advise his insurers of a pending case for negligence and this would mean they could no longer act for us in this matter, a statement I was later to find was not the case.

He pointed out however that if we did brief another solicitor it would take a long time and we had court hearing dates set. He said it would be very expensive to start again with another solicitor and that Carswell's were not as expensive as others.

Pagliarino interrupted to say "If you let me stay on the case I promise I shall do my very very best for you."

We said we would think about the matter over lunch. Sid and I discussed our firm belief that Pagliarino had deliberately withheld the ACCC letter so that he could continue in what appeared an important and protracted case and earn considerable fees.

He had told us earlier that he had sold his partnership in Carswell and Co preparatory to his retirement and was now employed as a consultant. However his retirement plans were put in disarray, he had told us, because he had been unable to sell his Hervey Bay house for the expected price. He sold it for much less and hence remained working. He told us he only had three major clients.

* * * *

With the next court hearing date set and so much work still left to do and Pagliarino having been involved for so long, we reluctantly decided it would be impossible for us to start again with a new solicitor, particularly as we were now hoping the matter could be resolved without a trial.

We both discussed our concern about the total alienation of the judge, for our barristers had had to request several delays in earlier hearings because we were overseas and we could not complete our affidavits, answering the mass of claims of the ACCC witnesses and making our own statements, in the time allowed.

We felt the judge might not permit a further delay for another solicitor to understand the case and start taking new affidavits on our behalf. For this reason we said Pagliarino should continue.

On the fax next day came a letter from Richards putting an incomplete version of what occurred at the meeting and asking Sid and I to sign it. We did not do so. Pagliarino asked us to do so on several subsequent occasions but we did not do so, as we did not agree with the version and still wished to reserve our right to take action on the matter.

* * * *

Our barristers then had meetings with the ACCC legal team, at which the matter of a settlement was raised.

We were told it would hinge on our agreeing to a statement of facts, and that the ACCC had incurred some $900,000 in costs in preparing the case against us. Knowing full well it was not likely the ACCC would accept an offer to settle for less than that, we offered $1,000,000 in settlement, to include the costs.

After meeting with the ACCC barrister, David Jackson told us this had been accepted provided we agreed to an ACCC statement of facts that we had behaved wrongfully. He explained we would have to give up our right to put our side of the case in court. We would have liked to explain why we did what we did, but not at a cost of $1.8million in legal fees at the very least, no matter the outcome.

We finally got to see the ACCC letter of September 16 2002 that Pagliarino had withheld from us. It was a request from the ACCC that we meet with a view to settlement, and, as encouragement, it indicated its costs could be reduced. Of course if Pagliarino had passed it on at the time, we would have been interested and would certainly have gone to a meeting to see what their offer was.

No wonder the ACCC had put so much subsequent effort into preparing a case against us when, as far as they understood, we had rudely ignored their offer to meet.

One of the issues in their case concerned the contracts we had offered tour operators, professional fishermen and island residents so they could have discounted fares on the barges. These stated that in return for the discounted fares and promise of a reliable service, they would use our barge service exclusively. These contracts had been drawn up by Pagliarino in the late 1980's and rewritten in December 2000 by John Richards.

When this emerged at our next meeting with our barristers on Oct 24 2005 David Jackson said the fact they had drawn up the contract for our regular barge clients with the word "exclusive" in and had not advised us this was unlawful we should definitely get another solicitor to advise us.

He said he had suggested to us before we get another solicitor to decide whether Carswell and Co actions demonstrated a conflict of interest and now he said he was going to put it in writing that we get another solicitor to decide whether we could continue to use Carswell and Co in this case.

As the solicitor's role was now minimal except as an obligatory but largely silent presence while we worked with the barristers on the statement of agreed facts, often in fact filled by Richard's student daughter as neither he nor Pagliarino were available, we felt it more urgent that we keep working consistently.

* * * *

It was a to and fro process taking some weeks. We would reject something the ACCC wanted in the statement they had prepared, primarily on our misuse of market power and predatory pricing, and the statement had to be taken back to the ACCC to see if it would accept our alterations. Several times they refused, and we were told we had to agree or forget about an out of court settlement.

At some of the meetings we were asked if we would agree to the sum of the ACCC costs and the fine being altered. Originally we were told the ACCC costs had been $900,000 which meant the fine would be $100,000.

However we were then asked if we would accept the costs as being $600,000 and the fine $400,000. Our response was that as long as it came to the $1million we had offered, it was up to the ACCC how it was allotted.

At the next meeting we were asked if we would accept a fine of $600,000 and costs of $400,000. Again we said it was up to the ACCC.

Finally we were asked if we would agree to the fine being $900,000 and the costs $100,000, a complete reversal of what we had first been told.

Again, and foolishly we were later to learn, we agreed, believing the same thing applied as we had been told about some portions of the statement of facts, that if we did not agree the ACCC would not reach a settlement with us. Otherwise why ask us to agree to this?

We asked why the ACCC would want to do this and were told it was to make their victory over us appear the greater and the penalty for our actions more punitive.

Pagliarino had produced our affidavits and the affidavits of our witnesses that we had taken for our defence. Soon afterwards we were advised that the ACCC would not read them unless we were prepared to pay another $60,000 in costs, as the ACCC felt certain it would have to undertake investigation of them and its many witnesses, whose affidavits ours contradicted.

So all the time and effort we and our witnesses had put in, in an effort to present a clearer picture of events to the ACCC and perhaps mitigate our actions, was totally wasted and of course none was presented in due course to the judge.

* * * *

We appeared in the Federal Court on December 15 and were given a stern lecture by the Judge Susan Kiefel, who accepted the settlement worked out between ourselves and the ACCC. The court found, as per the agreement we had reached with the ACCC, that we had had a substantial degree of power in the market for the supply of barge services at Inskip Point and took advantage of that power to eliminate or substantially damage a competitor, the consortium owning the *Manta Ray* barge.

This was achieved by a pricing policy of charging $10 less than our competitors and by eventually charging $20 which was below costs. It was a very low key affair and we emerged lighter in heart at having the matter put behind us and $1million lighter in pocket.

The case received very little attention in the media, until the Brisbane *Sunday Mail* was alerted by an ACCC press release, and two weeks later ran a full page story about the case. Sid and I had been warned if we were contacted by the media at all, we should say nothing to contradict the statement we had agreed with the ACCC, which had been put to the court. So we said nothing.

Ladas said little, except to complain he hadn't been paid any compensation, and most of the article quoted Tony Dean, son of Ian Dean and relieving skipper on the *Manta Ray,* who said the $1million was a drop in the bucket for Sid.

The ACCC could hardly claim it had achieved the public benefit of lower fares on the Inskip Point barges as they had quickly risen to the level Sid had been charging before the price war, and soon rose higher. What it did say in the article was that there were now four barges in use at Inskip Point, which provided a much better service.

* * * *

We did see another solicitor as David Jackson had suggested because we continued to feel particularly aggrieved over Pagliarino's not telling us the ACCC had sought a meeting with a view to settlement in September 2002, when all this stress and money could well have been saved.

When this new solicitor heard we had been questioning our witnesses and typing up their answers at Pagliarino's behest her response was that we had been very wise in pursuing a settlement as our involvement in this process would certainly have been to our detriment in court. Again we felt betrayed.

When we were told that a case against our solicitors could well be as lengthy and expensive as defending the ACCC case, we decided our freedom from the work it would involve was more important, and took no further action.

* * * *

Now Sid is a major player in the Gold Coast property market and has homes on the Gold Coast, in New Zealand and the Bahamas. At least six months of each year is spent travelling the world.

We have been back to Fraser Island only four times since we left, and then only for a couple of days each time to see the dwindling number of our staff who remain there.

Of them, May Jensen is now the assistant manager at Eurong Beach.

Don Caswell is marine manager for Kingfisher Bay. Harry Brutnell drives the *Fraser Venture* week about. Robyn Bostock is deckie on it.

At Rainbow Beach, Neil Grono is still skipper on the *Rainbow Venture* and Kosta Ladas on the *Manta Ray.*

Murray Reid is still carting supplies to Eurong Beach.

We still keep in regular touch with many of our other former staff and business friends, now scattered all over Australia.

There are changes since we left. There is a police station manned by two officers in the National Parks compound just north of Eurong Beach.

We saw a rescue helicopter land twice in one day, and were told that it was much more available.

Many of the National Parks staff are now flown to and from the island daily by Air Fraser, as they do not want to live on the island.

It looks as if the National Parks is softening in its attitude to tag-a-long tours for backpacker hostel owners and they may soon be allowed in their own right.

High wire fences to keep the dingoes out have been erected around Kingfisher Bay, Happy Valley and Eurong with cattle grids across the roads. A tearful Happy Valley resident said in a television interview it was like living in a prisoner of war camp.

The island roads are even worse than we remembered.